THE TRADES UNION CONGRESS & THE STRUGGLE FOR EDUCATION 1868-1925

THE TRADES UNION CONGRESS & THE STRUGGLE FOR EDUCATION 1868-1925

Clive Griggs
Brighton Polytechnic

The Falmer Press

A member of the Taylor & Francis Group

First published 1983

ISBN 0 905273 38 9 cased ✓

Jacket design by Leonard Williams

Phototypeset in Linotron 202 by
Graphicraft Typesetters Hong Kong
Printed and bound by Taylor & Francis (Printers) Ltd
Basingstoke
for
The Falmer Press
(*A member of the Taylor & Francis Group*)
Falmer House
Barcombe, Lewes
Sussex BN8 5DL
England

To Sheila

Contents

Illustrations

Abbreviations used

AESD	Association of Engineering and Shipbuilding Draughtsmen
ASCJ	Amalgamated Society of Carpenters and Joiners
ASE	Amalgamated Society of Engineers
ASRS	Amalgamated Society of Railway Servants (with two other railway unions formed NUR 1913)
ASW	Amalgamated Society of Woodworkers
AUBTW	Amalgamated Union of Building Trade Workers
CLC	Central Labour College
FBI	Federation of British Industries
GCEC	General Council Education Committee
GCTUC	General Council of the Trades Union Congress
GFTU	General Federation of Trade Unions
GUWTW	General Union of Weavers and Textile Workers
ILP	Independent Labour Party
ISTC	Iron and Steel Trades Confederation
IWMA	International Working Men's Association
LCC	London County Council
LRL	Labour Representation League
LSC	London Society of Compositors
LTC	London Trades Council
LWMA	London Working Men's Association
LSB	London School Board
LTEB	London Technical Education Board
NATSOPA	National Society of Operative Printers and Assistants
NCLC	National Council of Labour Colleges
NEL	National Education League
NUR	National Union of Railwaymen
NUT	National Union of Teachers
NUST	National Union of School Teachers
NUTGW	National Union of Tailors and Garment Workers
NUGGLU	National Union of Gas Workers and General Labourers' Union
NUTW	National Union of Textile Workers
PCTUC	Parliamentary Committee of the Trades Union Congress
RACS	Royal Arsenal Cooperative Society
RCA	Railway Clerks Association
SDF	Social Democratic Federation
SWMF	South Wales Miners' Federation
TGWU	Transport and General Workers Union
TUC	Trades Union Congress
TUCEAC	Trades Union Congress Education Advisory Committee
UPW	Union of Post Office Workers
WEA	Workers' Educational Association
WETUC	Workers' Education Trade Union Committee
WMCIU	Working Men's Club and Institute Union

Acknowledgements

I would like to express my gratitude to Dr. Roderick Floud, Professor of Modern History at Birkbeck College, for his continued help and advice in this study of the TUC. Grateful acknowledgements are also due to Miss Christine Coates at Congress House who made early material at the TUC Library freely available to me; Dr. Joyce Bellamy of Hull University who willingly helped to fill some of the 'gaps' that existed in Appendix I; Dr. Philip Bagwell, some time Professor of History at the Central London Polytechnic and Dr. Harold Silver, Principal of Bulmershe College of Higher Education, who both gave me advice and encouragement; and four more librarians who were most helpful in making relevant material available to me: Miss Rita Arkley of Brighton Polytechnic, Miss Iris Blake of the NSPCK, Mr. R. Ebsworth of the GMWU and Mr. David Horsfield of Ruskin College.

I should also like to thank my wife Sheila and Patti Grutchfield for typing the numerous drafts and final manuscript.

My thanks are also due to the staff of the following libraries:

Birkbeck College
Bishopsgate Institute
Brighton Polytechnic:
 (Eastbourne Site)
British Museum: State Paper
 Room & Newspaper library
Confederation of British
 Industry Archives
Department of Education
 & Science
Department of Health &
 Social Security
General & Municipal
 Workers' Union

The Guildhall
Lambeth Palace
London School of Economics
 & Political Science
Marx Memorial Library
National Museum of Labour
 History
National Society Archives
National Union of Railwaymen
National Union of Teachers
Public Record Office
Ruskin College
Sussex University
Trades Union Congress

Foreword

Dr. Griggs has produced a most readable work of scholarship, recording the genesis of the Movement's concern, policies, methods and influence in the world of education.

It is a moving story that gives new heart to those who strive to create education for all and who believe in the trade union Movement's compassion and concern for a better life; and it reveals the enormous difficulties – the persistent setbacks and the inevitable compromising – which the TUC has faced in helping to move forward the nation's education system.

The TUC has always been a force for radical change in education. Today, the TUC is in the forefront in shaping policies for a combined care and education service for the under-fives, in working for radical curricular reform in the schools to prepare young people for adult and working life, in contributing to practical policies to phase out the private sector in compulsory schooling, in demanding much more open access to higher education, and in detailing the priorities that could genuinely open up education opportunities to all classes and ages.

Dr. Griggs reveals in his book that the TUC's radical outlook on education is not an irresponsible populism created for the 1980s but rooted in trade unionism itself. It does not come from one stable of trade unionism, but embraces the Movement's strong, egalitarian traditions, the natural compassion of workers, the self-interest of occupational groups and the practical experience of workers from their jobs and their own schooling – or lack of it. These same forces continue to provide the powerful mix that shape TUC education policies.

Dr. Griggs has also given us a timely reminder that social reforms never come easy in our society and are always at risk. But in spite of the maelstrom in which education and training are currently caught up, education has come a long, long way since 1925 where his account ends. So we not only find inspiration from our history but also regain confidence in our ability to turn the tide in favour of better education for all. This is a book that can sustain all who engage in that fight and it is essential reading for all those who doubt the trade union Movement's commitment to social progress.

Clive Jenkins
Chairman, Education Committee of the Trades Union Congress

January 1982

Introduction

This study of the TUC and its attitudes to education covers the period from the formation of the TUC in 1868 to the year before the general strike; a time beginning with the last year of the mid-Victorian boom and ending with the first few years of the interwar depression. For many years, approximately from the mid 1870s to the mid 1890s, and again for much of the Edwardian era, trade was depressed. While the causes of such trade fluctuations are not the purpose of this study, these years of depression need to be borne in mind when one considers the economic climate in which trade unions had to survive and try to work for the benefit of their members.

Throughout the period the population drift from rural to urban areas continued and, annually, thousands emigrated to the Americas, Australasia and South Africa.[1] Industry grew in size and complexity as mergers took place[2] and work which had once been the preserve of the craftsman was broken down into a series of processes which could be handled by the growing numbers of semi-skilled workers. There were always examples of deplorable living conditions[3] far too common to be considered an exception; few working class children remained at school beyond the age of twelve years and even after 1902 few found their way to a secondary education. Even by 1925 the majority of workers received no annual paid holiday and, prior to 1918, seventy-two percent of the population were without the vote.

Daily life was always kept uncertain by the continued threat of unemployment, the arrival of another mouth to feed in the family and a lack of security at times of sickness or retirement. Yet it is also possible to show that in many areas there was gradual progress. This was certainly the case in education for, whereas in the 1860s the elementary education available was controlled by religious societies, was fee paying, voluntary and had insufficient numbers of places for the children below ten years of age, by 1925 the majority of elementary schools were controlled by the local authority, were free, and attendance was compulsory until fourteen years of age. Moreover, by the 1920s a whole series of related social services were also provided, such as medical inspections and school meals, to enable youngsters to benefit from the schooling provided.

Some will question whether the greater provision of education and social services can be regarded as progress: even more so whether local authority dominance in place of religious dominance is a matter of progress. Some may see any attempt to suggest that there were improvements merely as a liberal view of history. Yet there was little doubt among the numerous trade unionists[4] who were forced by economic circumstances to leave school in their early years for the world of industry that the experience was an unhappy one. At the TUC members with similar childhood experiences were keen to call for better educational opportunities for the next generation. Such active trade unionists certainly viewed the majority of developments which offered more education as matters of 'progress' and were willing to campaign for such programmes at Congress : how successful the TUC was in persuading others, including the Government, that such measures were beneficial and worth adopting is one of the issues this study will try to determine.

Notes

1 'Between 1853 and 1880 Britain sent out some 2,466,000 emigrants, of whom an unknown but probably small proportion returned. This amazing output had begun earlier and continued later than these dates . . .' THOMSON, D., *England in the 19th Century*, p. 164. '. . . emigration, increased again after 1900. In the last three years of peace it reached a record average of 46,400 a year.' THOMSON, D., *England in the 20th Century*, p. 20.

2 e.g. 1888 Salt Union, 1891 Alkali Co., John Brown & Co. throughout the 19th century and Lever Brothers whose growing monopoly power led to considerable criticism in the British Press in 1906.

3 Poor living conditions were shown by numerous social surveys of varying objectivity and sophistication : 1844 *Condition of the Working Class in Britain* by F.Engels, 1890s *Life and Labour of the People in London* by Charles Booth and *'Poverty'* Seebohm Rowntree's study of York, as well as books such as Jack London's *People of the Abyss* concerning Edwardian London and Robert Tressell's *Ragged Trousered Philanthropists* concerning Hastings during the same period.

4 See chapter 8

Chapter 1

Changes in TUC Attention 1868–1925

The TUC was initially formed as a debating society to which only a minority of skilled workers were invited. It supported the monarch,[1] imperialism,[2] and the Liberal Party until almost 1900, voted against an extension of the franchise in 1876[3] and in general accepted many of the values of Victorian society, including a desire for respectability. Yet this organization developed, by the late 1890s, a detailed education programme as radical as that of any other section of the labour movement,[4] including the Independent Labour Party and the Marxist Social Democratic Federation, and spent much time debating the matter and considerable energy in pursuing such a programme. It is this paradox which this study will attempt to explain.

It would be misleading to imply that the TUC ever gave first priority to education, even though at the second Congress the President, Mr. Wilkinson, told delegates that with reference to primary schools he believed it was not only an area for much needed reform but also that : 'On the solution of that question would depend, not only, the future welfare of England, but, to a large extent, of the whole civilised world'.[5] Unfortunately, there were often other issues, such as the Inquiry into Trade Unions which had produced majority and minority reports published in March 1869, that often claimed the attention of Congress delegates because their very existence seemed to be threatened on such occasions. It would however be less than charitable if it were not made clear that in spite of some very difficult times and many taxing problems the TUC did give considerable time, when conditions were favourable, to discussions of education. What may have started with no more than a series of strongly expressed statements in the early years developed by the end of the nineteenth century into a comprehensive programme of education and related social services; a programme which became even more detailed and all embracing in its response to continuing changes in the early decades of the twentieth century.

Throughout the period trade unionists were always a minority of the work force and in any one year no more than approximately eighty per cent of total trade union membership was affiliated to the TUC. For the first twenty years

Congress represented only the comparatively small number of organized skilled workers and whilst no accurate figures are available before 1886[6] total trade union membership, which may have passed the one million mark in the early 1870s, rapidly fell away and never achieved such proportions again until the 1890s. Rapid growth was experienced in the early years of the twentieth century when membership of all trade unions doubled between 1900 and 1914 from 1,972,000 to 4,145,000 and doubled again by 1920 before falling away rapidly to less than half the 1920 total by the end of the decade.[7] TUC delegates at first came from both trade unions and trades councils but the latter were excluded in 1895.[8]

However, whilst Congress never represented the majority of working people it did include in its ranks in general the best organized workers, the most highly skilled and best educated. TUC delegates were also most likely to have considerable experience of negotiating on behalf of their own trade unions, be members of school boards prior to 1902 or magistrates, and have had the experience, successful or otherwise, of standing for Parliament. Trade unionists were also most likely to be among those enfranchised in 1867 or later in 1884 so that, whilst trade unionists were a minority, the major political parties of the time could not easily afford to reject all proposals formulated by Congress.

It needs to be pointed out also that TUC delegates, whilst having trade union membership in common, were likely to represent between them a variety of religious and political philosophies, to such an extent that agreement on many issues would be difficult and there were times when such view points mattered. It is not difficult to find delegates who were practising Roman Catholics, Nonconformists or avowed agnostics;[9] neither is there any problem in listing delegates who supported the Conservative Party,[10] the Liberal Party, one of the smaller socialist parties or no political party at all.[11] To know that a person was a TUC delegate only informed one that he was a member of a trade union but in turn this was only likely to imply that he would act in a collective manner with members of his own trade but perhaps no more than that. Indeed he might be indifferent to or even in dispute with members of a different trade. To this extent it was difficult to get agreement among TUC delegates unless they believed a common danger threatened their union members or unless they felt that proposals being made would be of benefit to their own comrades or families.

General trends in terms of political influence can be observed: radical Liberals dominated the first few Congress meetings, then supporters of the Liberal Party (namely George Howell, Henry Broadhurst, and Charles Fenwick who between them held the secretaryship of the TUC during 1871–93) before growing support for some kind of independent Labour representation gradually took over. While arguments along political lines can be detected and were most bitter at times, especially during the 1890s, the over-riding philosophy to be detected throughout the history of Congress during the period under review was one of pragmatism; not pragmatism as an agreed philosophy arrived at through discussion, but an approach developed from the experience trade unionists had gained through their working lives in the production of goods or negotiations with employers. It was such a philosophy that prevented the TUC breaking up over points of particular philosophical theory and allowed the leadership to decide how best to cope with the problems which faced trade unionists and their families in both good and bad times of trade.

One key to the TUC's survival when previous failures to maintain a 'Parliament' of trade unionists are borne in mind was its federal structure which enabled delegates representing unions to reject the policy of the majority and still feel no wish or need to resign.Hence in the education debate, Lancashire textile delegates were constantly in a minority when the wish to raise the minimum school leaving age[12] was discussed, and similarly, James Sexton of the Liverpool dockers continued to argue against the wish for education in school to be only of a secular nature.[13] This federal structure could be seen as a source of strength in allowing members to follow their own policy or viewpoint contrary to adopted Congress policy and still maintain membership. In many cases, and the two examples provided fit into this category, objections were only raised to one clause or a detail within a particular clause, whilst there was general agreement with the main policy. In addition, over major issues affecting trade unionists in general, such as job protection or improved working conditions, most delegates held similar views. It is also true to say that very often the Parliamentary Committee, as will be shown later,[14] prepared the agenda carefully to avoid controversy whenever possible.

Formation of the TUC and Its Early Response to Education

The first Conference of the TUC which met on 2nd June 1868 at the Mechanics Institute in Manchester, was intended as merely a vehicle for debate. One reason was that previous attempts to bring together trade unions in order that they might plan future strategy, including such an attempt by William Dronfield himself, had been short lived.[15] Another reason was that Dronfield, after having read a paper in defence of trade unions to the ninth Annual Congress of the National Association for the Promotion of Social Science,[16] was disappointed and annoyed to find that is was excluded from the Association's Annual Report. In explaining the matter to Samual Nicholson, a fellow printer and President of the Manchester and Salford Trades Council, it seems that they concluded that they should have a Congress of their own. The original invitations sent out by Nicholson and W.H. Wood (Typographical Society), the Secretary of the Trades Council, makes this reasoning quite clear :

> It is proposed that the Congress shall assume the character of the annual meetings of the British Association for the Advancement of Science and the Social Science Association, in the transactions of which Societies the artisan class are almost entirely excluded; and that papers,

previously carefully prepared, shall be laid before the Congress on the various subjects which at the present time affect Trades Societies, each paper to be followed by discussion upon the points advanced, with a view of the merits and demerits of each question being thoroughly ventilated through the medium of the public press.[17]

It is, however, also apparent that there was no possibility of restricting such meetings to a discussion of papers in the long run for, in that same invitation, attention of delegates was drawn to legislation in the current session of Parliament which might prove detrimental to all trades societies. There could be no question of just listening to papers when the poor publicity trade unions had obtained in connection with the Sheffield Outrages of 1866 was considered, whilst the Hornby-Close decision of 1867 called clearly for some positive action from trade unionists.

During this time the London Trades Council, which had been formed in 1860 and by 1864 was dominated by those members which the Webbs were to call collectively 'The Junta',[18] was meeting secretly, often with professional advisers, in an attempt to decide how best they could influence the 'Royal Commission to Inquire into Trade Unions' which had been set up in 1867 following many of the fears expressed concerning trade unions. The leading members of the LTC were Robert Applegarth (Carpenters), William Allan (Engineers), David Guile (Iron Founders), Edwin Coulson (Bricklayers) and George Odger (Ladies Shoemakers), Secretary. They had not accepted the invitation to attend the first Manchester Congress, indeed only two delegates went from London, one of whom was George Potter, well known as editor of the *Beehive* and a constant critic of the activities of the Junta. The small gathering of thirty three delegates, mostly from areas surrounding Manchester, elected Potter as Chairman and Secretary for the following year and the success of their rival must have been one reason why the LTC decided to attend the second Congress. Another reason was that it seemed Congress was determined to continue because provincial trade unionists had felt themselves excluded from the workings of the Junta who had begun to take on the role of representing English trade unionism. However justified they may have been through the sound manner in which they had organized the newly emerging amalgamated societies, trade unionists from outside the capital wished to contribute to the trade union movement which was now showing a new lease of life.

The Junta duly sent several members to the second Congress at Birmingham: Odger, George Howell (Bricklayers), Thomas Connolly (Stonemasons), William Cremer and William Harry (both representatives of Marylebone and Chelsea Working Men's Association). In 1871 a Parliamentary Committee was established as an executive committee of Congress to prepare the agenda each year, seek to lobby Parliament and put up MPs of their own choosing. By 1873 of the nine elected members four were from the LTC, of whom three held key positions; Guile was Vice-Chairman, Allan was treasurer and Howell was elected Secretary. In addition, the Chairman, Alexander MacDonald of the National Miners' union, was a clear supporter of their views. Only John Kane of the Amalgamated Iron Workers' Association, who came from the north-east, could be described as somewhat critical of their views.[19]

In 1874 the Parliamentary Committee put forward thirteen trade unionists as candidates in the General Election, two of whom were successful: MacDonald stood at Stafford and Thomas Burt, a miner, stood for Morpeth, an area surrounded by mining villages. Although these men stood as Liberals, (they were in fact the first of what were to become known as Lib-Lab MPs) and whilst the TUC had supported this Party in 1868, now the pragmatism of the leaders came to the fore and they told trade unionists to vote for those candidates who had answered favourably to the 'Test Questions' sent out by the PCTUC, whether they were Liberal or Conservative. By this time the cautious lobbying and negotiating policy of the LTC had been firmly taken up by the PCTUC. It would be expected that change within the TUC in these early years, from what might be considered the radical leadership of Potter to the more prudent domination by the Junta, would be reflected in changes of attitude towards education. In fact this is not strictly the case and the changed attitude towards education when the first LTC members made their appearance was almost the opposite of what might be expected.

When the first TUC met, the sixth of twelve items for discussion on the agenda was technical education and it is perhaps to be expected that a meeting of skilled workers might well see this as the main aspect of education to focus attention upon. Two papers were read providing a historical sketch of the development of classes by trade unions in carpentry at Manchester and Birmingham respectively and considerable support was afforded to demands for greater provision of technical education in the country. Yet the rationale for such further knowledge was not an appeal to enhancement through greater skill or interest gained but rather in terms of a warning concerning the international competition the country faced in manufactured goods.[20] According to George Potter, '... if continental countries excelled us in the quality of their manufactures it was because their governments had fostered technical education, which ours had not done'.[21] In some form this was to be the most common plea by trade unionists whenever technical education was advocated[22] and whilst this form of education did not gain most attention there was steady support for it from the first TUC to the end of the period under consideration.

The new Liberal Government which came to office in 1868 was pledged to consider the general question of how to provide some form of basic education to the majority of children – the issue that had captured the attention of those interested in education in general and those who could see the need for greater education from a political point of view since the franchise had been extended in 1867.[23] Robert Lowe was not alone in disliking democratic institutions, having contempt for working people whilst at the same time seeing the sudden need to expand the education system to embrace as many children as possible;[24] the MP, Edward Potter of Carlisle, wanted a strong education bill which would make schooling compulsory to make an impression on trade unions.[25]

With such national discussion in mind C. Hutchinson (Boilermakers and Shipwrights Society) suggested that in discussing technical education they were starting at the top of the tree whilst W.H. Wood claimed that they should be considering a 'national and compulsory system of elementary education' whereupon he was called to order by the President who thought a discussion on general education would take too long. This did not prevent Wood from attempting to pass such a resolution on the following day calling for 'a national system of secular education for the poor' but no seconder was forthcoming.

The following year the situation had changed. By now it was known that W.E. Forster was making preliminary preparations for a possible Autumn Bill on Education. Due to some dissatisfaction with the statistics of the Newcastle Commission of 1861 he had sent out experienced inspectors to report on Birmingham, Leeds, Liverpool and Manchester, for it was the urban areas which were considered to have the poorest records of school attendance and yet these towns' need had not been included in the Newcastle Commission's survey.[26] When Congress met at Birmingham in 1869, members of the Provisional Committee of the National Education League addressed delegates,[27] even though the NEL's inaugural meeting was still two months away, so that the delegates had the importance of elementary education put before them in detail. As many prominent delegates, such as Applegarth and Odger, had already held preliminary meetings with NEL organisers, elementary education was assured of the attention of Congress and the chairman stressed its importance in his opening speech. A motion introduced by Cremer almost repeating Wood's unsupported demands of the previous year calling for 'a system of national unsectarian and compulsory education' was easily passed. Within twelve months the artisans' somewhat restricted view of education had been broadened into a concern for the provision of basic education for all children. Not for the first time at the TUC was a pressure group to attract trade unionists who would take their ideas before Congress and gain enough support from delegates for such sentiments to be adopted as the official TUC outlook. Nor would it be the last time that a stereotype of certain TUC members was shown to be misleading: the Junta image of the Webbs was helpful as a generalization but too restrictive to give a full picture of the individual members included. There is here at least some suggestion that it was the 'prudent craftsmen of the amalgamated unions' who had a wider image of education than some of the TUC members considered more radical in the past.

Forster's Education Bill was introduced into the House of Commons on February 17th 1870, and came into force the following August. It is not possible to assess direct TUC response for Congress was postponed that year. It had been decided to hold it back until the Trade Union Bill was before Parliament so that delegates could lobby MPs with a view to pressing for any amendments considered necessary.[28] Hence the next TUC was not held until March 1871, but the attitude of some TUC members can be gauged from a large meeting of Working Men which met halfway through June of that year in Exeter Hall, London. It was called in order that working men might 'signify their opinions on the Government Education Bill'. Chaired by the Rev. C.H. Spurgeon and attended by several MPs including Professor Fawcett, George Dixon, C. Reed and Winterbottom, a number of trade unionists were on the platform scheduled to speak. They included Cremer, Guile and T. Mottershead (Silk Weavers) all of whom were from the TUC although not acting in an official capacity.

Cremer was not slow to point out the strange way in which the Bill was receiving support in Parliament 'from those who had always been opposed to the people' and he feared the extent to which the original aims to expand education would be compromised in order to placate the interest of religious groups. It was Cremer who moved the first resolution, seconded by Guile, criticizing the Bill because it would not satisfy '... the want of proper educational provision for the people ... [which] ... cannot be supplied, except by the establishment in every parish or district of free schools, at which attendance shall be compulsory, and the teaching entirely free from anything of a sectarian character'.[29] The meeting decided to send a deputation to wait upon the Prime Minister and Forster, to put before them the views that had been expressed and the resolution that had been passed by 'an overwhelming majority'.

The date agreed for the deputation was early in July but as the Rev. Spurgeon was unable to go, it was left to Cremer to lead those chosen to represent the meeting. Their anxiety was expressed to the Prime Minister. They wanted an education bill but one stronger than the present one before Parliament. Cremer explained that 'as a tree was known by its fruit, so the Bill was known by its supporters, and hence he saw the Bill was receiving its greatest support from the Opposition benches'.[30] To be of most help to the working classes Gladstone and Forster were told that the Bill should make education free and compulsory. According to the *Beehive*, whilst the deputation was treated politely by the Prime Minister, 'Mr. Forster almost treated the men who went up to him like children' telling them that their ideas were based upon 'utter delusion, and altogether erroneous'. The men were not really in a very strong position. They did not have one working class MP to put forward their ideas in Parliament and the Bill did offer them a national system of education of a sort; something tangible enough to build upon in the future. There was no hope of getting free education as Church Schools needed the income from fees and most ratepayers would not be willing to pay the full cost of educating the poorest section of the nation's children. Compulsory education at the time was probably impracticable as there were insufficient school places even if attendance could have been enforced.[31] These were all arguments the TUC would take up as a body in later years. It is clear that in 1870 the TUC represented only the views of a small section of organised workers but it is also important to note that the principles stated by Cremer in his resolution amounted to more than a slogan. They were a series of minimum conditions which some members of the organized working class considered were necessary for the education of working class children. Their breadth shows that not all the craft union leaders had a narrow outlook, at least with regard to education.

When Forster's Education Act was passed in 1870 many of Cremer's expressed fears were seen to be well founded. Elementary education was to be neither free nor compulsory but it would seem that the promise of a system of elementary education, especially the development of board schools, with an elected membership, which would be of great value in urban areas, was sufficient to satisfy most trade unionists. The hopeful expectations together with the urgent need to discuss the 1871 Trade Union Bill combined to ensure that education no longer commanded an important place at Congress. When delegates met in London during March 1871, education was tenth among fifteen items for discussion with prime place being awarded to trade unions and legislation. A whole series of matters affecting basic living conditions, such as a Mines Regulation Bill, the 'Truck system, employment of women and children in Agriculture and Factories, were all well above 'Education, Primary and Technical'. In the event, even allowing for the fact that Congress adjourned at 4.30 pm each day so that delegates could '. . . devote the evening to waiting upon Members of Parliament',[32] when education came to be discussed it was found that no paper had been prepared. To cope with this embarrassing situation, Potter, as Chairman, quickly suggested he move the following resolution from the Chair:

> That we, the representatives of various trade unions in the Kingdom, in Congress assembled, cannot separate without recording it as our opinion that primary education should without delay be applied to every child in the Kingdom, and that in addition to this a good technical education should be open to every person engaged in connection with the industry of the country.[33]

In 1872 although a paper on Forster's Education Act had been prepared by A.W. Bailey of the PCTUC, time ran out so that the Chairman, W.H. Leatherhead (Organized Trades Association) suggested that this paper together with several others be taken as read and handed to reporters, and that a resolution be moved and seconded without discussion. From that year until 1885 no paper or discussion directly related to education with the exception of the National Society Textbook controversy[34] and an isolated call for the establishment of technical schools in all industrial areas[35] came before Congress.

1875–1884 Fallow Years for Education at the TUC

To understand the fallow years of education at the TUC it is necessary to recognize a series of factors, some economic and social, others in terms of individual personalities, which changed around the mid-1870s. Economic depression broke the short-lived Agricultural Labourers' Union of Joseph

Arch and forced other established unions to perform no more than a holding operation wherever possible. To assume that trade unionists in general would have taken a different path overlooks the view that some were content with their position as it was.

Applegarth had been forced to resign the secretaryship of his union in 1871 but had he remained at the TUC there is no evidence to suggest that the ideas expressed by himself and Charles Hibbs, a Birmingham Gunmaker, would have received much support at Congress: '... it was incumbent on the intelligent artisan to speak for the whole of the working class, to agitate for education for all and even compel the uneducated to recognize the value of education'.[36] Throughout this period trade union membership never rose above half a million and these skilled members did not look upon themselves as part of the larger working class of unskilled workers; they did not consider the very poor as being qualified in any way even for membership of the working class. More and more the minority of skilled workers were becoming a special and privileged group separated off from the rest of the workers.[37]

By 1875, some trade unionists, by pointing to the spate of reforms commencing with the second Reform Act of 1867 and continuing through Forster's Education Act of 1870, the Trade Union Bill of 1871 and ending with the Employers and Workermen's Act of 1875, felt that the major part of what they had campaigned for had been achieved. Even the title of the last named Act compared with its forerunner, The Master and Servants Act, suggested a clear up-grading of workmen by Parliament. Certainly George Howell thought that there was no more to be done in the way of trade union legislation and resigned the secretaryship of the Parliamentary Committee at the Glasgow Congress of 1875 because '... he thought that legislation with respect to Trade Unions was now perfect'.[38]

Howell, Broadhurst and Fenwick, who held the secretaryship of the Parliamentary Committee in turn between 1871 and 1893, were all members of the Liberal Party; all advocated more working class members going to Parliament, but as Liberals and not as independent working class representatives. All three became Liberal MPs loyal to Gladstone. Once established at the TUC if they failed to seek fundamental reforms[39] it was for a combination of reasons. They felt no wish to change radically a society in which they had gained some respect and recognition; even though it is probable that some of their acceptance was based upon political expediency, in that they were able to deliver the working class vote. For reasons which can only be described as social snobbery they were not entirely accepted[40] and in later life both Broadhurst[41] and Howell[42] felt the gap between their own upbringing and that of new colleagues at Westminster and Whitehall. As loyal Liberals they were hesitant to question their own Party and at times, through their position on the Parliamentary Committee, attempted to stifle pending criticism.[43] However, the policies they pursued and the ideas they expressed were supported by the majority of delegates at the TUC: at first from conviction, as most shared a common outlook from their position as skilled artisans seeking their just place in the Victorian hierarchy[44] and, later, from loyalty to leaders who had served them well in difficult times.[45]

The attitude of leading TUC members can also be illustrated by the incident involving the 'Prize Essay' of 1875. Alexander MacDonald offered a prize of £50 at the 1874 Congress for the best essay on 'Trade Unions; their objects, their fitness to obtain those objects; their influence on the trade of the country; and their moral influence on those who belonged to them'.[46] He believed the prize would be sufficient to tempt the highest intellect in Britain and Germany to enter the competition. The essay which was awarded first prize by the PCTUC had been signed 'Fidelity' and perhaps in order to add a little drama to the January Congress of 1875 a sealed packet was opened in the presence of all delegates attending to ascertain the name of the winner. The Chairman read out to delegates: 'The essay signed "Fidelity" was written by me. I am a grinder by trade, and for many years I have refused to join the unions, because I don't concur in their restrictive policy and I would not be an assessory [sic] to their unlawful deeds'.[47] The note was signed John Wilson, an infamous opponent to trade unionism who had spoken against the movement before the Royal Commission at Sheffield in 1867. The prize was given but the essay was not read out to delegates as it was decided the author was insincere.

Yet an examination of the contents shows precisely how the TUC leaders regarded their role in the community. The essay claimed that the unions

> ... must show that in their very nature they have the desire and power to prevent strikes.... Strikes as a rule are a dernier ressort and are more frequently discountenanced by the general secretary than approved of. Indeed it is the boast of most Trade Union secretaries that they have prevented more strikes than they have originated.[48]

The TUC leaders had not only recognized the image of trade unionism described by the writer but clearly approved of it; a view of moderate men resisting militant action wherever possible.

There is little evidence to suggest that TUC delegates felt deeply concerned about the education system in Britain between the early 1870s and the mid 1880s. There was certainly no attempt to form any coherent detailed policy on education during these years. Most references to education seem to be either in the form of generalized statements which required nodding approval rather than any action, or discussion which arose primarily from some other topic being debated.

Thus in the second Congress of 1875 during October at the City Hall, Glasgow, P. MacIver (ASRS) told a mass meeting in the evening that there was a great future for the working man because he saw '... how education would elevate, how a spirit of self-reliance would nerve him for all duties and difficulties...'.[49] Two years later, in his Presidential address, D. Merrick (Boot and Shoe Finishers) told delegates, '... workmen as a rule have learned to respect themselves, to improve their homes and give attention to the education of their families ... put their spare money in the bank, or devote it to the purchase of a house, or a piece of land, or entering into business'.[50] Such a speech could just as easily have been made by an employer or a temperance leader. Finally, in 1880, Dr. Ingram read a paper to Congress on political economy in which he stressed 'the importance of adequate wages, a well regulated home and education'.[51]. The common sentiments in all of these pronouncements advocate the necessary requirements for progress within the contemporary social system.

Apart from a general satisfaction at the progress being made in the provision of schools, a progress that could be witnessed by the building programme in many cities, education was not seen as a necessary weapon in the struggle for working people. At the time it was seen as a practical means of improving skill within the artisan class and only later as a possible tool for social mobility. Hence there were no calls for deep thinking about the purpose of education: less still was the curriculum considered a matter for discussion.

From the passing of the 1870 Education Act, when trade unionists saw the promise of schooling far better than anything they had experienced in their own childhood,[52] the only union which could have pointed out the detailed problems within the system was the best organized white collar union of the time, the National Union of Elementary School Teachers,[53] founded in June 1870 following a meeting by some hundreds of teachers at Kings College, London University.[54] This union usually supported TUC aims in education,[55] even if through no more than self interest, for most unions wished to see improvements in the education system which could only be introduced by improving conditions for teachers.

However, the one factor which prevented them from adding their experienced voice to that of other unions in matters of education was the refusal of their members to affiliate to the TUC; a resolution to this effect was lost at the 1895 NUT Conference by a two to one majority. This union could have explained the hard realities behind the revised code teaching, known everywhere as 'payment by results', a system which aroused no show of disapproval at the TUC. The reluctance of the NUT to join with other unions meant that TUC delegates in turn were not enthusiastic in welcoming teachers to their own discussions on education. Hence when the Paris School Teachers Trade Union wrote for credentials to attend the International Congress of Trade Unions being organized in London by the TUC, its application was refused by the PCTUC.[56] They made it clear that they would not put the matter to a vote and that should this stance be ignored at the meeting, 'they will refuse to take any further part in the proceedings and will give notice to the proprietors of St. Andrew's Hall that they will no longer be responsible for any damage which may be done to the premises'.[57] There was no further argument but it is almost certain that their attitude towards the French teachers had been coloured by their experience of the NUT in England. As late as 1901 when Congress met in Swansea, and the Honorary Secretary of the Reception Committee, W.C. Jenkins of the NUT, told delegates that '. . . the children of the toilers were being robbed', the first response was a question from the crowd asking about affiliation, to which a reply was shouted from another member of the crowd, 'Oh, we're too respectable for them'.[58]

1885–1902 TUC Moves Towards the Development of an Education Policy

The restoration of education to the agenda of the TUC in 1885 was not a direct product of the new socialist movements springing up, such as the Democratic Federation established by H.M. Hyndman in 1881, still less of the Fabian Society founded three years later, in the same year as Hyndman's organization was renamed the Social Democratic Federation and took upon itself the task of promoting Marxist ideology. Supporters of such groups were still to arrive at the TUC as delegates, whilst their election to the PCTUC was, as yet, many years away. In any case the initial reappearance of education as a topic for discussion was as a call to make it free and this was largely prompted by the fact that the Education Act of 1880 had made school attendance compulsory, so it was argued that this was causing hardship among poorer families.

However, the measure of free education was to be one example of how unquestioned support for the Liberal Party could no longer be guaranteed at Congress. Unemployment was widespread as the trade depression which had begun in the 1870s reached its nadir. Extension of the franchise to two million more males in 1884 added potential strength to labour although, even with the guarantee of the Secret Ballot Act of 1872, there was no evidence that many rural workers were attracted to radical political ideas. Nevertheless Congress was disenchanted enough with Liberal inaction over free education to force the PCTUC to add this demand to their draft alongside the Payment of Election Expenses and Payment for MPs.[59]

Despite such occasional successful challenges to the PCTUC's faith in Liberalism it would be unwise to exaggerate such moves. When Hardie accused Broadhurst in 1889 of having shares in a company which practised sweated labour he could find few to support his challenge of the Secretary, delegates voting by 11:177 in favour of the latter. The 'New Unionism' of 1889 did not produce delegates to Congress before 1890[60] and few were elected to the PCTUC: only Will Thorne secured a permanent place, Tom Mann was never elected, and John Burns[61] and Ben Tillett[62] lost their seats after only two years, and twenty-seven years later when the latter gained a seat on the General Council he had softened considerably.

It was not until after the mid 1890s that more than a small number at Congress were to show impatience with the leadership's cautious approach, although revolutionary remarks were expressed in speeches occasionally before then. For example, R. Ritchie of the Dundee Trades Council told Congress the enactment of the Eight Hour Day would not be a permanent adjustment to the social machine but it would be a move in the right direction:

... a stop gap until such times as education shall have spread the light and enabled the people to grappel [sic] with and sweep away the real causes of the oppression of labour. It will then go hard with the gambler on the Stock Exchange, who draws from the wealth of the country without having added anything thereto; with the land monopolist, and with the receiver of rents and royalties.[63]

It might be thought that such radical talk was linked to the new successes of the unskilled workers such as the Match Girls with their victorious strike of 1888 and the Gasworkers' Eight Hour victory in August without any industrial action and after being in existence for only three months as a trade union. Indeed, as Ritchie spoke the Dockers' Strike in London was at its height but the TUC did not seem to be enthusiastic about such events. It is more likely that the leadership was rather concerned about the success that militant action was having. As some measure of TUC involvement, whilst thousands of pounds were donated by overseas unions in support of the dockers the TUC could only raise £10, and that was collected from the attending delegates. Congress could applaud the criticisms of the stock exchange at the beginning of Congress but still rally to Broadhurst when he was under attack for his shares in Brunner Mond. The 'old guard' were still firmly in command at the PCTUC and could list a string of real benefits realised by the efforts of their Parliamentary representatives for trade unions: the Corrupt Practices Act of 1883; Extension of the Franchise in 1884; the redistribution of seats in 1885 and the County Councils Act of 1888. In return, the TUC had for some years been accepted as a responsible institution in Victorian society. For example, in 1891 they were asked to appoint a representative to the Governing Body of the Imperial Institute,[64] another small success for those seeking respectability.

By the early 1890s socialist ideas were beginning to spread through the trade union world, especially through the trades councils. Just as at the end of the 1860s NEL members of trade unions had brought their education policies before Congress, so now members of the SDF and ILP as trade unionists brought forward the policies of these socialist organizations via trade union resolutions. Hence Thorne (SDF) and J.R. Clynes (ILP), both from the Gasworkers Union, put forward the first resolution upon education which was a little more than an immediate response to the current situation. Apart from calling for a rise in the school leaving age to fifteen years and the abolition of night work for all young people under eighteen years, Thorne demanded the democratic control of education; a criticism in fact of the religious schools which received public money but were not accountable in the same manner as the board schools. He also stressed the need for 'equality of opportunity' to be the principle behind future developments in education; not an egalitarian ideal but some step towards such a view and one which would be easily recognized by the able trade unionists who often felt that in spite of their proven skill their social background prevented them from receiving the recognition, promotion and income due to them.

In the very year that Thorne introduced the resolution from the Gasworkers Union, who were to be in the vanguard of TUC education policy formation for the next ten years or more, the trades councils, the largest source of socialist support, were excluded from the TUC. Burns, who had been an independent Labour MP for Battersea since 1892 secured their exclusion, ostensibly because such a system sometimes meant that a trade union might be represented more than once, although there were others who believed it was one more attempt by the PCTUC to prevent socialist influence from spreading within the TUC.[65]

In spite of the removal of radical support, the Gasworkers Union's educational programme, which had many proposals similar to the SDF and ILP programme, received the support of Congress with the exception of reservations expressed by the Lancashire Textile trade unionists[66] concerning any raising of the school leaving age and the dispute which arose among a minority who wished to retain sectarian teaching in schools.[67] There is little doubt that most trade unionists thought that more education was in itself inevitably a good thing to support, especially as so many had been denied the opportunity for any period of continuous schooling when young.[68] To add to this feeling of neglect, which they were determined should not be experienced by their own children and grandchildren, support for Thorne's annual resolution was reinforced when it appeared that the newly elected Conservative Government of 1895 wished to change the path along which the education system had been travelling steadily since 1870. Whilst improvement had been slow it had at least been visible: compulsory attendance in 1880; the removal of fees in most elementary schools in 1891 and the development of some kind of secondary education in the form of 'Higher Grade' schools especially in the 1890s.

Conservative moves were a shock to many trade unionists because, impatient with Liberal policy, many working class people had voted Tory, seeing them as the obvious alternative to the Liberals. The lack of widespread support for socialist ideas became apparent when all twenty-eight ILP candidates were defeated and only nine Lib-Labs held on to their seats. It now seemed as if the Conservatives were quite willing to antagonize many of the working people who had voted for them although it can also be argued that they were rewarding the Religious Societies who supported them regularly.

The 1896 Education Bill was described as a means of rationalizing the present system. In reality this meant providing fresh aid for religious schools whilst restricting the amount of rate which could be spent on board schools. As Thorne had warned in his first resolution on education before Congress in 1895, there was a danger that public money would be spent in education without public control. This is precisely what would happen if more financial assistance were to be given to religious schools which did not possess democratically elected 'boards' for their management. Disillusion with the new Conservative Government among trade unionists did not take long. J. Mallinson (Edinburgh Trades Council), in his presidential address told delegates that

... although the present Government had been in office for fifteen months, it would be difficult to point out any one really tangible and beneficial measure passed in the interests of labour ... while other measures of a retrograde and questionable character, such as the Education Bill ... have been fully occupying the time of Parliament ...[69]

It was not easy to forget some of the promises made at the time of the election, such as the shortening of hours of labour and old age pensions, but these never came to fruition as much of the energy of the Tory Government was taken up by its policy of Imperialism. Enough opposition was aroused in Parliament for the Bill to be withdrawn although a similar Bill giving further financial aid to religious schools was passed the following year.

During the last few years of the nineteenth century, attitudes concerning education were to polarize once more. The Church of England, supported to some extent by the growing Roman Catholic Church, wished to restore as far as possible its traditional control over education which had been challenged severely by the school board system. The Conservatives wished to re-introduce the separation of secondary education from elementary education on social as well as academic grounds for, whilst this had always been the practice, the development of 'Higher Grade' schools had helped to undermine it in certain areas. Both were therefore inevitable allies with a common enemy: the board school system.[70] The defenders of the board schools were the non-conformists and most sections of the labour movement including the TUC. The latter worked hard to focus attention upon the central issue as they saw it; the need to defend the system of locally elected boards over which they might have some control. The attention of the non-conformists and the news media in general focused upon the religious dispute involved. In the end the Conservative Party was able to abolish the school boards with its 1902 Education Act, hotly disputed but finally forced home with the use of the newly introduced guillotine.

1902–1914 The Struggle of the TUC for Secondary Education

The early years of the twentieth century saw the British labour movement increasingly involved in political battles as the Edwardian period brought a setback to the improvements in living conditions experienced by many working class people in the late 1890s. Demands were made for an eight hour day for coal miners and the number of strikes rapidly increased in the period leading up to World War I. The trade union world had at last been convinced that it could no longer leave the Liberal Party to look after its interests. Following an intense debate at the 1899 Congress upon a resolution from the ASRS to bring various sections of the labour movement together to sponsor their own MPs, a narrow victory by 546,000 votes to 434,000 authorized four representatives from the PCTUC (Sam Woods – Miners, W.C. Steadman –

Bargebuilders, Will Thorne – Gasworkers and Richard Bell – Railwaymen), to meet two representatives from the three socialist parties: SDF, ILP, and the Fabians. The result was the foundation of the Labour Representation Committee[71] in February 1900 which put up fifteen candidates in the 'Khaki Election' of that year, of whom two were elected, Kier Hardie and Richard Bell. Six years later it returned twenty-nine MPs thereby giving notice of the potential voting power of the developing labour movement.

The trade union movement suffered two severe setbacks in the first decade of the twentieth century, both as a result of legal decisions. In 1901 the Taff Vale decision awarded damages of £20,000 against the Amalgamated Society of Railway Servants for losses suffered by the Taff Vale Railway Company during a strike and in 1909 the Osborne judgement prohibited trade unions from giving money to the Labour Party. The latter had implications for education:

> Sidney Webb believed that not political action alone but 'any work of general education; the formation of a library; the formation or management of University Extension or WEA Classes; the subscriptions for circulating book boxes; the provision of public lectures; the establishment of scholarships at Ruskin College, Oxford, or any other College' were plainly ultra vires and illegal.[72]

Education, once more, had to give way at the TUC to matters concerning the very existence of the labour movement. Yet both the PCTUC and TUC continued to give time to education not only by lengthy discussion at Congress, but in the case of the PCTUC, by using a variety of methods to get their views on the subject known and promoted. They encouraged all branches of the labour movement to bring pressure upon local government; the main means of doing this was through the organization of the trades councils. They were willing to work with other bodies where similar views were held upon a topic; in the field of education this was often the NUT.[73] As the number of Labour MPs increased so their views became more widely known, especially when Will Thorne presented an Education Bill in 1906 which was a replica of TUC Education Policy.[74] Finally, the PCTUC began to send deputations regularly to the Board of Education to outline their policy and plead the justice of their case directly to the President of the Board of Education.

For several years following the 1902 Education Act, TUC Education resolutions were introduced by the statement that: 'This Congress condemns the Education Policy of the Government, and desires to formulate a constructive educational programme based upon the principle of equal opportunities for all'.[75] The major problem facing the labour movement was the means by which their children could really gain a share in the secondary education system which was barred to most children by fees and entrance examinations. Government Ministers might agree, when meeting trade unionists, with the sentiment of 'equal opportunities for all' but they would not countenance the corollary of TUC Education policy which required, 'That all grades of education shall be free and State maintained',[76] a condition that the TUC felt was imperative if lofty phrases were to be translated into political reality.

Following the passage of the 1902 Education Act there was widespread agitation for its repeal. The Liberals claimed they would bring in legislation to deal with the aspects of the Bill found to be most offensive to non-conformists, just as they pledged themselves to change the law to prevent the possibility of another 'Taff Vale' decision being made to the detriment of the labour movement. The TUC continued to search for a solution to the religious issue by advocating secular education and, although they also gave attention to other educational matters such as the introduction of the metric system into British schools,[77] their interest in the field of education became increasingly focused upon the greater provision of secondary education.

There were three associated problems to be overcome if more children from lower income groups were to obtain a secondary education. The physical provision of more places within the secondary system was one obvious requirement but in addition there were financial and social problems also to be overcome.

> Although secondary education became available to a limited extent after 1890, in practise, large numbers of parents found that their children were unable to take advantage of it, and intelligent children frequently won scholarships which they could not accept. Even if they actively commenced their studies at secondary school, there was no guarantee that they would remain there for the length of time which would be of permanent benefit to them and many left at fourteen.[78]

To combat this problem the TUC fought for financial assistance for young scholars in the form of maintenance grants and the fairer use of Educational Endowments.

To overcome another factor which prevented numerous children from attending secondary school, namely, poor health, the TUC struggled to obtain legislation which would compel local authorities to provide school meals, medical inspection and treatment. Such demands were part of a comprehensive policy designed to enable more children to benefit from secondary education. Moreover, the granting of one part of this policy without the other inevitably meant that young people would not gain fully from the extension of secondary school provision, yet unfortunately it can be seen that development in related areas of social policy was uneven historically and geographically, and in many cases unfair.[79]

TUC demands for secondary education in some ways were ambiguous for they varied from support for egalitarianism to a meritocratic principle although members never seemed to realise the two were incompatible in the long run. There were traces of dual conflicting demands in the Bryce Memorial of 1895[80] but similarly they were to be found in TUC resolutions. In 1895 Thorne called for trade unionists, '... to secure the democratic principle of equality of opportunity'[81] without further elaboration but two years later TUC education policy had been extended to add to this earlier statement, that members 'should not be satisfied until the highest educational advantages which the country affords are within the reach of all'.[82] Yet in spite of the additional phrase it was still not clear whether secondary education was being called for for all or just those who could 'reach it'.

Slight variations on the theme are to be observed in the following years: 'scholarships available for those parents who are anxious to continue the education of their children',[83] in 1902; 'all children whose usefulness would be enhanced by an extended education'[84] in 1903; and 'for all those who desire to avail themselves of it'[85] in 1906. The wording changed but a selective element remained whether it be through the wish of parents or some assessment of the child which would make it known whether 'his usefulness could be enhanced' by such an education. It was not until 1907 that it was proposed that secondary education should 'be an essential part of every child's education',[86] but whilst such thinking suggested an open policy of secondary education for all in theory, much of the discussion by trade unionists when they visited the Board of Education suggested an acceptance of restricted entry for working class children based upon some measure of academic achievement. It was not academic competition TUC delegates argued against but the way in which school fees acted as a social barrier to secondary education.

One can find the rare objection to examinations and competitive schooling[87] but trade unionists lived in a world of craft and skilled hierarchies separated by differentials in pay, fought for by skilled workers and largely accepted by the 'unskilled' workforce. Competition therefore, with some reward system attached, usually in the form of improved job prospects, especially in terms of pay and security, readily became acceptable to Congress so that by 1921 one section of the education resolution called for free access to secondary education 'Whenever he or she has passed the qualifying examination'[88] and by 1924, with such a principle firmly established, Congress could only call for 'more scholarships'[89]; it would be some years before the influence of Tawney's 'Secondary Education for All' pamphlet had a major impact upon the labour movement.

In some ways one can see a repeat of the situation following the 1870 Education Act when the TUC pressed for improvements within a system which had potential for such developments; such as making elementary education compulsory and then largely free. In the Edwardian era, once it became obvious that the 1902 Education Act was firmly established, and believing that when returned to Office the Liberals would reverse the situation just as they promised to do for Taff Vale, so trade unionists worked to make improvements within the framework of the system as it was. They were rewarded by Parliamentary legislation, often of a permissive kind, such as the Provision of Meals Act of 1906, and the Education (Administrative Provisions) Act of 1907 requiring local authorities to examine children in elementary schools medically at least three times during their school career. On other issues, such as demands for an inquiry into endowments, which trade unionists believed had been diverted from the purpose of their original founders, there was no progress to report at all; partly because the Board of Education had no jurisdiction over private education, and one suspects, from an examination of the social background of past Presidents of the Board of Education, that they had considerable sympathy for the private system of education which they had in any case experienced themselves.[90] It has to be realized, however, that if improvements were slow it was partly because the Board of Education was not powerful enough to demand the money required – for free secondary education, for example, or the associated welfare services which were needed. The President of the Board of Education was not a member of the Cabinet during this period. The trend towards improvements which had been made, however, came to an end with the outbreak of the First World War.

1914–1925 The TUC Fight Against Cut-Backs in the Education Service

In the early years of World War I education was considered of secondary importance by the Government. The waging of war received top priority so that child labour began to increase considerably, especially in rural areas. TUC deputations to the Board of Education could complain that farmers were taking advantage of the system by employing children at lower rates of pay but the 'exceptional' situation was reason enough as far as Arthur Henderson, President of the Board, was concerned. This was a reply which trade unionists found doubly disagreeable coming from a trade unionist who had once been in their ranks.

Only towards the end of the war was there a change in attitude, even if not in practice, as many began to realise that better educational opportunities would be an important part of the new society which servicemen had been frequently told they were fighting for. An indication that the Government also believed this to be true was the appointment of H.A.L. Fisher to the Presidency of the Board in 1917. He was a proven academic and Liberal who was known to be keen on education expansion and sympathetic to working people. In fact, like most previous presidents, he had no experience of schools, other than private schools, either as pupil or teacher and later made it clear that whilst he was interested in the post it was not his first choice, nor the one to which he thought he was best suited.[91]

The TUC welcomed him at the Board and certainly felt that they had a sympathetic ally who approved of many of their proposals. 'We are hoping – I do not know whether our hopes will be realized – a great deal from you, because you fully understand the question of education from top to bottom' Thorne told Fisher when leading a Parliamentary Committee deputation to the Board.[92] This faith seemed to be justified as Fisher prepared the Education Bill of 1917 for, whilst the TUC were not particularly keen on the idea of Continuation Classes, they fully supported the raising of the school leaving age to fourteen years without exception. It was the FBI which was to oppose parts of the Bill,[93] and hence the President found that his plans were more fully supported by the labour movement than by the world of industry.

The early euphoria of the TUC was short lived for before the Act could be fully implemented there were already demands for cut-backs in certain areas, especially the proposals for part time education of young people from fourteen to sixteen and then later from sixteen to eighteen years. By 1921 Thorne was informing Fisher that TUC deputations had been receiving sympathy enough but of a negative kind:

> Some Ministers have gone even further than that and have told us that in consequence of decisions or undertakings arrived at by the Cabinet, it would be foolish on the one hand, and unfair to them on the other, to lead us to believe that they could do anything along the lines that we suggest ... we feel that it is a very great disappointment and will create, when it is generally known, a great revulsion of feeling amongst the workers of the country ...[94]

Only a matter of months later an *ad hoc* committee was to be set up by the Cabinet under the chairmanship of Sir Eric Geddes to advise on specific economies: those of defence and the social services. It proposed cut-backs of eighteen million pounds in Education.[95] From this time onwards the TUC could only complain bitterly as they saw the promises of the 1918 Education Act gradually abandoned as part of a Government campaign to try to restore the economic conditions of Edwardian times. As the cut-backs bit deeply into all sections of the economy the TUC once more was forced to consider the basic welfare of trade unionists – their very jobs if they were to survive the impending economic slump. Education once more became of less importance – small wonder as a General Strike was only months away.

1900–1925 The TUC's Involvement with Adult Education

There is no doubt that economic factors pushed schooling to the background as more attention was given to economic themes at Congress in the 1920s. At the same time adult education[96] was also a factor which began to capture Congress attention, increasingly at the expense of education for children. Appeals from several organizations for financial aid were made to Congress; at first from Ruskin College and the WEA and later from their rivals, the Central Labour College and the NCLC. The arguments between these rival organizations, all offering education to trade unionists, forced the TUC to consider the vital area of curriculum in the matter of education for trade unionists.

To confuse the issue, different unions supported different colleges so that at Congress the arguments between the two groups were put before delegates. Support Ruskin College and the WEA because they educated workers in a 'neutral' manner? Support the Central Labour College and the NCLC because they would show workers, from a socialist point of view, how capitalism continually cheats them and would provide trade unionists with the knowledge as to how and why such an economic and social system should be replaced with a socialist society? The TUC listened and provided financial assistance to both groups.

In the 1920s moves were made by the TUC to bring Ruskin College and the Central Labour College together under one roof to form a TUC College. Easton Lodge was offered to the TUC by the Countess of Warwick but agreement could not be reached for a variety of reasons. The fundamental differences in political philosophy between the organizations, especially the very outspoken NCLC, made it virtually impossible to bring about agreement. In addition, strong reservations were expressed by Ruskin College as to the suitability of a TUC College in the wilds of the Essex countryside. Finally the PCTUC called the idea off. Whatever the problems of rival ideologies the financial costs of Easton Lodge would have been more than substantial. The TUC could never have continued them past 1926 when the General Strike demanded both the attention and the funds of the three major unions who had financed trade union education: the National Union of Railwaymen, the National Union of Mineworkers and the Iron and Steel Trades Confederation.

The TUC and Technical Education

TUC attention in education had been concentrated upon elementary education in the nineteenth century and secondary education after 1902. However, from its first meeting in 1868 well into the 1920s, technical education received considerable support from the TUC[97] and very often at times when it was completely ignored by other sections of society. It is inevitable that a movement of craft trade unionists should take an interest in a form of education which was related to the apprenticeship system they had all known, at least in content.

This first claim might be seen as the approach of Robert Applegarth who urged in 1870 that it was necessary for workmen to be able to master machinery. A strong supporter of such education, he began a new campaign forty years later when seventy-seven years of age, demanding 'industrial education' as an important part of the school system. In the nineteenth century trade unionists supported technical education because they knew that skilled workers received higher wages and better job security. Yet the reason frequently given was in fact the fear of foreign competition, especially that of Germany.[98]

The craft element within the TUC and the economic factors concerning skilled workers remained strong enough for technical education to receive continued support. By the twentieth century however, there was a change in emphasis. Technical education was not abandoned but took second place to secondary education. It is possible that by this time trade unionists saw that technical education might well allow a workman to become skilled and get promoted to a foreman's grade but at the same time ensure that he was not promoted any further. The kind of curriculum offered by secondary schools seemed to offer the opportunity for intelligent working class pupils to avoid the factory floor and enter the office, offering even better security than that of skilled workers plus the benefits of sick pay and superannuation – facilities unavailable to most blue collar workers at the time.

Trade union support for technical education was recognized enough for Bradford Technical College to approach Congress, when it met in their town in 1888, to ask whether they would be willing to support three scholarships. The PCTUC agreed on condition that they were called 'Trade Union Congress Scholarships' and limited to 'none but the sons of mechanics or labourers'.[99] Alternatively, in the same year, Hull Trades Council could make no impact upon the local authority to provide technical education in schools,[100] but trades councils did receive some encouragement from the Technical Instruction Act of 1889 which enabled them to discuss local courses with Technical Instruction Committees.[101]

Such activity was, however, dampened by the development of secondary education, following the 1902 Education Act, clearly along the lines of the public school syllabus; the syllabus known and experienced by the architects of this Act, namely Robert Morant and A.J. Balfour. The status of this type of secondary education was seen to outweigh the usefulness of a technical course by those who looked to education as a means of social mobility. For all its warnings about the importance of technical education in the competitive world the TUC was largely ignored. In 1911, H. Elvin, as a member of the PCTUC delegation to the Board of Education told W. Runciman, President of the Board, that there was more to worry about from Germany's schooling than her dreadnoughts;[102] a warning repeated by the TUC President to Congress delegates in 1916.[103]

In fact, out of Fisher's 1918 Education Act, came the promise of Continuation Classes which received initial support from the TUC but later cautious criticism. When seen as an offer to extend education for young people over fourteen years of age in terms of part-time study they were welcomed, whether they were of a technical nature or not. Later there were doubts when it became apparent that they might be provided as a substitute for secondary education among working class adolescents or so vocationally orientated, if provided by a particular company, that they would enable young people to be qualified only for work carried out by that company. Therefore, whilst trade unionists were genuinely attracted to technical education because they were interested in the skills and knowledge involved, in engineering for example, they also hesitated in the twentieth century when they feared that vocational training might be used on a class basis to keep them in their 'proper place', within the social hierarchy.

Demands of Trade Unionists for Education

It is possible to recognize certain themes behind demands for improved educational provision at times. Yet when one considers the reasons sometimes given, either to Congress or Government Ministers or to the public through the platform of some other body such as the NEL in the early years of Congress, it becomes obvious that trade unionists often supported education for completely different reasons to their colleagues. Indeed, at times, for almost contradictory reasons. Foreign competition as a threat has already been mentioned, so too has the lack of education experienced by so many of the delegates prior to the turn of the century. Applegarth advocated education to combat crime,[104] a witness to the Newcastle Commission suggested it was the key to a better paid job[105] whilst Joseph Arch declared it would make trade union organization easier.[106] It was advocated to improve safety in mines in 1871[107] whilst W.J. Davis, who could not be described in any way as a radical, nevertheless believed that education had been withheld 'to keep the industrial classes in a state of ignorance'.[108]

Whatever their disagreements on other matters, trade unionists tended to support more education for the young. They did so for a variety of reasons and motives, including the wish to keep them at school and off the labour market. It would seem they were able to reach agreement because they wished for the same result for different reasons. They could disagree about the reasons but still support the same resolution. This is one major explanation as to how a cautious, some might even say conservative, trade union organization ended up with a radical education policy. The other is because more radical elements were able to present to the TUC what were in effect the policies of radical organizations twice removed from Congress which were able to put their programme on the agenda via an affiliated trade union. This might be the explanation of how the resolution made its way to the agenda but it is because resolutions could be interpreted in so many ways, so that each delegate was able to give it support for a different reason, that radical educational ideas were pioneered by Congress.

Notes

1 DAVIS, W.J. *The British Trades Union Congress: History and Reflections*, 1868–1887, Vol. 1, p. 60, also HAMILTON W. *My Queen and I*, Ch. 4.
2 At least no major criticisms of Imperialism were made: 'During the years of Disraeli's premiership the Trades Union Congress gave no consideration to the momentous issues raised by his foreign policy. No resolution appears on the agenda, nor in the debates is reference ever made to any aspect of the "Eastern Question", in spite of the fact that during these years Gladstone was rousing radical opinion against the Tories with his campaign on the Bulgarian atrocities. Disraeli's imperialist wars in Afghanistan and South Africa were not mentioned, but the Parliamentary Committee invited a Lancashire industrialist in 1879 to read a paper on the potential markets offered to British exports if the continent of Africa was

opened up to foreign trade. Henry Crompton who was present at this, asked the delegates not to support such a scheme, which would involve England in the crimes and horrors of wars of conquest; he received some support, but Congress, with mass unemployment in mind, gave the paper a cautious approval.' ROBERTS, B.C. *The Trades Union Congress 1868–1921, pp. 99–100*. Acceptance of imperialism was largely reflected in sentiments expressing support for investments or technical education to beat foreign competition in trade and commerce e.g. presidential addresses by Threlfall T.R. and Ritchie R. in 1885 and 1889 respectively, both stressed the need to win the 'industrial race'. In 1906 Ben Tillett wanted better schooling made available for children, '... in order to make them worthy of this great Empire.' TUC Report 1906, p. 175.

3 '... a resolution in favour of manhood suffrage was thrown out by a large majority.' DAVIS, W.J. *op. cit.*

4 For the purpose of this book the Labour movement will be understood to mean the broadly accepted section of organized Labour including TUC, Co-operative Movement, ILP, SDF, Labour Party and Communist Party; the latter only being in existence for the last five years under consideration.

5 TUC Report 1869, p. 19.

6 A problem which confronted the Webbs when providing statistical tables for their *History of Trade Unionism*, for, as they point out, until 1886 when John Burnett was appointed Labour Correspondent to the Board of Trade no attempt was made to collect accurate figures of the movement.

7 These figures are taken from G.D.H. Cole's *A Short History of the British Working Class Movement 1789–1947*, and whilst they do not accord exactly with the Webbs' figures they do provide total trade union membership compared with affiliated TUC membership.

8 See p. 26.

9 For example James Sexton (Roman Catholic); Henry Broadhurst (Methodist); W.A. Appleton (Church of England); John Burns (Freethinker).

10 See LEE, A.J. 'Conservatism, Traditionalism and the British Working Class 1880–1918' in MARTIN, D.E. and RUBINSTEIN, D. *Ideology and the Labour Movement*.

11 Some idea of the variety of political views held can be gained from the following examples of political allegiance: Conservative: BIRTWHISTLE, T., ENTWHISTLE, F., MAUDSLEY, J.; Fabians – STEADMAN, W.C., CROOKS, W.; ILP – BARNES, G., CLYNES, J.R., CURRAN, P., HARDIE, K., THOMAS, J.H.; Liberal – BROADHURST, H., CREMER, W.R., HOWELL, G., FENWICK, C., APPLETON, W.A.; SDF – BURNS, J., THORNE, W., BEVIN, E.; Communist – COOK, A.J., MANN, T.; Labour – SEXTON, J., TILLETT, B. Many changed parties, or were members of more than one party. After 1900 most trade unionists joined the Labour Party. There were, however, trade unionists who believed it was possible and preferable to exclude any discussion of political matters e.g. The National Amalgamated Union of Labour which claimed in November 1890 that '... as a society of working men this organization is non-political'. CLEGG, H.A., FOX, A., and THOMPSON, A.F. *A History of British Trade Unions Since 1889*, Vol. I., p. 95. In 1888 within the Hull Trades Council a proposal to amend the rules in order to allow political matters to be discussed was defeated early in the year, although later a similarly worded resolution was passed but there were still members who believed that only 'trade matters' should be discussed at such meetings. See BROWN, R., *The Labour Movement in Hull 1870–1900 with Special Reference to New Unionism*, M.Sc. Thesis, University of Hull, 1966, pp. 93–4.

12 See chapter 2.

13 See chapter 3.

14 E.g. The Sunday Opening of Museums Debate. See chapter 3.

15 The International Working Men's Association formed in 1864 under the leadership of George Odger, supported by W. Cremer and heavily influenced by Karl Marx. The London Working Men's Association formed in 1866 by George Potter to support the 1867 Reform Bill lasted about twelve months. The United Kingdom Alliance of Organised Trades established by W. Dronfield effectively to resist lock-outs collapsed in 1867.

16 See MUSSON, A.E. *The Congress of 1868*, chapter 1.

17 *Ibid.*, p. 32.

18 WEBB, S. *The History of Trade Unionism*, p. 215.

19 The other elected members were Peter Shorrocks, William Owen, Thomas Plackett and John Odger.

20 Lyon Playfair had visited the 1867 Paris Exhibition and written to the Taunton Commission about the comparative decline of British manufacturing which he attributed to a lack of technical education in England. This view was verified by other observers. See LAWSON, J. and SILVER, H. *A Social History of Education in England*, p. 303.

21 FROW, E. and KATANKA, M. (Eds) *1868 Year of the Unions*, p. 34.

22 TUC 1885, 1886, 1889, 1893, 1906, etc.

23 Typified by Robert Lowe's often quoted statement: 'I believe it will be absolutely necessary to compel our future masters to learn their letters.'.

24 Robert Lowe's 'pathological loathing of democracy' and his determination to make certain that education provided for working class children would ensure that they knew their place in the hierarchy of the Victorian era is well explained in: SIMON, B. *History of Education 1780–1870*, Vol. 1, pp. 354–356; STURT, M. *The Education of the People*, Ch. 12; FRASER, W.H. *Trade Unions and Society 1850–1880*, pp. 155–156.

25 SIMON, B., Vol. 1, *op. cit.*, p. 359.

26 MARCHAM, A. J. 'The Birmingham Education Society and the 1870 Education Act' *Journal of Educational Administration and History*, 8 (1) January 1976, pp. 11–12.

27 '. . . Dixon approached the second Trades Union Congress with a request that Charles Hibbs, a Birmingham gun-maker, be allowed to put the League case to delegates . . . trade union speakers whilst making clear that the League's policy did not necessarily meet all their wishes, supported it on the grounds that it stood for a national system, backed by compulsion.' McCANN, W.P. 'Trade Unionists, Artisans and the 1870 Education Act.' *British Journal of Educational Studies*. 17 (2) June 1970, p. 137.

28 A Congress was originally planned for October 1870 (see *Beehive* 6. 8. 1870). There is also some suggestion that the LTC were not keen to call the third TUC because they preferred to have the major say in lobbying MPs. ROBERTS, B.C., *op. cit.*, pp. 61, 62.

29 *Beehive*, 18.6.1870.

30 *Beehive*, 2.7.1870.

31 See Chapter 2.

32 WEBB, S. and WEBB, B. *op. cit.*, p. 265.

33 TUC Report 1871, p. 87.

34 See Chapter 3.

35 TUC 1874, see Appendix II.

36 McCANN, W.P. British Journal of Educational Studies 1970 *op. cit.*, p. 147.

37 MORTON, A.L. and TATE, G., *The British Labour Movement*, p. 120.

38 DAVIS, W.J., *The British Trades Union Congress History and Recollections 1868–1887*. Vol. 1, p. 52.

39 For a list of minor reforms pursued 1875–80 see ROBERTS, B.C. *op. cit.*, p. 96.

40 George Odger, Robert Applegarth and George Howell all found early attempts to

become MPs thwarted by Liberal Party opposition. See FRASER, W.H. *op. cit.*, p. 138.
41 See Chapter 8.
42 *Ibid.*
43 As, for example, their attempt in 1885 to exclude the demand for free education from the PCTUC programme in case it should embarrass the Liberal Party. See Chapter 3.
44 See HOBSBAWM E.J., 'The Labour Aristocracy in Nineteenth Century Britain' in *Labouring Men.*
45 Such as the support shown for Broadhurst in 1887 and 1888 when challenged by Hardie and the re-election of Fenwick to the secretaryship of the PCTUC in 1892 even though he was known to be against the Eight Hour Day policy of Congress.
46 TUC Report 1874, pp. 18–19.
47 TUC Report 1875, p. 46.
48 JEFFEREYS, J.B. (Ed) *Labour's Formative Years 1849–79*, p. 42.
49 DAVIS, W.J. *op. cit.*, p. 51.
50 *Ibid.*, p. 63.
51 TUC Report 1880, p. 27.
52 See Chapter 8.
53 It dropped the 'Elementary' from its title in 1889 for matters of status as some of its members were teaching beyond the elementary stages by then.
54 See TROPP, A., *The School Teachers*, Chapter 8.
55 It took the opposite line over the 1902 Education Act as many of its members taught in religious schools.
56 PCTUC Minutes 23.10.1888.
57 PCTUC Minutes 1.11.1888 and 5.11.1888.
58 TUC Report 1901, p. 27.
59 WEBB, S. and WEBB, B., *The History of Trade Unionism*, pp. 359–360.
60 Ben Tillett was on the PCTUC 1892–94.
61 Will Thorne of the Gasworkers was one of the first to attend in 1890.
62 John Burns was a member of the PCTUC 1890, 1893–94, but it was his own action in 1895 which led to his expulsion.
63 TUC Report 1889, p. 16.
64 PCTUC Minutes 1.6.1891 and 8.2.1891.
65 For full details of Burn's involvement and possible motives see ROBERTS, B.C. *The Trades Union Congress 1868–1921*, pp. 146–155; PELLING, H. *A History of British Trade Unionism*, pp. 108–109.
66 See Chapter 2.
67 See Chapter 3.
68 See Chapter 8.
69 TUC Report 1896, p. 20.
70 See Chapter 6.
71 Known as the Labour Party from 1906 onwards.
72 BAGWELL, P.S., *The Railwaymen*, p. 252.
73 Whilst the NUT held back from affiliation to the TUC the Union formed for Uncertificated Teachers (NUST) joined and were able to be included in PCTUC deputations to the Board of Education thereby putting forward their own complaints concerning security and pay. See Chapter 8.
74 See Appendix V.
75 TUC Report 1904, p. 119 and TUC Report 1905, p. 142.
76 TUC Report 1905, p. 142.
77 From 1905 onwards the TUC collaborated with the Decimal Association to introduce the metric system into British schools. PCTUC Minutes, 19.1.1905.
78 ELLIS, A.C.O., 'Influences on School Attendance in Victorian England', *British*

Journal of Educational Studies, 21 (3) Oct. 1973, p. 318
79 See Chapter 5.
80 For discussion of Trades Council Memorial to Bryce Commission see Chapter 4.
81 TUC Report 1895, p. 55.
82 TUC Report 1897, p. 97.
83 TUC Report 1902, p. 71.
84 TUC Report 1903, pp. 86–87.
85 TUC Education Bill 1906, Clause 4. See Appendix V.
86 TUC Report 1907, p. 186.
87 TUC Report 1897, p. 50. Thorne alone was consistent in opposing competitive examinations.
88 TUC Report 1921, p. 369.
89 TUC Report 1924, p. 418.
90 With the exception of Arthur Henderson, the ex-trade unionist, all the Presidents of the Board of Education 1900–25 were educated privately:

Duke of Devonshire	Private Tuition	Trinity, Cantab.
Marquis of Londonderry	Eton	Christ Church, Oxon.
Augustine Birrell	Amersham Hall	Trinity, Cantab.
Reginald McKenna	Kings Coll. School	Trinity, Cantab.
Walter Runciman	South Shield High/ Private Tuition	Trinity, Cantab.
J.A. Pease	Tottenham Grove House	Trinity, Cantab.
Arthur Henderson	Local elementary school	
Lord Crewe	Harrow	Trinity, Cantab.
H.A.L. Fisher	Winchester	New College, Oxon.
E.F.L. Wood	Eton	Christ Church, Oxon.
C. Trevellyan	Harrow	Trinity, Cantab.
Lord Eustace Percy	Eton	Christ Church, Oxon.

91 See FISHER, H.A.L. *An Unfinished Autobiography*, p. 97.
92 PCTUC Deputation to the Board of Education Minutes, 15.2.1917
93 FBI Deputation to the Board of Education Minutes, 21.11.1917
94 PCTUC Deputation to the Board of Education Minutes, 10.2.1921
95 For full details see SIMON B., *The Politics of Educational Reform 1920–40*. Vol. III, Chapter 1, Part III.
96 See Chapter 7.
97 See Appendix II.
98 For example, TUC Report 1893, p. 30: also 1896, 1905, 1906, etc.
99 PCTUC Minutes, 6.9.1888.
100 BROWN, R. *The Labour Movement in Hull 1870–90 with Special Reference to New Unionism*, M. Sc., (Econ.) Hull 1966, p. 117.
101 CLINTON, A. *Trade Councils from the beginning of the Twentieth Century to the Second World War*, Ph.D. London 1973, p. 82.
102 PCTUC Deputation to the Board of Education Minutes 16.3.1911.
103 TUC Report 1916, p. 62.
104 McCANN, W.P., *British Journal of Educational Studies*, 1970 *op. cit.*, p. 147.
105 *Report of the Commissioners appointed to inquire into the state of Popular Education in England* (The Newcastle Report) 1861, Vol. 1.
106 ARCH, J. *Autobiography of Joseph Arch*, pp. 90–91.
107 TUC Report 1871.
108 DAVIS, W.J. *The British Trades Union Congress History and Recollections*, Vol. 1, p. 2.

Chapter 2

Child Labour, Raising the School Leaving Age and Continuation Schools

Child Labour: Some Categories

Child labour, for most of the period under consideration, can be divided into numerous categories. The most obvious is that of children working full time for some wage and there is evidence to suggest that the total number in this category declined towards the close of the nineteenth century for two main reasons. In the first place the minimum school leaving age for children was gradually raised from ten years in 1876, to eleven years in 1893, twelve years in 1899 and fourteen years in 1918. This meant that more children were excluded from those numbers who had previously been allowed to work full time; at least in areas where the law was effectively applied. In the second place, the changing nature of industry meant that, in certain branches of manufacturing where heavy machinery was introduced or greater technical skill required, young children were no longer regarded as an asset in the factory. Whether child labour fell because machinery made young children less useful in factories or whether machinery had to be introduced into factories to compensate for the reduction in child labour resulting from the Factories and Workshops Extension Act of 1867 and the Education Act of 1870 it is difficult to decide. At least some of the decline in earlier opposition to raising the school leaving age can be attributed to this factor although in certain industries, such as textiles and agriculture, the wish to preserve child labour remained very strong.

Another category of child labour was that which became known as the 'Half-Time' system whose origins lie in the provision of Factory Acts passed earlier in the century[1] in order to combat excessive child labour.[2] It was prevalent in textile areas, especially Lancashire which contained approximately half of all half-timers and to a lesser extent in Yorkshire and Cheshire. In textile areas children went to the mill in the morning from 6 a.m. until 12.30 p.m., then to school between 2 p.m. and 4.30 p.m. The following week they attended school from 9 a.m. to noon and then went to the factory from 1.30 p.m. to 6 p.m. It can be seen that half-time was a misnomer for when the hours at work and school were totalled up over two six-day weeks, sixty-six hours were spent at the factory compared with only thirty hours at school.

Homework was another form of child labour which included forms of domestic work, especially staying at home to nurse young children if a mother was working, but also included work undertaken at home, as for example in London where the manufacture of matchboxes was one of the most widespread of these tasks[3] – often carried out in appalling conditions and not liable to inspection before 1891, and even then only after an inspector had obtained a warrant from a magistrate.

Work undertaken before and/or after school was widespread in towns, again especially in London, where children were used extensively for fetching and carrying errands or selling cheap items on street corners.[4] Both homework and before and after school work were extremely difficult to check on[5] and by the late nineteenth century had become the most exploited forms of child labour in terms of wages earned. Some aspects of such work were both described and condemned by W. Sherwood of the Gasworkers in promoting a resolution to raise the school leaving age without exemption to fifteen years of age in 1901:

> He instanced cases where boys under thirteen years of age were making glass bottles, working in an atmosphere which must degrade them ... there were boys and girls engaged in slimy cellars in the nauseous work of sorting out eggs ... little children were being sent to the fields to work at 4 o'clock in the morning.... Children ought not to be allowed to pester people to buy their wares late at night in the street ... the exposure itself must have a pernicious effect.... What was the use of sending children to school at 9 o'clock if they had been working since five and returned to work after school hours?[6]

There was plenty of casual work in rural England for children: beating for shooting parties; gathering flowers for sale; picking blackberries, collecting acorns for pigs, as well as harvesting crops such as cereals, potatoes, hops and apples. Indeed, on examination the log books of a sample of West Sussex rural schools for the period 1870–1918 show that absence from school for various kinds of rural work were to be found for every month of the year with the exception of May.[7] It is true that with the exception of harvesting such rural tasks were only extended over a few days but rural teachers were further frustrated in the knowledge that the school managers often knew of such work and made little attempt to stop it. The 1873 Agricultural Childrens' Act, which had been introduced to extend the earlier coverage of Factory Acts to 40,000 children connected with agriculture, was frequently ignored.[8] Illegal child labour in rural areas continued well down into the 1890s.

One of the hardest forms of child labour was related to the gang system found most commonly in East Anglia, in which farm work was contracted out to a gang leader who in turn paid a group of working men, women and children to perform the necessary task. These gangs included children down to four years of age and apart from such hard blistering and strenuous work as pulling turnips, children were expected to walk to and from work journeys of up to ten miles.[9] To read of the tasks involved, the journeys undertaken, the pittance in wages and the sleeping conditions endured is to wonder at the survival of any of these children into adulthood. The Gangs Act of 1867 prohibiting children under eight years of age from being employed in such work and giving magistrates the power to regulate the distances young children could walk to work checked the worst abuses of this system but it was not until the passing of the 1876 Education Act forbidding children under ten to be employed in agricultural work that the gang system began to fade as far as children were concerned.

Many industries provided peculiar problems for juveniles. One more example must suffice to indicate the complexity of the problem trade unionists were trying to combat.

In 1875 George Smith had drawn attention to the problems confronting children on canal boats[10] of whom there were about 25,000 with an estimated maximum permanent population of 100,000 persons. The following year he denounced the overcrowded conditions and drew attention to the '40,000 illegitimate children' crammed into boats 'scarcely the size of a gentleman's dog kennel'.[11] He recommended that children should neither sleep nor work on the boats but be forced to attend school at least until they had reached the second standard.

In 1877 a Government Bill was introduced which made the registration of boats compulsory and required each vessel to carry a certificate giving full details of the occupants. It also provided local school attendance committees with full jurisdiction over the boats in their area but a considerable part of the problem was the transitory work of the boats. It was virtually impossible for an authority to check on children who might be miles away the following day.

Broadhurst, when Secretary of the TUC and MP for Stoke, wrote to Smith in 1887 offering to help by introducing a further Bill into Parliament. He succeeded in putting forward a Private Members Bill with the support of John Cobbett, Samuel Morley and Albert Pell. It was intended to tighten up the provision of the 1877 Act and also to limit the hours of permissible child labour. However, the opposition on behalf of the canal companies blocked the Bill in its second reading. At the end of the century, in 1899, when the canal boat population had markedly declined, Sir John Gorst was still despairing at the lack of schooling these children were receiving, a problem which would not be remedied until they were no longer allowed to travel in canal boats.[12]

There is no way of gaining a comprehensive picture of child labour although it is known that it remained a substantial part of the work force throughout the nineteenth century.[13] Some measure of child labour in factories became known through the Inspectors of Factories Reports but in the twilight zones, where a combination of unscrupulous employers, selfish, ignorant or sometimes just destitute parents and those in official positions[14] who turned a blind eye to the labours performed by children, many of the grizzly descriptions of novelists such as Charles Kingsley, Arthur Morrison and Jack London were proven to be far from fictitious.[15] Indeed, they were substantiated by the social surveys of Charles Booth and Seebohm Rowntree.

The Child Labour Experience of Trade Unionists

For most trade unionists neither novels nor social surveys were needed to inform them of the conditions inflicted on children at work for they had the 'benefit' of their own childhood experiences upon which to judge. This is one of the major reasons why most trade unionists were opposed to child labour: they were only too well aware of its results and were determined that as far as they were able, they would not allow present and future generations of working class children to undergo the rigours of the workplace until they had received sufficient schooling and grown well into adolescence.

Nearly all the trade unionists listed in appendix I were at work before the passing of the 1870 Education Act. Early work on the farm, down the pits or as errand boys are seen to be fairly common for first time employment. The loss of the father was a common factor which forced many to earn money as early as possible to supplement the family budget. Examples of the several categories of child labour illustrated, with the exception of homework, can be found from the trade unionists listed. W.A. Appleton,[16] Keir Hardie and Frederic Rogers all began work as errand boys; Hardie at the tender age of seven, the other two at the age of ten years. Rogers described how he worked for an ironmonger from eight to eight each day, except on Saturday when he carried on until 10 p.m.[17]

J.H. Thomas provides an example of a young boy who had to work before and after school; two hours before and two hours after as well as all day Saturday. He had been left by his mother and was brought up by his grandmother. At nine years of age he began his part-time job as an errand boy for a chemist shop and at twelve years of age went to work full-time in the shop where he stayed for three years until becoming an engine cleaner on the Great Western Railway.[18] At least three of the trade unionists listed in appendix I started work as half-timers: J.R. Clynes became a half-timer at ten years of age working as a 'little piecer in a textile mill',[19] D.J. Shackleton began at a similar age at Hull Carr Cotton Mill; whilst Ben Turner, who became a strong critic of the system later, had experience of it in the woollen industry from nine years of age.[20]

The colliery was a common beginning for many trade unionists. Some started at the surface working on the colliery farm. This was the experience of Charles Fenwick and Tom Mann at nine years of age and Tom Cape at ten years.[21] Fenwick and Mann were underground the following year; Cape not until he was twelve years of age. Sam Woods was underground at six years of age with his father and Normanwell at seven years, rising at 3 a.m. to get to the colliery where he was employed underground 'pushing corves or tubs along the roadway in the mine by forcing them forward with his head in company with another young boy.' He returned home between six and seven in the evening.[22]

Tom Mann was similarly employed underground and described the nature of the work years later:

> There were boxes known down the mine as 'dans', about 2′6″ long and 18 inches wide, and of a similar depth, with an iron rung strongly fixed at each end. I had to draw the box along, not on rails; it was built sledge-like and each boy had a belt and chain. A piece of stout material was fitted on the boy around the waist. To this there was a chain attached and the boy hooked the chain to the box and, crawling on all fours, the chain between his legs, would drag the box along, and take it to the 'gob', where it would be emptied. Donkey work it certainly was.[23].

Mann underwent such experiences for two years, between 1866–68, although this work was supposed to have been stopped by the 1842 Factory Act. Alexander MacDonald and Keir Hardie also went down the pits when young, MacDonald at eight years, Hardie at ten working as a 'trapper'.[24] Thomas Burt also started as a trapper at ten years of age.[25]

Will Thorne began work at six years of age in a brickyard, thereby experiencing the same kind of child labour as George Smith who was to campaign so hard for canal boat children, Joseph Arch was nine when he began full time work:

> My first job was crow scaring, and for this I received four pence a day. This was a twelve hours one.... From crow scarer to ploughboy was my next step ... when I was between twelve and thirteen years of age I could drive a pair of horses and plough my own piece.[26]

George Howell also started work in a rural area scaring birds and drawing the plough at eleven years before starting work with his father the following year in the building trade, walking five miles to start a twelve hour stint which began at 6 a.m.[27]

Rather more novel beginnings were experienced by James Sexton who after working part time in the market with his parents, who were hawkers, took a job punching holes in clog irons at eight years of age. The following year he was working a twelve hour shift at the local gas works and three years later stowed away to San Francisco.[28] Ben Tillett went to sea in a more orthodox manner; he joined the Royal Navy at thirteen years of age after having spent five years working in a circus.[29] The comparatively few trade unionists whose early childhood work experiences are on record do not present an unusual picture of Victorian adolescence. On the contrary, their experience of hard manual work for long hours when very young was the common experience of working class children at the time and for many years later; indeed with certain exceptions, such as Mann's experience underground, most of these tasks described were being carried out down to the turn of the century at least, even if the children employed were a year or two older due to rises in the school leaving age.

The Threat of Child Labour to Adult Employment

Child labour was always seen as a threat to adult employment by trade unionists;[30] the lower rates of pay offered being an attraction for employers to hire children, often forced to work through the poor financial situation of their family. At the second Congress of 1869 the limitations of apprentices was discussed and fears expressed that there were times when employers would hire young people under the title of apprentice when in fact they were offered no training but merely used as a source of cheap juvenile labour. George Odger of the London Trades Council wished to know whether they were to refuse young boys who wanted to learn a trade. Congress provided an answer by passing a resolution which declared, '. . . that in trades where the supply is in excess of the demand that the limitation of apprentices is justifiable, a fair proportion being allowed in keeping with the number of men employed to teach them'.[31]

In the years when craft unions dominated Congress and when such workers received better pay and enjoyed greater security than the larger number of 'unskilled' workers, it is perhaps inevitable that TUC delegates supported in principle an apprenticeship system which they had experienced for themselves as the best way for new entrants to be prepared for the trade. The long period of training was partly a guarantee that not just any worker could be called upon to fill a vacancy; so a measure of scarcity helped to preserve the higher rates of pay for skilled workmen. However, the requirements and conditions of the numerous trades differed so widely and were carried on in such a variety of locations that it was very difficult for skilled workers to gain the control they would have liked to have over entry to a trade.[32]

At the 1880 Congress abuse of the apprenticeship system was again raised. Mr. Nannetti, a printer from Dublin, described his own local situation in which his establishment catered for six to eight apprentices whilst across the street, in a similar printshop, thirty-five apprentices were engaged in the production of a morning newspaper. Many delegates were willing to suggest that each trade looked after its own apprenticeship system but the majority of delegates wished to agree upon some common principles which would protect both young children and skilled workers.

It was quite clear that some youngsters were being offered apprenticeships under false pretences. Where a number of boys were brought into a trade and not indentured they ended up merely as a source of cheap labour. As one delegate explained:

> There were certain portions of the details of a trade which were more remunerative to an employer, and boys were kept employed at that portion, so that when their time was completely served they were thrown upon a trade without being able to earn a fair and honourable wage.[33]

It was suggested that parents ought to be able to sue employers for the non-performance of the convenants of an indenture and the failure to instruct an apprentice in 'the mysteries of his trade'. A part of the premium should be paid to the artisan who did the instructing and a resolution from Mr. Nannetti was passed calling for '... a regular system of indentured apprenticeship extending over a stipulated period as the best means of furthering the development of technical knowledge and increasing the skill of the workmen of the United Kingdom'.[34]

It was quite clear that in the areas of work in which children were most widely used, most adults employed in that industry, with the possible exception of certain skilled hands, were also poorly paid.[35] The paradoxical situation was that whilst children remained in an industry it was difficult for many adults also employed doing routine work to demand higher pay; yet whilst the wages of adults in such industries were low this forced many of them to send their own children into the industry to supplement their own inadequate income.[36] In turn they resisted the attempts of others to reduce child labour which they saw, sometimes regretfully and sometimes not, as a threat to their own existence.

The fact was that whilst the conditions for many working children were appalling and their rates of pay abysmal there was no lack of 'volunteers'. Necessity was the driving force, as Adamson, M.P. for Fife was to explain to the House of Commons in the debate upon the 1918 Education Act:

> At the age of eleven I had to leave school and go to work in a coal mine. Does anyone imagine that it was because I was anxious to leave school at that early age to work in a coal mine, or that my mother was less anxious to provide her son with as good an education as other parents were providing for their children? ... the stern necessity, the economic necessity of the family were such that at an early age I was put to work...[37].

The less scrupulous employers were fully aware of such a situation and could exploit it; partly because many of the worst employers would not allow membership of a trade union, or allow a trade union to operate within their plant or, if they did, might at least refuse to recognize them for negotiating purposes.[38] This often meant that both knowledge of poor child labour conditions and ability to deal with them were limited for trade unionists. Complaints about the use of child labour to reduce costs were frequent from trade unionists. Richard Bell of the Amalgamated Society of Railway Servants told the Congress in 1896 that the railway companies '... seemed to take children immediately they were able to leave school, and to employ them for the sake of the low wages they were paid'.[39]

Convincing fellow trade unionists was one thing; persuading Government Ministers that this was the case was more difficult. During the First World War, at a time when regulations concerning juvenile labour had been relaxed, W.B. Walker, Secretary of the Agricultural Workers Union, in a TUC delegation to the Board of Education, pointed out that the situation was being abused by farmers wishing to cut their costs. There was, he said, 'no evidence that there is a shortage of labour, especially in Eastern Counties – partly because farmers were not cultivating land as it might be farmed. If shortage arose they could pay adults to work overtime, but instead the employers fall back on the cheaper labour of women and children'.[40] Indeed, many farmers 'preferred to hire the cheap labour of school children than pay an adult wage to women workers'.[41]

A ruse to keep wage bills down by the employment of child labour was also explained to Lord Percy when called upon at the Board of Education by a deputation from the General Council of the TUC in 1925.[42] Mr. Hallas told him how large numbers of fourteen-year-olds sought work each year and how in Birmingham, where there were a great variety of industries having simple repetitive processes readily learned by youngsters, school leavers were frequently recruited. Preference was given to them because whilst they were under sixteen years of age they were not insurable and once they reached that age they were dismissed. He wished to see these youngesters kept at school so that the sixteen-year-olds might be employed more easily.

Trade unionists were not slow to point out that the Government itself could not escape criticism over the use of young school leavers. H.H. Elvin of the National Clerks, in a PCTUC Deputation in 1914, told the President of the Board of Education, J.A. Pease:

> We regret to remind you that the Government are sinners in this respect. I understand that as many as something like 2,500 boy clerks are employed in the Government Service, a very large percentage of whom, it is established that something like three quarters, on reaching the age of eighteen are without further employment.[43]

J.A. Pease admitted as much but claimed that 'great efforts are made to find them jobs' and that a Royal Commission on the Civil Service might provide an answer to the problem.

Juvenile Employment Detrimental to Health

Part of the protests by trade unionists concerning juvenile employment as a result of the effects it had in depressing adult wages and employment. They also protested because they were aware of the harmful effects it sometimes had upon the health of the child. In 1874, during a debate at Congress over the Nine Hours Bill, the subject of child labour arose. Mr. Brown from the Derby and Nottingham coalfield maintained that no child should be at work until '... their sinews and bones had been strengthened' which meant for him, at least twelve years of age, whilst Mr. Yates from Manchester said that, '... it would be the best day's work ever done in this country if the children were to be withdrawn from the factories at eight years of age and sent to school for three or four years longer, then they had a better chance of getting on instead of being crippled in a mill...'[44]

More than twenty years later, Richard Bell, Organizing Secretary of the Amalgamated Society of Railway Servants again pointed to the dangers children faced at work:

> He referred to the large number of fatal accidents which occurred to children working on the railways, and said numbers of them were employed almost entirely on night duty, which for years his society had been endeavouring to get abolished. The nature of their employment stunted the growth of the lads so much that when they reached an age at which they were entitled to promotion, they were found to be below the required standard of height.[45]

Increasingly trade unionists began to use supportive evidence from various reports to underline the deleterious effects which accompanied juvenile labour in order to try and persuade both colleagues and Government that it should be brought to an end. J. Vernon of the Typographical Society in his presidential address tried to persuade textile workers of the injurious effects of the half-time system on their children pointing out that, 'Dr. Francis Warner, who examined 52,000 children of the factory centres for the local Government Board, declared that the great majority had been weakened and crippled seriously by the conditions under which their earlier years were spent, and they had all been affected by these conditions, physically, morally and mentally.'[46]

Will Thorne in a debate on education claimed that, 'in every one of the districts where child labour is employed the infantile mortality is higher than anywhere else'[47] and W.F. Dawtrey of the Steam Engine Makers put forward figures to J.A. Pease, President of the Board of Education, to show that accident rates for part-time juveniles were higher than for full-time adults who worked nearly twice as long.[48]

In fact, poor health was not a direct product of young children working as such but the result of a combination of unsuitable work, long hours, low wages, poor nourishment, appalling housing conditions and a childhood history of the last two factors which meant that they were often of poor physique when they began work and that the arduous conditions they then underwent further undermined their health. A Home Office investigation of the LCC area in 1905 pointed to 55,000 school children actually known to be in some form of employment, the percentage of children working rising as the poverty of the district increased. 'The Investigator, Chester Jones, pointed out that medical evidence from the LCC was such as to suggest that all juvenile employment, other than selling newspapers, should be forbidden in London. County Council witnesses made clear that child labour was harmful both to health and to education.'[49]

Resistance to the Abolition of Child Labour

Trade unionists were not surprised to find themselves opposed by groups of employers in the struggle to abolish juvenile labour. It was less heartening to know that in some areas parents, too, wished to retain the practice of child labour. Most disheartening and embarrassing of all was to find that there were also trade unionists who spoke out against all attempts to raise the minimum age at which children might start work. This last group created considerable tension and hostility among the majority of delegates at the TUC. Mr. Gould of Hull expressed the view of many when he told Congress that, '... in former times they had had to fight the employers on matters relating to factory work, but now they had to fight their fellow-workmen who were interested in keeping the children at work'.[50]

The Board of Education were fully aware of this situation and on more than one occasion confronted TUC deputations calling for the raising of the school leaving age with a suggestion that a major obstacle to such a move was the workers themselves. 'The Government are prepared tomorrow to raise it to fifteen or sixteen', Mr. Pease, President of the Board of Education in 1914 told TUC representatives

> if public opinion would support it.... As a Board we are willing. It is for the workers in this country to realize that instead of turning their children into the streets to sell newspapers during their dinner hours, or often to sell little articles before the children go to school, and wasting the vitality of their children, they ought at the moment to be specially reserved and the child's whole attention devoted to his educational work.[51]

Such remarks, whilst accurate enough in themselves, failed to make any distinction between parents who were so desperately poor that they had no option but to send their children out for work whenever it was available and those who could manage financially but were either indifferent or ignorant. In some cases it was asking too much for parents who had received so little education themselves to grasp what relevance it might have for their children.

The attack on child labour at the TUC took three forms. There was the criticism of child labour *per se* which raised no direct opposition. Then the attack directly or indirectly on the half-time system which was consistently resisted by representatives from the textile areas. Finally there was the demand to raise the minimum school leaving age without exemption, which by itself would automatically phase out the employment of children at work below an agreed age. The clear connection of the latter is shown by the fact that occasionally the other side of the same coin was promoted; namely resolutions supporting a minimum age for employment at work.[52]

If they were not the first in the labour movement to call for the abolition of the half-time system[53] the TUC were the first to draw attention to it by calling for the raising of the minimum age at which children might be recruited to part-time factory work from eight to ten years of age. This demand was contained in a resolution in connection with the Nine Hours Bill at the 1873

TUC when a call was made to reduce the working hours of women and young persons to fifty-four per week:

> ... in order to afford additional facilities for education purposes, the ages of children of both sexes becoming half-timers [to be] altered from eight years as at present, to ten years, and that no young person of either sex may be employed as 'full-timers' under the age of fourteen years...[54]

This resolution received unanimous support at a time when elementary education was not compulsory and children could work at virtually any age, except in coal mines.

Between that date and 1891 there was little mention of child labour but only suggestions that evening classes should be available in order that youngsters at work might continue with some education after leaving day school. However, in 1891, there was an International Labour Conference in Berlin attended by representatives from the TUC. Child labour was discussed and British delegates had been led to believe that their Government would support a minimum school leaving age of twelve years if other countries agreed to adopt such a measure.[55] Accordingly the British delegates voted for such a measure but upon their return it became obvious that the government was reluctant to make such a move in this direction until a hostile vote in the House of Commons[56] forced them to accept the raising of the minimum age for half-timers from ten to eleven years of age. In a debate in the same year referring to Factory Inspection, David Holmes, who together with Joseph Cross was to prove a constant supporter of the half-time system, tried to move an amendment to delete the request to raise the minimum age at which children might work to twelve years but he was heavily defeated by 79:301 votes.

In 1895, J.R. Clynes of the Gasworkers Union put forward a resolution calling for, '... the abolition of child labour until the age of fifteen, and all night labour until the age of eighteen'.[57] It was accepted, after a request from Mr. Bland representing Bradford textile workers, to reduce the minimum age of work for children to fourteen years. So far demands for raising the school leaving age put before Congress were accepted by all, even if a little reluctantly by some of the textile workers. There was little specific debate around the half-time system as such because it did not follow that changes in this direction would inevitably effect the system unless such legislation denied exemptions. In fact the school leaving age was most complicated because the permissive nature of Government legislation meant that the situation varied from one local authority to another depending upon the bye-laws.

In 1880, out of 4,794 sets of bye-laws 237 ceased to require attendance after twelve years, 13 after eleven years and 39 after 10 years. Of 133 boroughs under school boards, for total exemption from school of children over ten years, 11 adopted standard VI, 93 standard V and 29 standard IV, whilst for partial exemption 6 adopted standard V, 50 standard IV, 44 standard III and 15 standard II.[58] Exemption clauses were to enable child labour to continue legally in some form well down until 1918.

Perhaps the main change in 1895 was the nature of the language used to introduce the legislation for raising the minimum school leaving age. It was very emotional and provocative to those who in any way supported child labour. The Gasworkers' resolution was prefaced thus:

> Considering that the employment of children in factories and work-shops and their consequent exploitation by the capitalist is injurious to the children, unjust to their parents, and a crime against the human race; considering the infamous fact that the children of the working class have not the same opportunities for the classroom and the play-ground as the children of the capitalist class; considering that in this connection Great Britain is behind other countries; considering that the unhappy parents under an unhappy system are actually willing, and even anxious, to have their children torn from school and hurled into the factory – this Congress is of the opinion that the time has come for Great Britain to cease building its empire upon children's hearts, to give up coining its wealth out of children's wasted lives...[59]

A similarly worded paragraph prefaced resolutions on this subject in the years 1897, 1898 and 1899 and delegates also resorted to vivid expressions, although shorter in length, to describe what they considered were the ills of child labour. In his presidential address in 1898 J. O'Grady of the Cabinet Makers told delegates that those who still acquiesced in '... this abominable traffic of child labour ... [were] ... accessories to the fact of legalized child murder'[60] and A. Bowman of the Belfast Flaxdressers argued in 1900 that it was wrong to believe that the textile industry had to depend '... in the slightest degree upon the degradation and practical murder of our children'.[61] Such language brought objections from the Lancashire textile delegates: Shackleton from Darwen protested to no avail in 1899[62] and the following year Holmes asked Bowman to withdraw the charge of 'technical murder' after the resolution had been passed; a request which Bowman agreed to.

When W.F. Dawtry of the Steam Engine Makers took up the battle against the half-time system at Congress from 1908 to 1913, he did not spare the feelings of those who still supported the system, describing it 'as being cruel and unjust to the children and future citizens, wastefully both morally and financially, a blot upon our professed civilization ... a survival of barbarism'.[63]

The supporters of the half-time system at Congress were not without their reasons for defending a system with which they were so familiar.[64] These reasons in many ways coincided with those put forward by mill owners in particular but also with those who found favour for child labour in some forms.[65] One familiar claim made for the system was that unless children went into the mills at an early age their fingers were not flexible enough to learn the work, as D. Holmes explained in 1897:

In Lancashire the workers simply could not afford to let the age be raised to fifteen, because if the young people did not learn to deal with delicate fibres before they were fifteen they would never become efficient work people, and would never be able to make a living for themselves.[66]

A somewhat surprising argument from a trade union point of view was expressed by Joseph Cross from Blackburn. Answering a charge of cheap labour he explained that '. . . it must be remembered that the great bulk of the products of the mills was exported, and that they had to compete against foreign labour, which was much cheaper from top to bottom than British labour, although that was cheap enough'.[67] Clearly Lancashire mill owners had no problems with a work force whose leaders so readily accepted that wages needed to be low to compete with the textile industries of the Far East. Such trade union leaders seemed to ignore associated problems in their industry: the continued use of old machinery which was not being replaced due to lack of sufficient investment or even that whilst cheap child labour was available there was less incentive or urgency for owners to re-equip the mills. Productivity was never mentioned in these debates.

As for the suggestion that the education of half-timers suffered in comparison with children attending school full-time, this was flatly denied. Addressing the Congress in 1897 Holmes reminded delegates of what he had told them the previous year, '. . . that both in local and national competitions the half-time children carried off the highest prizes'.[68] The quality of half-time schooling was similarly praised by E.H. Carlile, a Tory MP who had been a manager of such a school in Lancashire. He told the House of Commons that '. . . no school could produce, from an educational point of view, the good results that were passed by the half-time school'.[69]

All of these claims were disputed by TUC delegates. For example, J. O'Grady, when President of Congress, devoted most of his address to the problems of child labour quoted Mr. George Harwood, MP for Bolton and himself a cotton spinner and employer of labour, who had told his constituents in December 1897 that:

> . . . it had been said that if children were not sent to the mills and workshops early enough they did not acquire the requisite skill. His experience was to the contrary. For years he had refused to take half-timers, and he found those who went at thirteen years of age picked up the manual skill, the handicraft, more quickly than those going at eleven years of age. He had tested that over and over again, and he was certain about it.[70]

T. Hirley, Oldham Gasworkers, suggested that the special pleas of textile workers were no more true for their trade than any other industry. Young children were not needed to maintain any industry effectively.[71]

As for D. Holmes' claim that half-time schools produced better results, this was publicly challenged by N.B. Stringfellow, vice president of the Half Time Council of Teachers, a pressure group aimed at the abolition of the system. He had written to the Manchester Guardian declaring that Holmes' statements were without foundation: his letter had produced no response so he wrote again pointing out that:

> From his position [that is Holmes'] as a member of an important School Board, and as the official representative of an influential body of workers, his public utterances, carry with them a certain amount of public influence. It is not the first time he has stated that half-time children obtain better educational results than those who attend the whole day, but he has never given any evidence in support of his statements. His silence tends to show that he has none to give.[72]

It was difficult to argue that a child in the half-time system who had started work at 6 a.m., three hours before a day school pupil, was as fresh as the latter for afternoon school.[73] There can be little doubt that the working conditions in the mills were bound to reduce the effective learning of children who went on to afternoon school. In earlier years it is true that '... the enforced regular attendance of many part-timers could compensate for their lack of previous education [and] ... given the problem of securing regular attendance at elementary schools generally, factory children may have had a better record than full-timers'.[74] However true this may have been in earlier years, by the 1890s at the latest, attendance at elementary school had greatly improved, especially in the towns.

The group of children who were similarly disadvantaged in terms of tiredness at school were those who worked before and after day school, a point made by the Commissioners examining attendance at continuation classes and day schools:

> A serious drain upon the energies of many Day School pupils is caused by exhausting or demoralizing employment out of school hours. This prejudicially affects the pupils' training in the Day School and impairs their capacity for the continued education which should follow it. Many children are grievously overworked out of school hours, and, in consequence, are too tired to profit by their instruction in the Day School, and are rendered unfit for further education later on...[75]

At the same time it was not quite so easy to show that elementary day school pupils reached better standards in all schools because the limitation of the curriculum did mean that some half-time children were able to reach the required standard in their district after a comparatively short spell at day school and such an argument was used by supporters of the half-time system in its defence, and even accepted by those completely opposed to it. Mr. J. Geere of the Bolton Spinners contended that, '... the children were able to reach the limit of possibility so far as their elementary education was concerned before the period of half-time exemption arrived' and quoted the circumstances of his own three children who had passed all the standards by the age of twelve years.[76] He suggested that if they wished to abolish the system they should provide the opportunity for their children to be properly educated. Such a view had also been put forward by W.A. Appleton, Secretary of the Lacemakers, two years earlier:

> The bright children of the working classes who have been able to pass the sixth standard are very frequently in schools where there is no provision for teaching beyond that particular standard. The law says that they shall not leave school, and the authorities refuse to provide further facilities.[77]

This was an issue increasingly focused upon later in criticism of the separateness of elementary and secondary education.

This claim was reinforced when a PCTUC Deputation called upon W. Runciman, President of the Board of Education, in 1911. W. Mullin of the Cotton Spinners informed the President that '. . . many textile workers object to full-time school because once a child has reached Grade VII he does not learn any more'[78] and went on to give an example of such children being used by teachers to run errands. When questioned by the President, Thorne, a staunch opponent of half-time, agreed that children who had reached the top were used in this way.

Certainly by the Edwardian era the half-time system had declined in the textile trade. Government figures provided in the 1898 TUC Report showed that the textile trade used the system most and that it was concentrated in Lancashire. Of the children aged eleven to fourteen still attending school[79] in the country almost 120,000 were half-timers (see table 1)

Table 1

County	No. Under the Factories & Workshop Act	No. not Under the Factories & Workshop Act	Total	%
Lancs.	30,578	35,930	66,508	56
Yorks	15,382	16,586	31,968	27
Rest of Eng/Wales	8,531	12,740	21,271	17
Total	54,491	65,256	119,747	100

However by 1906–7 the average number of partial exemption scholars had been reduced to 47,360 of whom 34,306 were employed in factories. Among the factory part-timers, 20,302 were in Lancashire and 10,517 in Yorkshire but the statistics for this later period do not allow for easy comparison with those of the late 1890s. It is nevertheless clear that the total number engaged in factories in both Lancashire and Yorkshire had declined.

In 1909 the Cotton Operatives Amalgamation decided to ballot their members to ascertain attitudes within the factories towards raising the minimum age for half-timers. The results, which were forwarded to the Committee investigating Attendance in Continuation Schools, were reproduced in an appendix to their final report[80] (see table 2)

Table 2

	In favour of present age	In favour of increasing age from 12 to 13	Neutrals & those not voted
Cardroom Weavers	29,161	5,963	1,139
Spinners	15,296	3,166	
Weavers	98,104	22,378	7,017
Overlookers	3,144	890	
Bleachers & Dyers	1,490	851	
Mill Warpers (Men)	210	92	
Beamers, Twisters & Drawers	3,318	628	1,342
	150,723	33,968	9,498

It could be seen that the cotton workers were in favour of retaining the system as it was, so that trade unionists representing these workers did not feel that they had a mandate to support TUC policy on this matter.

There is some evidence to suggest that some trade union representatives from the cotton industry whilst opposing TUC policy on these grounds did not personally support the system. Hence W. Marshland of the Cotton Spinners speaking on the matter and opposing the TUC resolution stated that '... they could not legislate in advance of public opinion. They were trying to educate the rank and file, and in the near future meetings among the operatives would be held for that purpose'.[81]

The results of the poll were a setback to the TUC and an embarrassment when the PCTUC Deputation called upon W. Runciman at the Board of Education in 1911 to discuss, among other things, the raising of the school leaving age. Will Thorne suggested that 'the ballot said nothing' because he claimed it 'was taken at a time when work was slack, with hungry children and low wages and the increasing cost of living, parents dare not vote against half-time'.[82] More to the point would have been the fact that voting rights were given to all operatives down to ten years of age and whilst this might have been laudible in the sense that those concerned could vote it is also probable that considerable pressure to conform was bound to take place in a situation where management, most parents and workers supported such a system. In any case many schools did not present a particularly attractive alternative to factory work even if the hours of 'labour' were more restricted.

Whilst the half-time system was by no means the worst form of child labour and was found in areas and occupations other than textiles, such as shops and agriculture, it was nonetheless heavily concentrated in textile mills, especially those of Lancashire. The Union representatives from these mills, especially Holmes and Cross, may have had doubts as to the suitability of the system by the late 1890s yet resented criticism from other trade unionists in jobs which bore no relationship to those of the cotton industry. Holmes protested on more than one occasion of the lack of understanding, as he saw it, for their situation. 'Other trades were filled with adult labour. They, however, had 64% of young persons and females...'[83] Certainly such a work force was less adequately equipped to challenge management's conditions of work than unions, such as the Gasworkers, Dockers and Railwaymen, composed exclusively of male adults and becoming increasingly aware of how rapidly they could affect the economy of the country through industrial action. However, if the union representatives of textile workers believed such unions should not interfere, they were even less likely to listen to the pleas of the National Union of Teachers, a non-affiliated union which might be considered to have a vested interest in getting more children into schools. Richard Waddington, NUT President in 1898 spent many years campaigning for the abolition of the half-time system and if this was not to the liking of the textile unions it was a matter of common purpose between the TUC and the NUT; their views coincided on this issue in particular and they co-operated to bring the system to an end.[84]

There was more likelihood that cotton workers would be persuaded against the system by fellow textile workers who had experienced similar conditions and problems and since abandoned the system. The two textile representatives who were outspoken opponents of the system who fitted such a description were Ben Turner of the Batley Weavers, a half-timer himself when a boy, and Allen Gee. Turner opposed the system at the International Textile Workers Congress at Berlin in 1900 and seconded W.F. Dawtry's resolution at the 1912 TUC to abolish the system. On the last named occasion he explained to delegates the changes which had taken place in the woollen trade of Yorkshire:

> ... in Yorkshire the half-time system has almost disappeared. When I was a lad, forty years ago, there was not a town in Yorkshire that had not its half-timers. Now there are only two areas. The worst area is Bradford and the other is Halifax. All the great sections of Yorkshire have completely abolished the half-time system. I remember them contending in the early days that they could not do without the lads and lasses with their delicate fingers to do the work. That has all gone by the board in the woollen trade and in the cotton district of Huddersfield they have no half-timers in the mills. If it can be done without in the towns and cities I have named, it can be dispensed with throughout the trade.[85]

Allen Gee, Secretary of the General Union of Weavers and Textile Workers, supported Turner at the Berlin Conference[86] and was a member of the Committee[87] set up to examine attendance at Continuation Schools, as also was Holmes. One further textile representative opposed to the Lancashire delegates was A. Bowman of the Belfast Flaxdressers who like Turner, had emphasized his own engagement in the textile industry and who, at the 1900 TUC, seconded a resolution aimed at abolishing all child labour and, hence, the half-time system.

A further blow to the half-time system came from the Report of the Consultative Committee on Attendance at Continuation Schools which recommended that '... the time is now ripe to raise throughtout England and Wales the limit at which children can obtain any exemption from attendance at day school to thirteen years of age, and they suggest that Parliament should fix a not distant period at which this age of exemption would be yet farther raised to fourteen'.[88] This Committee also praised the support of Labour leaders who had campaigned for raising the school leaving age but on a note of caution pointed out that:

> A distinction must be made ... between resolutions passed at such meetings as those of the TUC and the real attitude of the average labour mind. While it is safe to assume that the TUC resolution represents the ideals of those work people who voted for it, and has a distinct effect on public opinion among the workers, such a resolution must not be taken as an index of the practical measures which working men as a whole are actually prepared to accept.[89]

This was an acknowledgement of the results of the poll held by the Cotton Operatives Amalgamation (which was printed as an appendix in the report) and of the influence of Joseph Cross on the Committee.

Supported by the recommendations of the Consultative Committee's Report in 1911, W. Runciman had introduced an Education Bill which, among other things, recommended the abolition of partial exemption, the raising of the school leaving age to fourteen years (with local education authorities having discretionary powers through bye-laws to vary this one year either way), and the suggestion that continuation classes be established after school for young people up to sixteen years of age. Unfortunately this Bill had to be withdrawn without discussion owing to a lack of time and the more pressing matters of unemployment and health insurance.[90]

By 1913, although the half-time system was slowly withering and Dawtry was proposing its abolition for the fourth time in the last five Congresses,[91] it still lingered on, faintly supported by Joseph Cross.[92] Like all child labour, though, it attained a new lease of life in the first World War and did not finally disappear until the 1918 Education Act was passed raising the school leaving age to fourteen years without exemptions. Whilst that was the end of the half-time system it was not the end of part-time education for a new form of this began to be discussed under the title of Continuation Schools.

A Trade Unionist as President of the Board of Education

In May 1915, Arthur Henderson rather reluctantly accepted the position of

President of the Board of Education; a dual role for he was also to be responsible to the Ministry of Munitions and to the Admiralty on Labour matters. This 'part-time' appointment provides some indication as to the importance attached to education in the early years of the first World War.

There were several things which differentiated this President from his predecessors. He was the first to have had direct experience of an elementary school, namely as a pupil. He was the first to have come from the trade union movement, being an early member of the Iron Founders Union and an executive member of the Labour Party. He was also the first President to refuse to receive a deputation from the TUC to discuss their Education Programme, instead offering only to consider their views on child labour. Mr. C.W. Bowerman, Secretary of the PCTUC received a letter from the Board of Education of informing him of the President's decision:

> It appears to him [that is Henderson] that the Resolutions under the heading of 'Education Policy', though dealing with questions of great importance, relate without exception, to matters which involve either legislation, often of a highly contentious character, or substantial new grants from public money or both.... It is clear that legislation and additional State aid for Education are out of the question so long as the War lasts.... On the other hand, the First Resolution relating to Child Labour touches a matter which he has much in mind.... He would therefore be very glad to receive a Deputation representing the Congress to discuss this Resolution...[93]

In fact Henderson could offer no more hope in the direction of child labour than he could on any other aspect of education. The Government had drawn up a five point code on child labour which was so general and vague that it offered no effective barrier to the employment of children. They were as follows:

1 Employment of children must be regarded as an exceptional matter, only to be availed of when no other form of labour is available.
2 That all reasonable efforts must be made to secure adult labour, especially by payment of reasonable wages.
3 Every case to be considered on its merits and no general relaxation.
4 Employment suitable to the age of the child.
5 The exemption that was granted to be granted for a limited period only.

Henderson read out these points to the PCTUC Deputation when they called upon him and admitted that 8,000 children in agricultural regions had already been exempted from school. He claimed that 'the Board of Education does not have the authority to dictate policy to local Education Authorities.... There are signs that the position is going to get worse[94] ... all we have really is moral suasion ... and we regret that the numbers are greater than we expected'.[95]

Henderson was already under criticism at the TUC for his lack of effective action in this matter. Jack Jones of the Gasworkers at the 1915 Congress said to delegates: 'I must say that it seems a most extraordinary thing that when Labour gets into the Government and becomes represented at the Board of Education we should immediately have entered into a reactionary education policy'.[96] It is not possible to know whether Henderson had been manoeuvred into the Presidency at a time when cutbacks in education were considered necessary by the Asquith Government; if so he was not the first member of the Labour movement to find that upon his appointment to ministerial rank he should be called up to defend to past comrades the very reactionary policies he had earlier attacked.[97]

Henderson was conscious of the uncomfortable situation in which he found himself and in July 1916 wrote to Prime Minister Asquith suggesting that someone else should be appointed as full-time President to the Board of Education:

> It is said by Lord Haldane, by speakers in the House of Commons, and by the public, that the Board of Education is without a Head.... I think you will agree with me that, apart altogether from my personal feelings and credit, it is a matter of consequence to the Government that, at a time when public interest in our educational future is keener than it has been for many years, the Department should not be left to a Minister who is necessarily in large measure an absentee, who is not in a position to lay plans for the future and who appears in Parliament (and in his own Party) principally as the defender of reactionary policies inherited from his predecessor.[98]

A month later Henderson wrote again asking the Prime Minister to accept his resignation.[99] Lord Crewe was appointed to the position but by the end of the year, Lloyd George had taken over as Prime Minister from Asquith and asked H.A.L. Fisher to become President of the Board of Education.

Raising of the School Leaving Age

It has been shown how demands to raise the school leaving age had often been linked in resolutions, as well as in the minds of trade unionists, with the need to end child labour. The first World War to some extent provides a convenient but not rigid division between the campaign concentrating upon the worst aspects of child labour to a new approach relating more directly to schooling. Once the minimum school leaving age of fourteen years had been reached in 1918 the pressure from the TUC began to be focused upon extending that age and pushing for more children to spend their extra school years in a secondary school instead of an elementary school.

Demands at the TUC to raise the school leaving age can be traced back to at least 1891 when they were incorporated in the one resolution on education put before Congress. A separate call for the abolition of child labour often mentioned a school leaving age but this was usually directed towards the abolition of the half-time system. At the same time the more comprehensive resolutions on education promoted by the Gasworkers in the 1890s included a clause calling for the raising of the school leaving age and providing a specific age which should apply to all children. For three years, from 1895 to 1897, there was a call at Congress to ban nightwork for all young people under eighteen years of age; at the same time there were calls to raise the minimum school leaving age but these did not remain constant for, although the call was usually for fifteen years, in 1895 it was reduced by an amendment from T. Glover, representing Lancashire textile workers, to fourteen years. As can be seen from Appendix II demands for raising the school leaving age differed in their manner of expression but a summary would show the following pattern:

TUC 1895	15 years (amended to 14 years)
TUC 1896–1900	15 years
TUC 1901	15 years – expressed in reverse manner – prohibition of child labour below 15 years
TUC 1902–	No maximum leaving age to be fixed
TUC 1903–1905	15 years
TUC 1906–1908	Secondary and Technical Education for all children up to 16
TUC 1909	16 years plus Daytime continuation classes 16–18 years
TUC 1910–15	16 years
TUC 1916	14 years with LEA bye-laws for 16 years
TUC 1917–18	16 years
TUC 1919–25	15 years plus continuation classes 16–18 years

The fluctuations follow the optimistic approach of the TUC from 1895 until World War I when there was pressure to make gradual improvements, the feelings of future success from 1916 with H.A.L. Fisher at the Board of Education followed by the uncertainty and deteriorating conditions after 1920.

H.A.L. Fisher at the Board of Education and His Relationship with the Trades Union Congress

The Trades Union Cogress was genuinely pleased with Fisher's appointment to the Board of Education. At their first meeting, when a Deputation from the PCTUC called upon the President, will Thorne congratulated him and expressed both his pleasure and expectation:

> ... I recognize, that for the first time, I think, for the last fifteen years we have got what I call a practical educationalist as President of the Board of Education. We are hoping – I do not know whether our

hopes will be realized – a great deal from you, because you fully understand the question of education from top to bottom.[100]

How far such hopes were to be realized will be seen later but two years on Thorne was still showing just as high a regard for the President as an education expert: '. . . I do not think any of us can attempt to teach you anything about education, because you know all about it from A to Z'.[101]

To a group of trade unionists who had only managed to obtain a few years of elementary education before being pushed out into the world of work at an early age, an Oxford Don must have seemed to be the very epitome of what they considered an educationalist to be. In fact Fisher was no such thing and made this quite clear in his autobiography later:

> Popular opinion pronounced me to be an 'educationalist'. That was a delusion. I had never, save for a week when I was an undergraduate, taught in a school nor addressed myself to a serious study of pedagogic literature. . . . My true field of study was and had long been the history and literature of Europe, and I should have been more in place as Under Secretary for Foreign Affairs, a position for which I was afterwards considered, than as President of the Board of Education.[102]

Only the promise of financial backing from Lloyd George for educational reform persuaded Fisher to accept the post.[103]

To begin with, the feeling of good will flowed in both directions. Fisher had been genuinely moved by the reception he had received when addressing a group of dockers in Bristol on the subject of education and believed that the Labour Movement's support was a key factor if child labour was to be abolished and greater educational provision made for all young people. The PCTUC must have been impressed by the sympathetic reception they were given by Fisher in February 1917, especially when compared with that of Henderson a year earlier. The resolutions of the TUC of 1916 which had been forwarded to Fisher for discussion were welcomed by the new President who told them:

> I cannot overstate the importance which I attach to the interest which trade unionists are taking in educational reform. We here at the Board who are anxious to promote educational reform, are conscious that in the last resort we cannot outstep public opinion; and it is upon the trade unionists of the country in a very large measure that the direction of public opinion into useful channels will depend.[104]

Fisher went through the points raised by the Delegation explaining the enormity of the task before them in improving the education system; new buildings, more, better and higher paid teachers and told the TUC that their task was to persuade their fellow workers and push the local bye-laws to their limits, for already much could be achieved through present permissive legislation. Most previous demands for improvement by the TUC had been met by questions of raising finance. On this Fisher's response showed no trace of such an attitude. He told the delegates, '... that anything which the nation really wants, it is rich enough to pay for, and that if the nation really wants a good system of education, this country, war or no war, is perfectly rich enough to pay for it'.[105]

This meeting can probably be seen as marking the honeymoon period between Fisher and the TUC, with still a good couple of friendly years to come before a time of some disillusion set in, probably on the part of both parties. TUC delegates expressed disappointment with Fisher's stance from 1921 onwards and Fisher felt let down by the Parliamentary Labour Party if not by the TUC as such. As members of the PLP were also sometimes members of the PCTUC, Fisher's feelings of annoyance with the former may well have flowed over to the latter. The reasons for this disillusionment were twofold. Whilst the TUC were not greatly enamoured of all of Fisher's education proposals they supported him in the belief that most of them were advantageous. However, when he began to go back on the promises made in the 1918 Education Act, admittedly under pressure from the Cabinet, he nevertheless lost much of the support of the TUC. A more fundamental problem, which would inevitably have affected the relationship in the long run is that the TUC wanted more radical changes in education than Fisher was either able (due to financial circumstances later) or willing (due to his own liberal views) to put forward. This was to become apparent over a whole series of issues ranging from secondary school provision and school fees to endowments and continuation classes. In 1917 however, Fisher was a most welcome member of the Board of Education as far as the TUC was concerned.

Fisher's Education Bill was welcomed by the TUC in general, as the report of the parliamentary Committee to Congress in 1917 made clear.[106] They welcomed the final ending of fees in elementary schools and the raising of the school leaving age to fourteen years without exemptions but with regard to the issue which was to prove most controversial, namely continuation classes, they were a little hesitant. In fact, whilst they gave them qualified support in 1918, in the early 1920s they criticized certain aspects of them but by the mid 1920s they were fighting desperately to have them introduced throughout the country.

Like many general terms used in education, both secondary schools and continuation classes had meant different things at different times. At least some of the gradual disenchantment of the TUC towards Fisher can be explained by their different interpretations of these terms. Continuation Classes in the 1862 Code had referred to education following on from elementary education for children but, by the 1890s, was being used generally to describe adult evening classes as well. Secondary education cannot be so easily classified for although it might be claimed that it referred to the schools described by the Taunton Commission of 1868 the term was not actually used in the Report. There was no 'secondary system' as such and whilst the Taunton Commission had produced a three-fold classification of schools largely relating to the social class of the pupil's parents, in fact the schools varied widely in quality. Suffice to say that even the most modest referred to by the Taunton Commission as 'the third grade of education' catering for 'smaller tenant farmers, small tradesmen and superior artisans' were distinguished from elementary schools by both the higher scale of fees and a wider curriculum. Of all the trade unionists listed in Appendix I only one may have attended a secondary school;[107] one reason why references to such schools at the TUC were infrequent until the twentieth century. A further reason was that in the last decade of the school board era working people saw the higher grade schools as a form of secondary education which had the advantage of being cheap or even free. Once these schools were removed by the 1902 Education Act those wishing for something beyond the limited curriculum offered by the elementary school inevitably began to turn their thoughts towards secondary schools.

It is possible to show that demands for secondary education at the TUC were actually reduced in scope between the late 1890s and early 1920s. In 1897 for example, the TUC called for the State to '... place secondary education within the reach of every worker's child'[108] but by 1903 this demand had been reduced to secondary education for '... all children whose usefulness would be enhanced by an extended education'.[109] Again, in 1897 the TUC condemned

> the system of providing secondary education only for the very small proportion of the workers' children who can come to the top, after severe competition with their school fellows ... on educational grounds, and, in that it tends to foster feelings of antagonism and jealousy, which are such a serious obstacle in the way of that union among the workers which their highest welfare demands, and which it is the object of trade unionists to promote.[110]

By 1902 competition had become the accepted way of progress towards secondary education, for the resolution concerning scholarships suggested that they should be distributed according to the '... intelligence and attainment of the child'.[111]

Whilst the Labour Party was calling for secondary education for all, from 1922 onwards the TUC's demands for secondary education were still linked to a view that only the most intelligent of the working class children could go to secondary schools; an acceptance given quite meekly to Walter Runciman, President of the Board of Education in 1909, when discussing the matter with a PCTUC Deputation:[112]

W. Runciman: Of course, it must be known that it is not every child who can take advantage of these facilities.

D.J. Shackleton: Oh, no; we quite understand.
(Chairman PCTUC)

W. Runciman: You cannot expect to capture every child for secondary education.

It is possible to find demands for secondary and technical education prior to

World War I[113] but what the demand for secondary education meant to some delegates was not always clear, hence a request from Mr. Hackett of the ASRS for some agreement as to what was meant by the term 'secondary' education. He wanted secondary 'day' school inserted to make the meaning clear to distinguish it from the evening classes which some delegates might have had in mind.[114] By the 1920s the TUC firmly linked availability of secondary schools with ability to pass qualifying examinations; at least as far as working class pupils were concerned. A selective system was accepted whilst it is true that demands were constantly made for the gates of entry to be opened more widely[115] there was general acceptance that there should be gates to pass through; '... as was said on the last occasion of Congress', Alderman A.W. Tapp J.P. of the Ship Construction and Shipwrights Union reminded delegates, 'it would be absurd to send to a child to secondary school unless it reached a standard to benefit by receiving that education'.[116]

If demands for secondary education were not so prominent at the TUC after 1918 it was at least partly because the attention of many trade unionists had been diverted a little to consider the offer of continuation schools outlined in the 1918 Education Act. This was not Fisher's own idea but came from the recommendations of the Report of the Departmental Committee on Juvenile Education in Relation to Employment after the War, finally published in 1917 and soon known as the Lewis Report.[117] It called for the raising of the school leaving age to fourteen years without exemptions and attendance at day continuation classes for most young people between the ages of fourteen and eighteen years of age, for not less than eight hours per week or 320 per year. Both measures were incorporated in Fisher's Bill although the time was considerably reduced by an amendment.

The TUC had shown an interest in Continuation Classes several years earlier. It can be shown that, in 1909, at the TUC, H.H. Elvin (National Clerks) had successfully moved a resolution which stated: 'that from the age of sixteen to eighteen years classes shall be provided during the day time to enable the students to learn thoroughly the the theoretical and practical side of their work, and that employers shall be compelled to allow their employees the necessary time off to attend such classes'.[118] It was in effect an attempt to move the education offered in evening classes to a time during the day when it was felt that youngsters would be better fitted to benefit from the teaching provided. This was considered necessary because of the early hours worked by young people on the railway[119] for example and the length of the working day for many others.[120] H.H. Elvin, as the major promoter of continuation classes at the TUC suggested in a Deputation to J.A. Pease, President of the Board of Education, that they might copy the German model of compulsory day part-time education for fourteen to eighteen year olds because youngsters were '... too tired at the end of the day's work' and sometimes missed meals to get to classes and therefore had no food from noon to 9 or 10 p.m.[121]

He continued his demands to the President when they met in similar circumstances two years later pointing out the wastage involved in evening classes due to the poor attendance of so many; 40,000 out of 130,000 students in London attending so infrequently in 1913 that their studies were considered ineffective.[122] Elvin claimed that the circumstances of some youngsters discouraged evening study:

> ... the youngsters are very keen on improving their educational standard, and they enter with enthusiasm ... but they find owing to the position in which they are in the office or elsewhere, the abnormal hours they have to work, in some instances it has been shown that something like 58 hours a week – it is absolutely impossible for them to attend the classes in which they have enrolled...[123]

The President agreed that day schooling was best.

By 1917, although both Fisher and the TUC supported Continuation Classes, they did so for different reasons: Fisher saw them as an extension of elementary education for the masses as he had no wish to provide secondary education for all children. The TUC saw continuation classes as an improvement on evening classes both in terms of the possibility of young people learning more and because by making them compulsory it would ensure that all adolescents received some further education; voluntary evening classes appealed only to the most energetic and dedicated youngsters. Hence Fisher and the TUC were agreed upon the provision of these classes but for different reasons. The TUC were to express two major reservations in later years: the first was that they might become so vocational in curriculum that far from expanding a young person's horizon they might actually limit them to a particular job or even a particular company; the second was that they might gradually be used as a cheap substitute for full-time secondary education for working class adolescents.

In 1917 Fisher could rely upon the TUC for support. The main critics of his Continuation Class proposals were to be found in the world of commerce and industry, orchestrated through the newly formed Federation of British Industries. This body, formed in 1916, had a sub committee on education which in August 1917 circulated a questionnaire to members and affiliated associations inviting responses to Fisher's Education Bill; 2,000 replies were received and a memorial on education giving the FBI's views on recommended future developments in education was forwarded to the Board of Education. A Deputation from the FBI was then arranged to wait upon the President in February 1918.

The Memorial ran to several pages and expressed general agreement with Fisher's ideals as expressed in the Education Bill. It gave approval to calls to improve elementary education and supported full-time selective secondary education of gifted working children but in the key area of compulsory continuation classes it expressed complete opposition:

> ... they will welcome any well considered development of educational facilities for all children without distinction throughout the country

... which they believe to be most urgent; firstly, the improvement of elementary education; secondly, the provision of a full secondary education for the more able children, and, only after these measures have been taken, an improved general education for the remainder. ... The Committee are not, however, in agreement with Mr. Fisher's proposal to impose compulsory part-time education at the present on all children in this country up to the age of eighteen ... in every industry this proposal is viewed with great alarm.[124]

Industries employing large numbers of juveniles, especially the Lancashire textile trade, lined up behind Sir Henry Hibbert, who led the opposition to continuation classes in the House of Commons. One of the major objections continually made by the FBI in its fight against any move to reduce the working hours of juveniles by introducing continuation classes was that the country could not and would not be able to afford it; at least not in the forseeable future:

... the employer sees the disorganization of his work system, and an all round increase in the cost of production at the very time when the industrial position will be most difficult, and foreign competition most formidable.[125]

Yet there is also evidence, both in the Memorial and in remarks made later, that the FBI also feared the power of education to make young people doubt the wisdom of continuing employment in some mills and factories. The Memorial recorded that,

... there seems to be a general feeling among employers throughout the country that there is a distinct danger of those children who take advantage of these facilities being ultimately lost to industry, and accordingly more generous support would probably be given to some system whereby the employers would provide financial assistance on behalf of young persons in whom they were interested and who might be expected in the ordinary course to return preferably to their own works but at any rate to the industry.[126]

Before his meeting with the FBI, Fisher circulated their Memorial to several members of his department for their comments. The responses were all unfavourable. One wrote: '... is strongly biased throughout towards the vocational aspects of the subject and its effects on production and virtually ignores the strong demand of wage earners and others for the better education of young persons as citizens'.[127] Another came to a similar conclusion: 'The root difference between them and their opponents is that they regard education as purely a means to an end. ... They don't regard it as necessary or desirable to educate the great mass of the working class for their leisure or citizenship'.[128]

Professor Gilbert Murray, Oxford Don and adviser to Fisher, wrote detailed notes on the FBI Memorial. With regard to the concern of the FBI about the effect of compulsory continuation classes upon industries employing large numbers of juveniles he remarked that '. . . the Federation rest their case . . . on the dislocation which their withdrawal for eight hours a week would cause. To this the only possible answer seems to me to be that these particular trades are parasitic upon the young life of the community as a whole...'[129] He also criticized the FBI's recommendations for 'the more promising children' who might stay on at school, for only a minority of these were to be offered secondary education whilst a larger proportion would be sent to junior technical schools to be 'fitted for a particular industry'.

With such considered advice beforehand and a team of eight including J. Herbert Lewis (Parliamentary Secretary), Sir L.A. Selby-Bigge (Permanent Secretary) and Sir E. Phipps, H.A.L. Fisher faced the three representatives from the FBI: F.W. Gilbertson, C.A. Cochrane and J.W. McConnel. The minutes of the meeting suggest a polite but firm stand by the Board with the FBI speakers being forced to admit that they had not worked out the details for particular industries which, in their own proposals, they had claimed would be greatly disturbed. What comes through more than anything however is the fear expressed by the FBI that greater education for young people would lead them to turn their back on industries which had previously enjoyed a 'captive labour market': '. . . one of the great dangers of this Bill', F.W. Gilbertson argued, 'is that you are going to destroy our industry by dislocating us from the young labour; and if we are going to have . . . compulsory education without expense up to fourteen, we must have that qualification that while boys and girls are being educated, it is an education which will lead them into coming into the mills, and make them more useful when they come into the mills . . . the place where the industry is carried on is the place for them to be taught'. Gilbertson did add that '. . . we do not wish to be thought in the least reactionary'.[130] Yet such motives for the education of adolescents, clearly expressed by the FBI team, were precisely those feared by TUC delegates later: a reservation for vocational education that was to be a constant fear in the labour movement; that education would be precisely tailored to the child's future role in society – education as a determining factor rather than a force for wider choice.

To some extent, the reactions of Fisher and his colleagues were the responses of those who believed in a liberal education and shared little respect for industry or commerce. One has only to consider their own educational backgrounds to realize the truth of such a view, but even allowing for this prejudice there was also a genuine feeling, especially in the last years of a War which had claimed so many lives and for which so much sacrifice had been made, that working people deserved something better than to be treated as mere industrial fodder; linked to a company by both work, and part-time study strictly related to that work, which might make them more efficient in one particular company whilst at the same time making it very difficult for them to obtain work elsewhere.

When the FBI's views were made public they helped to provide a rallying ground for all those opposed to the 1918 Education Bill. The FBI was schizophrenic over the press reception of its Memorial, telling its members in February that it had been 'favourably commented upon in the Press'[131] but some weeks later claiming that there had been a 'widespread misrepresentation in the Press of the Memorial on Education issued by the Federation'.[132] Support for the FBI was provided by an unsigned 'Employer of Labour' in the *Times Educational Supplement*: 'To impose this additional burden [this is Continuation Classes] on industry just at the time when it will require the whole of its strength to grapple with the terrible problems of reconstruction may ... prove economically a fatal error.'.[133] However, in leading articles *The Times*, *Times Educational Supplement* and *New Statesman* all supported Fisher's Bill.

The most savage criticism of the FBI proposals was written by R.H. Tawney for the *Daily News*[134] entitled 'Keep the Workers in their Place'. It appeared just a week after the FBI Deputation had visited Fisher. Tawney saw the Memorial as an attempt to intimidate the Government over its Education Bill but which had, in effect, 'revealed the motive and social policy which lie behind the opposition to the extension of higher education'. If Fisher's liberal minded colleagues had noticed the FBI's educational designs for working class children so, too, had Tawney and his attack went to the core of an argument that was to dominate secondary education in England and Wales for decades to come:

> Behind the objection based on the convenience of industry lies another objection based on the theory that all except a small minority of children are incapable of benefiting by education beyond the age of fourteen. It is not actually stated, indeed, that working class children, like anthropoid apes, have fewer convolutions in their brains than the children of captain of industry. But the authors of the Memorandum are evidently sceptical as to either the possibility or the desirability of offering higher education to more than a small proportion of them.[135]

The FBI Memorial is important for three reasons in connection with the TUC. In the first place it provided a view of education related to industry which was the very opposite of that desired and proposed by trade unionists. In the second place it showed precisely from which quarter opposition to Fisher's ideas for an improved education for all children originated. Finally it outlines the very views which trade unionists were later to warn would become the reality behind proposals for continuation classes. In spite of a much closer approach between the educational ideals of Fisher and the TUC compared with Fisher and the FBI, in spite of the sympathy Fisher showed towards the trade union movement, in spite of the initial support from the Press for Fisher's Bill in its early stages and the withering attack by Tawney on FBI proposals – in the long run it was the TUC view that was defeated, Fisher's Bill amended in parts[136] and discarded in others so that the FBI view finally won the day.

In January 1918 Fisher had sent a copy of the FBI Memorial to Sir H. Llewellyn Smith at the Board of Trade, to consider the impact the proposals might have on industry. In his reply to Fisher, he ended his letter by saying, 'I think the Federation is a body which carries a good deal of weight and that its opposition might be formidable'.[137] The truth of this statement was seen, as pressure was built up by the FBI both in the country[138] and in Parliament,[139] and Fisher began to make concession.[140] F. Goldstone of the National Union of Teachers, speaking in the House of Commons, believed that Fisher had given in too easily to pressure:

> It seems to me that the right Hon. Gentleman capitulated far too soon, and there did not seem to me either in the House or in the country that volume of opposition to his original proposals which warranted so early a capitulation to the interests which have forced him into the present position.[141]

Fisher's concessions meant that continuation schools would not come into effect for the sixteen to eighteen year olds until seven years after the appointed day on which the continuation school provision came into force, nor would it include those who had reached the age of sixteen years by then. Instead of 320 hours per year for fourteen to sixteen year olds local authorities could reduce this to 280 hours. Fisher informed the House that his amendments would 'be more to the advantage of the industrial interests' than some of their own amendments.[142] In this he was probably correct. He salvaged only the raising of the school leaving age to fourteen years without exemption and agreements to increase the salaries of teachers[143] from his original radical proposals.

The struggle for the Education Bill in Parliament led to some disenchantment between Fisher and the Labour Movement:

> In fighting my Bill through the House of Commons I had hoped to receive effective support from the Labour Benches, for education was a prominent plank in the labour platform. In that hope I was disappointed. My personal appeals to Labour Benches were unanswered.[144]

It was the Parliamentary Labour Party he criticized in particular but this obviously referred to TUC members sitting as Labour MPs at the time. Will Thorne, one of the champions of education at the TUC for many years and Labour MP for West Ham had little to say during the debate although he did claim that the continued support of the TUC had helped Fisher to reintroduce the Bill in 1918.[145] Perhaps more annoying to Fisher was the behaviour of J.H. Thomas of the National Union of Railwaymen who gave a lengthy talk on the need to support education when calling upon the former in a PCTUC Deputation in 1919 although his voice had not been heard much in the House of Commons on this topic. This led Fisher to record in his diary that at the Deputation Thomas made an eloquent speech but 'why the deuce didn't he make it in the House when the Bill was going through'.[146]

In fact the small Parliamentary Labour Party was divided. The rank and file of the Party demanded raising of the school leaving age to sixteen years, just like the TUC, but the PLP accepted fourteen years in line with Fisher's proposal. A major source of division remained in Lancashire where, 'an inter-party alliance of Lancashire MPs ... worked to limit the inroads which the reform might make into the hours and years for which a child might be available for paid employment'.[147] Indeed the amendment accepted by Fisher[148] restricting continuation schools in the first place to those below sixteen years and only after seven years to the sixteen to eighteen year age group was supported by Lancashire MPs who bowed to the pressure of their constituencies whilst Labour Party members such as 'Bruce, Parker, Hodge, Walsh and Wardle, all of whom held Government office, voted against one or more of a series of labour, or labour supported, amendments designed to give local Education Authorities the power to raise the minimum leaving age beyond the age stated in the Bill, to sixteen'.[149]

It did not seem to occur to Fisher that some of the lack of enthusiasm among trade unionists might be because they believed the Bill did not go far enough.[150] Yet it is apparent that, whilst the Bill seemed radical enough to the FBI, when compared to the TUC Education Programme Fisher's Bill did not seem to offer a great deal. The school leaving age was two years below that demanded by the TUC in 1906, the continuation classes now only referred to juveniles up to sixteen years of age whereas the TUC had demanded such classes for young people up to eighteen years since 1909 whilst secondary education seemed almost as remote in 1918 as it had done in the Edwardian era. Above all, the vocational aspects of continuation schools fully desired by the FBI and rejected at first by Fisher and his advisers gradually came to dominate the curriculum of such classes, especially when they were run by individual companies: the limitations that such an education offered were bitterly resented by trade unionists increasingly as these classes became established after 1918.[151] The Conservatives in general supported such classes.[152]

When the TUC met in 1918 they spelt out the conditions they wished to see regulating continuation school:

a) That the education given in continuation schools be directed primarily to the strengthening of character, physique, and intelligence, and only secondarily, and after the age of sixteen, to imparting training for industry.

b) That continuation classes held on the premises of employers be not recognized as continuation schools within the meaning of the Act.[153]

As C.T. Cramp of the NUR explained:

We do not object to technical education but we believe that our educational system should be directed primarily to the bringing forth of healthy, happy and intelligent human beings...[154]

In March 1919 when the PCTUC called upon Fisher they were still voicing full support both for him and his Education Act.[155] In return the Minister now had little to offer them apart from a short reading from the Introduction to the Code on the Aims of Elementary Education, which upon examination seemed hardly realistic in the light of elementary school provision at the time,[156] and a plea for patience. 'In education', he told the TUC representatives, 'we cannot expect to advance very rapidly; but the pressure must all be in the direction that you desire, and you may be quite certain that the Board will have that object constantly in view'.[157] As for the request for smaller classes,[158] because many elementary school classes exceeded fifty pupils, again patience was required until sufficient teachers could be trained and new buildings constructed.

The Board might have had the aims of the 1918 Education Act in mind but just as pertinent was whether the Cabinet did also. Fisher has told how Lloyd George as Prime Minister agreed to provide the finances for his educational plans when he was appointed to the Board in 1917 and wrote later that 'the PM was as good as his word'.[159] Yet by the end of 1919 the Treasury was calling the Cabinet's attention to the rise in expenditure in education.

> In December 1919, in response to instructions, Fisher placed a Memo before the Cabinet in which he explained that the recent increases in the cost of staff salaries and equipment were owing simply to inflation. His statement failed to satisfy the Treasury, however, for in January, 1920, Austen Chamberlain, as Chancellor of the Exchequer, called 'the serious attention of the Cabinet to the immense growth of expenditure on education since the Act of 1918...'[160]

It is noticeable that cutbacks in education were already being planned long before Lloyd George appointed the Geddes Committee in 1921; with the Prime Minister's approval and much to the great disappointment of Haldane,[161] Chamberlain told the House of Commons early in December 1919 that only with fresh Cabinet authority could schemes already authorised be carried out, otherwise they were to remain in abeyance and at the end of the month he wrote to Fisher telling him to economize as much as possible.

The two years immediately following the Armistice of November 1918 had been years of industrial struggle and a record number of strikes, including an unprecedented one by the police as well as threats by miners and railwaymen.[162] The Government had been frightened and backed down after confronting both the miners and the railwaymen although the striking policemen were dealt with more ruthlessly.[163] By the winter of 1921 the post war boom had halted, wholesale prices fell and unemployment rose. The Government were now confident enough to consider tackling the social unrest which had followed the War in attempts to get back to 'normal'; which for employers meant the situation prevailing in the Edwardian era. Others believed that such a situation was hardly just reward for those who had taken part in one of the most savage wars in history.

The appointment of the Geddes Committee illustrates the new found confidence of the Government; confidence which had already been boosted by an 'anti-waste' campaign stimulated by the 'Daily Mail' and acted upon by a series of circulars issued by the Board of Education (1190, 1225 and 1228) all demanding that local authorities should confine their expenditure to necessities. Even W.A. Appleton, Secretary of the General Federation of Trade Unions, was caught up in the mood and, in a book, advocated economy in education:

> The losses and extravagances of the past seven years must restrict immediate educational efforts. Only that which will assist the present and the imminent future can be attempted.... Economy and practicability must be the watchwords of those who would educate the people but who are reluctantly compelled to put existence before adornment; bread before erudition.[164]

The Geddes Committee, consisting entirely of businessmen,[165] recommended that £18 million be cut from the £50 million provisional education estimates for 1922–23; such reductions to be achieved by a series of changes including the raising of the school starting age from five to six years, an increase in the size of classes in order to reduce the demand for teachers, a raising of secondary school fees, an end to university state scholarships and the newly introduced teachers' pension fund to be put on a contributary basis. Comments by the Committee about increases in recent educational expenditure took no account of the inflation responsible for at least a large part of the increase.

It was by now becoming clear to the TUC that they were no longer faced with the offerings of the 1918 Education Act which many had believed were meagre enough but a move, under the cry of 'economy', to take back the provisions the Act had made for the gradual improvement of juvenile education. For many TUC delegates their worst fears of continuation classes were being born out. For the first time at Congress a separate resolution was moved devoted solely to Continuation Schooling. Repeating the principles outlined in the 1918 TUC Education programme the resolution ended by stating that the TUC, '... strongly condemns all schools or classes controlled by the employers ... as antagonistic to the interests of the working classes'.[166] Mr. R.J. Lappin of the Engineering and Shipbuilding Draughtsmen's Association who moved the resolution stated:

> It is useless to claim ... that control by employers in a manner adverse to the educational interests of the scholars is entirely precluded; the relationship between paying the piper and calling the tune is well established, and, besides, such influence is already well known in connection with evening classes.[167]

J. Houghton of the Scottish Union of Dock Labourers, seconding the motion implied conspiracy; that one of the reasons for continuation classes being established was, '... in order to give the employers the opportunity to go to the young people in connection with their works and get their minds moulded to the Manchester School of Economics...'.[168]

The special relationship the TUC once had with Fisher was gone. In the short run changed circumstances had soured it. Fisher did not approve of the cutbacks but, like Henderson before him, he was seen to defend Government policy in public or at least make excuses for it. His protests in the Cabinet, especially over any suggestion to cut teachers' salaries, helped to reduce the full effects of the Geddes Committee's recommendations so that instead of the proposed £18 million cutback this became reduced to £6$\frac{1}{2}$ million. Probably more convincing to Lloyd George than Fisher's arguments were the Labour victories in by—elections at Manchester and Camberwell where the threatened Geddes cutbacks and their specific effect upon working class children was an issue made much of by the successful candidates.[169]

Fisher who had considered resigning, may have helped to divert the worst blows of the 'Geddes Axe' from education but he was not seen in the role of a saviour by the TUC; on the contrary he appeared as at best an apologist for Government policy which was directly affecting working class interests in an adverse manner. At the 1922 TUC Fisher was personally criticized in the Education debate. 'Our friend Tom Myers', John Hill of the Boilermakers told delegates, 'put a question in the House a week or two ago when he asked Mr. Fisher, the Minister for Education, what was the justification for the Government having taken on 100 untrained teachers when there were hundreds of trained teachers idle at the time. The reply of Mr. Fisher was that the justification was that of economy'.[170] This must have come hard for Fisher who had argued the need for more qualified teachers to an uncertificated teacher who formed part of a TUC delegation in 1920.[171]

Under the general pressure of cutbacks delegates were beginning to ask some fundamental questions as to why their children were the ones to be affected rather than those of Government Ministers or the Middle-Class. Why was there a shortage of school buildings when there were unemployed bricklayers or why were there still classes of fifty in elementary schools when there were unemployed teachers? The awe in which TUC leaders, especially Thorne, had once held Fisher was gone, to be replaced by jibes in Parliament. Mr. C.J. Ammon of the Post Office Workers provided an explanation at the TUC for both the recent changes in Government attitude towards education and the apparent failure of Fisher as Education Minister:

> Mr. Fisher, the Minister of Education, and the Government, had their marching orders from their masters prior to taking this step! The Federation of British Industries issued a circular objecting to the standard of secondary and other education given to the children of the workers of this country. Following on that we had the Geddes Report, then the action that has since been taken by Mr. Fisher. The Minister of Education, who has hitherto had a reputation of being the leading educationalist in the country, has proved to be the weakest and most reactionary of Education Ministers. In the House of Commons I ventured to describe him as the most pathetic spectacle in British public life.[172]

If such words from trade unionists seemed unkind and even unfair they were partly a result of the knowledge born of experience that whatever the cutbacks might be in education it would be their children who would be bearing the brunt of it.

It has been stated that disillusionment with Fisher by the TUC was a result of recent changed circumstances in education; that is, the negation of much of the 1918 Education Bill. However, in the long run some friction was inevitable for whilst Fisher may have felt his views were nearer to those of the TUC than the FBI they were in effect the views of a liberal stateman[173] who might have sounded radical in Edwardian times but no longer did so in the aftermath of a World War and the Russian Revolution. Mr. Adamson, MP for Fife, had reminded the House of Commons that the proposals of the 1918 Education Bill did not match up to the demands of the working class and when compared with the Bradford Charter it could make little claim to be very progressive.[174] Like so many proposals for social welfare hatched during the War they were really related to pre-war thinking and conditions; in the changing circumstances they now even seemed conservative to some.[175]

Fisher's Bill was the limit of his thinking in education matters. It was not the first stage to greater reform. When writing his autobiography more than twenty years later he made it clear that he considered his policy of 1918 was all that was needed because it had not been superseded since then.

> The Education Act of 1918, supplemented by the Teachers' Super-annuation Act which was passed in the autumn of the same year, as nearly as possible exhausted the power of Parliament to promote the public system of education. Nor ... has any legislative change been thought necessary since ... the work had been done.[176]

Hence even if the 1918 Education Act had been fully implemented Fisher would still have been out of step with the labour movement by 1922 when Tawney's 'Secondary Education for All' was published, for he did not believe in this concept in the 1920s any more than he had when explaining his Bill to the Commons in 1917, when he had made it clear that staying on at school to fourteen years of age (or fifteen where local education authorities approved) for most children would be undertaken in elementary not secondary schools.[177]

By 1922 the trade union movement was on the defensive. The TUC had reorganized itself so that the PCTUC had given way to the General Council in 1921 but at that Congress, whilst progress in terms of such reorganization could be announced, affiliated membership had dropped by 87,000 from a record high in 1920 to 6,417,910. This fall announced the first step in a general decline of an affiliated membership which reached 4,366,000 in 1925 and continued downwards to its lowest total of 3,295,000 in 1933. The TUC was not to recover its 1920 membership numbers until the Second World War. In 1922 a General Election recorded an increase in Labour Party votes by nearly two million giving it now 142 seats in the House of Commons but the Conservative Party clearly won the election.

Contraction in educational spending and provision had now become the policy of the Government and in this the new Conservative administration was reinforced by a deputation of Conservative MPs who urged the Cabinet to reduce expenditure on education further.[178] Baldwin as Prime Minister and Chancellor of the Exchequer duly squeezed the education system further, causing such discontentment that early in 1923 strikes by the National Union of Teachers, lasting several weeks, took place at Southampton, Gateshead and Lowestoft.[179] At the end of the year another General Election was called and whilst the Conservatives survived with the largest number of MPs (258 in total), the Liberals with 158 and the Labour Party with 191, if combined, could out-vote the Conservatives. In January 1924 a minority Labour Government took office with Charles Trevelyan, formerly a Liberal, appointed to the Board of Education.

The Board of Education Under a Labour Minister

The economic situation had not changed for the better but Trevelyan did start to reverse the post war cut-backs in education. He withdrew circular 1190 which had been instrumental in ruthlessly pruning educational expenditure; he encouraged the extension of secondary education but told the House of Commons that it was not possible at the time to introduce secondary education for all.[180] The TUC expressed approval of his first moves, prefacing their education resolution with the comment 'that this Congress welcomes the new spirit shown by the Labour Government towards the question of Education', but then went on to list a whole series of suggested improvements, including a demand for 'education in continuation schools to be made obligatory in the employers' time up to eighteen years'.[181]

The Labour Party was only in office for nine months so that Trevelyan's attempts at gradual expansion in the face of Conservative opposition did not have time to make substantial progress.[182] He did gain valuable experience and learned that the Labour Movement needed to control local authorities as well as central government if their plans for education were to bear fruit. He received no encouragement from Philip Snowden,[183] who turned out to be the most orthodox of Chancellors with little concern for education in general and no interest in Tawney's 'Secondary Education for All', which had been adopted by the Labour Party but not the TUC at this stage. Upon leaving office, Trevelyan pleaded that all parties should keep education out of politics.[184] The naivety of such a view is well illustrated by the different attitudes of the Labour and Conservative Parties towards raising the school leaving age. Trevelyan would have liked to raise it but believed it was not possible at the time[185] whereas the Conservatives opposed the idea because they believed that a concession of one year would lead to another, knowing full well that some members of the labour movement had eighteen years as the ultimate goal in mind.[186]

Continuation Schools Fade Away

In the same year that Trevelyan's brief spell in office ended, the Conservatives returned to power and the aristocratic Lord Percy took over at the Board of Education and one orthodox Chancellor was replaced by another. Percy lacked the drive of Trevelyan but that did not matter so much as he also lacked the desire to introduce any sweeping changes. The Chancellor, Winston Churchill, not only favoured retrenchment in nearly all branches of Government expenditure but positively disliked formal education[187] so that any appeals for greater consideration in this area of social services would have been largely wasted.

A deputation from the General Council of the TUC to Lord Percy in 1925 made no progress whatsoever. Mr. Titrterington suggested that raising the school leaving age to fifteen would solve '... both an educational and an economic problem, by protecting the child from industry and relieving industry from a type of labour "distinctly pernicious"'[188] but Percy could only plead that while he had asked local education authorities for any plans they might have to raise the school leaving age he could not force their hand. He explained that he could only meet proposals with the money he had available; a true statement in fact and one also in line with his own intentions which were, like the FBI, to improve elementary education first because, he told the deputation, '... he could not ask parents to keep their children for an additional year in schools incapable by general consent, of giving proper advanced elementary education' for the persent situation for children in such schools 'was just as much a blind alley as blind alley employment in industry'.[189]

It was a difficult answer for the TUC to confront. Children should not stay at school because the education was not good enough but it was not likely to improve either as the Government would not spend the necessary money on it. The idea put forward by Tawney,[190] that at eleven years of age all children should proceed to a secondary school, had received the approval of the Labour Party and many members of the TUC, although it was not yet Congress policy. However, at no time during this period or for many years afterwards was such a view accepted by the Conservative Party.[191] Percy merely reflected the views of his Party and their followers, as he was to explain later: 'Not long after Baldwin formed his Government, Neville Chamberlain said to me that, in his judgment, public opinion – at any rate Conservative public opinion – would welcome more expenditure on health and housing, but was in favour of economies in education'[192] a euphemism for cuts in the financing of education.

As for Continuation Classes, the idea was rapidly fading as far as the Government was concerned. Birmingham and London had informed the Board of Education that although their appointed days to introduce such schemes had been fixed they did not intend to pursue the proposals. The TUC, at one time not particularly enthusiastic supporters of such schemes, were now prepared to fight for them or any other part of the 1918 Education Act which could be salvaged. H.H. Elvin, who had advocated such classes since 1909, tried to persuade Percy that the failure to develop such classes was a factor in our inability to hold the markets of the world; yet at the same time wished to make it clear that 'they regarded continuation classes as only a temporary expedient during progress to a complete secondary system'.[193]

By 1925 it was apparent that there was no way in which the TUC could persuade contemporary Conservative Governments that it was in the nation's interest, least of all the interests of working class children, to move away from a policy in education which still basically reflected pre-war society. Whatever the disagreements the TUC might have had with Fisher in 1923 there had at least been some points of general agreement, some common ideals, even if they could not be realized for financial reasons. In 1925 the TUC and the President of the Board of Education had positively nothing in common. As Percy told the General Council Deputation: 'The Council's resolution did not touch the problem with which he was concerned'.[194] From his answers to their discussion the TUC must have felt exactly the same about the President's answers.

The apparent futility of sending a deputation may have been the reason that the General Council of the TUC turned down an offer from the WEA a month later to join in a similar gathering to discuss the raising of the school leaving age with the President of the Board of Education.[195] Far from collaborating with the TUC, there were a growing number of Conservatives in the Cabinet and elsewhere who believed that the trade union movement needed teaching a lesson. That time was not so far away in 1925.

Notes

1 FROW, E. and FROW, R., *A Survey of the Half Time System in Education*, p. 11.
2 SILVER, H., 'Ideology and the factory child: Attitudes to half-time education' in McCANN, P. (Ed) *Popular Education and Socialization in the Nineteenth Century*, p. 141.
3 RUBINSTEIN, D. *School Attendance in London 1870–1904: A Social History*, p. 61.
4 *Ibid.*
5 'A return of wage earning children in 1899 had shown that at least 144,000 children who were making a full time attendance at school were employed for wages out of school hours; about 40,000 were employed for more than 20 hours per week, and fully 3,000 for more than 40 hours. A few worked for more than 50 or 60 hours weekly.' DUNLOP, J. and DENMAN, R.D. *English Apprenticeship and Child Labour*, p. 26.
6 TUC Report 1901, p. 65.
7 GRIGGS, C. *The Development of Elementary Education in a Rural Area*, M.A. (Educ.) London 1969 Appendix 3, p. 134.
8 HORN, P.L.R. 'The Agricultural Children Act of 1873' in '*History of Education*', 3 (2) 1974, p. 30.
9 For further details see PINCHBECK, I. and HEWITT, M. *Children in English Society*, Vol. 2, pp. 391–394.
10 MACLEOD R.M. 'Social Policy and the Floating Population 1877–99' *Past and Present*, No. 35 1966, pp. 106–129.
11 *Ibid.*, p. 108.
12 *Ibid.*, p. 129.
13 'Child labour remained surprisingly important in this country, showing no significant tendency to diminish in important industries until very late in the century' HOBSBAWM, E.J. 'The Labour aristocracy' in *Labouring Men*, p. 293.

14 LOWNDES, G.A.N. *The Silent Social Revolution*, p. 22 and RUBINSTEIN, D. *op. cit.*, p. 99.
15 For example, Charles Kingsley *The Water Babies* (1863); Arthur Morrison *Child of the Jago* (1896); Jack London *People of the Abyss* (1903).
16 *Seventy Years of Trade Unionism*, p. 43.
17 ROGERS, F. *Labour, Life and Literature*, p. 5.
18 BLAXLAND, G. *J.H. Thomas: A Life for Unity*, p. 17.
19 CLYNES, J.R. *Memoirs Vol. 1.*, p. 29.
20 TURNER, B. *Short History of the General Union of Textile Workers*, p. 179.
21 *Seventy Years of Trade Unionism op. cit.*, p. 49.
22 *Various Labour Biographies*, p. 134.
23 MANN, T. *Memoirs*, p. 10.
24 COLE, M. *Makers of the Labour Movement*, p. 204.
25 BURT, T. *Thomas Burt: An Autobiography*, p. 32.
26 ARCH, J. *op. cit.*, p. 30.
27 LEVENTHAL, F.M. *Respectable Radical: George Howell and Victorian Working Class Politics*, p. 2.
28 SEXTON, J. *Sir James Sexton: Agitator*, p. 28 & p. 39.
29 TILLETT, B. *Memories and Reflections*, p. 39.
30 This view was frequently expressed by trade unionists. To take but one example from a debate on the half-time system at the TUC, J.C. Gordon of the Sheet Metal Workers seconding a resolution said: '. . . in some districts where the half-time system was existing it would make a great difference to the unemployed problem if the children were kept at home instead of being sent into the factories'. TUC Report 1909, p. 190.
31 TUC Report 1869, pp. 116–118.
32 FRASER, W.H. *op. cit.*, pp. 35–37.
33 TUC Report 1880 p. 37.
34 *Ibid.*
35 PINCHBECK, I. and HEWITT, M. *op. cit.*, p. 404.
36 See *Justice*, 1.8.1896.
37 *Hansard*, 1918, Vol. 106, Col. 1898.
38 The Railways refused to recognize trade unions for negotiating purposes for years. See BAGWELL, P.S. *op. cit.* The industry was run like a military organization with wage deductions for 'misdemeanours' such as 'wilfully greasing the floor of the engine drivers' room' (plate 3) or whistling on duty (p. 26). It was not until 1907 that the railways recognized the trade unions which had been in existence in their industry since at least 1872 when the ASRS was formed.
39 TUC Report 1896, pp. 71–72.
40 PCTUC Deputation to the Board of Education, 17.2.1916.
41 MARWICK, A. *The Deluge: British Society and the First World War*, p. 96.
42 GCTUC Deputation to the Board of Education, 25.5.1925.
43 PCTUC Deputation to the Board of Education, 12.2.1914.
44 TUC Report 1874, p. 24.
45 TUC Report 1899, p. 72.
46 *Ibid.*, p. 45.
47 TUC Report 1907, p. 189.
48 PCTUC Deputation to Board of Education, 15.2.1912.
49 RUBINSTEIN, D. *op. cit.*, p. 74.
50 TUC Report 1897, p. 42.
51 PCTUC Deputation to Board of Education 1914.
52 TUC Report 1901. Resolution to prohibit employment of children under fifteen years of age in all factories; carried by 171:71 votes., pp. 65–66. Repeated 1902. TUC Report 1902, pp. 24, 25.

53 SIMON, implies that the Social Democratic Federation were the first to do so. See SIMON, B., *Education and the Labour Movement 1870–1920*, Vol. 2, p. 139.

54 TUC Report 1873, p. 2.

55 A Report from the PCTUC to the 1891 Congress described how: 'The proposal to raise the age of "Half-Timers" from ten to twelve years, was rejected through the obstinate resistance of the Home Secretary, notwithstanding the pledge given by British Delegates, on the authority of the Government...' TUC Report 1891, pp. 28–29. British trade unionists wished for co-operation from other countries so that no country might have the 'advantage' of cheap child labour in the manufacture of its products.

56 An example of an MP on this occasion trying to gauge trade union opinion on the matter is provided by Seymour King, Conservative MP for Central Hull, who wrote to the Secretary of the Hull Trades Council informing him that textile workers had written to him asking for resistance to the raising of the age for child labour beyond ten years. The Secretary replied that the Council felt that '... a child of ten years was too young to be pushed into the struggle for existence'. BROWN, R. M. Sc. thesis, University of Hull, 1966, *op. cit.*, p. 213.

57 TUC Report 1895, pp. 56–57.

58 SUTHERLAND, G. *Policy-Making in Elementary Education 1870–95*, p. 156.

59 TUC Report 1895, *op. cit.*

60 TUC Report 1898, p. 30.

61 TUC Report 1900, p. 89.

62 TUC Report 1899, p. 72.

63 TUC Report 1910, p. 165.

64 In fact Marx also supported the half-time system, at least in theory. The tenth point of the programme of the Communist League prepared by Marx and Engels, published in 1848, read: 'Free Education for all children in public schools. Abolition of children's factory labour in its present form. Combination of education with industrial production'. *The Communist Manifesto*. This makes it clear that he opposed child labour as it was but believed that it was necessary to bring theory and practice together if man were to be a complete person. Engels should have had first hand knowledge of the system and would have known of its virtues and vices but when Vol. I of Capital was published in 1867, three years prior to Forster's Education Act, and therefore arguably at a time when the half-time system was ensuring that factory children were getting some education, Marx not only continued to support the system but for some reason used evidence of a most dubious nature. (See *Capital Vol. I*, pp. 482–484). This strange phenomenon was first questioned by Harold Silver in 'Aspects of Neglect: The Strange Case of Victorian Popular Education' *Oxford Review of Education*, Vol. 3, No. 1, 1977, pp. 63–64, and again later in his essay 'Ideology and the Factory Child: Attitudes to Half-Time Education' *op. cit.*, pp. 154–157.

65 Charles Booth, whilst not in favour of the factory half-time system thought the principle might be beneficially applied to girls so that they might carry out domestic work at home for some part of the day. His argument was based upon the need to improve the quality of cooking and nutriment in many working class homes. *Evidence to the Inter Departmental Committee on Physical Deterioration*, Vol. II, 1914, pp. 50–55.

66 TUC Report 1897, p. 41.

67 *Ibid.*, p. 42.

68 *Ibid.*, p. 41. In a separate debate upon TUC Education Policy, Mr. F. Thomas from Bromley '... declared amidst much laughter, that Lancashire, in which the half-time system prevailed, was acknowledged to be far more intellectual than any other part of the country'. He received no support for this view. TUC Report 1897, p. 50.

69 *Hansard*, 1909, Vol. 3., Col. 1782.
70 TUC Report 1898, p. 29.
71 TUC Report 1900, p. 89.
72 Correspondence quoted in *Justice*, 31.10.1896.
73 See SILVER, H. 'Ideology and the factory child: Attitudes to half-time education' *op. cit.*, p. 157 for illustration of 'Half-Timers asleep at their desks'. Tom Mann drew attention to the problem as revealed by the Labour Commission of 1892: 'Six thousand child half-timers worked in a temperature of eighty to 110 degrees in the morning and went to school in the afternoon. By 3.30 "They could no longer be stopped from dozing off."'. TORR, D. *Tom Mann and His Times*, pp. 162–163.
74 SILVER, H. 'Ideology and the factory child: Attitudes to half-time education' *op. cit.*, p. 149.
75 *Report of the Committee on Attendance, Compulsory or Otherwise, at Continuation Schools*, 1909, Vol. I., p. 217.
76 TUC Report 1909, p. 191.
77 TUC Report 1907, p. 187.
78 PCTUC Deputation to the Board of Education, 16.3.1911.
79 The Census returns of 1891 showed that there were 3,223,600 children in the age group ten to fourteen years; in 1901, 3,341,800. See MITCHELL, B.R. and DEANE, P. *Abstract of British Historical Statistics*, Table 4, p. 12. However as the minimum age of employment was only raised to eleven years in 1893 large numbers of this age group were legally employed.
80 *Report of the Committee on Attendance, Compulsory or Otherwise, at Continuation Schools*, Appendix 4, p. 287.
81 TUC Report 1909, pp. 190–191.
82 PCTUC Deputation to the Board of Education, 16.3.1911.
83 TUC Report 1901, p. 65.
84 The NUT requested the PCTUC to send three representatives to a meeting to discuss the half-time issue: W.J. Davis (Chairman), Sam Woods (Secretary) and Will Thorne of the PCTUC were chosen. PCTUC Minutes, 6.2.1899.
85 TUC Report 1912, p. 186.
86 TURNER, B. *Short History of the General Union of Textile Workers*, p. 82.
87 *Consultative Committee on Attendance at Continuation Schools*, reported in 1909. The Committee which met sixteen times and examined fifty-two witnesses was under the chairmanship of Charles Trevelyan. In addition to A. Gee and D. Holmes, the membership included Lord Clifford, Lord Sheffield, W.R. Rea MP., H.M. Lindsell, G. Bellhouse, Tom Garnett, Mark Oldroyd and C.E. Sykes as Secretary.
88 *Ibid.*, p. 216.
89 *Ibid.*, p. 142.
90 ANDREWS, L., *The Education Act 1918*, p. 8.
91 Ben Turner described the gradual decline of the Half-Time system in the Woollen Trade and suggested the Lancashire cotton industry should follow suit. TUC Report 1912, p. 186.
92 By 1914 Thorne could report in a PCTUC deputation to the Board of Education that '... our friends the textile workers are not giving us the opposition they did in years gone by, and we are unanimous in this...' PCTUC Deputation to the Board of Education 12.12.1914. In 1907 there were 112 LEAs in England and Wales which allowed for no partial exemption in their byelaws.
93 Letter to C.W. Bowerman, Secretary PCTUC, from Board of Education, 10.2.1916.
94 This was a promise the Board of Education did keep! H.H. Elvin in a deputation from the PCTUC the following year showed how child labour in agricultural areas had risen to 15,753 in May 1916, and was still 14,915 in Oct. 1916.

95 PCTUC Deputation to the Board of Education, 17.2.1916.

96 TUC Report 1915, p. 414.

97 For example, Henry Broadhurst appointed Under Secretary at the Home Office after eleven years as Secretary of the PCTUC was called upon to deal with the Trafalgar Square Demonstration of 13.11.1887 '... by no means a pleasant initiation for me into official life' although one he seemed to be quite willing to deal with. See TORR, D. *op. cit.*, p. 228.

98 Henderson to Asquith, 26.7.1916. Correspondence quoted in HAMILTON, M.A. *Arthur Henderson: A Biography*.

99 Henderson to Asquith, 8.8.1916. Correspondence quoted in HAMILTON, M.A. *Arthur Henderson: A Biography*.

100 PCTUC Deputation to the Board of Education, 15.2.1917.

101 PCTUC Deputation to the Board of Education, 1.3.1919.

102 FISHER, H.A.L. *op. cit.*, p. 97.

103 Fisher's appointment was part of Lloyd George's campaign for reconstruction which he had inherited from Asquith and breathed new life into. The idea of reconstruction was voiced as early as 1915 and taken up in 1916: 'It appeared early because, after all, the war was expected to end early ... the first foreshadowing of social reconstruction, the extension of war pensions, grew directly out of the military war and its very high casualty rate ... the widely publicized reconstruction programmes of 1917, in which education and housing had star billing, were in part designed to allay warweariness and discontent.'. MARWICK, A. *op. cit.*, pp. 258–259.

104 PCTUC Deputation to the Board of Education, 5.2.1917.

105 *Ibid.*

106 'During a long series of years Congress has by resolution and deputation endeavoured to induce successive Presidents of the Board of Education to accept the Trade Union education programme. Although many Education Ministers have been sincerely sympathetic towards that programme, it has remained for the present Minister – the Right Hon. H. Fisher – to make a real attempt to give effect to it.... Within a few days of the termination of the recent sessions of Parliament, Mr. Fisher introduced a Bill.... The Bill has for its object the provision of enlarged and enriched opportunities of education to the children of the poor ... it will be seen that the Bill is based on broad comprehensive lines, amply justifying the time which Congress has year by year devoted to the consideration of educational matters during the past quarter of a century.' TUC Report 1917, pp. 91–92.

107 Ben Pickard – school given as Kippax Grammar School in the *Dictionary of Labour Biography*, but Colliery School only mentioned in the *Dictionary of National Biography*, see Chapter 4.

108 TUC Report 1897, p. 50.

109 TUC Report 1903, pp. 86–87.

110 TUC Report 1897, p. 50.

111 TUC Report 1902, p. 71.

112 PCTUC Deputation to the Board of Education, 2.3.1909.

113 'That attendance in primary and secondary schools shall be compulsory ... children to continue school until sixteen years, or until such age as the university course begins....' TUC Report 1905, p. 142. 'That secondary and technical education be an essential part of every child's education ... all children to be full-time day pupils up to 16 years.' TUC Report 1906, p. 175 and similar demand, TUC Report 1907, p. 186.

114 TUC Report 1905, p. 143.

115 See Chapter 4.

116 TUC Report 1921, p. 370.

117 In fact a Bill was presented to Parliament by Chiozza Money in 1911 designed to

raise the school leaving age from twelve to thirteen years and after that time allow children to stay on at day school until fourteen years or attend part-time continuation classes until sixteen years. It was withdrawn owing to pressure of time. See SIMON, B. Vol. II, *op. cit.*, p. 292. H.H. Elvin referred to the Bill in the PCTUC Deputation to the Board of Education, 12.2.1914.

118 TUC Report 1909, p. 191.
119 A.F. Chandler (Railway Clerks) '. . . he had seen children . . . run for a train at half past four in the morning. What was their chance of education?' TUC Report 1909, p. 191.
120 Official reports of youngsters too tired to study after work in the evening went back many years. 'In 1871 an Inspector had pointed to the futility of trying to teach children in rural areas who had already been plodding through a stiff clay furrow for six or seven hours.' McCANN, W.P., Elementary Education in England and Wales on the Eve of the 1870 Education Act *Journal of Educational Administration and History*, 2 (1) 1969, p. 23.
121 PCTUC Deputation to the Board of Education, 15.2.1912.
122 These claims were completely born out in the Lewis Report 1917. 'In 1911–12 there were about 2,700,000 juveniles between fourteen and eighteen years, of these about 2,200,000 or 81.5% were enrolled in neither day schools nor evening schools.... Here, then are the two great causes of educational wastage; general disregard of the facilities by evening schools completes what early withdrawal from day schools began ... quite apart from the question of half-time exemption, many children, during the later years of their day-school life, are employed outside school hours in ways and to an extent which seriously interferes with their educational progress.' Lewis Report 1917, Vol. 1, pp. 3–5.
123 PCTUC Deputation to the Board of Education, 12.2.1914.
124 FBI Memorial on Education, p. 3.
125 *FBI Bulletin*, 9.5.1918, p. 290.
126 FBI Memorial on Education, pp. 8–9.
127 Memo to H.A.L. Fisher from W.N.D., 25.1.1918.
128 Memo to H.A.L. Fisher from F.H.D., 2.2.1918.
129 Memo to H.A.L. Fisher from Prof. G. Murray, 28.1.1918.
130 FBI Deputation to the Board of Education, 6.2.1918.
131 *FBI Bulletin*, 14.2.1918, p. 221.
132 *FBI Bulletin*, 25.4.1918, p. 284.
133 *Times Educational Supplement*, 28.2.1918. An article supporting Fisher's Bill was also included 'by a correspondent – unsigned.'
134 *Daily News*, 14.2.1918.
135 *Ibid.*
136 'The object of the amendments was, first, to remove the requirements for continuation education altogether, and then, if these efforts failed, to attempt to limit the continuation proposals by granting exemption to young people in certain industries, or by reducing the hours of attendance a week to eight, four or even two.' ANDREWS, L. *op. cit.*, p. 50.
137 Sir H. Llewellyn Smith to H.A.L. Fisher, 30.1.1918.
138 'As 1917 progressed, opposition to continuation schools among the commercial interests, stiffened. In an awkward meeting with the Bradford Chamber of Commerce, Fisher was clearly told that they would only support continuation schools held in the evening out of work hours and then because they would keep juveniles from mischief.' DEAN, D.W. 'H.A.L. Fisher, Reconstruction and the Development of the 1918 Act' *British Journal of Educational Studies*, 18 (3) 1970, p. 264. At a meeting of the Mining Association, Textile and other manufacturing trades held on 9th May 1918 under the auspices of the FBI: 'A resolution was passed expressing the belief that the proposals in the English and Scottish

Education Bills with reference to continuation classes were calculated to injure unnecessarily the industrial and commercial interests of the country, to increase the cost and reduce the volume of production...' *FBI Bulletin*, 23.5.1918, p. 309.

139 ANDREWS, L. *op. cit.*, pp. 52–54.

140 Mr. Whitehouse MP complained about the pressures which had forced Fisher to make concessions: 'I greatly regret that vested interests in this matter have compelled the President to make such drastic changes in the Bill'. *Hansard*, 1918, Vol. 106, Col. 1671.

141 *Hansard*, 1918, Vol. 106, Col. 1658.

142 *Hansard*, 1918, Vol. 106, Col. 1644.

143 See Chapter 7.

144 FISHER, H.A.L. *op. cit.*, p. 110.

145 Speaking at his union's biennual Conference Thorne told them: '... educational propaganda work at the TUC for many years had made it possible for Mr. Fisher to introduce his extraordinary Bill'. Report of the 17th Biennial Congress National Union of Gasworkers and General Labourer's Union 1918, p. 85.

146 DEAN, D.W. *op. cit.*, pp. 264–265.

147 BARKER, R.S. *The Educational Policies of the Labour Party 1900–61*, Ph. D. Thesis (Lond.) 1968 p. 81. For full details of the PLP's attitude and actions towards the 1918 Education Bill see BARKER, R.S. pp. 78–88.

148 Ramsay MacDonald stated that 'the concession that has been given really destroys the whole scheme'. *Hansard*, 1918, Vol. 106, Col. 1651.

149 BARKER, R.S. *op. cit.*, p. 82.

150 All sections of the Labour Movement had reservations about Continuation Classes: 'In WEA circles and at Labour conferences, proposals were made for a school leaving age of sixteen, universal free secondary education, and an extensive supply of scholarships to the Universities. Continuation Schools were seen as ... a rather shabby way of avoiding these programmes.' DEAN, D.W. *op. cit.*, p. 267.

151 Opposition to vocational training had already been declared at the 1918 Labour Party Conference, British Socialist Party Conference and TUC of same year.

152 'Most Conservatives unashamedly advocated a severely vocational education within the schools, and argued that since 1870 there had been a steady erosion of practical subjects as the more bookish academic subjects crept in.' DEAN, D.W. 'Conservatism and the National Education System 1922–40' *The Journal of Contemporary History*, 6 (2) 1971, p. 155.

153 TUC Report 1918, p. 304.

154 *Ibid.*, p. 305.

155 See p. 51.

156 Fisher read at some length to the TUC delegates from the Code, part of which was as follows: '... teachers can yet do much to lay the foundations of conduct. They can endeavour, by example and influence, and by the sense of discipline which should pervade the school, to implant in the children habits of industry, self control and courageous perseverance in the face of difficulties; they can teach them to reverence what is noble, to be ready for self sacrifice, and to strive their utmost after purity and truth; they can foster a strong sense of duty ... while the corporate life of the School, especially in the playground should develop that instinct for fair play and loyalty to one another which is the germ of a wider sense of honour in early life'. PCTUC Deputation to the Board of Education, 12.3.1919.

The aims read like something out of Tom Brown's schooldays: it is surprising to learn that such views were ever seriously put forward as even remotely realizable in the overcrowded elementary schools of the time and it says much for Fisher's naivety that he could seriously lecture the very adults who had passed through such schools and knew them at first hand, unlike himself or most of his department.

157 *Ibid.*

158 Clause 2(a) of the Education Policy of the TUC approved by Congress stipulated: 'That the maximum number of children allowed on the register of any class in a public elementary school be reduced to 40, and within a period not exceeding five years, to 30'. TUC Report 1918, p. 304.

159 FISHER, H.A.L. *op. cit.*, p. 92.

160 THOMS, D.W. 'The Emergence and Failure of the Day Continuation School Experiment' *History of Education*, 4 (1) 1975, p. 44.

161 'The failure of Lloyd George to institute fully a programme of educational reconstruction ... was to push Haldane much further to the left of the political spectrum and he later joined the Labour Party because he saw it as the only political group committed to large scale educational development.' SHERINGTON, G.E. 'R.B. Haldane: The Reconstruction Committee and the Board of Education 1916–18' *Journal of Educational Administration and History*, 6 (2) 1974, p. 22.

162 For a vivid description of such events see HUTT, A. *The Post War History of the British Working Class*, Ch. I-IV.

163 See REYNOLDS, G.W. and JUDGE, A. *The Night the Police Went on Strike*, Chs. 13 & 14.

164 APPLETON, W.A. *What We Want and Where We Are: Facts not Phrases*, pp. 155–156.

165 Sir Eric Geddes, Shipowner (Chair); Lord Inchcape, wealthy industrialist; Lord Farringdon, Sir Joseph Mackay and Sir Guy Grant. 'Labour made much of the fact that leading critics of educational expenditure seemed to come largely from business quarters, and they were hostile to the composition of the Geddes Commission...' DEAN, D.W. *The Political Parties and Development of their attitude to Educational Problems 1918–42*, M.Phil. Thesis (Lond.) 1968, p. 67.

166 TUC Report 1920, p. 371.

167 *Ibid.*

168 *Ibid.*

169 SIMON, B. *op. cit.*, Vol. III, pp. 44–51.

170 TUC Report 1922, p. 413.

171 See Chapter 8, p. 211.

172 TUC Report 1922, p. 416.

173 'The appointment of Fisher as President of the Board of Education certainly helped to provide further impetus towards educational change. But it did not initiate a new era in educational policy, as has sometimes been supposed. Although a liberal committed to social reform, Fisher had no desire for radical change. In general he fitted in easily with the attitude of the chief Board officials.' SHERRINGTON, G.E. 'The 1918 Education Act: Origins, aims and development.' *British Journal of Educational Studies*, 24 (1) 1976, p. 74.

174 *Hansard*, 1918, Vol. 106, Col. 1897.

175 'The reconstruction plans of Lloyd George's Coalition Government were mostly continuations and expansions of welfare institutions established, or projected, before the war. In this sense his reform programme was itself essentially traditional and nostalgic; in this sense also ... it was inappropriate for the nation that emerged from the conflict. Lloyd George was a conservative reformer and the post war solutions of his administration were answers to pre-war questions.' GILBERT, B.B. *British Social Policy 1914–39*, pp. 1–2.

'In general terms, the 1918 Education Act did not set out to reconstruct or even reshape English education. Instead, much of its intention was conservative.' SHERRINGTON, G.E. *Ibid.*

176 FISHER, H.A.L. *op. cit.*, p. 109.

177 *Hansard*, 1917, Vol. 97, Cols. 802–811.

178 DEAN, D.W. *Journal of Contemporary History, op. cit.*

179 TROPP, A. *op. cit.*, p. 221.

180 BARKER, R.S. *op. cit.*, p. 172.
181 TUC Report 1924, p. 418.
182 The Labour Government continued the work of the Consultative Committee on the Education of the Adolescent which was appointed by the previous Conservative Administration. Its report produced in 1926 and known as the Hadow Report supported most of the ideas proposed by Tawney's 'Secondary Education for All' providing extra evidence of the need to end the social division between elementary and secondary schools.
183 PERCY, E. *Some Memories*, p. 94.
184 PARKINSON, M. *The Labour Party and the Organization of Secondary Schools*, p. 20.
185 BARKER, R.S. *op. cit.*, p. 172.
186 DEAN, D.W. *op. cit.*, p. 93.
187 'I found the Chancellor of the Exchequer an even more archaic colleague than the Minister of Health [i.e. Neville Chamberlain] ... Churchill's feelings about education have often reminded me, then and since, of Possun's famous comment on Gibbon's attitude to Christianity; he seemed to "hate it so cordially that he might seem to revenge some personal injury"'. PERCY, E. *op. cit.*, p. 96.
188 GCTUC Deputation to the Board of Education, 25.5.1925.
189 *Ibid.*
190 TAWNEY, R.H. *Secondary Education for All*.
191 'The Conservative Party remained, throughout the inter-war period, fundamentally unsympathetic towards measures designed to level up the educational experience of the mass of children outside the grammar schools.' BARKER, R.S. *op. cit.*, p. 154.
192 PERCY, E. *op. cit.*, p. 95.
193 GCTUC Deputation to the Board of Education, 25.5.1925.
194 *Ibid.*
195 GCTUC Minutes, 25.6.1925.

Chapter 3

The TUC and the Religious Issue in Education

The Church of England and Trade Unions

The religious issue, which dominated national debates concerning the development of an educational system for England and Wales during the nineteenth
century, was never solved to the satisfaction of all the contending parties. Both
the 1870 and 1902 Education Acts have been seen by some as a wise
compromise in the circumstances[1] and as victories for the Established Church
by others.[2] The TUC tried to refrain from involvement in religious matters but
there were times when this was not possible. Congress debates upon education
during the nineteenth century in particular were bound to involve some
discussion of religious attitudes already incorporated into the educational
system. The nearest to neutrality the TUC believed it was possible to get was to
support the call for secular education during school hours and leave religious
instruction, whether by parents or clergy, to be undertaken outside school
time. Only when the TUC considered its own interests were directly under
attack by a religious body was it prepared to make an issue of the topic and
tackle the organization concerned in a prompt manner.

The attitudes of delegates towards the religious issue were coloured chiefly
by the manner in which they believed the Church had acted towards trades
unions. 'The Church' in this instance was seen as the Church of England, for a
different attitude was shown towards Roman Catholicism and Non-
conformity in general. Catholicism, whilst it was the only christian sect to
increase its membership among the working classes in the nineteenth century,[3]
largely from Irish immigration, was mainly restricted to Lancashire and South
East London, the very areas in which the Irish had settled; it was therefore less
likely to be involved in a trade dispute on a national scale. Trade unionists of a
religious persuasion were likely to be Non-conformists[4] which meant that their
views of the Church of England would be influenced by the attitude of this
Church towards Non-conformity.

It was difficult for trade unionists to regard the Church of England as an ally.
At school board elections the Established Church sided with the Tories against

candidates representing Liberals, Non-conformity and Labour. Even without this direct confrontation the Church Hierarchy and individual members of the clergy were believed to be antagonistic towards organized labour. Editorials in the *Church Times* viewed trade unionism unfavourably until after the Dock Strike of 1889, claiming that working people were foolish to join organizations which attempted to go against 'the laws of nature'. The benefits of unions were considered to be illusory although they brought considerable 'evil', for workers 'often erroneously thought that capital was their enemy, failing to realize that without it they would be unemployed'.[5] Even the TUC was considered to be 'a most formidable and possibly dangerous character' by this Church of England journal.[6]

It was in rural areas that trade unionists most suffered the hostility of the Established Church. Although they were a minority of trade unionists, throughout the period of this study the migration from countryside to town continued so that such workers often took their attitude towards the clergy with them. There was undeniably a strong link between the clergy, landowners and farmers. The Oxbridge education of the priest[7] was likely to be shared only by some of the landowners; this inevitably resulted in some cultural affinity. Apart from usually being members of 'the Church' the landowners and farmers were also the financial providers for the local church, with obvious consequences:

> ... many of the clergy instinctively identified themselves with the landowners and farmers and the old hierarchy.... It is probable that many of them were afraid to offend the farmers ... on whose co-operation they depended for so much that was to be done in their parishes.[8]

Hence when labour disputes broke out in rural areas, especially the widespread lock-outs of 1872, the clergy found themselves forced to take sides and most frequently came down on the side of their social, cultural and financial allies. Widespread resentment was aroused when two magistrates, who were also clergymen, sentenced sixteen labourers' wives, some with children at the breast, to prison for seven and ten days of hard labour. The women were alleged to have insulted and abused two blackleg farm workers sent to Ascot Village during the dispute. The sentences led to rioting, national coverage in the press, meetings and donations, so that upon their release the newly formed National Agricultural Labourers' Union arranged a celebration and presented each of the women with five pounds.[9]

The trade union farm workers who travelled from village to village holding meetings and recruiting members were described as 'agitators' by Dr. Ellicott, the Bishop of Gloucester, who suggested at a meeting of the Gloucester Agricultural Society in September 1872, that the village horsepond was the appropriate place for such men.[10] Joseph Arch, the founder of the National Agricultural Labourers' Union, summed up the general experience of his union during these years of unrest:

... there was a parson here and there who went with us openly; but the majority were against us, and others blew now hot now cold, and flew round like weather cocks as squire or farmer or villager grew strongest at the moment.[11]

Clerical allegiance to landowning interests died hard in some areas. As late as 1914, in Norfolk, a unique combination of events led to a school strike that was to last for twenty-five years.[12] Mr. and Mrs. Higdon, both teachers, were appointed to Wood Dalling Elementary School in April 1902. Tom Higdon was the son of a farm labourer from Somerset; both were non-conformists, christian socialists and members of the NUT. On arrival Mr. Higdon set about organizing the local farm workers into a branch of the Agricultural Workers' Union and encouraged them to take an active part in the parish elections, with the result that they captured the seats previously held by local farmers and the vicar.

The Chairman of the School Managers complained to Norfolk Education Committee about the attitude of the Higdons, who had also come into conflict with local farmers over the problem of child labour. Indeed in October 1902 Mr. Higdon had sent a note to a leading farmer in the area, Mr. Gamble, that he was employing a boy under age without a labour certificate. The note was ignored but shortly afterwards Higdon observed the boy working in a field opposite the school. He marched into the field to get the boy, quickly became involved in an argument with Mr. Gamble, and the quick tempered teacher knocked the farmer to the ground with the result that he was charged with assault and fined forty shillings with 12/6d costs. Eighteen months later Mr. Gamble became a manager of the school.[13]

The Higdons were removed by the Norfolk Education Committee to Burston village in 1911 where upon Mr. Higdon repeated his success of organizing the farmworkers, capturing the parish council seats in the elections of 1913 at the expense of the local farmers and the new parson, the Reverend Eland, who came bottom of the poll. However, the Reverend Eland, his wife and his friend the Reverend C. Millard from nearby Shimpling Village were all on the School Management Committee and complaints of rudeness to the school managers were brought against Mrs. Higdon who was dismissed on April Fools Day, 1914. Upon learning of this decision, Violet Potter, a thirteen year old girl at the school, led sixty-five of her fellow pupils out of a total of seventy-two school children out on strike in support of the Higdons.

The conflict developed into one in which the Reverend Eland and local farmers were opposed to the Higdons and the majority of the villagers. Parents were taken to court and fined for their children's non-attendance at school until the court accepted that the education being given by the Higdons, who continued to teach the children, was satisfactory. (Mrs. Higdon had received good HMI reports at both Wood Dalling and Burston Schools). The Reverend Eland evicted three supporters of the strike from Glebe lands, including blind Mr. Sandy who had provided the Higdons with a temporary school room. The trade union movement became involved with donations being sent by the miners, railwaymen, gasworkers, carpenters and joiners, typographical society, London vehicle builders and various trades councils.[14] Meetings of support were held in London, addressed by such figures as Tom Mann and George Lansbury, and in all over £1,000 was collected out of which a new school house was built. The 'strike school' as it became known, lasted until 1939 when Tom Higdon died.

If such a situation was unique it was because, in general, farm labourers voted by custom at parish elections for the landowners and vicar and school teachers rarely made an attempt to quarrel with local managers if only because their situation was so precarious in the rural schools of the Church of England. Even the Reverend C. Fisher, who was vicar of Burston when the Higdons first arrived and who was in general on good terms with them, expressed disapproval at their absence from Church even though he knew they were nonconformists. Rural custom and hierarchical order held a dominant influence over agricultural workers. The clerical link with landowners and farmers can be said, at its best, to have worked for the *status quo* but such a situation was in need of considerable change as far as agricultural trade unionists were concerned so the parson often appeared as one of a group of people standing out against improvements in living conditions sought by farmworkers.

There were, of course, always exceptions to such clerical behaviour and trade unionists expressed their gratitude to those Churchmen who supported organized workers during labour disputes. The two most notable Church leaders in this category were Cardinal Manning and Bishop Fraser of Manchester, both of whom supported the agricultural workers in the 1872 lock-out. 'Manning', wrote Joseph Arch, '. . . ever proved himself the working man's friend. He was a practical friend to us for he sent a subscription of £10 in 1878, and again one of the same amount in 1879'.[15] The cardinal was welcomed by the leaders of the London Dock Strike in 1889 as a man sympathetic to their situation and one who could be trusted as arbitrator.

Bishop Fraser, whilst not completely agreeing with the principles of trade unions, believed they had been forced upon workers by the harsh conditions of labour they had faced.[16] Although he opposed strikes he sent £20 towards a relief fund set up to help striking workmen in Bolton[17] and, in a reply to a letter from Broadhurst, wrote that concerning these social problems:

> Christianity, if it cannot solve them, yet ought to be able to help in their solution . . . and in what you are pleased to say I have done in the matter, I hope I have not stepped beyond my province as a Minister of the Gospel . . . I remain, Sir, in entire sympathy with [every] *really upward* aspiration of the working people of this country.[18]

During the early 1890s the vicar of St. Agatha's Finsbury, the Reverend Freeman C. Wills, befriended local book binders who were on strike. In the depths of winter when the only possible meeting place seemed to be a public house, he provided a disused school room in which he kept two coal fires alight for the men. He never commented upon the strike, but was seen as a friend in need by Frederick Rogers, President of the Book Binders Union at the time.[19] The vicar of Upholland raised the question of the bible being produced by sweated labour at the Liverpool Diocesan Conference of 1898 and wrote to Sam Woods the TUC Secretary informing him of his action.[20] The Bishop of Birmingham also spoke out against the 'sweating' system and was also instrumental in re-establishing negotiations between the Brassworkers Union and the Employers Association by helping to rehabilitate the necessary Conciliation Board in 1909.[21]

Whether through indifference or hostility to the Established Church few urban workers attended church services. It has been argued that, because the Church had neglected the towns for years, by the time they did begin to make greater provision through the abolition of rented pews and the construction of more churches in urban areas, most working people had simply given up the habit of going.[22] There is, however, little evidence that there was a great demand from the urban working class for a programme of Church building anyway. Some of the more able working men felt little affinity with an organization which largely denied them any opportunity to share in its management even though many had shown considerable organizational ability in the establishment of both trade unions and co-operative societies.[23] The numerous 'missions' established by schools and colleges in the 1880s had little success;[24] most of the well-meaning missionaries having no real understanding of the life style, attitudes and problems of the 'natives' they had come to help.

The major problem for the members of the Established Church was that they thought the established economic and social system should go on for ever and were therefore constantly working to uphold the social system; in doing so they inevitably came into conflict with trade unionists who wished to see changes made in the economic order of the time. Hence, in the London Dock strike, Bishop Temple was considered to have given an 'unfortunate impression of indifference'[25] whilst at the turn of the century a local clergyman gave a 'special service of thanksgiving to Almighty God' when Will Crooks was defeated at the polls in Woolwich.[26] The general picture of an Established Church led by a hierarchy whose background and sympathies were allied to those in power was hard to deny.[27]

Religious Sermons at the TUC

Whatever the hostility or friendship shown to trade unionists by individual members of the Church and in spite of some uncomplimentary remarks made about various denominations in particular or religion in general by some TUC delegates during debates, in 1872 the Reverend F. Morse was asked to provide a short religious address when Congress met at Nottingham. From that year onwards a pre-Congress sermon became an annual feature, so much so that in some years it was included in the front of the conference report.[28] It was not unusual on such occasions for ministers to praise the efforts of trade unionists in seeking to improve their living conditions. For example, in 1898 at Bristol Cathedral, the Reverend G. Estwick Ford told delegates that it was most appropriate that they should seek the blessing of God on their deliberations 'for that great object of organizing themselves ... to secure fair and righteous dealings between employers and workmen, and to abolish conditions of life and labour which involve hardship and wrong to the poor'.[29]

The three London Bishops, although absent from the capital when Congress met there in 1902 nevertheless sent a joint message of greeting informing delegates that they were themselves 'frequently engaged in urging upon other classes of the community their responsibility towards those engaged in labour with their hands', and recognized how much the welfare of vast numbers of industrial workers in their dioceses had been improved 'by the societies which you represent'.[30]

At Leeds two years later Mr. C.T. Dimont, the Vice Principal of Leeds Clergy School told Congress the Christian law demands 'that it shall be possible for every man to find work ... that he shall be paid a just wage',[31] sentiments that bore no relationship to the fatalistic remarks appearing in the editorials of the *Church Times* implying that economic laws were beyond the province of man to alter. There were times when the clergy were more revolutionary than the TUC congregation who may have warmed to a sermon by the Reverend John Gleeson in Ipswich when he reminded them of the dignity of labour and that Jesus too was an artisan but were surprised to find him quoting the German socialist Carl Liebknecht to them: 'Christianity is the religion of private property and of the respectable classes.'.[32] Ironically, by this time, not a few of the leading trade unionists belonged to the respectable classes even if they lacked the ownership of much private property. Few showed much sympathy for the philosophy of continental socialists and for many their first introduction to Liebknecht would have been by a Congregational Minister.

Sunday Opening of Museums and Art Galleries

TUC leaders were wary of confronting religious societies over issues believed to be of little fundamental importance to the livelihood of workers, whatever their personal views of the past or present role of various denominations had been. They had enough enemies without needlessly antagonizing sections of society which contained within them at least some members friendly to their cause. This is well illustrated by the question of the Sunday opening of museums and art galleries after 2.00 p.m., placed before the Standing Orders Committee in 1882. A complaint that it had not been put on the agenda of Congress received no satisfaction but when the matter was repeated the following year an explanation was provided by the Chairman; ' ... it would involve a discussion on the Sunday question, and introduce a religious element into their debates which was not useful'.[33] When the event was repeated for a third year a proposal was made by W. Inskip from Leicester to let Congress decide whether the measure should be discussed, and Congress decided that it should by forty-six to thirty-eight votes.[34]

The case for Sunday opening was presented as an educational measure. Museums and art galleries would act as a counter attraction to the public house and Sunday was the one free day[35] when the families of working people could make such visits. These places, paid for by the public were 'elevating in tone, and recreative to mind and body'.[36] Amendments aimed at extending the opening hours during the week instead ignored the long hours worked by many people so that they were in no mental condition to enjoy the galleries and museums after a nine to ten hour day. Religion was rarely mentioned in the debate, except to say that it was not the issue,[37] for those against Sunday opening argued that they were against any further extension of hours of work. One delegate pushed the argument to the extreme conclusion by proposing that they vote against all Sunday working, including taxis, trains and policemen.[38] At the 1887 TUC Sunday opening was approved by forty-five to twenty-four votes,[39] the major argument winning over most delegates being the view that working people were being excluded by their hours of work from publicly provided places that others were able to enjoy.

Unsectarian and Secular Demands at the TUC

There were two phases of discussion concerning religious education at the TUC. The first took place in the early years surrounding the 1870 Education Act; the second from the early 1890s to 1912. In the first period there were unanimous demands for unsectarian education; in the second period a large majority supported secular education. In 1869 the issues seemed to be clear cut; trade unionists had only experienced education in some form of religious school. By the 1890s however, there was the greater possibility that increasing numbers had no experience of sectarian education for, as the movement of population from countryside to town continued, fewer children experienced the education of the one elementary school district which was most likely to be Church of England. In addition the growth of the urban board schools meant that the children of artisans were more likely to experience unsectarian education. As they grew up they lacked the bitter personal school experiences of the older trade unionists and whilst the majority were against the intervention of religious bodies in education it was largely because such activity seemed inappropriate by the 1890s.

Cremer's successful resolution calling for unsectarian education at the 1869 Congress owed something to the influence of the NEL but there were other factors involved as well. There was a positive dislike of the Established Church by trade unionists who had attended their schools. Arch, referring to his own school experiences of the 1830s, saw the schooling as specifically designed to keep working people in their place:

... he might learn his catechism; that, and things similar to it, was the right, proper and suitable knowledge for such as he; he would be more likely to stay contentedly in his place to the end of his working days.[40]

He called them Parson's schools and wrote, 'I should like to see them swept away from off the face of the country'.[41] Frederick Rogers believed that all the religious schools pursued the same course: ' ... in fact, the aims of the various religions was less to educate than to proselytize'.[42]

At a time when Church of England influence in education (such as the university entrance requirements at Oxbridge) and in the area of Teacher Training was only slowly being challenged, discontent among non-conformists was strong and such feelings were echoed in the labour movement. At a meeting in Exeter Hall in 1869, Applegarth told the audience it would be quite possible to raise the money for a national system of education if the Church were disestablished and dissendowed.[43] A few years later, at his election address at Morpeth in January 1874, Thomas Burt declared his support for the disestablishment of the Church and unsectarian education,[44] whilst Robert Elliot, a fellow pitman wrote a ballad at the time including these views, which was sung by Burt's supporters. Bishops were particularly singled out for criticism:

An' then thor's the Bishups, them chaps thit can say
A poor man is weel paid wi' two shillin a day,
An thit he's a villin the fokes mauna spare
That wad set some poor fellows a striking fur mair

and it ended with the suggestion:

So Tommy mun tell them te pack up thor kit
As soon as they can, an' git ready te flit;
Becaas i' the futor, as sartin as fate,
They winna git paid fra the funds iv the State.[45]

The ballad was popular enough to go through twenty editions.

Potter's *Beehive* was another influence working on the newly formed TUC: both in letters and editorials the case for unsectarian education was stressed. Samuel Morley was informed in an open letter that, 'the working men have no hostility to religion.... They hate priest-craft. They revolt from sectarianism. They despise theological strife'.[46] This probably summed up the view of many trade unionists who thought that the only way to avoid the religious strife they had witnessed was to press for unsectarian education; and attitude which was to reappear among trade unionists towards the end of the nineteenth century. Cremer told an audience of working men gathered in Exeter Hall to discuss the 1870 Education Bill, that they would never allow Mr. Gladstone ' ... to hand over the education of their children to the clergy of the Established Church',[47] and put before them a resolution calling for schools in every parish which shall have ' ... teaching entirely free from anything of a sectarian character';[48] a motion carried by an overwhelming majority. The only objections made were to the suggestion that the Bible be read, a minority of the audience claiming that it was not suitable for children. The deputation from this meeting which called upon the Prime Minister was reported and commented upon by *Beehive*:

> We do not need Mr. Gladstone's assurance that the religious powers are great powers; we have found them such; and we have found them apt to exert their potency for what they deem to be their own denominational benefit.[49]

One searches in vain at this time for any support expressed by trade unionists for the work the Established Church had performed in the schools. Even allowing for the non-conformist influence it seems as if organized labour was either hostile to the Church in particular or blamed all denominations for squabbling among themselves whilst working class children lacked education. However simplistic or erroneous the view might have been there was very strong feeling that this had been so.

As board school elections got under way following the 1870 Education Act candidates were impelled to express their views on the religious issue as this was an issue which created strong arguments among electors. In a full page of advertisements in *Beehive*[50] devoted to elections for the London School Board, not one of the twenty-three candidates who had paid to put forward their views objected to Bible reading in schools although not all were as enthusiastic as J.R. Morrison who stated that 'the with-holding of the Gospel from the poor [would be] the death knell of a country'. Most, however, advocated unsectarian education, such as J. Wallace, standing for Southwark, who, although claiming to be a 'zealous advocate for education based upon religion', advocated that all religious instruction be given at home or by a minister of their own denomination outside school. By the time the board school system was firmly established, urban trade unionists were well pleased with these 'unsectarian' institutions, so much so that they were likely to forget the problems faced by their rural brethren who were still dominated by a network of schools controlled by the Church.

Declining church attendance alone is evidence enough to illustrate the general indifference to organized religion among so many of the working people.[51] Even attempts by some to get up Labour Churches in the 1890s met with little success[52] whilst active secularism enjoyed little sustained appeal[53] even though some trade unionists, such as John Burns, had learned their platform oratory at such meetings. Not one TUC delegate dealing with the religious issue in an education debate declared himself an atheist: it was safe enough to oppose the Church of England, or even suggest there were faults with many of the different Christian sects but disbelief in a God was not a sensible declaration in political terms. There was considerable respect for the integrity of Charles Bradlaugh within the labour movement, whether people shared his views or not in private, but association with him in public was a matter for individual judgement and conscience. Arch appreciated Bradlaugh's support for his union and shared the platform with him on several occasions although neither then nor in private conversation did the latter ever broach the subject of religion. 'I honoured and respected Charles Bradlaugh' wrote Arch, '... he had a great struggle all through his life, but he fought like a man for what he believed to be right'.[54]

Another leading trade unionist, like Arch also a practising non-conformist, had considerable doubts when asked to share a platform with Bradlaugh. The miners had invited Bradlaugh and Broadhurst to address them and the latter wrote to a Wesleyan Minister who was a friend asking for advice because he was worried about his reputation, claiming that the Tories had used smear tactics during the 1880 General Election when he had spoken on the same platform as Bradlaugh, calling him a 'Bradlaughite'. Broadhurst's Wesleyan friend advised him against attending if possible:

> In principle there is nothing to prevent you from going to the meeting, but *policy* would say *no*! I am sorry that the miners have invited him to take part in their meeting ... I feel it difficult to advise you ... the meeting is of great importance, and you have promised to address it; still I shall be glad if something transpires to prevent you from going.[55]

Broadhurst was, of course, opposed to atheism but it was the politician in him that made him doubt the value of any association with Bradlaugh if he wished to maximize his vote. Yet at the same time his non-conformity was enough for him to oppose sectarian education, a view he strongly expressed in conversation with Cardinal Manning, much to the surprise of the latter, who, it seems, assumed that all practising Christians would approve of such teaching.[56]

The SDF and ILP supported secular education and it is interesting to note that a considerable number of trade unionists who introduced or supported such a demand at the TUC were also members of one of these two parties. The three leading Gasworkers' delegates were: Thorne, (SDF) J.R. Clynes and Pete Curran (ILP). It would be misleading however to over-simplify such influences, for one of the strongest opponents of secular education, James Sexton, was also in the ILP whilst G.H. Roberts who spoke out strongly against the religious influence in schools on several occasions had by 1923 joined the Conservative Party. Moreover, while small socialist groups, especially the uncompromising SDF, could afford the luxury of antagonizing many, survival in the larger more general trade union movement required a little more diplomacy. Trade unionists did criticize the Church but none quite matched the total condemnation by the SDF in their weekly paper *Justice*, which, in referring to the Education Bill of 1896, declared: 'Clericalism is the enemy; the enemy of education; the enemy of progress; the enemy of humanity'.[57]

The first resolution in the 1890s which introduced secular education provided, within the relevant clause, an explanation for such a demand:[58]

> That sectarian strife should be dissociated from the question of education, and this can only be done by debarring theologians from

raising sectarian strife and by the State providing for the teaching of secular subjects and social duties, leaving the teaching of creeds and dogmas to the religious denominations.[59]

This resolution, introduced by Pete Curran and Ben Turner, both ILP members, came from the Gasworkers Union which was in turn heavily influenced by London Branches containing a considerable portion of active ILP and SDF members. A similar resolution was repeated annually at the TUC, with slight word changes, until 1905 when the explanation was dropped and the demand left by itself: 'That education in all State supported schools shall be secular'.[60] The following year the demand for secular education had been incorporated in a general clause containing other demands as well, such as free education. In 1912 the subject was removed from discussion because it was the one area which prevented unanimous agreement being reached upon TUC Education Policy.

The arguments supporting secular education at Congress were many; those opposing it few. On all occasions that a vote was taken support for secular education was overwhelming.[61] By far the largest category of arguments for secular education were based upon the expressed despair of seeing any agreement reached between the disputing religious bodies. This was the argument Thorne constantly used at Congress when supporting secular education:

> The only solution to the religious controversy that had always raged – and would continue to rage – round the education system was to have a system of secular education pure and simple.[62]

Keir Hardie explained such Congress thinking to the House of Commons during the debate on Birrell's Bill:

> The great majority of the members of the Congress were men like himself of the Christian faith; but they supported the secular solution because of the impossibility of finding a common denominator of the Christian religion which all could accept.[63]

The 1907 Congress debate on education was dominated by the religious issue during both the morning and afternoon sessions. It contained virtually all the arguments which were to be repeated at various meetings later, with W. Pickles echoing once more the views of Thorne and Hardie:

> ... the difficulty by which they were confronted was the fact that the various religious denominations could agree upon nothing themselves. Until they could come to an agreement Congress had a right to say 'Keep your quarrels out of our schools.'[64]

Congress saw the danger early on of being dragged into what they considered a dangerous diversion. Not only had they kept out of the religious argument surrounding the 1902 Education Act, leaving the non-conformists to pursue this issue so close to their hearts and concentrating instead on the issue of control over local schools, but in 1904 the PCTUC issued a circular which was widely distributed, including 100,000 copies in London alone, warning that:

> Trade unionists should see to it that 'education' is not relegated to the position of a side issue – that it is not swamped by controversy over the religious difficulty.[65]

This view was taken a step further by G.H. Roberts in 1908 when he explained to the Congress that,

> Unfortunately, I am compelled to think that those at the present time fostering this question are not doing so from disinterested motives. The governing classes are glad to see any apple of discord thrown into our midst in the hope that we may be set at others' throats.[66]

There were delegates who protested in particular about the rate aid which went to religious schools following the 1902 Education Act. Appleton, was one of the few leading trade unionists who was also a practising Anglican. He contributed regularly to the education debate and constantly advocated secular education on the grounds that the delegates were all rate-payers and therefore should not pay for the teaching of one Christian sect;[67] neither should any religion be taught by proxy.[68] The PCTUC had objected in 1900 to the outcome of the 1896 Education Act because it had given, '. . . huge doles to the clerical schools until they are now almost entirely supported by public money . . . [and] . . . covered the country with clerical organizations . . . giving them power to make the schools more sectarian'.[69] If the frank message seemed in its hostility to approach the harsh verdict of *Justice* on this Act it would be wrong to think it was due to the same degree of anti-clericalism; the TUC reserved such language for occasions when they thought trade unionists were directly threatened and in this instance acted in defence of the school board system which the Church of England was actively working to undermine.

There were outright denunciations of Church influence by delegates. Referring to the 1902 Education Act, C.W. Bowerman declared '. . . that it was designed to place their children in the fetters of clericalism',[70] and J. Wignall of the Dock and Riverside Workers several years later spelt out to delegates the nature of such fetters:

> It was the teaching of priests and parsons that had enslaved the people, the teaching that 'you have always the poor with you', to 'be content with your lot', 'honour your Masters'. That had been the religious teaching in the schools and secular education was the only means of getting freedom in the schools and giving the children the best possible education free from the shackles and bondage of religious teaching.[71]

This argument, echoing the writings of Joseph Arch twelve years earlier, summed up the feeling of so many trade unionists that whatever individual priests might have said or done the record of the Church of England was largely one of support for those who were opposed to organized labour. Time and again it was the personal experiences of trade unionists which were related to denounce religious education. Stories from Ireland of the difficulties faced by trade unionists when religious teaching of opposing denominations fostered disunity[72] and of the constant squabbles among the religious groups themselves, as witnessed by those who had served on both school boards and the new local authorities[73] were related in support of secular education.

There was however a minority at the TUC who argued against secular education. A few argued from a religious point of view, such as J. Kent of the Scottish Typographical Workers who believed that his countrymen were favourable to religious teaching as '. . . the fear of the Lord was the beginning of wisdom',[74] and W. Vandy of the London Compositors argued that 'the basis of all true education, ethics and morality was to be found in that grand old Book to which they were all so deeply indebted'.[75] It was James Sexton however who protested most frequently at Congress against secular education which he argued was also a 'distinct sect' in itself.[76] Sexton was a Roman Catholic himself and conscious of the fact that seventy-five per cent of his members in the Liverpool Dock area were also members of that religion. It was impossible for him to support secular education at Congress and still obtain the votes of so many Irish Catholics in his union, whatever his religious beliefs might have been. Both his Catholicism and his pragmatic trade unionism left him with no other alternative than to oppose secular education. At the same time he was aware that neither his particular religion nor his stance were particularly popular among delegates; hence he never argued his case from a strictly religious point of view. 'There was plenty for Congress to do without quarrelling about religion',[77] he claimed, fully aware that he would never get his own members, whom he told Congress had joined the Labour movement for Labour purposes, to back secular proposals.[78] For large numbers of working class Catholics in Lancashire their own Church was not seen as part of the establishment opposed to organized labour; indeed there was evidence from recent history of considerable discrimination against Catholics and this together with the fact that most of the Catholics were comparatively poor meant that followers, if anything, saw their Church as on the side of working people. In fact, in the late nineteenth century, the Roman Catholic Church was moving into an informal alliance with the Church of England over the matter of education, for by its very nature the former Church could not envisage a situation in which it did not control the education of its followers as anything less than disastrous. Sectarian education might benefit the Anglican Church in the short term but it was also obvious that if the principle of religious education was lost the effects would be disastrous also to the Catholic Church in the long run.

Even if religious belief seemed to be in decline and the influence of the Established Church curtailed, there were still delegates who worried about the image the TUC might present in supporting secular education. R. Toothill of the Machine and General Union thought 'the passing of such a resolution would give people the idea that the Trades Congress was an irreligious and Godless body'.[79] There was plenty of hostility toward trade unionism throughout the period and, whilst there is no evidence to show that their standing was greatly enhanced when secular education was dropped from their education programme in 1912, some trade unionists felt there was no point in antagonizing any group if it could be avoided. Against that, one had to measure any religious teachings or influence which might have fostered feelings of anti-trade unionism among children.

Some of the leading Conference delegates may have been concerned with the TUC image over such matters but the working class in general were not agitated by theoligical disputes which many felt belonged to a past age and had no relevance to their daily lives. Keir Hardie told the House of Commons in an education debate following the Liberal victory of 1906 that:

> It was one of the greatest fallacies to assume that parents cared the toss of a brass farthing concerning the religious instruction in the schools. It showed how completely out of touch were honourable Members with working class opinion that an idea of that kind could prevail ... the bulk of the working class were indifferent ... because they saw what little good had come to the country from the religious instruction of Church and chapel alike.[80]

Ben Tillett similarly told Congress delegates that '... the various religious bodies had neither helped them in their unions nor in Parliament'.[81]

Enough has been shown to provide some foundation for such an attitude towards the Anglican Church but there is also evidence to show that within the Nonconformist Churches not all showed empathy with working class movements.[82] In the long run it was their trade union experience which united delegates rather than their theological, or even political, views. The rather sceptical remarks of J. Galbraith of the London compositors summed up the views of so many trade unionists and working class people who lived from week to week and saw little point in making long term plans:

> Heaven forbid that he should say a word against the Church; but as a Trade Unionist it was his immediate duty to see that the lads had an opportunity of getting a living in this world, and chance the next.[83]

The argument over secular education lasted from 1896 until 1912. As some kind of solution in 1910 J. O'Grady of the Furnishing Trades proposed that all affiliated societies should be balloted as to the retention of secular education as part of TUC Education Policy, but the resolution was lost. The debate did however provide some indication of the animosity the issue aroused between Thorne as the champion of secular education and Sexton who always vehemently opposed it.

J. Sexton: 'our friend the enemy, the Right Honourable William

Thorne, Minister for Education', was a very modest and retiring young man. Congress might have noticed his euphorious introduction of himself as a revolutionary Trade Unionist constitutional Democrat.

W. Thorne: I said nothing of the kind.

J. Sexton: ... Mr. Thorne himself during Congress week has vociferously applauded and endorsed the proposed unification of Trade Unions.

W. Thorne: As a matter of fact I was not in Congress when it was discussed.

J. Sexton: But surely you do not object to it?

W. Thorne: That is another question. Let us have truthful statements at all events.

President: You have only three minutes altogether Mr. Sexton. You had better get to the point.

J. Sexton: Well, then, may I ask friend Thorne, this political Pooh-Bah, where this question is going to land us?[84]

Congress was to face one more bitter debate over the issue in 1911; a debate in which Sexton was later severely criticized for the manner in which he protested but which still ended in a comfortable victory for those supporting secular education by 717,000 to 120,000 votes. Yet the following year the Gasworkers Union dropped the demand for secular education from the resolution on education they put before Congress. Sexton could not contain his delight nor resist a jibe at Thorne who was President of Congress that year. 'It is a courageous man who admits he was wrong.'[85] When Thorne replied that this was not so he was cheered by the delegates. The supporters of sectarian education had won a hollow victory. It was an occasion at the TUC when an overwhelming majority gave way to a minority in order to overcome a source of constant disunity.

To some extent trade union leaders could afford to give in to the religious sects because they no longer had such an influence over the lives of the majority of the people. In March 1911 a PCTUC Deputation waited upon W. Runciman, the President of the Board of Education, to discuss TUC Education Policy. Thorne drew the President's attention to TUC demands for 'free and secular' education and expressed regret over the 'Liberal Government's inaction over reversing the education policy of the last Tory Government'.[86] Thorne argued that they wanted 'complete freedom from ecclesiastical control' and assumed that the Government intended to redeem the pledges it had given to the country in 1906 to settle the religious difficulty. No promises were made by Runciman, who could in any case plead that the Government's attention was taken up by the constitutional crisis, but it seems that by now the Liberals did not wish to revise the religious issue again. In general the country had lost interest in the subject. This was one more piece of evidence for TUC leaders that religious education was no longer an important issue and that instead of spending time arguing about opposing religious forces of the past there was a greater need to face up to opposing secular forces of the present.

Speeches criticizing religion had been made at Congress; sometimes the PCTUC had added their weight to the debate, although when they did so it was primarily in defence of board schools rather than as attacks upon religious schools. However, when the PCTUC felt that the interests of trade unionists were under some threat, whatever its source, they drew close together and strongly opposed it. There were two occasions when the PCTUC felt they were under pressure directly from religious bodies. One occasion was of a minor nature when the Roman Catholic Federation attempted to put pressure upon the PCTUC; the other, a controversy over a reading book used in Church of England Schools achieved major prominence due to the publicity the issue received in the national press.

Roman Catholic Federation Pressure upon the TUC

During the years 1908–11 the Roman Catholic Federation attempted to put pressure upon the PCTUC to drop their support for secular education. In September 1908 the RC Federation sent a deputation to state their case to the PCTUC,[87] and the following January protested to the Committee who it thought proposed to discuss secular education with the President of the Board of Education when the next TUC deputation called upon him.[88] The PCTUC informed the RC Federation that this was not the case; their deputation was primarily intended to raise the question of free secondary education; secular education was to be considered for a future Parliamentary Bill. This reply gave the RC Federation no satisfaction for they were clearly opposed to any move towards secular education. They thought that secular education had been excluded from the deputation's discussion through their own request; a construction the PCTUC Secretary was quick to point out was quite erroneous.

A steady flow of letters throughout the year protesting against secular education reached the TUC offices from the RC Federation[89] culminating in one which claimed that the Chairman at the 1909 Congress, W.J. Shackleton MP, had directed the debate on secular education in a partial manner and not permitted a card vote at the end. In fact, as always, the resolution had been carried by a large majority and the PCTUC were angry at the continued attempts of the RC Federation to interfere with TUC policies. The Secretary was instructed '... to write expressing the regret of the Committee at such a letter, pointing out in strong terms the futility of the charges, also disclaiming their right to interfere'.[90]

This did not prevent the RC Federation from continuing to pressurize the

TUC. They formed a Catholic Federation of Trade Unionists, probably in the assumption that protests from fellow trade unionists would be received more sympathetically by the PCTUC. However, as most of the trade unionists involved were those who annually argued against secular education at Congress and regularly lost, the PCTUC was not disposed to give their repeated pleas special consideration. The Catholic Federation of Trade Unionists passed resolutions at their own meetings[91] condemning secular education but the PCTUC refused to meet a deputation from this body[92] to discuss a matter which Congress had already democratically voted upon.

The National Society and the School Text Book Controversy

The years between 1875 and 1884 have been referred to as fallow years concerning education debates at Congress. In fact they witnessed two debates which although not related to the formation of an education policy were involved with education; one indirectly was the Sunday Opening of Museums and Art Galleries,[93] the other concerned a text book used widely throughout the National Society Elementary Schools of the country. It is this latter controversy which was to become a matter for public discussion in a way that neither the TUC nor the National Society could possibly have envisaged.

The matter was brought to the attention of the 1879 Congress at Edinburgh by A. Simmons of the Kent and Sussex Agricultural Labourers Union. He had obtained a copy of the National Society's Standard V Reading Book containing numerous pages on political economy. The particular section which had attracted his attention was that part describing and explaining the role of trade unionists. He proceeded to read out to the Congress relevant extracts from the book which claimed that although most of the people of the UK thought of themselves as free men and preferred that they would die rather than submit to slavery, in fact many

> ... submit to be ruled by tyrants who do not allow them to choose how they shall employ their time or their skill or their strength. These unhappy persons are those who have anything to do with trade unions and combinations. There will generally be found among the workmen some able and ill-disposed persons who feel envy, and endeavour to excite others against everyone who earns more than the usual wages. In this way they often persuade a great number of their fellow workmen to form themselves into a combination and appoint these agitators under the title of committee men. The business of these committee men is to make laws for the government of the combination, and to punish all who break them.[94]

The trade union members apparently paid a weekly subscription of which

> a part, often a large part ... is taken by the committee men for

themselves. The committee men, who have thus acquired the power, keep it by intimidation and violence to the persons and property of those who oppose them or refuse to join them, and any master who disobeys them is punished by what is called a strike ... most of these trades are completely ruined.[95]

Simmons claimed that there were fourteen pages of this 'nonsense' in a book issued by the National Society whose President was the Archbishop of Canterbury. This Society's income was £25,000 per annum and it was the representative of the Church of England in the work of education. There were $2\frac{1}{4}$ million copies of the book in this issue, but what surprised Simmons was that in conversations he had held with the clergy he had frequently been told that they did not consider trade unionism to be within their sphere of duty.

The 1879 Congress showed little sympathy towards the National Society during the debate and some delegates, apart from denouncing the statements recorded in the school book, criticized the Church of England which they felt was ultimately responsible. Mr. Williams brought laughter to the Conference by pointing out that although the school book claimed trade unionists were unhappy men he had never been happier since he became one of them. He declared, 'The Church of England was a most powerful trade union in itself, and the most complete in its organization. While they paid for their own trade unions, the clergy of the Church of England made other people pay for theirs'.[96]

Whilst all were agreed in condemning such books as being used '... to poison the minds of the children', Conference was uncertain to which authority a delegation from the PCTUC should be sent. Some suggested the Archbishop of Canterbury, although Joseph Arch was quick to ask, '... if the trade unionists were to circulate such statements, respecting the Church of England whether the Archbishop of Canterbury would request them to receive a deputation from the Church of England?'.[97]

It was finally agreed, after Congress had sat well past the normal hour, to pass a resolution condemning the use of such a book in schools and to send a delegation to the Education Department. In fact, apparently unbeknown to Congress, a group of clergy had been working on their behalf on this very issue and having read a report of Simmons' speech next day in a newspaper, the Reverend Walter Cunningham, curate of St. Mary's the Great and lecturer on political economy at the University of Cambridge, wrote to the Chairman of the TUC asking to address Congress that day. He explained to delegates that he was a member of the Clerical Committee which included amongst its members the Bishop of Durham, Mr. John Oakley and Brook Lambert, who were sympathetic to working people and had been meeting regularly during the winter of 1878–79, in order to study a mass of semi-religious literature with a view to correcting mis-statements which appeared in text books, especially with regard to political economy. They had already met with some success by getting the SPCK to withdraw some of its publications and early in 1879 turned their attention to the National Society.

The workings of the Clerical Committee had been a 'behind-the-scenes' affair. A memorial from them had been sent to the National Society protesting about certain passages in text books being used in the Society's schools and the reply received was ambiguous enough to prompt John Oakley to write again on behalf of the Committee to the Reverend J. Duncan, Secretary of the National Society:

> Hoxton
> March 12th 1879

Dear Mr. Duncan,

Let me thank you at once for your courteous and satisfactory letter in reply to our memorial. If we understand you to say that the passages of which we complained *will be omitted* from the new Reading Book (I am sure) our Committee will be satisfied.

But you will see that your letter at present omits to give us that assurance. And the feeling expressed, both in and out of our Committee, about the (said) extracts has been so strong, (and I venture to think so just) that I hardly think we shall all be content to leave the matter in any uncertainty.

We were aware that the passages in question were written by the late Archbishop of (Dublin). They expressed the intellectual formalism of the earlier school of English Political Economy; and the hard temper of a logical Protestant irritated by contact with what he thought the pure irrationality of Irish Roman Catholicism.

It is impossible to make use of them in an Educational Text Book. We meet on Friday the 21st. Can you satisfy me about these before then?

> J. Oakley[98]

The Secretary of the National Society was able to give such satisfaction to the Clerical Committee:

> 15th March 1879

Dear Mr. Oakley,

What I intended to say and what I thought I had clearly implied in my previous letter was that as soon as the National Society's new series of Reading Books now in course of preparation, is published the Old Series will be withdrawn bodily. The new books are in no way founded upon the old and will certainly not contain the extracts from Archbishop Trench (sic)[99] to which objection has been made.

> Very truly Yours
> J. Ducan[100]

The writings which the Clerical Committee were referring to and those which were to receive the attention of Congress six months later belonged to Richard Whately, one time Professor of political economy at Oxford University and Archishop of Dublin, who had been dead now some sixteen years.

They dated from material originally written in 1833 when he had produced 'Easy Lessons on Money Matters for the Use of the Young' for the SPCK; the section on political economy being extended by him the following year. Whately had convinced the SPCK Committee of General Literature and Education, that the children of the lower orders should be acquainted with political economy and produced for them a text containing sections under the titles of Money, Exchange Commerce, Coin Value, Wages, Rich and Poor, Capital, Taxes, Lettings and Hirings: '. . . a simple, orthodox exposition of classical theories, dogmatically expounded as unchangeable laws.'.[101] The section on wages, which was to be widely reproduced in various texts in the years ahead, '. . . "demonstrated" that wages were determined by the laws of supply and demand; that efforts to restrict entry into a trade, to combine against employers, or attempt violence would act against the interests of the workers'.[102]

There can be no question of such sections having been overlooked by the religious societies for the Church of England, Nonconformists and Roman Catholics all had special committees to examine in detail any text proposed as a school reader. The remarkable thing is that in an age of continuous religious friction all of the religious societies readily accepted Whately's writings, or similar versions based upon them. They clearly all agreed with Whately that '"correct" economic doctrines must be taught to the poor, beginning with their children',[103] even if they could not agree upon anything else.

Whately's writings dominated the elementary schools of Britain with book sales running into hundreds of thousands[104] and '. . . virtually every advanced reader published by religious bodies from the late 1830s to 1880 had its quota of Whately, or imitations or adaptations of his articles',[105] There can be little doubt that the official committees of the various religious societies were as keen as he was to convince the working people during their school days that the free play of economic forces was inevitable and of benefit to all; it therefore followed that combinations to raise wages or improve conditions were both pointless and foolish.

How far such views influenced the children it is difficult to know. Many of the pupil teachers and assistant teachers themselves could not understand political economy and doubtless used the books as 'English Readers' in which the reading and comprehension of the language was the important matter in hand, rather than concepts in political economy. Such an approach was also quite common with History and Geography texts. It has been shown that, between 1872 and 1873, of 111,275 children examined not one chose political economy as a subject;[106] some indication of its difficulty and popularity. Yet however little teachers or pupils grasped the principles espoused, these texts were read and some of the simplistic generalized statements remembered. By 1879, when the protests of the TUC began to be heard, some version of these texts had been in the schools for nearly fifty years. It was not surprising therefore to learn that the National Society at least was planning to introduce a completely new text.

There is no record of a TUC deputation to the Board of Education in 1879 but one did call upon the Archbishop of Canterbury. The entry in Archbishop Tait's diary gives no indication of the size of the deputation nor the importance he attached to it, being merely a short factual entry amidst other such official and personal meetings during that week: 'Deputation at Lambeth from Trades Unions on the subject of certain extracts used in the National Society's Reading Books (fifth standard) and taken from Whately's easy lessons on money matters'.[107] The deputation, in fact numbered around fifty,[108] was led by Broadhurst and included Simmons. The former read a few selected passages to the Archbishop, especially Whately's description of a strike:

> ... if the strike lasts several weeks ... they are forced to part with their bedding and furniture and even their clothing; they give up their cottages and sleep three or four families in one room with hardly food and firing enough to support life. All this time the door of the factory is open to them.[109]

Whately had claimed that the reasons the men suffered such deprivation was through '... fear of being assaulted and perhaps murdered by ruffians hired by their tyrants.... No one who ventures to disobey the orders of the committee is sure of his life for a day'.[110]

The Archbishop suggested that Whately's writings referred to a bygone age when such things had taken place. He said he had a great deal of respect for the Bishop, '... a foremost man in every matter of importance for the progress of the people and the advantage of the age in which he lived, for he was – an unusual thing in those days – a most liberal Churchman'.[111] The trade unionists pointed out that in such times trades unions were illegal and working in completely different circumstances. The point was that such books were being used at present by the National Society; these books should be withdrawn from the schools. 'It was not right to teach children such erroneous and prejudicial matters about concerns in which their fathers might be engaged.'[112]

The *Times* reported the deputation at some length but made the mistake of assuming that a second deputation of the clergy was from the National Society.[113] In fact it was the Clerical Committee who wished to support the TUC; the *Times* reporter had misunderstood or perhaps even assumed that such a group was bound to be against trade unionists! The Archbishop was seriously concerned about the matter and wrote to Duncan at the National Society:

15th November

Mr dear Mr. Duncan,

I received, as you are aware, on Thursday last, a Deputation from the Trade Unionists and another from a Committee of Clergy – both with reference to Standard V Reading Book now withdrawn from sale.

I should be glad to have an opportunity of laying before the Committee of the National Society my views as to the action, if any,

> which ought to be taken in consequence of these Deputations, and I
> am also anxious to obtain from the Society such information as is
> available with reference to copies of the book now in circulation...[114]

The matter was discussed with the Archbishop at the next meeting of the
National Society on December 3rd.[115]

Unfortunately for the TUC, within the same month that their deputation
visited the Archbishop of Canterbury, at which they proclaimed they were
peaceful hard-working men, an incident occurred in Sheffield which cast grave
doubts upon such a claim. A strike had taken place at the Birley Vale Colliery
and bitterness increased when a few non-union men continued to work.
Frustrated by this 'scabbing' some union members tried to frighten those who
refused to support the strike and used a portion of gunpowder one night which
destroyed part of the kitchen of one of the non-union men. Fortunately, no
physical harm came to any of the occupants.

The Times, taking up the story from the *Sheffield Telegraph*, ran a sarcastic
editorial linking up the TUC deputation concerning the school text book with
the violence in Sheffield:

> The Secretary of a Trades Union who went in a deputation to the
> Archbishop of Canterbury the other day, assured the prelate that
> Trade Unionists never commit outrages. We must confess to having
> been under a contrary impression; but it is, of course, necessary to
> place implicit reliance upon so august a personage as a Trade Union
> Secretary protests. The stories of outrages of workmen reported in the
> *Sheffield Telegraph* and, therefore, of course, based upon an incorrect
> supposition. This journal supposed that some recent unsuccessful
> attempts at murder and successful attempts at injury were caused by
> Unionists.[116]

There then followed a description of the events in which Taylor was named as
the man who had worked during the strike and suffered damage to his home.
Then the sarcasm continued:

> ... the only remaining possibility is that the offence was committed
> by the cat, an evil-disposed beast with a dislike to honest labour....
> The diabolical animal went to the home where Taylor and three other
> men who were working at the colliery lived together, and having
> procured a tin bottle, capable of containing about $2\frac{1}{2}$ lb. of gun
> powder, had inserted this explosive through a hole which it had made
> in the back kitchen window. A fuse had been arranged and to this the
> cat set fire.[117]

More in this vein followed and the editorial ended with a warning: 'Clearly
such a cat should be carefully looked after, but at the same time and in spite of
assertions of the Secretary above quoted, it would be as well to keep an eye on
the Unionists'.[118]

The news of the colliery dispute in Sheffield, together with the arguments raised by the National Society text books, brought more correspondence to the National Society criticizing the arguments put forward by the TUC deputation and the Clerical Committee who had been working on the matter for many months:

November 26th

Dear Sir:

Is not the outcry against Archbishop Whately's condemnation of the tyranny of Trades Unionists, somewhat premature?

Today's *Times* gives an account of doings at Sheffield, for which, I think, John Oakley and Henry Jones should be asked by the National Society to account on the theory they have publicly maintained that such outrages were things of the past, things for which Trades Unions were in no way responsible, and for which therefore they were in no way to be condemned in our teaching.

I, for one, was very sorry the Nat. Society yielded to the clamour.

I am dear Sir
Very Truly Yours
J.W. Ayre[119]

A longer letter from the Reverend H.R. Baker of Woolwich expressed surprise at the conciliatory statements made by the Archbishop and the National Society and argued that this was the wrong course to follow:

I have known a good deal of, and mixed with, working men of all sorts, for years, and I have no hesitation in saying that every word of this quotation made from the book by Broadhurst, and objected to by him, is *absolutely* and *entirely true.*

For my part I think the Society has made a great mistake in withdrawing the book, and had I known that such withdrawal was contemplated, I should have strongly opposed it. I have known these Trades Unions to be the causes of great wretchedness (and) many of the best class of working men would tell you so. They will be the ruin of the country.[120]   (italics in original)

The meeting of the National Society attended by the Archbishop agreed that the sale of the book should cease and that a few months later it should be withdrawn from circulation; no easy task when the number of books involved was considered. When the TUC met the following Autumn satisfaction with the work of the deputation was expressed but as to the promise to remove the books, Simmons pointed out that '. . . although he had made every enquiry,. . . . so far as he could ascertain, no steps had been taken for their withdrawal'.[121] Another year passed and once more there was no evidence of action from the National Society so Simmons again pressed the issue in a resolution claiming that 'the Congress is surprised that no effort has been made by the National Society connected with the Church of England to withdraw the objectionable book issued by the Society ... containing statements the most misleading and unjust to Trade Unions; ... the Congress regrets to observe the apparent disregard of the Society, as to that which is taught in their schools be true or false'.[122]

In fact the National Society had issued a new text but only withdrew the old reader as new supplies made possible. This new reader in Political Economy was published in 1880 and drew upon the writings of Alfred and Mary Marshall,[123] Millicent Fawcett,[124] W. Stanley Jevons[125] and Maurice Block.[126] Mrs. Fawcett had written a short piece on 'Trades Unions – Strikes' which showed both greater understanding and sympathy for trade unionists:

> A Trades Union is a society formed by the workmen engaged in any particular trade. This society generally fulfils the double purpose of a benefit club and organization for protecting the interests of the workmen, by obtaining for them the highest possible rate of wages.[127]

More approval was given to the former function than the latter. Trade unionists were compared with corn merchants who will only sell their goods at a certain price: the hardship involved to trade unionists themselves during strikes was mentioned and the right of working men to belong to such organizations was stressed. The article still showed some agreement with Whately's views for it ended:

> They have not generally been content with the right of combination, but they have used force and violence to compel those workermen to join their societies who would otherwise have been unwilling to become members of trades unions.[128]

The new book edited by R.H. Inglis Palgrave had been published in 1880 but the extracts on trades unions came from a book by Mrs. Fawcett entitled 'Political Economy for Beginners' published about 1872. Legislation within those few years had helped to change attitudes a little towards trade unions but in 1880 such organizations were not looked upon favourably by many working people and Mrs. Fawcett's writings probably represented a general liberal view of unions at the time. The whole issue gradually faded as new books replaced the old controversial readers of Whately but far from being 'bodily withdrawn' as Duncan had told the Clerical Committee in 1879 copies remained in the schools for many years to come, an echo of the whole affair being heard at the 1892 Congress when for the last time a resolution on this matter was put before delegates condemning '... the pernicious teachings with regard to trade unionism and trade unionists which are taught in the fifth book in use in the National and Model Schools....'.[129] One can only assume that the remaining copies faded away after this date as no more was heard of the matter. Text books once established did go on for years as the syllabus prior to 1902 tended to be very limited in the Elementary Schools. The 'new' National Society text referred to, although published in 1880, was still selling just prior to World War I.[130]

Trade Unionists Questioned on the Religious Issue by the Cross Commission 1887

The constant complaints of the religious sects, led by Cardinal Manning and supported by the Church of England, concerning the position of their schools led to the appointment of a Royal Commission to enquire into the workings of the Elementary Education Act of 1870. Conflicting views on nearly every issue resulted in the publication of a majority report supported by fourteen members and a minority report signed by eight members. The division of opinion on the Commission reflected divisions within the country but not in proportions represented on the Commission whose membership was heavily weighted towards the religious sects, seven of the 22 members being ordained priests,[131] whilst by contrast there was only one trade unionist, George Shipton, Secretary of the London Trades Council. The Commission sat in May and June and examined sixty-eight witnesses of whom only three were described as 'a representative of the working classes', which gives some indication of the importance attached to the opinion of those whose children actually attended the elementary schools.

The three working class men chosen were all artisans and lived in London. They were T.E. Powell, Secretary of the Bookbinders and Machine rulers and Consolidated Union; Thomas Smyth, a plasterer representing the London Trades Council; and H. Williams a printer who made no mention as to whether he was a member of a trade union. Smyth and Williams answered questions about the religious issue; the former at some length. Williams had far less to say and the answers he did provide seemed to lack any factual basis. He told the Commission he was a Sunday school teacher and favoured religious instruction in schools although he did not know the religious denomination of the school to which he sent his children. He criticized the board schools but when questioned admitted that he had no knowledge of them.

By contrast Smyth's ideas were clearly formulated showing how the London Trades Council he represented had carefully considered the issue of religious instruction in schools. The 'conscience clause' he argued, was unworkable because if parents withdrew children they made martyrs of them: the child, '... would be removed out of the class; he would be marked off and put aside; he would be in a manner pointed at, and pointed out as a boy who was different from the rest'.[132] He wanted religious instruction to be removed from all schools and believed that board school teachers, too, without realising it preached their own particular faith so that teaching became sectarian. This is probably true as most elementary school teachers who had received training had done so in a religious college. Smyth thought that religious teaching should be carried on outside the school by parents and pastors of the various religious sects.

The Commissioners questioned Smyth in detail when he implied that religious instruction was not essential to teach morality:

Smyth: ... they should be taught morally from the highest point of view.

Q: By whom?

Smyth: In the schools or by the teachers only.

Q: But I thought that you objected to a teacher giving such instruction...

Smyth: Yes, if it was a religious question; but I believe that a teacher would be able to inculcate morality, the higher morality, without the aid of religious teaching at all.

Q: Do you think it is possible to teach a child his duty towards his neighbour without teaching him his duty towards God?

Smyth: Yes, I do.

Q: You would exclude religion?

Smyth: That is all.

Q: Would you not also exclude morals without meaning it?

Smyth: No, I think morals come to a very large extent under scientific modes of life; a well regulated life is certainly a moral life.

Q: There is a great deal of truth in that, but is it enough?"[133]

The replies of two working class men from London can hardly be put forward as representative of the views of the working class or trade unionists, although Smyth's view might have a greater claim to represent trade unionists as he was there in an official capacity for the London Trades Council. Smyth's answers suggest they were the considered policy of the largest and most important of the trades councils in Britain but how far the rank and file members supported such views it is impossible to say for the opinions of such people were rarely sought by official commission.

TUC Policy Concerning the Religious Control over Teaching

In 1900, of the forty-three residential teacher training colleges in the country, thirty were Anglican, three Roman Catholic, two Wesleyan, six British and Foreign School Society and two were unaffiliated.[134] The Anglican dominance was greater than this spread of colleges suggests for, as the British and Foreign School Society and undenominational colleges imposed no religious tests, approximately one third of their places were taken up by Anglicans.[135] The new day training colleges had gone some way to improving opportunities for non-Anglicans but one continued grievance of many who desired to take the first step towards becoming a teacher was that in single school areas Anglican schools would only accept those who were members of their own sect as pupil teachers.

The TUC was the first section of the labour movement, with the exception of teachers' unions, to show an interest in teacher training. In 1897 a tortuously worded resolution[136] called for improved methods of educating teachers but a few years later Congress paid some attention to the control of teachers' colleges by religious bodies. Clause (d) of the Education resolution put before delegates in 1901, after calling for adequate provision added that '. . . such colleges to be free from sectarian bias or control'.[137] This call was repeated the following year[138] but on neither occasion did any discussion follow, probably because the question of religious influence had already been exhausted in discussions arising out of the call for secular education in schools.

Teacher training continued to be discussed in later years[139] but largely in terms of supply, distribution and wishes for it to be more closely linked to the universities. The question of religious control was not raised again, except concerning employment within the education service, for in the TUC's own Education Bill of 1906, clause three read '. . . no theological or denominational tests shall be applied to any of the staff or officers of the school or of the educational authority'. It is perhaps a little surprising that those at the TUC demanding secular education within the schools should have paid comparatively little attention to the teacher training colleges which, by controlling entry, were able to favour prospective teachers who were at least nominally members of their own sect. Once more the traditional privileged position of the Anglican Church gave them an influence in the supply of teachers out of proportion to their following.

Conclusion

There can be little doubt that calls for unsectarian education in the early years and secular education were later initiated from those who were also members of organizations working outside the TUC – the NEL and small socialist parties respectively. However this factor does not explain why the majority of delegates who were not members of any of these organizations should have strongly supported such resolutions. The answer to this lies in the general feelings of trade unionists, usually based upon experience, that, with the exception of certain individuals, the dominant Anglican Church at least had done little in the past to help them. Speaking in 1906, J. Thickett of the ASRS asked delegates '. . . who is there among us who would dream of retracing our footsteps, of going back to the original and inadequate voluntary system?'.[140] This is what so many delegates felt; that they could not support a school system for their children which they believed had failed them in earlier years.

As for opposition to religious sects, apart from the comparatively few who might be thought of as agnostics, TUC delegates seemed to judge the situation on its merits. Hence they could accept a religious service at their Congress enough to have it printed as the first item in their annual report whilst at the same time voting for a resolution to exclude religious services and lessons from schools. The withdrawal of the secular clause from Congress education policy in 1912 cannot be seen as a victory in any way for religious interests; if anything it is one more example of pragmatism in the trade union movement. Whether leading trade unionists, by the Edwardian era, had begun to realize that the most industrialized and urbanized country in the world, in spite of maintaining an established church, also seemed to have become the most secularized society as well is not clear. What is noticeable is that even though the supporters of religious education were small within the labour movement, certainly too small to cause any major breach, the British trade union movement, unlike its continental counterparts, did not split along religious lines. The major factor here was probably the general indifference of so many working people to organized religion but, in a small way, the TUC's pragmatism and diplomacy also helped to keep trade unionists united.

Notes

1 BARNARD, H.C., *A History of English Education* (2nd edit.) p. 117 & p. 211; MUSGRAVE, P.W., *Society and Education in England since 1800*, p. 75.
2 MORRIS, M. *The People's Schools*, p. 15. See also *Beehive*, 30.7.1870.
3 INGLIS, K.S. *Churches and the Working Classes in Victorian England*, p. 16.
4 See. Chapter 8.
5 MAYOR, S.H. 'The Relations Between Organized Religion and English Working Class Movements 1850–1914'. Ph.D. M'ster. 1960 p. 162. In his conclusion Mayor points out that to varying extents 'all denominations were out of touch with the working classes'. p. 660.
6 *Ibid.*, p. 161.
7 Mr. Galbraith expressed some disapproval of the Oxbridge training most priests received: 'If clergy were a little more educated they would not be so prejudiced against the working classes'. TUC Report 1879, p. 38.
8 CLARK, G.K. *Churchmen and the Condition of England, 1832–85*, p. 258.
9 COLE, G.D.H. *A Short History of the British Working Class Movement 1789–1947*, p. 258.
10 WEBB, S. and WEBB, B. *The History of Trade Unionism*, p. 318; ARCH, J., *The Autobiography of Joseph Arch*, p. 64.
11 ARCH, J. *op cit.*, p. 57.
12 The most recent detailed account is to be found in EDWARDS, B. *The Burston School Strike*. See also GROVES, R. *Sharpen the Sickle*, pt. 3, Ch. 5; and a contemporary pamphlet by CASEY of the *Labour Leader*, *The Burston School Strike*, c. 1912.
13 *Ibid.*, pp. 51–53.
14 For the balance sheet showing a complete list of donations, EDWARDS, B. *The Burston School Strike*, Appendix 2. The NUT paid the Higdons money for 'victimization'.
15 ARCH, J. *The Autobiography of Joseph Arch*, p. 66.
16 MAYOR, S.H. *The Relations Between Organized Religion and English Working Class Movement 1850–1914*, p. 149.
17 *Ibid.*, p. 151.
18 *The Broadhurst Papers*, London School of Economics, 25.10.1877.

19 ROGERS, F. *Labour, Life and Literature*, pp. 192–193.
20 DAVIS, W.J. *The British Trades Union Congress History and Recollections* Vol. II, p. 152.
21 DALLEY, W.A. *The Life Story of W.J. Davis*, p. 267.
22 THOMPSON, P. *Socialists, Liberals and Labour*, p. 18.
23 INGLIS, K.S. *Churches and the Working Classes in Victorian England*, p. 115.
24 *Ibid.*, p. 30.
25 MAYOR, S.H. *op cit.*, p. 315.
26 CLYNES, J.R. *Memoirs Vol. I, 1869–1924*, pp. 144–145.
27 'Most of the higher clergy were themselves products of the landed group, and even when they weren't, their loyalties to it were strong.' NISBET, R.A. *The Sociological Tradition*, p. 178. 'The general impression gained about social background of the bishops was that they came from the Upper or Middle class... Their education was usually gained at one of the major Public Schools and Oxford or Cambridge... All five of the Archbishops of Canterbury between 1848 and 1902 had been headmasters of a Public School.' POOLE M.D.W., 'Prelacy and Privilege: Anglican bishops and the public schools 1830–70' in *History of Education Society Bulletin* No. 14 Autumn 1974, pp. 16–17. A Church of England Committee appointed by the Archbishop of Canterbury to consider how best the Church could commend the teachings of Christ to those involved in industrial life published a report in 1918. It included a chapter critical of the role of the Church in the past: '... in the past the Church has shown an undue subservience to the possessing, employing and governing classes, and its deeper fault may have been a want of faith in its own principle'. *Labour Leader* 26. 12. 1918.
28 In the nineteenth century only in the 1898 Report; in the first 25 years of the twentieth century it was published in Reports of 1904, 1908–13, 1922–25.
29 TUC Report 1898, p. 25.
30 TUC Report 1902, p. 28.
31 TUC Report 1904, pp. 39–43.
32 TUC Report 1909.
33 It is impossible to know which delegates did see the issue as a religious one; Broadhurst who spoke against Sunday opening mentioned in his autobiography that his speech enlisted the 'hearty sympathy and support' of Cardinal Manning, implying some religious empathy between the two.
34 TUC Report 1884, p. 38.
35 One speaker in the 1885 Sunday opening debate pointed to the example of Manchester which had opened public libraries on Sundays but provided staff with another free day. Meacham has pointed out that for many working people the real luxury of Sunday was being free to do precisely nothing. (See MEACHAM, S. *A Life Apart*, pp. 119–120.) It is probable that, as usual, trade unionists were thinking of themselves, not the larger number of people outside the trade union movement and in the 1880s it was the artisans who were largely represented at Congress; the very men who would take their families to museums and galleries on a Sunday.
36 TUC Report 1885, p. 37.
37 *Ibid.*, p. 38.
38 *Ibid.*, p. 39.
39 TUC Report 1887, p. 46.
40 ARCH, J. *op cit.*, p. 28.
41 *Ibid.*
42 ROGERS, F. *Labour, Life and Literature*, p. 58.
43 Applegarth described the meeting many years later in the *Weekly Times* 12. 6. 1910.
44 GREEN, H. 'A Howkie Gans to Parliament' *Marxism Today*, 18 (3) March 1974, p. 96.
45 JEFFERYS, J.B. *Labour's Formative Years 1849–79*, pp. 154–155.

46 *Beehive*, 30.7.1870.
47 *Beehive*, 18.6.1870.
48 *Ibid.*
49 *Beehive*, 2.7.1870.
50 *Beehive*, 26.11.1870.
51 The complex issue of the decline in numbers of practising Christian and associated falling away of church attendance throughout the nineteenth century is discussed in: BEST, G. *Mid Victorian Britain*, p. 170.; INGLIS, K.S. *Churches and the Working Classes in Victorian England*; PICKERING, W.S.F., 'The 1851 Religious Census – A Useless Experiment?' *British Journal of Sociology* 18(4.), Dec. 1967; PELLING, H. *Popular Politics in Late Victorian Britain*, pp. 26–27.
52 INGLIS, K.S. *op cit.*, pp. 216–221. A Labour Church was functioning in Hull in 1894 and providing meals for children in the accompanying Sunday School Classes. BROWN, R. M.Sc. (Econ) 1966, *The Labour Movement in Hull 1870–1900 with Special Reference to New Unionism*, p. 366.
53 THOMPSON, P. 'Liberals, Radicals and Labour in London 1880–1906' in *Past and Present* No. 27, 1964, pp. 31–32.
54 ARCH, J. *The Autobiography of Joseph Arch*, pp. 65–66.
55 Broadhurst Papers, 22.4.1880.
56 BROADHURST, H. *Henry Broadhurst MP: From Stonemason's Bench to Treasury Bench*, p. 300.
57 *Justice*, 23.5.1896.
58 In fact in 1895 secular education was implied in Thorne's resolution but not stated specifically until the following year.
59 TUC Report 1896.
60 TUC Report 1905, p. 142.
61 See Appendix II.
62 TUC Report 1903, p. 86,
63 *Hansard* Vol. 167, Col. 440, 12.12.1906.
64 TUC Report 1907, p. 188.
65 TUC Report 1904, p. 68.
66 TUC Report 1908, p. 180.
67 TUC Report 1905, p. 142. Appleton stated in the 1906 debate: 'I am supposed to be a member of the Church on England. I admit I am not a very worthy member. But for twenty-five years I have repeated its services, Sunday after Sunday; and I think there is no better service on God's earth. But I do not think the Jew and the Catholic should be compelled to pay for its teachings....' TUC Report 1906, p. 176.
68 *Ibid.*
69 PCTUC 'Important Circular' August 1900.
70 TUC Report 1902, p. 71.
71 TUC Report 1910, p. 176.
72 '... the reason the workers had up to the present been divided was because of the religious teaching in the schools.' Bob Smillie of the Miners Federation speaking at Congress. TUC Report 1907, p. 188.
73 TUC Report 1905, p. 143.
74 TUC Report 1903, p. 86.
75 TUC Report 1904, p. 120.
76 TUC Report 1906, p. 176.
77 TUC Report 1909, p. 189.
78 TUC Report 1908, p. 180.
79 TUC Report 1909, p. 189.
80 *Hansard*, Vol. 167, Col. 440, 12.12.1906.
81 TUC Report 1909, p. 190.

82 'A Methodist historian has concluded that in the early nineteenth century the movement drew "its largest number of adherents" from among the middle classes who had made and been made by the industrial revolution. Methodism was helping many people up the temporal ladder; but there is little evidence that in any form it was extending its ministry far into the great body of working class people who attended no religious worship.' INGLIS, K.S. *op cit.*, pp. 117–118.

83 TUC Report 1904, p. 120.

84 TUC Report 1910, p. 175.

85 TUC Report 1912.

86 PCTUC Deputation to the Board of Education. Mins., 16.3.1911.

87 PCTUC Mins., 4.9.1908.

88 PCTUC Mins., 20.1.1909.

89 For example, PCTUC Mins., 8.2.1909 and 16.6.1909.

90 PCTUC Mins., 15.12.1909.

91 Resolution passed at Meeting of Roman Catholic Federation of Trade Unionists held at Manchester on 29th May 1911.

92 PCTUC Mins., 19.6.1911.

93 See Chapter, 3, p. 82.

94 *Manchester Guardian*, 19.9.1879.

95 *Manchester Guardian*, 19.9.1879.

96 *Ibid.*

97 *Ibid.*

98 Oakley to Duncan 12.3.1879. National Society Archives. Italics in orginal.

99 The correct name of Whately was written over the top in pencil.

100 Duncan to Oakley, 15.3.1879.

101 For a full discussion of the influence of Richard Whately in School Text Books see GOLDSTROM, J.M. 'Richard Whately and political economy in school books 1833–80' *Irish Historical Studies*, Vol. XV, 1966–67. Also in less detail GOLDSTROM, J.M. *The Social Content of Education 1808–70*, Irish University Press.

102 GOLDSTROM, J.M. *Irish Historical Studies op. cit.*, p. 134.

103 *Ibid.*, p. 133.

104 *Ibid.*, p. 136.

105 *Ibid.*, p. 137.

106 *Ibid.*, p. 145, footnote 45.

107 *Tait Diaries*, Vol. 65, 1879 Aug. 24 – Dec. 9, 13.11.79.

108 Parliamentary Committee – Secretary's Report (i.e. H. Broadhurst) printed in TUC Report 1880, p. 9.

109 *The Times*, 14.11.1879.

110 *Ibid.*

111 *Ibid.*

112 *Ibid.*

113 W. Walsham Bedford, Bishop Suffragan wrote a letter to *The Times* pointing out their mistake. *The Times*, 15.11.1879.

114 Archbishop of Canterbury to Rev'd. Duncan 15.11.1879 National Soc. Archives.

115 Rev'd. Duncan to Archbishop of Canterbury 18.11.1879 National Soc. Archives.

116 *The Times*, 26.11.1879.

117 *Ibid.*

118 *Ibid.*

119 J.W. Ayre to Rev'd. Duncan 26.11.1879 National Society Archives.

120 Rev'd. H.R. Baker to Rev'd. Duncan 20.11.1879. National Society Archives.

121 TUC Report 1880, p. 12.

122 TUC Report 1881, p. 35.

123 MARSHALL, A. and MARSHALL, M. *The Economics of Industry.*

124 Mrs. Fawcett wrote with her husband a book entitled *Essays and Lectures on Social*

and Political Subjects to which she contributed eight of the fourteen essays. MacMillan and Co.

125 *Primer of Political Economy*, MacMillan and Co.

126 *Petit Manuel D'Economie Pratique*, J. Hetzel et Cie, Paris.

127 PALGRAVE, R.H.I. (Ed) *Political Economy Reading Book*, pp. 161–162.

128 *Ibid.*, p. 163.

129 TUC Report 1892, p. 70.

130 The actual copy referred to is inscribed For Miss Gracie Oliver Aug. 31st 1913. Other details include that Miss Oliver was aged nine years and lived at 'Sunny Side', Wallington, Sussex.

131 That is. Cardinal Manning, Dr. Temple-Bishop of London, Rev. J.R. Rigg, Rev. R.W. Dale, Canon Robert Gregory, Canon B.F. Smith, Rev. T.D. Cox-Morse.

132 *Report of the Royal Commission on the Elementary Education Acts*, (The Cross Report) 1888, Vol. 17, pp. 379–380.

133 *Ibid.*, pp. 381–382.

134 SCHOFIELD, J. *The Labour Movement and Educational Policy 1900–31*, M.Ed. (Manchester) 1964, p. 122.

135 MURPHY, J. *Church, State and Schools in Britain 1800–1970*, p. 89.

136 'That such reforms be at once made in the method of training the teachers of the nation's children as shall ensure that in no case shall the difficult task of training the minds of young children be entrusted to those whose minds are undeveloped.' Clause 4 Education Resolution. TUC Report 1897, p. 50.

137 TUC Report 1901 (clause d), p. 72.

138 TUC Report 1902 (clause e), p. 71.

139 1907, 1909, 1918, etc..

140 TUC Report 1906, p. 176.

Chapter 4

Free Education, Endowments and Scholarships

Free education, endowments and scholarships are closely related; they are a response to the same issue in education – that of a system of fee paying. At the beginning of the period under review access to all forms of education was through the payment of fees. After 1891 most elementary schools ceased to charge fees and from 1907 a small proportion of 'free places' were made available in secondary schools. The Education Act of 1918 finally abolished fees in all elementary schools but even by 1925 most places in secondary schools were reserved for fee paying pupils and the majority of children received only an elementary education. As for higher education, this was virtually out of the reach of most working class pupils[1], who lacked the opportunity to study for entrance examinations, had to compete for a small number of scholarships and, even if they surmounted such hurdles, still faced the problem of maintaining themselves during the years ahead at college and university. Academically successful children were a double burden to working class families. If they continued in education, at the least their maintenance had to be financed and at the same time the family lost the potential earnings of the young person studying.

Free Education

In general the supporters of free education were to be found in all sections of the labour movement, among many Nonconformists and some Liberals (especially Joseph Chamberlain) and, of course, the National Education League which was in existence from 1869 to 1876. Those largely opposed were the Board of Education[2], the Conservative Party, the Gladstone wing of the Liberal Party, the Established Church and the Roman Catholic Church. In terms of personalities, free education was publicly opposed by Herbert Spencer, Henry and Millicent Fawcett and Cardinal Manning.

It has been shown in Chapter two that there was some resistance among a minority of trade unionists and the poorer strata of the working class to compulsory education. There is, however, little evidence to show that there was similar resistance to the call for free education from such groups of working people. This is not the same as saying that all working class parents objected to paying fees; indeed a small minority saw differing school fees as one way of choosing a school which would ensure that their own children would not be forced to mix with the poorest children in the area. This would enable their children to avoid picking up the bad habits or anything else which might prove infectious from the poor.

Free education was an early demand in the British Labour movement and can be traced back to at least 1851 when a Chartist Convention adopted a programme which included gratuitous education.[3] Within the mainstream of the education debate free education was understood to be limited to elementary schools and demands for this reform are seen to have centred upon two Education Acts which were passed within a decade of each other. The build-up to the first, Forster's Education Act of 1870, stimulated the debate for free education whilst it was the consequences of the second Act, Mundella's Bill of 1880 making education compulsory for all children under ten, which led to the second wave of demands for free education.

The first campaign for free education surrounding the proposed 1870 Education Act went well beyond the confines of the labour movement being largely orchestrated by the NEL. The TUC as a body made no reference to free education at this point although individual members such as Applegarth spoke on behalf of trade unionists within the NEL and supported the idea.[4] At this time, when the TUC was composed largely of artisans, the school pence required were no major worry to their members. More important to them was the provision of sufficient school places for their children and it was this aspect of the 1870 Education Bill which was likely to gain most of their attention. There were some, however, who believed that fees were unfair for poorer-paid unskilled and casual workers, hence the support given to the idea within the NEL by certain prominent trade unionists.

The 1870 Education Act did not provide free education in elementary schools. Indeed such schools were permitted to charge up to ninepence per week although the average fee charged at the time was around twopence. There was a clause in the Act which permitted fees to be remitted if parents pleaded poverty but, as religious schools were included in this provision, Noncon-formists disliked this 'back-door' method of subsidizing such schools from the rates. In fact, by 1872, only forty three school boards were making these payments which covered 13,265 children.[5] Forster had claimed in 1869 that free education would prove too costly but, for the NEL, the inclusion of fees in the Act remained a major source of irritation.[6] In 1876 an Act was passed which transferred the payment of poor pupils' fees from the school boards to the poor law guardians. They were, of course, already responsible for the fees of pauper children but Section ten of the new Act made it clear that in applying for aid with fees a parent would not automatically be classed as a pauper. In practice, the Guardians, in London at least, were far from charitable in this sense. They rarely paid paupers' fees[7] and, in 1878, '. . . at Wandsworth and Charlton offered the workhouse to mothers applying for the childrens' fees'.[8] Among the thirty metropolitan Boards of Guardians, eighteen refused to provide fees for non-pauper children.[9]

Following the 1870 Education Act, opposition to school fees began to be expressed more often among sections of organized labour. In December 1871, the Birmingham Trades Council set up a sub committee to consider education and came out strongly in support of free and compulsory schooling[10] and in October 1873 the Westminster Workers passed a resolution declaring that the education system would only be successful if it made schooling compulsory and free.[11] At this stage, however, the opposition to free schooling was far too strong for such demands to influence either of the major political parties or the Established Church.

The Church of England supported fees because they feared that if free education were introduced and they received even greater financial support from central or local taxes there would be accompanying demands from the community to have some say in the management of these schools; whilst they showed no reluctance to receive financial assistance from the community they wished to retain full control of the schools for themselves. To ensure the maximum income from fees '. . . they deliberately set their fees high to exclude those children who were likely to be poor payers, or to depend on the Guardians for the money to pay the fees'.[12]

As for Disraeli's Tory Government they not only supported fees but sought to get them raised wherever possible. In 1876 the Manchester School Board applied to open a free school in each district but this was rejected, as was the attempt of Norwich School Board to charge a farthing and later one penny in most of its schools. The Tory administrators forced them to raise the fee to two pence by threatening to withhold the annual grant and in 1878 began to undertake a survey of school boards whose fees were considered too low with a view to demanding that they be raised.[13]

Mundella's Act of 1880 was the second impetus in the campaign for free education. It now became more difficult than ever to justify the payment of fees for children to attend school when such attendance was compulsory by law. This was precisely the point made by Thomas Powell, a first class visitor of the London School Board in Southwark and one of the three working class representatives asked to give evidence to the Cross Commission in 1886. He agreed that fees were not great but still believed that free education would be an improvement:

> *Question*: Are you in favour of free education?
>
> *Answer* : Entirely so.
>
> *Question*: On what grounds?
>
> *Answer* : . . . I think it logical and fair that education being compulsory should be free. . .

> *Question*: But the wearing of clothes is compulsory in all citizens; you
> would not propose that their clothes should be provided by
> the State?
>
> *Answer* : If a man had none I should, if he were unable to get them
> otherwise.[14]

Powell argued that as the State demanded a citizen's services when necessary
they had responsibilities to keep him fit for such service and this included the
provision of free education. T. Smyth, too, argued that the State had responsibilities to its future citizens:

> I am not prepared to say whether or not it would be well for the State
> even to provide houses and clothes and food and everything else as
> well as education; but I do say that if the State insists that we shall have
> an educated people the State should provide the means of educating
> them. The State does not insist that we shall have good houses or that
> we should have good clothes; therefore we cannot call upon the State
> to provide them.[15]

In the early 1880s within the Liberal Party only the Radical wing was
pushing for free education and Joseph Chamberlain was unable to convince
Gladstone that '... in the matter of school fees people should not have to
accept as alms what was their privilege as citizens'.[16] Chamberlain argued that
unless the Liberals promised to introduce free education they would lose the
working class vote. He had good reason to believe that organized labour was
seeking this reform. With the impending election, towards the end of 1885,
sections of the labour movement were pressing for free education. The SDF
Manifesto displayed in *Justice* included a demand for free education in all board
schools[17] and John Burns, standing as an independent Labour candidate with
the support of the local SDF branch in Nottingham issued a ten point political
programme in which the first listed demand was for free education.[18] The Hull
Trades and Labour Council used the TUC election manifesto to ascertain the
attitudes of local candidates towards a series of issues including free education.
Unfortunately for them the one candidate who agreed with all their aims, W.S.
Saunders, the Liberal MP for Hull at the time, was narrowly defeated by a local
Tory shipowner.[19]

The radical TUC election manifesto used by Hull Trades and Labour
Council was not the manifesto originally planned by the PCTUC. Indeed
nothing illustrates the correctness of Chamberlain's analysis of the attitude of
organized labour towards free education more than the friction which arose
when the PCTUC Election Manifesto was presented to the 1885 TUC. The
first sign of disagreement came half-way through a lengthy presidential address
to Congress, by T.R. Threlfall of the Typographical Association. He turned his
attention to the matter of education, which he argued had been restricted in the
past:

... we wish the children of the future to partake of free education. As our Education Acts are now framed they inflict great privation upon vast multitudes of the poorest parents, because school pence, paltry as they may well be to the well-to-do, is a considerable sum when taken from a family whose weekly income amounts to less than one pound a week.[20]

There were of course many families earning far less than this who saw education not as a blessing but as another demand upon their meagre income. In spite of Threlfall's plea, when the election manifesto was drawn up by the Parliamentary Committee for approval by Congress it was found to be a timid document, reflecting precisely official Liberal Party policy with no mention of free education. Henry Broadhurst, as Secretary of the PCTUC, was a loyal supporter of Gladstone and did not wish to include any demand which might embarrass the Prime Minister. Whether he also failed to assess correctly the views being expressed in the SDF and Trades Councils and their potential influence at Congress is not known but when challenged over the omission of free education and the payment of MPs he explained to Congress that although he too favoured such ideas this was not the time to advocate them. Congress disagreed and a resolution proposed by G. Bisset from Aberdeen and seconded by Richards from Southport was promptly passed stating:

That in the opinion of this Congress the time has arrived for the Government to establish a thorough system of national education, and that in order to accomplish this object the public elementary schools must necessarily be made free.[21]

The resolution was carried unanimously and the PCTUC forced to include it in their election manifesto together with the payment of returning officers and MPs, plus a demand to enfranchise women. This sharp rebuttal of Liberal Policy by the TUC should have served as a warning to Gladstone but there is no evidence that it did.

Once the demand for free education had been included in Congress Policy in 1885, it was reinforced over the next couple of years. A delegation from the TUC attended an international meeting of trade unionists held in Paris in 1886 at which Mr. Jones' call for 'gratuitous, compulsory, secular education' was greeted with cheers.[22] The British Congress in the same year once more heard a President supporting the call for free education, this time F. Maddison who, like his predecessor, was also a member of the Typographical Association. He told delegates that '... as experience has proved it necessary in the interests of the children, to make their education compulsory it is equally necessary that education should be free. Free education, then, must be one of the planks of our platfrom'.[23] This view was supported later by a resolution proposed by Robert Knight of the Boilermakers which included a demand for admission to board schools to be free of charge[24] followed the next year by a similar resolution stating that '... in the opinion of this Congress a truly national system of free education is not only desirable but necessary ...'.[25]

There were signs that the opposition to free education was beginning to weaken. The stern views of the Fawcetts, who argued that those who could not afford the necessary school pence should be classed as paupers or that the poor needed to pay fees in order to retain their independence and dignity, were held less frequently. These views had always been strongly criticized by Robert Applegarth and others in the Labour movement.[26] There was still a strong belief among the more prosperous members of society that every service offered should be paid for fully by the customer and an inability or unwillingness to accept that some people were poverty stricken through no fault of their own but through illness, loss of the 'breadwinner' by death or – the most common cause of poverty revealed by Booth's survey of the 1890s – low wages. The fact that the London poor '. . . had too little money to pay school fees without depriving their families of food and clothing'[27] was beyond the comprehension of many who had never known such worries.

In practical terms the attempt to collect fees from poor pupils was leading to chaos in some districts. The London School Board tried various schemes to overcome the problem. How could they force children to pay fees when their parents simply could not afford them?[28] One scheme tried by the LSB was to refuse entry to children who had not brought their fee and then fine the parents for non-attendance. Not only did this help to defeat the work of the attendance officers but it was also unsuccessful in Court. By 1886, arrears in LSB fees were not much below £10,000 a year, which represented nearly ten per cent of the fees actually collected[29] and a few years later there were reports of six London schools in which on average 46.1% of the fees had to be remitted.[30] In 1887 at the TUC during a discussion upon the Truck Amendment Bill a Report by Alexander Redgrove, Chief Inspector of factories was quoted; this revealed that deductions were being made from the wages of workmen employed in an ironworks, for the education of their children at a board school. Among three cases cited deductions of 4s 2d, 5s 2d and 8s 2d per month were given as examples of continued truck.

It is true that when the Cross Commission reported in 1888 it did not recommend free education; that was hardly to be expected from a Commission containing so many prominent Churchmen who were known to be antagonistic to such an idea, such as Cardinal Manning, Dr. Temple the Bishop of London, Canon Robert Gregory, Canon B.F. Smith, Reverend J.R. Rigg, Reverend R.W. Dale, etc. More significant in the long run was the Enfranchisement Act of 1884 which greatly enhanced the voting power of organized labour. The Conservatives realized the significance of this factor quickly and in the best opportunist fashion considered that if free education was now inevitable they might just as well introduce the reform and get the credit for it. The fact that they had always opposed such a view was no deterrent for they were aware that many voters had short memories. In addition, a further advantage would be that they could shape the legislation to their own taste and thereby build in protection for their Church of England allies as well as the

Roman Catholic minority who would support them if the measure was moulded to accommodate religious interests. If Disraeli could 'dish the Whigs' over the franchise in 1867 there was no reason why Salisbury, a strong opponent of free education, should not play a similar game with the Liberals in 1890. The vote of the LSB in January of that year supporting free education[31] by twenty-four to sixteen votes could only have provided further impetus to the Tory leader[32] and a compromise Bill was finally passed in 1891; this made elementary education free for the majority of children. The immediate response from the TUC was appreciation of a move in what they considered to be the right direction tinged with regret that evening classes had not also been included within the Bill.[33]

In fact a substantial number of children in elementary schools were still paying fees years later; 800,000 in 1894 and 150,000 still in 1912. Hence specific demands for free elementary education continued to be made in TUC resolutions until 1906 after which they were included in demands for the abolition of fees in other sectors of the educational system. Demands to remove fees from the remainder of elementary schools also continued to be made by other sections of the labour movement[34]: a Conference at Manchester in 1894 attended by representatives from trades councils, the ILP, the Building Industries Federation and the Associated Society of Engineers, drew up a ten point 'Labour Programme' which was headed by a demand for free education in all schools.[35] Similarly, a meeting two years later convened by the LTC passed a resolution put forward by the executive of the SDF, moved by Harry Quelch and seconded by J. Kent, which included a demand for '. . . a system which shall provide for every child free access to the means of education, from the elementary class to the university'.[36] For all the limitations of the 1891 Education Act, the abolition of fees in a majority of the elementary schools did lead to an immediate improvement in attendance, especially among infants and older children.[37]

By the turn of the century the TUC was less concerned with fees in elementary schools. Demands for their abolition were regularly featured in education resolutions throughout the Edwardian era[38] but most children were in easy reach of a free elementary school; the schools which continued to charge fees were usually located in the more prosperous areas of towns and used their fees to retain some measure of social exclusiveness. Fee paying elementary schools were continuing to decline in numbers and it only remained for the 1918 Education Act to deliver the final blow. It is true that some Conservatives continued to support the principle of fees in such schools for the very reason already mentioned; as for example Mr. Evelyn Cecil, who told the House of Commons during the 1918 Education Bill debate that some fee paying elementary schools should be retained because, 'sometimes parents desire to remove their children from a particular school, because they find that the children in it are, I am sorry to say, dirty or use bad language. . .'.[39] Lord Percy even considered restoring fees in elementary schools as late as 1925[40] but this would have proven most unpopular politically and in any case, in terms of their contribution to the cost of education, fees had always been a tiny proportion.

The only strong reaction to fee paying outside the secondary school system at the TUC prior to the First World War was over the charging of industrial and reformatory school fees. A comparatively small number of these schools had been established under regulations in the 1870 Education Act[41] and complaints were raised at Congress in 1909 and 1910 by James Sexton concerning examples of working men who had been imprisoned for non-payment of such fees. The problem was largely confined to casual labourers whose earnings were very low. A resolution asking the PCTUC to bring the matter to the attention of the Home Office was passed unanimously in 1909 but the following year a lengthy debate arose. Sexton claimed he could provide 'typical cases representing hundreds even thousands of others' who were in a poor plight. Apparently labourers with four or five children were earning no more than ten shillings a week, which meant that the wife had to leave the children in order to obtain work to supplement the scanty wage of her husband. This meant that the children might be left to their own devices, get into trouble and be sent to an industrial school; the extra pennies they had earned through street trading vanished once the child attended such a school.

Sexton told TUC delegates how a labourer could get behind with school fees and be sent to prison. A rather sad farce then followed.

> While he is in gaol, the wife and children ... are taken to a work house in a cab – the only cab ride they may have in their lives and are kept there at the expense of the ratepayers to the tune of twenty-five shillings per week while the father is in prison. When the man's time has expired, notice is sent to the Poor Law Authority; and they hire another cab and take the wife and children, and dump them down in the street outside the gates of the gaol, telling the man when he comes out that he must find a home for them. But the home has been broken up...[42]

F.W. Booth of the Typographical Society from Hull claimed that Sexton's story was neither typical nor true and went on to tell delegates that parents were given every opportunity to pay the fees of approximately four pence per week but he received little support from Congress. Even G.H. Roberts of his own union suggested that '... he must have thought he was addressing a conference of Poor Law Guardians'[43] and the resolution asking the Home Office to relieve poor parents of these fees was agreed to. The following year a PCTUC Deputation visited the Home Office to discuss a series of items, of which industrial school fees was the last mentioned on a list of ten.[44]

Before the passing of the 1902 Education Act the TUC made little reference to secondary schools but greater interest began to be shown afterwards. Support had been removed from the Higher Grade schools which many working people had seen as a form of secondary education available to their children. In addition, interest in technical education declined. Technical education had been an inevitable demand in the early days of Congress when craftsmen dominated the unions and although skilled workers still earned above average rates of pay and enjoyed greater job security it was becoming apparent that technical education also had its limitations, given the society of Edwardian Britain. Technical knowledge might raise a worker to the rank of foreman but it was secondary education in the mould cast by Robert Morant and A.J. Balfour which was more likely to provide the social mobility needed to join the ranks of the white collared workers.

When H.A.L. Fisher told the House of Commons, in introducing his Education Bill in August 1917, that working people did not want education 'in order that they may rise out of their own class, always a vulgar ambition' he displayed a complete lack of knowledge of working class life, for whilst it is true that this was not the only motive for gaining a secondary education, such education was almost the only means by which a boy could escape the common destiny of his peers in many communities; especially was this true in mining areas and in those reliant upon one major industry. An increasing amount of time and energy in discussions concerning education in the labour movement between 1902 and 1944 was taken up by demands to open up access more freely to secondary education and the TUC was no exception in this matter.

It was all very well for headmasters of traditional grammar schools to complain that children from working class families would be turned towards wretchedly paid clerical work[45] through a secondary school education instead of becoming skilled artisans by attending elementary school and then following in their father's footsteps. What they failed to grasp is that, although there were poorly paid clerical posts, many of these were more likely to contain better promotion prospects within a company. In general, white collar workers, even when paid lower rates initially, were often in jobs where there were incremental advances of salary, payment for sickness and some form of pension scheme. To be a member of the 'salaried staff' as opposed to a 'wage earner' not only meant that you could not be given one hour's notice of dismissal as was common with many manual workers[46] but were also usually guaranteed greater job security in general. Although there were always exceptions to this generalization and whilst many craftsmen and 'semi-skilled' workers often despised 'pen pushers'[47] they were nevertheless often keen for their youngsters to attend secondary school so that they might obtain one of these 'secure' jobs. In the working class household financial insecurity was a fact of life; by contrast a secure clerical post seemed like a prize well worth striving for.

Immediately following the passing of the 1902 Education Act the Board of Education pursued a policy of high fees and few scholarships in secondary schools and normally refused to recognize as a secondary school, one which did not charge fees. HMIs were extremely critical of local efforts to expand secondary education, for example at Nottingham and Bradford,[48] where it became obvious that the views of the LEAs and the Board of Education differed widely as to what should constitute secondary education. The former argued that the system needed gradual building up alongside parental encouragement whilst the latter tended to judge the schools as they were at the time and in comparison with well established traditional grammar schools in the belief that this would ensure quality as opposed to quantity. It was not until the return of a Liberal Government in 1906 and the resulting free place legislation requesting secondary schools to make up to twenty-five per cent of their places available to elementary school children in return for an increased grant, that the strict post-1902 Education Act secondary school regime was relaxed. Even so, it seemed to the labour movement that a school system had once more been established which related to the social class of the pupils rather than any other criteria and they were frequently to make such views explicit.

Endowments

Whether intended or not school fees acted as a social barrier. In the state-financed secondary schools after 1902, attempts to allow some clever working class children into such schools were made by the offer of scholarships and after 1907 through the establishment of the free place system. Before dealing with this method of entry to secondary schools it is convenient to consider a related issue concerning fee paying schools in general, but particularly independent schools; this is the question of endowments. TUC delegates frequently expressed the view that the endowments of many private schools had originally been intended either for scholars with poor parents or, at least, not for the children of parents with above average incomes.

Cries against the misuse of charities and endowments went back at least to the House of Commons Committees of 1816 and 1818 under Henry Brougham and abuses in the major public schools had been readily exposed by the Clarendon Commission of 1864. The Taunton Commission performed a similar function for another 791 of the further 3,000 or so private, proprietary and endowed schools in 1868. The pocketing of £127,700 gathered in fines or renewal of leases, during the twenty years preceding the Clarendon Report, by provosts and fellows of Eton was an example of theft on the grand scale but embezzlement and misappropriation of income, admittedly in a more modest manner, were also found to be rife in many of the minor private schools, as was exposed by the reports of the Taunton Commission,[49] which constituted 'a massive indictment of the schools'.[50]

How far trade unionists knew of the findings of these commissions or of later attempts to gather together the small endowments of some of the poorer schools to provide some system of fee paying secondary education for the sons of the middle class is not easy to assess. Certainly no evidence from these sources was quoted by TUC delegates whether at Congress or when confronting presidents of the Board of Education. Yet it can be shown that there was a strongly held belief among many trade unionists that there was money available which could and should be used to provide secondary education for working class children. George Odger, speaking on a National Education League platform, as early as 1870, '... attacked the rich who had, he alleged, filched the schools from the people of England and now supported these institutions with money left for the education of the poor'.[51] In the same year R. Applegarth in a letter to *The Beehive* also mentioned how '... the middle class ... had a monopoly of free education afforded by enormous and misused endowments...'.[52] A few years later the Labour Representation League suggested that the State had a right to interpret the bequests of original benefactors and that the time was now opportune to settle the whole question of endowments.[53] It is probable that most of these remarks emanated from the general discussions which arose from the publication of the Clarendon and Taunton Reports.

The first mention of endowments at the TUC came in 1881 from a reference to 'attempts being made to confiscate the rights of the poorer classes in some of the educational institutions in Scotland'. Mr. Fairbairn from London supported the accompanying request by Scottish delegates for the PCTUC to take the matter up, claiming 'that £56,000 a year was taken away from the funds of the London charities for the benefit of the parson'.[54] Four years later the matter gained greater prominence when T.P. Threlfall in his opening presidential address turned his attention to the matter of education and told delegates;

> We have a right to demand free education; for do we not pay above our
> fair share of taxation, according to every shilling of our earnings? ...
> If the money argument is gone into, let me ask a question or two. What
> has become of the vast sums of money which have been left in bygone
> times for education, for help to the poor? The records of the City
> companies are a sample of the uses to which this money has been put.
> The modern interpretation seems to be that the money was left for the
> poor in spirit – not the poor in worldly goods. It never would have
> been bequeathed if the ancient donors could have forseen its uses for
> costly banquets, middle class education and other foreign purposes.[55]

The result of Threlfall's statement was that in the TUC Circular prepared by H. Broadhurst and distributed to trades councils for presentation to candidates in order to test their attitudes to TUC policy in the forthcoming General Election of 1886, one of the points included was a demand for 'the restitution of educational and other endowments to the service of those for whom they were originally intended'.[56]

That the matter was steadily gaining the attention of trade unionists can be illustrated by the fact that, almost immediately following the publication of the TUC Circular, the Labour Representation Association of Manchester and Salford, which had only been established in January 1885, published their own circular just after the November municipal elections outlining their aims for the consideration of parliamentary candidates intending to stand for election the following year. Among these aims was one 'to secure that the educational endowments intended for the benefit of the working classes shall be applied to the purposes for which they were designed, subject to such modification in matters of detail as the altered circumstances of the time may require'.[57]

The representative of the London Trades Council before the Cross Commission, Thomas Smyth, also discussed the issue of endowments with the Commissioners in 1887. He argued that the State should bear the full cost of education but that in doing so it should '... absorb to itself for such purposes all funds and endowments left for educational purposes'.[58] Questioned by Cardinal Manning as to whether the state should provide education for all classes, Smyth claimed that the upper classes received free education through the system of endowments:

> *Smyth*: ... At present I believe most of the higher education, at least there is a tradition among us that all the higher education, is practically free for the upper classes. The State provides it largely at, the universities and grammar schools, and all sorts of places to which the poor have no access.
>
> *Cardinal Manning*: You would contend that at the present moment the education of the highest class is provided by the State by means of old endowments; for instance the universities possess land and endowments, and that being, you say national property, the upper classes are receiving education freely.
>
> *Smyth*: Yes.[59]

In 1895 the Trades and Labour Councils and Co-operative Societies presented a Memorial to the Bryce Commission signed by two ex-secretaries of the TUC, George Howell and Henry Broadhurst, both now Liberal MPs, together with representatives of various trades councils and co-operative societies. The second item put forward views which, it was claimed, were largely shared by the wage earning workers of the country concerning secondary education in general and endowments in particular:

> We cannot but think that the immense endowments which now sustain most of the grammar and other secondary schools of the country would, if such endowments were wisely distributed and effectively applied, prove almost, if not wholly, adequate to the establishment and maintenance of a secondary school in every district of the country – if such a secondary school was rigorously confined to Secondary Education, and did not provide primary education as well...
>
> As these endowments ... were in most cases originally bequeathed for the education of poor children, we hope the principle will be universally adopted, which has been generally enforced by the Endowed Schools Commissioners, and more lately by the Charity Commissioners, in new schemes which they have approved for the reorganization of endowed schools...[60]

The Memorial recognized what the Commission was to show, that there were endowments reserved to support both secondary and primary education; approximately £735,000 excluding the value of sites and buildings for the former and approximately £100,000 for the latter.[61] With elementary education now free in most areas it made sense to ask that endowments be concentrated on the provision of secondary education but it is difficult to understand why trade unionists should have approved of the manner in which endowments had been treated following the Endowed Schools Act of 1869, for such action which had taken place provided no evidence to suggest that 'poor gifted children' would gain much help from a continuance of past policy. Even allowing for the complexity of the operation in dealing with the antiquated provision of some benefactions there was evidence to show that there had been 'rationalizations', which had resulted in local children being abandoned in favour of one or two exhibitions which local boys had little chance of gaining without having attended a preparatory school first.[62]

Either the Memorial's authors did not fully comprehend the extent to which the 'middle classes' had captured the secondary schools or they were deluded into believing that it would be possible for a considerable number of clever working class children to gain entry to these schools. The influence of two important elder statesmen of the trade union world well known for their general acceptance of the *status quo* must have been considerable to gain the general acceptance of the other members of the labour movement who had added their signatures to the document; especially as their children were not likely to have gained anything from the past work of the Commissioners. It is even more difficult to understand how such approval of past activities could have been given by trade unionists who in the same document recommended that '... it would be highly beneficial to all classes of the community if their children were to attend a common school'.[63] The work of the Commissioners had resulted in the very opposite of such an ideal being implemented within the educational system.

No more of this issue was heard at the TUC until the turn of the century but from 1904 onwards a reference to endowments began to be incorporated into the TUC Education Programme. It started with just a phrase in 1904 when the sixth point of Congress Education policy included a call for the '... proper management of educational endowments'.[64] The following year this had become expanded within a demand for the National Exchequer to foot the total bill for education, part of the revenue to come from 'the restoration and democratic administration of valuable misappropriated educational charities and endowments'.[65] In 1906 and 1907 similar demands were included in the TUC Education Programme[66] whilst at the 1906 National Union of Gas-workers Biennial Conference the education resolution introduced by Will Thorne which alluded to this matter put the demand in more challenging terms calling for the 'restoration of the educational endowments which have been stolen from the people'.[67] For all this strength of feeling from Thorne no reference was made to this matter in the TUC Education Bill he put forward in Parliament during the same year.

During these years resolutions relating to endowments brought little response from delegates probably because they agreed with the view expressed. Ben Tillett added his support in 1906 telling delegates that 'the people have been robbed. If these bequests were looked into, we should take away from the middle and upper classes some of the schooling that really belongs to the poor'.[68] He suggested that a Government Inquiry should be held regarding endowments, a suggestion that was taken up by the TUC three years later when Will Thorne introduced the Education Resolution which included a clause on endowments in which he called for '. . . the Parliamentary Committee to press the Government to appoint a Royal Commission to inquire into and report upon the educational endowments of the country'.[69] Like Tillett, Thorne relayed to Congress the view that 'it was well known that many of them [endowments] although left solely for the education of poor children, were being used for the education of the middle and upper classes'.[70] A Royal Commission would make revelations 'of a startling character as to the way endowments were being administered'.[71]

The remarks made about endowments by trade unionists in the Edwardian era were certainly more critical than those made by H. Broadhurst and G. Howell in the Memorial to the Bryce Commission in 1895. Yet there was little sign of any positive response to trade union demands. In Parliament, after 1906, Ramsay MacDonald, Philip Snowden and J.R. Clynes all attacked the Government over the question of endowments[72] but whilst it seemed to some members of the labour movement that the Commissioners had been unfair in dealing with educational endowments since 1869 it was clear that their activities had been legal.

The request by the PCTUC for the setting up of a Royal Commission to examine educational endowments was put before three different Presidents of the Board of Education to no avail between 1910 and 1919, twice to W. Runciman (1910, 1911), twice to J.A. Pease (1912, 1914) and once to H.A.L. Fisher in 1919. It was Thorne who usually put the TUC cases but whilst he could claim a long history of agitation by his own union on this issue he rarely provided a coherent argument to the Board of Education. In 1911 he told W. Runciman how the Blue Coat School (Christs Hospital) founded by Edward VI for the education and maintenance of the poorest children of London had recently let half an acre of land belonging to the Foundation in Shaftesbury Avenue at a yearly rental of £7,300. Instead of following this up with some analysis of the type of children accepted as present day scholars or the range of fees, he went on to suggest that such money would provide medical treatment for poor London children. Whilst this was true, the kind of detailed knowledge of the school which was needed to show that in some way it was cheating the poor or not spending the endowments as originally prescribed was not forthcoming. He provided isolated bits of information that a school, which he did not name, had sold land for £200,000 but he did not show how this was vital to the TUC case concerning endowments.[73]

When arguing the case for a Royal Commission Thorne could only repeat demands for an Inquiry which many in the labour movement[74] believed would reveal 'that the money is being spent for the purpose of educating the sons and daughters of the wealthy classes who can well afford to pay for their own education'.[75] He added the threat that '. . . in the face of the discontent and labour unrest it is not safe to withhold them' [the endowments]. In 1914 Thorne could only repeat the TUC demands and inform the Minister that 'nothing will satisfy the organized workers until we get a Royal Commission'.[76]

If Thorne's presentation of the TUC case lacked well marshalled evidence it was partly because the kind of detailed evidence necessary from private schools was not readily available and the collection of such material was not likely to be a high priority at TUC Headquarters.[77] Neither was Thorne well supported by his colleagues. Only in the 1919 Deputation did any of them speak up in support and on that occasion J. Cramp of the NUR could only state 'I have not gone sufficiently into that question to be able to speak with authority. Generally speaking I know, as we all know, that very many endowments have gone astray and are not today being given to the objects for which they were originally intended'.[78] However true this may have been, an open confession of ignorance of a subject which was part of his own trade union's original resolution hardly strengthened the TUC argument on this occasion.

J.H. Thomas, who had the most to say about education on this occasion, also spoke on the question of endowments but whilst he spoke longer than Thorne or Cramp his contribution also lacked any analysis of the situation and he could only repeat views similar to those already expressed:

> I refuse to believe today that the endowments made were class en-dowments . . . to believe that people . . . interested in education, left their wealth and money for the purpose of endowing education, merely left it for the endowment of class education . . . but there can be no doubt that by custom . . . today's endowments are made class endowments, that is to say class in the sense that a particular and special class benefit from them. . .[79]

However it needs to be said that there was little in the attitude of the Presidents confronted to suggest that even if the TUC case had been presented in a more factual manner their request would have been granted. The Ministers concerned were all products of the system that was being criticized: W. Runciman had attended South Shields High School and received private tutoring before proceeding to Trinity Hall Cambridge, J.A. Pease had attended Tottenham Grove House Quaker School before going to the same Cambridge College, whilst H.A.L. Fisher's education had been received at Winchester and New College, Oxford.

Runciman suggested that claims concerning the scale of endowments, were exaggerated as dozens of smaller schools had little money available, yet he came nearest among the Education Ministers to suggesting that some kind of Inquiry might be useful:

... it may be necessary that we should consider the changed condition of education and finance and the way in which endowments which are not supposed to be used in relief of rates are becoming more and more restricted in the objects to which they can be applied. It may be necessary to have an enquiry into the effect of endowments on education as a whole, but I cannot say whether the Prime Minister would agree to have a Royal Commission appointed for the purpose.[80]

Runciman was aware of the strong feelings aroused by the endowment issue which he believed was 'coming more and more to a head'; he knew the TUC were determined to push their claim and probably believed that they might achieve some measure of success. He told the PCTUC representatives:

I should therefore hope that any enquiry for which you press would be one to know how far endowments for the purpose of education can best be used for education ... [and] ... would urge that educational advantages which may have been provided ... for the people as a whole should not be restricted to any one class, either your own or the class of anybody else....[81]

J.A. Pease was against the idea of a Royal Commission on the two occasions on which he met the PCTUC. He did not think the charges against endowments could be sustained. Changes which had taken place had been made merely 'in accordance with the changed conditions in which we now live'.[82] He explained that the Board of Education had no power over private schools:

... large public schools, Eton and Winchester ... have endowments but those endowments ... we at the Board of Education have no control over ... it would require legislation to give us any power over schools of that character.[83]

This was precisely what the TUC hoped that a Royal Commission would lead to: most of them knew already that private schools were independent of the Board of Education, a view that was made quite explicit in the TUC Education resolution of 1915.[84] Pease claimed that the Board of Education was in full sympathy with recent attempts by the Charity Commissioners to try and extend the endowments of some of the well known schools for the 'benefit of the children of the poor' but suggested that schools had such strong support that the demands of the TUC could not be realized:

St. Pauls ... and one at Tonbridge, a similar school, are controlled by Governors who are closely connected with City Companies ... I want to point out to you that, in the event of any scheme being put forward it is open to either House of Parliament to reject any such scheme, and unless we feel that such a scheme can be put forward and carried through both houses, I do not think one should be encouraged to make an effort in that direction, because our efforts would be doomed to failure.[85]

Two years later Pease showed less patience and told the PCTUC Deputation '... not to frighten off private contributions to education – for Universities and Public Schools ... who have the right to donate money how they please'.[86]

When the TUC request for a Royal Commission was put to H.A.L. Fisher in 1919 he answered at length but evaded the full question and dealt only with the universities. Referring to Oxford and Cambridge, he agreed that there was feeling in some quarters that the time had come for a fresh inquiry into their finances and constitution but suggested that in fact 'there is a very considerable movement for reform within the Universities themselves'.[87] They would, he told the Deputation, compare favourably with the contribution to learning of any university abroad. The real grievance, the endowments connected with private schools, was ignored. Between 1910 and 1919, the views of Education Ministers towards the TUC request for a Royal Commission to examine educational endowments moved from a point where sympathy was expressed and an indication given that some kind of inquiry might be undertaken when Runciman was at the Board of Education to a time when the idea was rejected by Pease and ignored by Fisher.

Little more was heard about endowments after the PCTUC Deputation to H.A.L. Fisher in 1919. It was raised again at the 1920 Congress when H. Evans of the Journeymen Butchers reminded delegates that, 'it is desirable to take into consideration the amount of money which has been left to charities for the purpose of education' and pointed to Manchester Grammar School which he gave as an example of a past charity 'being utilized to-day by the very people who are in a position to pay for the education of their children'.[88] His demand for Congress to consider the matter further received widespread support but no further action was taken largely because questions of finance in secondary education had gradually become concentrated upon the issues of scholarships, free places and free secondary education.[89]

Scholarships, Free Places and Free Secondary Education

The changing use of words in education has already been mentioned in connection with 'secondary education'. Another word which underwent some change was 'scholarship' which became generally used in the twentieth century to refer to a place gained at a secondary school without the payment of fees. Trade unionists in their discussions sometimes used it in this manner. In fact it would be more accurate to use it to refer to the few places made availabel by competitive examination at secondary schools following the Endowed Schools Act of 1869. The number of working class pupils entering for these examinations and the even smaller number who were successful was negligible. When the Liberal Party was returned to power in 1906 the newly emerging Labour Party, now with some fifty seats in Parliament, brought pressure on the Government to make secondary education more easily available to working class children. The result was the introduction of the 1907 Secondary School

Regulations which allowed secondary schools to receive a higher rate of grant if they would offer up to twenty-five per cent of their places free to elementary school children.[90]

These 'free places' as they became known, unlike the scholarship places, were not intended to be available through competitive examination but merely by a qualifying examination designed to indicate that a youngster was capable of benefiting from the education provided by a secondary school. In fact, as the number of children qualifying rapidly outstripped the number of free places available the tests soon became highly competitive.[91] The Trades Union Congress had originally asked for secondary education to be made available to all children[92] but by the turn of the century had changed its policy to fit in with the idea of children attending if they had qualified, but not necessarily in terms of a competitive examination. Indeed there were several instances of trade unionists arguing specifically against competitive examinations and in 1897 such a view was incorporated in TUC Education Policy; clause 3 stating:

> ... that the system of providing secondary education only for the very small proportion of the workers' children who can come to the top, after severe competition with their schoolfellows, is to be strongly condemned
> a) on educational grounds, and
> b) in that it tends to foster feelings of antagonism and jealousy, which are such a serious obstacle in the way of that union among the workers which their highest welfare demands, and which it is the object of trade unionism to promote.[93]

However it was not so much this ideal of non-competitive mankind that led others to oppose the examinations for non-fee payers wishing to go to secondary education; it was rather that many trade unionists considered the system to be unfair. As early as 1905 the TUC were calling for a form of continuous assessment, though such a term was not used. Referring to the selection of children from elementary schools they stated, 'that the standard of capacity shall be judged by work previously accomplished, and not by competitive examination'.[94] This suggestion was incorporated by Will Thorne in the TUC Education Bill he presented to Parliament the next year in a clause which included a reference to secondary and technical school entrance by, 'all who have fitted themselves by their previous work'.[95] In 1908 Thorne explained his objection to the situation as it stood:

> I am opposed to all kinds of competitive scholarships, because it is perfectly evident that if a man receives £3 per week he has a better chance of tutoring his children than if a man receives £1 per week.[96]

The plea for an overall assessment to replace competitive examinations was still being made ten years later by J. Jones of the General Workers who told Congress:

It would be far better to take the year's work of the students concerned for the purpose of passing them on to the higher school. Those who have gone into the system of scholarship examinations know that it is largely a matter of temperament, and those that get excited cannot do themselves justice. The best test would be the full result of the past year's work...[97]

Complaints had been made against the old scholarship system existing prior to 1907 and although Sidney Webb, chairman of the London Technical Board may have believed that London in 1903 had a more generous provision of scholarship than any German, French or American City,[98] these comparisons were of little interest to trade unionists. In the same year a circular issued by the TUC for all trades councils to put to candidates in the forthcoming 1904 LCC Election declared:

To an infinitesimally small proportion of the children of the industrial classes in London secondary education is made available by means of the London County Council's competitive 'scholarship ladder'.... The London 'scholarship ladder' must give place to a 'broad highway' – to a non-competitive system of maintenance scholarships, which will provide a secondary education scholarship for every child who can reach a certain standard.[99]

To Sidney Webb, who was more interested in efficiency than social justice, the competitive scholarship system seemed the obvious way of selecting the children who obtained the highest marks of scholarship. For the Labour movement the issue was not so straightforward. A TUC Circular of 1900 had pointed out that 'six-sevenths of the nation pass through the elementary schools: does anyone suppose that all the highest intelligence is confined to the other seventh?'.[100] Trade unionists knew that working class children were at a distinct disadvantage when compared with children from higher income backgrounds and this was a constant bone of contention. J. Wignall of Swansea speaking at the 1901 Congress claimed that '. . . the intermediate schools were out of the reach of the working man's child and eighty per cent or ninety per cent of the scholarships were gained by the children of people who could afford to pay fees'.[101] However there was nothing to prevent enterprising middle class parents from encouraging their children to gain scholarships which would save them from paying school fees whether they could afford them or not. As fee payers inevitably came from families with above average incomes, and so did most of the scholarship winners, secondary schools were to remain 'almost exclusively as middle class institutions'.[102]

It had been intended that the free place system would go some way towards opening up secondary schools to a wider social spread of pupils for, as Runciman explained to the PCTUC Deputation in 1911, 'the places are restricted to pupils from Elementary Schools and as these are attended by the Working Classes they should get the free places going'.[103] This seemed obvious enough but the situation in practice was far more complex. The working classes contained numerous strata in terms of occupations, income and life style; working class children who did achieve some academic success were usually from the families of skilled workers, shopkeepers or clerks. Trade unionists were quickly learning that the provision of educational facilities alone was not enough to guarantee that all children had a reasonable chance of benefiting from them; this was a lesson which educational administrators seemed to take much longer to understand. Organized Labour knew from its own experiences that the elementary schools deemed to be most suitable for them were poorer in every way than the secondary schools provided initially for higher income groups. W.A. Appleton told Congress that in one particularly poor school he said to a teacher that it would make a decent stable and received the reply that '. . . it might if it were better ventilated',[104] and a few years later A.W. Tapp of the Shipwrights listed the advantages of secondary schools:

> The standard of the teachers is much higher so far as their educational training and qualifications are concerned. There is more attention to the individual child. The classes are not nearly so large and in every way much better provision is made for a much wider education.[105]

The free place system probably worked to distract the TUC from earlier calls of secondary education for all. The PCTUC became involved in arguments over details, important enough at local level and as matters of principle, but details which took up much time and effort and brought only minor rewards. This is perhaps best illustrated by a discussion which took place between the PCTUC and the Board of Education when Runciman was President. D.J. Shackleton complained to the Minister that at both Colne and Nelson scholarships being given by 'outside' bodies were being included as part of the allowance towards the twenty-five per cent free places by local secondary schools:

> At Colne they have eleven free places – five provided by the county and six by co-operative bodies and generous minded people. It is a ridiculous position to be placed in, if the co-op societies and generous people are going to be made the means of saving the rates of the country.... Nelson has twenty-five free places provided, eleven by the Council and fourteen by outside authorities. Well we think these ought to be additional and that the time has come when twenty-five per cent of free places should be open without examination, other than the necessary test, to see whether the children are qualified to enjoy the facilities offered.[106]

Runciman agreed that there was a 'genuine grievance' here and promised to investigate the matter. By the Autumn the PCTUC were able to report[107] to Congress that '. . . the President of the Board of Education in the Regulations for Secondary Schools for 1909 has, to some extent, met the appeal made to him on your behalf by the Parliamentary Committee. . . .'.[108] The extra scholarships offered by outside bodies such as co-operative societies were to be independent of the twenty-five per cent allocation of free places. Yet the numbers concerned, six places at Colne, whilst important enough locally were not much of a concession when it is remembered that the TUC proposal to the President had been for free education from primary school to university throughout the country. This major claim of the TUC had been completely ignored.

Those who saw the twenty-five per cent free places as a base from which to increase this percentage later were to become disappointed from 1917 onwards. Arthur Henderson, as President in that year, had already been criticized by trade unionists for his defence of reactionary policies; he received further disapproval from Mr. Tapp for giving his consent to reduce the twenty-five per cent of free places to twelve and a half per cent.[109] it was also becoming apparent that any percentage offer was of no use if there was not a secondary school in the area to attend. Tapp, who spoke frequently at Congress on educational matters in these years told delegates,

> I come from a district entirely composed of the industrial classes. It has a population between 50,000 and 60,000 and yet we have no secondary schools in that town, although the Town Council has applied over and over again.[110]

There was evidence to show that secondary schools were less likely to be placed in areas populated by the industrial classes[111] for the bulk of their 'customers' were fee payers; hence the most prosperous areas were sought for possible locations as was made clear by LCC policy;

> When a new grammar school was proposed the Council's officials carefully examined the locality with a view to ascertaining its economic status and, above all, the number of potential fee payers. For example in 1909 the LCC Education Officer submitted a report on secondary school accommodation which contained much detail relating to the occupations of the inhabitants of the various boroughs along with the rateable values of the properties. From these he argued that certain boroughs would, or would not, be suitable for the expansion of secondary education.[112]

It was probably believed by most fee payers that they paid the full cost of secondary education. This was not true and trade unionists who were also members of local authority education committees were able to show what a small proportion of educational spending was covered by fees. In 1912, P. Walls as a member of the PCTUC Deputation to the Board of Education, told the President, J.A. Pease, that with regard to his Education Committee in Cumberland '... the fees are not a hundreth part of our cost of secondary education; they are not a two hundred and fiftyeth part of our expenditure on education, so they are infinitesimal from a financial standpoint. They seem to me to more or less serve as a barrier'.[113] When the FBI Deputation called upon the Board of Education in 1918 it became apparent that they were also under the illusion that fees covered the full cost of secondary education. They also seemed to imply that the greater the purchasing power of the parent the less intelligent the child needed to be in order to attend a secondary school. This was illustrated in the discussion between FBI spokesmen, who seemed a little confused among themselves at first, and H.A.L. Fisher and his colleagues at the Board of Education, including Sir L.A. Selby-Bigge, Permanent Secretary:

F.W. Gilbertson (FBI): I think the [FBI Education] Committee would like to see secondary education free for those children who were selected as capable of benefiting by it.

J.W. McConnel (FBI): I thought we had made that proposal.

F.W. Gilbertson: That was the idea. Take for example, a parent who had a child not able to pass the necessary exams, and who would be reported as not suitable for proceeding to the secondary school. That person obviously would have to pay the cost of the education; but those children selected as qualified to have the benefit have their education free.

Sir Selby-Bigge: But they are not to be admitted, are they, if they are not fit to go into it?

F.W. Gilbertson: It is rather difficult, is it not, to say that somebody who is prepared to pay all the expense of the education and the loss of the child's labour, should not have the opportunity?

Sir Selby-Bigge: The parent, or whoever it is, does not pay all the cost, because the State pays a great deal of it.[114]

It was this attitude, clearly expressed by FBI representatives, that trade unionists considered so unfair. Complaints that wealthier parents were able to pay teachers to give their children extra coaching were frequently made[115] as were protests that some children who were less intelligent but fee payers kept out brighter working class children.[116]

The variation in school fees from one local authority to another was also criticized.[117]

There was no suggestion by the Government or local authorities that secondary schools should become meritocratic institutions: only the scholarship system had originally been competitive, although the free place system had also rapidly turned into an academic competition.[118] To the Labour movement it seemed as if the meritocratic principle was only to be applied to working class children. This practice of the LCC was one of the attitudes so strongly condemned by R.H. Tawney in 1922:

> It is still possible for the largest education authority in the country to propose to erect inequality of educational opportunity into a principle of public policy by solemnly suggesting, with much parade of philosophical arguments, that the interests of the community require that the children of well-to-do parents, who pay fees, should be admitted to public secondary schools on easier intellectual terms than the children of poor parents who can enter them only with free places, and that the children who are so contemptible as to be unable to afford secondary education without assistance in the form of maintenance allowances shall not be admitted unless they reach a higher intellectual standard still.[119]

The middle class atmosphere of the secondary school was inevitable given its source of recruitment. Working class parents who had received at the most a basic elementary education often looked upon such places with suspicion. Some believed 'that further education might make life, in psychological terms, harder rather than easier for themselves and their children',[120] a view confirmed to some extent a generation or more later by some sociologists.[121] Others pointed out that gaining a free place at secondary school still left parents with extra costs to meet. J.W. Bowen of the Union of Post Office Workers voiced such problems in the TUC Education Debate centred upon the proposed Geddes cutbacks in 1922:

> ... the workers' child is not so acceptable in our secondary schools as we think he ought to be. The tone of those secondary schools, the expenses demanded of the parents in the maintenance of all kinds of accessories, is too big a drain on the worker for him to allow his child to go there.[122]

The composition of education committees was also considered to be unrepresentative of the community and P. Walls of the Blastfurnacemen referring to his own area in an early PCTUC Deputation to the Board of Education explained

> that the system of co-opting members to the Education Committees has a great deal to do with our troubles.... We have about a dozen co-opted members upon our Committee. We have a canon, a bishop and several retired gentlemen. I will be bound to say none of these people has ever come into practical personal contact with the industrial community in their lives. I hesitated a considerable time before entertaining the idea that there was any intention on the part of that Education Committee to make secondary education exclusive to the rich people. I have hitherto taken care not to insinuate in the least that that was so; but now I am forced to the conclusion that this is the object at which they are aiming.[123]

When the TUC complained about fees to Government Ministers the latter would always argue that whilst the Government was increasing its expenditure on secondary education some local authorities were more concerned with saving ratepayers as far as possible from the extra expenses involved in the provision of secondary schools. This was precisely the nature of the reply W. Runciman gave to the PCTUC Deputation in 1909:

> ... the main obstacle to extending educational facilities is the pressure that is now brought to bear upon the ratepayers ... the State is certainly not going backward in this matter. That is a charge which must be preferred against the local authorities, if against anyone.[124]

It was because trade unionists were aware of the varying degrees of enthusiasm for secondary education among local authorities that they frequently proposed that the State should pay a larger part of the costs of education;[125] or even all of it.[126]

For working class children, to gain a free place at a secondary school was an achievement. Whether they could actually take it up depended largely upon the financial situation of their parents. There were two sacrifices poor parents were called upon to make: the first was the foregoing of the small but sometimes vital wage which their adolescent son or daughter would bring home if they obtained paid employment; the second was to meet the extra costs involved in keeping a youngster at secondary school, such as the expenses of a school uniform. It was for this reason that the Labour movement gradually formulated its ideas on maintenance allowances for poor children who were offered a place at a secondary school. At the TUC, demands for maintenance grants usually accompanied those calling for more places to be available at secondary school or free secondary education. In 1897 the TUC Education programme included a demand for 'such maintenance grants provided by the State as shall place secondary education within the reach of every child'.[127]

The call for maintenance grants at the TUC in the years to follow was expressed in a variety of ways. In 1903 the wording was 'free maintenance scholarships to all children whose usefulness would be enhanced by an extended education';[128] in 1906 the first clause of the TUC Education programme called for 'the State maintenance of school children'[129] and in the same year the TUC Education Bill contained a clause including the demand for '... a sufficient number of free maintenance scholarships ... to enable all those who have fitted themselves by their previous work to continue their studies at technical institutions or universities',[130] a demand also made less precisely in 1905.[131] Similar demands were also made by the SDF in 1906 and the ILP in 1908. There was no discussion on the matter at the TUC because all delegates were agreed and although the matter was raised by the PCTUC Deputation to the Board of Education in 1914, J.A. Pease, as President, chose to ignore it.

In 1918 the matter gained greater attention due to the proposed raising of the school leaving age to fourteen years and with this in mind Philip Snowden tried unsuccessfully to include an amendment in Fisher's Bill '... to secure maintenance allowances for all children whose school career would be extended by the Bill'.[132] Instead a discretionary clause was included allowing local authorities to provide such grants if they chose to do so. It is another example of the 1918 Education Bill falling short of the demands of the Labour movement.[133] Nevertheless some progressive authorities were able to offer maintenance grants in accordance with the permissive legislation of the 1918 Education Bill and thus encouraged the TUC to keep up the pressure for such concessions to be given to every child 'desirous and qualifying for secondary education'.[134] In 1921, Miss Walsh of the Uncertificated Teachers Union, as a member of the PCTUC Deputation to the Board of Education talking in support of maintenance grants, said to H.A.L. Fisher 'if a country like Russia can do it, surely we can . . .'.[135] There was no response from the President. Far from widening the scheme of maintenance grants, under the threat of the 'Geddes Axe', the Board of Education later in the Autumn issued to all local authorities Circular 1238 which announced that 'from the moment of receipt the grant on maintenance allowances for children aged fourteen to fifteen must be regarded as withdrawn'.[136] This was a cruel blow for children who had already been allocated the grant just prior to the distribution of this Circular. Yet it was only one of a series of blows which fell upon the working classes and trade unions from the end of 1921 onwards.[137]

The only respite from the cutbacks in education came during the few months that Charles Trevelyan was President of the Board of Education in the short-lived minority Labour Government of 1924. He gave local authorities permission to increase the twenty-five per cent free places to forty per cent in June and the following month was able to gain a further £440,000 for educational expenditure, part of which he used in ' . . . lifting the past Geddes restrictions on the amount and duration of maintenance grants for pupils over fourteen and raising the Exchequer grant on these from a meagre twenty to fifty per cent'.[138] Approval was expressed at the TUC for Trevelyan's efforts to ease the recent restraints on educational expenditure but by the time Congress met in September insufficient time had passed for much immediate improvement to have become apparent and, as most of Trevelyan's legislation was permissive, local authorities could decide whether or not they would act upon them. Hence A.W. Tapp pronounced to delegates that 'in very few places are maintenance grants given, and where they are they are not adequate to meet the expenses involved'.[139]

Even the marginal improvements effected by Trevelyan disappeared under Eustace Percy's reign as President of the Board of Education. Mr Titrington's claims in a GCTUC Deputation to the President that 'children ought to be enabled to have any education from which they would benefit but in the present conditions of the working classes this would necessitate maintenance allowances'[140] brought no response or promise of concessions from Percy. As for requests from Mr. Hallam gradually to make secondary education free, the President made it clear that expenditure on education would largely be restricted to basic requirements. 'The freeing of secondary education' Percy explained, 'would place a burden of £600,000 a year on the rates alone and would therefore prevent other developments.'[141]

At the end of the first quarter of the twentieth century a book entitled *Social Progress and Educational Waste* and written by Kenneth Lindsay, set out to describe how far the policy of a competitive educational ladder for secondary education had been successful. Lindsay wrote:

> Perhaps two figures will give perspective to the whole problem and point to the heart of the matter. First, of the 550,000 children who leave elementary school each year, 9.5 per cent of an age group proceed to secondary schools, one third exempt from fees and two thirds fee-paying, while 1 per cent reach the university. Secondly, of 2,800,000 adolescents in England and Wales, 80 per cent are not in full-time attendance at any school.[142]

He went on to give evidence to show that '... at least fifty per cent of the pupils in elementary schools can profit by some form of post-primary education up to the age of sixteen....'.[143]

In 1925 pleas for the abolition of secondary school fees were likely to be met with the answer that the nation could not afford it. Only the previous year H.A.L. Fisher had told the House of Commons that '... if we look facts in the face and take account of the industrial circumstances of our age and our country as they are, we are driven to the conclusion that owing to poverty and industrial pressure the great mass of children must go out into industry after elementary schooling is over....'.[144] Fisher's outspoken views must have surprised those trade unionists who believed he was going to champion the cause of working class education back in 1917. It would be difficult now to separate the Liberal ex-President of the Board of Education from the bulk of Conservatives who also opposed secondary education for all and were against the principle of free secondary education; 'Behind all this kind of thinking was the assumption that a parent's determination to pay for his child's education was a crucial test of his desire to have it.'[145] It was difficult for trade unionists to convince a Government which held such views that there was anything unfair about the exclusion of approximately ninety per cent of elementary school children from the opportunity of a secondary school education. This was in spite of an earlier Board of Education Report in 1920 which recommended free secondary education as soon as possible.[146] For experienced trade unionists, however, the knowledge that they had been forced to fight for free elementary education was enough to inform them that a similar struggle would be required before secondary education was also made free. In the meantime, the majority of children in England and Wales were denied anything more than a basic elementary education.

Notes

1 TUC Report 1910, p. 176. J. Cuthbertson of the Metal Workers told delegates that 'as for Universities, we may as well consider them out of the question altogether so far as the workers are concerned'.
2 SUTHERLAND, G. *op. cit.*, p. 163.
3 SILVER, H. *English Education and the Radicals 1780–1850*, p. 82.
4 *Beehive*, 26.3.1870.
5 SUTHERLAND, G. *op. cit.*, p. 168.
6 A motion proposed by A. Herbert MP and seconded by Morrison MP at a June meeting of the NEL in 1870 read: 'That no scheme of national education can be regarded as a settlement of the question which does not include provision for the general and immediate establishment of elected school boards, for compulsory attendance of children at school, for free admission...'. *The Beehive*, 18.6.1870.
7 RUBINSTEIN, D. *op. cit.*, p. 87.
8 SUTHERLAND, G. *op. cit.*, p. 171.
9 *Ibid.*
10 SIMON, B. *op. cit.*, Vol. 2, p. 127.
11 WARD, L.O. *An Investigation into the Educational Ideas and Contribution of the British Political Parties 1870–1918*, Ph.D (London) 1970, p. 291.
12 SUTHERLAND, G. *op. cit.*, p. 175.
13 *Ibid.*, p. 170.
14 Cross Commission 1888, *op. cit.*, Vol. 17, para. 400.
15 *Ibid.*, para. 380.
16 WARD, L.O., 'Joseph Chamberlain and the denominational schools question' *Journal of Educational Administration and History*, Vol. V, No. 2, July 1973, pp. 21–22.
17 *Justice*, 8.8.1885.
18 KENT, W. *John Burns: Labour's Lost Leader*, p. 20.
19 BROWN, R. M.Sc. 1966, *op. cit.*, p. 95.
20 TUC Report 1885, p. 19.
21 *Ibid.*, p. 44.
22 International TUC Report by Adolphe Smith – TUC Report 1886, p. 21.
23 *Ibid.*, p. 22.
24 *Ibid.*, p. 46.
25 *Ibid.*, p. 47. Further support was provided in January 1888 by the publication of T.P. O'Connor's *The Star*, produced by the London Workers' paper. It included free education in its list of demanded reforms. WARD, L.O., Ph.D. 1970, *op. cit.*, p. 299.
26 A letter to the *Beehive* from Robert Applegarth concerning free education asked: 'By what process those who venture the opinion have arrived at the conclusion that free education would "degrade" the working classes I cannot imagine. Is it because the middle class, who have had a monopoly of free education (afforded by the enormous and mis-used endowments), have been degraded thereby?'. *The Beehive*, 26.3.1870. The Sub-Committee of the Birmingham Trades Council set up in December 1871 to report on Education had observed that it '... would not consider the adoptions of a totally free system of education any degradation, but would on the other hand view it as a wise distribution of a small proportion of the heavy taxation their toil is producing'. McCANN, W.P. *Trade Unionist, Co-operative and Socialist Organisations in Relation to Popular Education 1870–1902*, Ph.D. (Manchester) 1960, p. 493.
27 RUBINSTEIN, D. *op. cit.*, p. 84.
28 That some parents found it difficult to raise the necessary fees was confirmed when

'... a Board Inspector reported a sharp drop in attendance at a Tower Hamlets school when the fee was raised from one penny to two pence'. RUBINSTEIN, D. *op. cit.*, p. 85.

29 SUTHERLAND, G. *op. cit.*, p. 85.

30 RUBINSTEIN, D. *op. cit.*, p. 87.

31 *Ibid.*, p. 88.

32 The dithering of Salisbury and the various arguments within Cabinet over the design of the Bill to introduce free education are fully explained in SUTHERLAND, G. *op. cit.*, Chapter 10.

33 TUC Report 1891, p. 30.

34 Even among the wave of apparently spontaneous strikes by schoolchildren in October 1889 in a number of towns including London, Liverpool, Leeds Cardiff, Edinburgh and Hull, in the latter at least, one of the demands of the pupils was for 'free education'. BROWN, R., M.Sc. (Hull) *op. cit.*, p. 137.

35 BATHER, L. *A History of Manchester and Salford Trades Council*, Ph.D. (Manchester) 1956, p. 139.

36 *Justice*, 20.6.1896.

37 ELLIS, A.C.O. *British Journal of Educational Studies*, 1973, *op. cit.*, p. 323.

38 Congress education resolutions from 1903 to 1909 inclusively, made reference to fees in 'primary' or 'elementary' schools, as typified by one in 1907, Clause 4 of which read: 'A national system of education under full popular control, free and secular from the primary school to the university.'. TUC Report 1907, p. 186.

39 *Hansard*, 1918, Vol. 108, Col. 903.

40 DEAN, D.W. *The Journal of Contemporary History*, 1971, *op. cit.*, p. 159.

41 For full details of the development of these schools see ELLIOT, B. 'School Boards and Industrial Schools: a neglected aspect of the 1870 Education Act' *History of Education Bulletin*, No. 22, August 1978.

42 TUC Report 1910, p. 166.

43 *Ibid.*, p. 167.

44 PCTUC Mins., 16.2.1911.

45 BANKS, O. *Parity and Prestige in English Secondary Education*, p. 67.

46 Nothing illustrates the precariousness of manual employment better than Robert Tressell's (that is Robert Noonan) classic novel concerning the building trade in Edwardian Hastings, entitled *The Ragged Trousered Philanthropists*.

47 Disrespect for clerical work among many manual workers probably arose from two sources: one was a feeling that such work was not very 'manly' but a second was because such office work was often in close physical proximity to that of the 'boss' which meant that such workers were often seen to be with the employer rather than with the workers in an industrial dispute. To be fair it took great courage for a small group of office workers to stand up against an employer whereas for a factory work force of several hundred both unity and numbers help to maintain solidarity. It is true that many office workers in quite lowly positions did have illusions about their status, and it might well be argued that they were a prime example of 'false class consciousness' but there were notable exceptions; both teachers and railway clerks were organized into trade unions at an early date (1870 and 1897 respectively) and whilst the latter did not join in the rail strikes of 1911 and 1919 more than half supported the NUR and ASLEF in the 1926 General Strike.

48 BANKS, O. *op. cit.*, p. 62.

49 For details of the misappropriation of funds in many public schools see BAMFORD, T.W. *The Rise of the Public Schools*, Chaps. 7 & 8. For examples of how local boys were gradually excluded from numerous public schools (Harrow, Rugby, Repton, Oundle etc.) see SIMON, B. Vol. 2, *op. cit.*, Ch. 3.

50 LAWSON, J. and SILVER, H. *op. cit.*, p. 304.

51 McCANN, W.P. *British Journal of Educational Studies*, 1970, *op. cit.*, p. 140.

52 *Beehive*, 26.3.1870.
53 WARD, L.O. Ph.D. 1970, *op. cit.*, p. 292.
54 TUC Report, 1881.
55 TUC Report, 1885, p. 19.
56 Hull Trades and Labour Council recorded that they had submitted the circular to candidates standing at the General Election. BROWN, R. M.Sc. *op. cit.*, p. 95.
57 BATHER, L. Ph.D. 1956, *op. cit.*, p. 125.
58 The Cross Commission 1888, *op. cit.*, Vol. 17, para. 382.
59 *Ibid.*
60 *Report of the Royal Commission on Secondary Education*, (Bryce Report) 1895, Vol. V, p. 495.
61 *Ibid.*, Vol. I, pp. 307–309.
62 For details of the manner in which the Commissioners' recommendations and actions led to the end of free education in many schools over the years see SIMON, B. Vol. II, *op. cit.*, pp. 324–336.
63 Bryce Report 1895, *op. cit.*, Vol. V, p. 495.
64 TUC Report 1904, p. 120.
65 TUC Report 1905, p. 142.
66 TUC Report 1906, p. 175 and TUC Report 1907, p. 189.
67 Gasworkers Biennial Congress Report 1906, p. 44.
68 TUC Report 1906, p. 176.
69 TUC Report 1909, p. 193.
70 *Ibid.*
71 *Ibid.*
72 BARKER, R.S. *The Educational Policies of the Labour Party 1900–61*, Ph.D. (Lond.) 1968, p. 300.
73 PCTUC Deputation to the Board of Education Mins., 16.3.1911.
74 A. Mansbridge of the Workers Educational Association wrote to the PCTUC supporting their demands for a Royal Commission to Inquire into Endowments. PCTUC Mins., 18.7.1911.
75 PCTUC Deputation to the Board of Education Mins., 15.2.1912.
76 PCTUC Deputation to the Board of Education. Mins., 12.2.1914.
77 It was because the TUC failed to provide staff to equip the PC with all kinds of vital information that, according to the Webbs, '... the Fabian Society started in 1912 the Fabian Research Department to investigate and supply information...' WEBB, S. and WEBB, B., *The History of Trade Unionism 1666–1920*, Christmas 1919 ed., p. 571. It was later to become the Labour Research Department.
78 PCTUC Deputation to the Board of Education. Mins., 12.3.1919.
79 *Ibid.*
80 PCTUC Deputation to the Board of Education. Mins., 16.3.1911.
81 *Ibid.*
82 PCTUC Deputation to the Board of Education. Mins., 5.2.1912.
83 *Ibid.*
84 Clause 5: 'That in the welfare of the State, the finances of endowed public institutions be investigated, with a view to reform and bringing the government of public schools and universities under democratic control.' TUC Report 1915, p. 413.
85 PCTUC Deputation to the Board of Education. Mins., 5.2.1912.
86 PCTUC Deputation to the Board of Education. Mins., 12.2.1914.
87 PCTUC Deputation to the Board of Education. Mins., 12.3.1919.
88 TUC Report 1920, p. 368.
89 The last time the endowment question was raised at the TUC during the period under discussion was in 1922 when it was suggested that a Committee of Inquiry go into the details of the legacies and bequests being absorbed by the creation of an

increased number of scholarships and bursaries at the leading schools. TUC Report 1922, p. 229.

90 The financing of schools was highly complex, some would say irrational due to the gradual evolvement of the system. For a contemporary pamphlet exposing the chaos at the turn of the century, see YOXALL, J.H. (Gen. Sec. NUT) *The Coming Education Bill*, (1901), pp. 5–6.

91 ANDREWS, L. *op. cit.*, p. 37.

92 TUC Report 1897, p. 50.

93 *Ibid.*

94 TUC Report 1905, p. 142.

95 TUC Education Bill 1906, Clause 4.

96 TUC Report 1908, p. 180.

97 TUC Report 1918, p. 305.

98 BRENNAN, F.T. 'Educational engineering with the Webbs' in *History of Education*, 1 (2) June 1972, p. 181.

99 TUC Report 1904, p. 69.

100 TUC Circular (August) 1900. See Appendix IV.

101 TUC Report 1901, p. 72.

102 BERNBAUM, G. *Social Change and the Schools 1918–44*, p. 11.

103 PCTUC Deputation to the Board of Education. Mins., 16.3.1911.

104 TUC Report 1907, p. 187.

105 TUC Report 1920, p. 363.

106 PCTUC Deputation to the Board of Education. Mins., 2.3.1909.

107 Runciman informed the Chairman of the PCTUC that he had issued regulations ordering that any scholarship given by a co-op body or similar society should be made additional to the free places given by the local authority. PCTUC Mins., 19.6.1909.

108 TUC Report 1909, p. 71

109 The twenty-five per cent free places were restored again immediately following 1918, only to be cut back once more in 1920. This brought adverse comments again from A.W. Tapp at Congress in the Autumn (TUC Report 1920, p. 363) and protests the following Spring when the PCTUC visited H.A.L. Fisher at the Board of Education. E.L. Poulton, Chairman of the PCTUC Deputation informed the President: 'It was stated, Sir, at the Congress that the twenty-five per cent free places for the children had unfortunately, in some instances, been reduced to twelve and a half per cent. Now we look upon the twenty-five per cent as being quite inadequate, and we are very disappointed that that should have been further reduced'. Fisher did not deny this had happened but suggested that such issues were a matter for local authorities. He was satisfied with the twelve and a half per cent increase in the total number of free places in secondary schools within the last year and claimed that 'there was no country in Europe which had a better record in this respect'.
PCTUC Deputation to the Board of Education. Mins., 10.2.1921.

110 TUC Report 1917, p. 354.

111 For a detailed study of the relationships between urban catchment areas and related schools see MARSDEN, W.E. 'Urban education and social geography' in REEDER, D. (Ed) *Urban Education in the 19th Century*.

112 BERNBAUM, G. *op. cit.*, pp. 12–13. On p. 12 details of various London boroughs and their provision of secondary school places is given showing a correlation between number of places and prosperity of borough.

113 PCTUC Deputation to the Board of Education. Mins., 15.2.1912.

114 FBI Deputation to the Board of Education. Mins., 6.2.1918.

115 PCTUC Deputation to the Board of Education. Mins., 16.3.1911 and 15.2.1912.

116 A.W. Tapp: 'At the present time, though, there are a large number of children in

the secondary schools who are doing elementary work simply because their parents are wealthy enough to pay the fees. These children should be sent out of these schools to make room for children of the industrial classes who would benefit by secondary education.' TUC Report 1921, p. 370. '... unfortunately in our secondary schools today there are many children, juniors, doing elementary work which they might have been doing in the elementary schools, but are doing in secondary schools owing to their parents being better off. Consequently many bright children cannot get into the secondary schools because their parents are unable to pay their fees.' TUC Report 1922, p. 414.

117 PCTUC Deputation to the Board of Education. Mins., 16.3.1911.
118 BANKS, O. *op. cit.*, p. 69.
119 TAWNEY, R.H. *Secondary Education for All*, p. 27.
120 MEACHAM, S. *op. cit.*, p. 174.
121 See JACKSON, B. and MARSDEN, D. *Education and the Working Class*, Routledge and Kegan Paul (1962) A classic study of working class children from Huddersfield born in the early 1930s who attended grammar schools in the 1940s. The problems of such children in adjusting to middle class values are vividly illustrated and the penalties of failing to do so are revealed in their final academic results at school.
122 TUC Report 1922, p. 412.
123 PCTUC Deputation to the Board of Education. Mins., 2.3.1909.
124 *Ibid.*
125 In 1906 TUC Education Policy included a clause stating: 'That the cost of education shall be met by grants from the Imperial Exchequer and by the restoration of misappropriated endowments.' Similar demands were incorporated into the TUC Education Bill of that year. Such a statement seemed to imply that all education costs should be met by the State with some help from remaining educational endowments. In 1919 W. Thorne asked H.A.L. Fisher 'That not less than seventy-five per cent of the total average expenditure of local authorities upon education be defrayed from the National Exchequer' (PCTUC Deputation to Board of Education. Mins., 12.3.1919). This demand was contained in the Education policy of the TUC (Clause 7), moved by C.T. Cramp of the NUR. TUC Report 1918, p. 304.
126 J. Gordon of the Tinplate Workers told Congress 'That the whole cost of education should be a national charge'. TUC Report 1905, p. 143.
127 TUC Report 1897, p. 50.
128 TUC Report 1903, p. 86.
129 TUC Report 1906, p. 175.
130 TUC Education Bill 1906, Clause 4 v. Appendix V.
131 TUC Report 1905, p. 142.
132 BARKER, R. *Education and Politics 1900–51*, p. 31.
133 The 'Bradford Charter', the programme launched by the Bradford Trades Council in October 1916 included a call for an increase in the number of maintenance grants being provided. The 'Charter' was adopted by both the ILP and Labour Party as their Education Programmes for 1917.
134 TUC Report 1920, p. 363.
135 PCTUC Deputation to the Board of Education. Mins., 10.2.1921.
136 SIMON, B. VOL. III, *op. cit.*, p. 40.
137 A concise description of the setbacks suffered by trade unionism during the 1920s is provided in HUTT, A. *The Post-War History of the British Working Class*, Ch. 3.
138 SIMON, B. Vol. III, *op cit.*, p. 82. For full details of Trevelyan's attempts to restore past cutbacks in education and to expand educational and related welfare provision see pp. 78–84.
139 TUC Report 1924, p. 421.
140 General Council Trades Union Congress Deputation to the Board of Education.

Mins., 25.5.25.
141 *Ibid.*
142 LINDSAY, K., *Social Progress and Educational Waste*, p. 7.
143 *Ibid.*
144 DEAN, D.W. M.Phil. 1968, *op. cit.*, p. 49.
145 DEAN D.W. 'Conservatism and the national education system 1922–40' *The Journal of Contemporary History*, 1971, p. 156.
146 *Report of the Departmental Committee on Scholarships and Free Places*, 1920. This Committee recommended the freeing of grant aided secondary schools 'at a fairly early date' once the present state of the national budget had improved.

Chapter 5

Physical Education, School Meals and Medical Care

From their own personal experiences many trade unionists knew of the poor circumstances in which large numbers of children were forced to live in the growing conurbations of nineteenth century Britain. Even the 'aristocrats of labour' separated from the poor by their higher earnings and place of work had some knowledge of the squalid neighbourhoods housing the Victorian urban poor. The middle classes, however, whilst knowing that there were both people and places best avoided, probably had no comprehension of the extent of such poverty or of its far reaching effects. The surveys of Booth and Rowntree have already been mentioned as providing a general picture of the problem; more specific studies relating to children, in particular, provided the necessary details for the Government at least to be made more aware of the nature of child poverty, its consequences for the individual and its overall effect upon the nation.

Within just over twenty years of 1883, five studies covering the physical and mental health of children were published. Between them they built up a picture of ill-health among urban children. One group gravely concerned about such reports were those responsible for recruiting young men to the armed services needed to expand and defend a large empire. This theme will be returned to again later but first a few extracts and conclusions from the reports should be considered to illustrate the conditions, confronting many children, to which the Labour movement frequently attempted to draw attention. The Report of the Committee of the British Association published in 1883 showed a clear relationship between social class and standards of health:

> The average stature, for example, of boys between the ages of eleven and twelve at public schools was 54.98 inches, while of boys of the same age at industrial schools it was only 50.02 inches. There was thus a difference of 5 inches in the average stature of boys belonging to the two extreme classes shown.[1]

Similar correlations were to be found in subsequent reports.

A few years later Dr. Francis Warner carried out an enquiry (1888–91) concerning the physical and mental defects of children in 106 London schools and this was followed by another study (1892–94) of children in various areas outside London.[2] A greater proportion of boys were shown to be mentally or physically defective than girls and it was found that children of Jewish immigrants were less likely to be 'dull' or suffering from low nutrition, than 'English' children who in turn were better placed than children of Irish immigrants. It was stated that 'taking the average condition of the day schools and comparing with it the children of upper grade with those of poorer classes, there is a preponderance in favour of the lower class as less dull or defective'.[3] It was the economic message which was to prove most effective in the long run with Governments:

> The State becomes heavily burdened by the defectively made portion of the population which probably tends to accumulate under extensive emigration, leaving with us the weak, tending to pauperism, starvation, vagrancy and crime ... the field for recruiting the services is also limited ... it must be remembered that these feebly-gifted children are confined to no social class.[4]

Whilst 'dullness' might have been considered to be spread fairly evenly among the social classes (although it is doubtful whether the methods of assessment used at the time would have been considered valid in the second half of the twentieth century), surveys dealing with physical health consistently showed positive links between income, living conditions, nutrition and health. In 1904 the Committee on Physical Deterioration reinforced the findings of the British Association published a generation earlier: 'Physical infirmity' declared Dr. R.J. Collie, one of the medical staff of the late LSB, 'is practically confined to the poorest and lowest strata of the population, whose children are improperly and insufficiently fed and inadequately housed....'[5] The relationship between social class and health appeared time and time again. Infant mortality rates in Glasgow averaged 141 per 1000 births but within the city varied from 63 to 217 per 1,000. In London also, where the proportion of persons living in one or two roomed tenements exceeded thirty-five per cent infant mortality rates reached 223 per 1,000 births, whilst figures for the industrial towns of Preston were 236, Burnley 210, Blackburn 200 and Sheffield 201.[6] It was confirmed that whilst death rates in general had fallen in the last twenty-five years infant mortality rates had not.

The prime reason for physical deterioration given by Dr. Eichholz in the Report was 'food ... the point about which turns the whole problem of degeneracy'.[7] Elaborating further Dr. Eichholz pointed to three aspects of the food problem; the lack of it, the irregularity of meals and the non-suitability of much of the food. In a special investigation he had made of Johanna Street Board School, Lambeth, a school in 'a very bad district', he considered that 'ninety per cent of the children are unable, by reason of their physical condition, to attend to their work in a proper way, while thirty-three per cent during six months of the year, from October to March, require feeding'.[8] The

Report also echoed some of the findings concerning recruitment to the armed services of the earlier 1895 Report:

> ... of 14,848 candidates who had passed the recruiters as satisfying the standards of height and chest measurements, and were subsequently medically examined in Royal Marine Recruiting Districts in 1902–03, 25.7% were rejected, as against 23.1%, for the Army, and in three years, 1900–03, of 21,916 examined in London alone, 32.1% were rejected.[9]

The final study which helped to complete the picture of ill-health among children was the Report on Medical Inspection and Feeding of School children published in 1905.[10] This Report once more underlined the correlation between social class, height and weight but instead of the two rather extreme examples provided by the British Association in 1883, it gave a detailed study of the various strata found among working class children whose parents ranged from skilled artisans, clerks and shopkeepers to unskilled labourers. Six elementary schools in Salford were graded according to location and occupation of parents and the average height and weight of various age groups recorded. Taking just the example of eight year old boys the average differences in height and weight between the 'best' and 'worst' districts were 2.7 inches and 3.5lb respectively.[11]

The series of studies carried out between 1878 and 1905 which have been considered were hardly needed to convince members of the Labour movement as to the conditions prevailing among the children of the poor. Most teachers serving in schools surrounded by low income areas were also familiar with the plight of undernourished children. The reports did, however, provide much useful evidence to support trade union demands for the introduction of welfare services for children and also to bring home to many who had no conception of the problem some measure of the extent to which physical defects were to be found among children of poor parents.

Without wishing to exaggerate the virtues of leading trade unionists it can be shown that in the context of children's welfare they argued consistently for a variety of services which would improve the health and, consequently, the quality of life of many poor children. By contrast, at least in the early years, some part of the Government's provision of welfare services was related to the evidence concerning the poor health of many potential recruits to the army for both the Boer War[12] and First World War.[13] Military considerations were initially a factor in the inclusion of army drill in the curriculum following the 1870 Education Act and in the decision to pay grant, in 1871, for '... attendance at drill under a competent instructor for not more than two hours per week and twenty weeks in the year'.[14] The latter action may well have been influenced by the Franco Prussian War and there was a steady increase in the number of schools offering drill in the curriculum.[15] At the same time it must be said that the need to control large numbers of children often lacking in self discipline and confined to the restrictive boundaries of school buildings also seemed to be met initially by drill. Even picking up pencils and opening books was sometimes carried out in response to numbered commands.[16]

Initially, girls took part in drill but, following upon the invitation of the London School Board to Miss Lofving from Sweden in 1878, girls' physical education rapidly adopted the 'Swedish system' although attempts to get boys to follow this method in 1882 were resisted.[17] Girls were not considered as potential for the armed services; boys were and, for them, in addition to drill with broom handles or even sometimes dummy rifles and bayonets, military manoeuvres were also practised.[18] F.H. Spencer, later to become a school inspector, wrote in detail of the drill lessons he experienced as a pupil teacher in Swindon in 1885:

> ... we formed fours and moved to the right in fours.... As we wheeled into line, each company was as straight as a wheel spoke. Within a few weeks we were an armed force. The arms were broomsticks each with a red pennon; and every boy had bought his own, though pence, God knows, were scarce enough. It was a triumph of morale.... It explains the rise of Napoleon Bonaparte and Adolph Hilter. Within a few months we had got past forming squares in the playground and preparing to receive cavalry; we had attained proficiency in bayonet exercises and were skirmishing in open order ... it was all crude, and unsuitable, calculated no doubt to arouse a military spirit....[19]

Military drill remained a part of the school curriculum but, in 1894, schools were 'notified that higher grants for discipline would not be paid after August 1895 to a school not providing for the teaching of the Swedish system'.[20]

Yet, in 1902, the Board of Education, in consultation with the War Office, produced a Model Course of Physical Training based entirely upon military drill as outlined in a War Office publication entitled 'Infantry Training'. Two years later the Committee on Physical Deterioration recommended the payment of grants from the National Exchequer to '... all clubs[21] and cadet corps in which physical or quasi-military training, as an approved scheme, is conducted subject to inspection'[22] and in 1906 the Report of the Consultative Committee upon Questions affecting Higher Elementary Schools stated that 'physical exercises and drill are taken for granted ... where possible, rifle shooting should be encouraged'.[23] As might be expected, there was a call for more cadet training during the First World War: R.B. Haldane, for example, sought to develop a national system of Boy Scouts in elementary schools, cadet corps in secondary schools and OTC units in the universities.[24] In fact the Board of Education rejected the idea. The militarists had lost their influence over schools during the Edwardian era but how far this was due to the opposition of the labour movement in general and physical educationists in particular is not easy to estimate.

The Labour movement favoured physical exercise but firmly rejected military drill.[25] At the TUC in 1879 Mr. Bells 'drew attention to the spread of military instruction in schools'[26] and, in 1885, Mr. Morrison moved a resolution at Congress opposing the manner in which military drill, originally introduced for its physical advantages as had been claimed,

> . . . is now being followed up by the formation of cadet corps, the boys comprising which are to be dressed as soldiers and supplied with rifles by the War Office . . . a cunningly devised scheme by which the military authorities and a number of school boards have been step by step preparing the way for the pernicious continental system of conscription.[27]

Congress supported the resolution which argued that schools should be restricted to the task of developing '. . . the intellectual and moral faculties of children committed to their care'. John Burns pursued the issue in the House of Commons claiming that military drill, judging by his experience of army reservists within the Dock Demonstrations of 1889, did not encourage obedience or discipline. He recommended cricket, a game he was fond of as both participant and spectator, to develop the physique of school children.[28]

The NUT objected to the Board of Education's recommendations of 1902 for two reasons. They opposed the militarist flavour of army drill and also the consequences of the programme; namely, that teachers should themselves be put through drill courses by NCOs so that in turn they might teach the children. This had resulted in 'the pitiful spectacle in fields near big towns of school mistresses of fifty and sixty years of age, being compelled to undergo drill by a sergeant instructor'.[29] The ILP were strong opponents of military training in schools and Keir Hardie protested in Parliament that 'the churches and the schools were being used as recruiting agencies for popularizing the Army and familiarizing the youth of the country with military ideas and drills'.[30] By the year 1917, when H.A.L. Fisher was developing his Education Bill, the tragic results of the War in terms of human casualties were familiar to all and a conference called by the WEA and attended by representatives from the Labour Party, co-operative organizations, trades councils, individual unions and the PCTUC recommended the exclusion of military style training from the continuation schools outlined in H.A.L. Fisher's proposals. Yet when Mr. Whitehouse, a Liberal MP, attempted to amend the Bill in Parliament along these lines in May 1918, five Labour MPs, Barnes, Bruce, J.R. Clynes, Parker and Roberts joined with H.A.L. Fisher and successfully rejected the amendment.[31]

The NUR protested about the inclusion of military training at their 1918 AGM[32] and the Labour Party in the same month declared that their policy included 'the prevention of physical training in schools being of a military bias'.[33] The TUC were still protesting about the matter in 1920, J. Houghton of the Scottish Union of Dockworkers claiming that it would allow 'the privileged classes [to get] hold of the minds of our children in order to give them military training'.[34] Within a short time the issue was irrelevant because proposed plans for continuation schools, with the sole exception of Rugby, fell victim to the 'Geddes Axe'.

The resistance of the TUC and other sections of the Labour movement to military drill did not mean that they were opposed to physical training in schools. On the contrary, from 1905 onwards the TUC was demanding 'that efficient physical training shall become a necessary feature of school life';[35] a demand which was to be incorporated within a growing welfare programme for schools and repeated frequently in later TUC resolutions.[36] In the physical training sphere alone demands for organized games, playing fields and school baths had been added by 1918.[37] If the Board seemed slow in providing the necessary facilities both W. Runciman and H.A.L. Fisher, when Presidents of the Board of Education, expressed agreement in principle to the TUC programme, in discussion with PCTUC deputations in 1911 and 1917 respectively. They agreed with the need for physical training and promised increases in the equipment necessary to include physical education in the curriculum of student teachers.

If the TUC were slower to demand physical education to improve the health of children than the Government were to include drill in schools, it was because the former did not believe that a lack of exercise was the primary cause of physical deterioration. After all, some children were performing physical work outside school hours which was more strenuous than any drill lesson. The Labour movement, like Dr. Eichholz in 1904, believed that lack of food was the major cause of physical defects in children. It was for this reason that they campaigned for, organized and contributed to various local schemes for feeding children long before the Government accepted that there was a need. The SDF and the ILP both called for at least one free meal per day in board schools. John Burns included the demand in his election address at Nottingham in 1885[38] whilst the ILP were instrumental in getting Bradford to be the first local authority to provide school meals.

Local voluntary schemes sprang up in many areas: in Southwark, Mrs. E.M. Burgwin, headmistress of Orange St. School, provided dinners using a voluntary scheme in the 1880s;[39] Worcester provided one penny dinners in 1885[40] which were free for poor children; whilst the Labour Church in Hull provided food free for poor children once per week in 1894.[41] On a larger scale the London School Dinner Fund was set up in 1889 to try to cope with the problems of hordes of hungry children in the metropolis. There was no evidence to suggest that the Government had any grasp of the extent hunger was widespread among children. Even the Minority Cross Report seemed more worried about the possible undermining of 'self help' if the Government took measures to feed poor children and concluded that '. . . seeing the dangers of collective action and its certain indirect evils, we make no recommendations on this subject'.[42]

This cautious conservative view was not shared by *Justice* which launched a scathing attack on the officialdom which failed to respond in a humanitarian manner to the problems facing poor children:

A member of the LSB points out that a sum of £38,959 was spent by it last year in enforcing the laws for compulsory attendance. If this sum were applied towards the provision of free meals it would serve the double purpose of attracting attendance where now it must be compelled and of helping to build up a healthy instead of a stunted and starved population. As a matter of fact it would be better to rear up a nation of uneducated barbarians, provided they were tolerably healthy, than a nation of hospital patients possessed with a thorough knowledge of the 3 Rs.... We ought to take our rulers by the scruff and shake this miserable concession out of them....[43]

Justice suggested that the better attendance record of Paris (ninety-one per cent) compared with London (seventy-eight per cent) was related to the fact that free meals were provided for Parisian children.

Pressure from the Labour movement for free meals increased during the 1890s. The TUC in 1897 called upon Parliament to '... empower school boards to provide food for the many thousands of starving and underfed children who are to be found in the people's schools throughout the country'.[44] Mass meetings organized or supported by the Labour movement frequently passed resolutions supporting the provision of breakfast, a mid-day meal or both.[45] Hence a conference in Manchester supported by the Trades Council, ILP and ASE drew up a programme including free breakfasts for children in 1894 and two years later a mass meeting was held in Trafalgar Square, strongly supported by *Justice* which wrote an article the previous day claiming that:

Evidence of the poverty of parents can be gathered independent of Socialist sources. We printed in this paper (February 22nd) a memorial forwarded to the London School Board which showed that in Southwark one committee alone supported 150,355 dinners and 28,780 breakfasts, all free ... the National Food Supply Association supplied no less than 255,000 dinners ... and the London Schools Dinner Association supplied over 632,000 meals last year... Everyone is conscious that in certain areas of London, miles in extent ... the children are being murdered that capitalism and its profitmongers may thrive.[46]

All the voluntary meals organizations were limited in their ability to cope with the demand for want of funds. Trade unionists favoured free or cheap school meals because so many knew for themselves what it was like to be hungry as a child.

Pressure, through meetings and conferences, was maintained by the Labour movement. Keir Hardie tried to get a clause, authorizing free meals, inserted into the 1902 Education Bill but failed.[47] This failure of the 1902 Education Bill to consider the physical welfare of children brought further criticism from *Justice* which argued that 'a system of intellectual training is impossible if it is not based on a sound physical constitution, the product of good food, plenty of exercise, fresh air and escape from the foetid slums and fever-stricken hovels to which so many thousands are condemned'.[48] At the 1904 TUC the President referred to the findings of the Committee on Physical Deterioration which had recommended local authorities to provide meals for necessitous children but this was a matter of preaching to the converted.[49] The major task was to convince Parliament where all the familiar arguments about national welfare programmes undermining parental responsibility could be heard, a view to which Keir Hardie was quick to respond in 1905:

> As to the argument of parental responsibility, he ventured to say that the children of honourable Members on both sides of the House were sent to boarding schools where meals and accommodation were provided for them and the home life of the families broken up for six or seven months of the year. The provision of school meals for which the parents would pay when able would no more interfere with parental responsibility and family ties than did the provision for honourable Members' families at boarding schools.[50]

Sir George Bartley told Keir Hardie that the children's circumstances were due to the habits of their parents, such as drinking and gambling, so why should these habits be encouraged by rate payers?[51]

By this time, however, many of those still unfamiliar with the studies of Booth and Rowntree had digested the contents of the 1904 Report on Physical Deterioration and a Bill with severe limitations was passed in 1905 to provide some measure of support for the provision of school meals. This was followed by the Education (Provision of Meals) Act of 1906, a distinct improvement on its forerunner which had led some parents to believe that if they accepted free meals for the children the father might be disenfranchised. Even so the Act was typical of so much welfare legislation in that it incorporated the doubts and fears of the middle classes who were anxious that only the very poorest should receive free or cheap meals.

Hence the Act was permissive; even where local authorities agreed to introduce a scheme the regulations varied from one area to another. This led Thorne in 1912 to tell Pease at the Board of Education 'it is no answer to say that LEAs may feed the children; it is the duty of the Government to say they must feed them'.[52] Some authorities had investigators checking men's wages with employers; others left it to teachers to decide who should qualify for such meals which meant that the fate of some children might be decided by the attitude of the teacher towards school meals. It is doubtful whether administrators ever realized the humiliation and indignity they forced upon so many working class families in their quest to ensure that only those who were willing publicly to own up to their poverty should receive benefits for their children:

> The procedures outlined made good sense to middle class administrators, anxious to keep poor children from starving yet responsible for the level of the rates. But the regulations demanding a willingness to

open one's life to others and an ability to master 'rational', 'standard' language and rhythms of bureaucracy, undoubtedly deterred many respectable mothers from applying. What they feared most was the stigma attached to participation in such a programme.[53]

It would be fair to say that the Labour movement had provided the main driving force in the country to provide school meals; indeed it was the major triumph of the Parliamentary Labour Party.[54] After this Labour and many Liberal MPs worked hard to extend the provisions of the Act, '. . . introducing bills in every year but one up until the outbreak of war in 1914'.[55] At the TUC the early demands for a mid-day meal had been extended by 1912 to include provision during the holiday period as well. These wider demands were stimulated by the knowledge gained from a study in Lancashire which showed that when children were weighed before and after the Summer vacation many were found to have lost 3 – 4lb.[56] Bradford chose to finance such a system from the profits of the Gasworks but in south West Ham where W. Thorne was a councillor, provision of meals outside school time was declared illegal and councillors provided with the bill. W. Thorne told J.A. Pease, President of the Board of Education that,

> In consequence of the extraordinary position which we have taken up in South West Ham I have a piece of blue paper hanging over my head for, I think it is, a sum of £245. That is because we took it upon ourselves to feed the children between the Friday night and Monday morning. But I can assure you I have no intention of paying it, and I do not think any of my colleagues have. . . .[57]

After the First World War demand for school meals increased rapidly, until in 1922 under the Geddes cutbacks it was decided to reduce the grant to local authorities from £1,030,000 to £300,000 in spite of the protests of Dr. Addison, the former Minister of Health.[58] In May 1922 the Board of Education issued Circular 1261 informing local authorities that:

> The unprecedented expansion of the number of free meals provided by LEAs under the Provision of Meals Act during 1921–22 has made it necessary for the Board to consider carefully the arrangements made by Authorities for the administration of the Acts.[59]

The guidelines given by the President of the Board of Education in the House of Commons (4.4.1922) were reproduced in which he had claimed '. . . it is impossible to acquiesce in a continuance of the present arrangement, under which, in abnormal periods, a considerable part of the burden of poor relief may be thrown on the education rate and the Vote of the Board of Education'.[60] The abnormal periods referred to were the coal stoppages of 1912–13 and 1921–22 and the first winter of the War. Local authorities were then informed of the decision to limit the grant for such purposes during 1922–23 to £300,000.

The Board of Education informed local authorities in the Circular that it sympathized with the 'valuable and disinterested service given to this work by many Authorities and by large numbers of their officers and teachers, especially in times of national or local emergency and distress' but it was made clear that such action would not receive the support of the Board in future. Just as the figures, to show how the number of school meals provided had doubled between 1919–20 and 1920–21, were included in Appendix A of the Circular so, too, was a list of local authorities which had never provided school meals at all since the 1906 Education Act.[61] There were five County Boroughs, fifty-six Non-County Boroughs, thirty Counties and seven Urban Districts: areas in general to be found in the Home Counties, East Anglia, the West Country and West Wales. They were largely under Conservative control.

Obviously local authorities did not respond to the Board of Education as expected for, in July 1922, Circular 1273 was dispatched stating that:

> Although estimates have not been submitted by all Authorities it is clear that the sum of £300,000 will be exceeded by £138,000.... Unless therefore Authorities themselves take the initiative and further revise their estimates, the Board will be under the necessity of disallowing for the calculation of grant so much of the estimated expenditure of Authorities as is necessary to bring the total expenditure ... within the £300,000.[62]

The Board of Education circulars were of great importance to trade unionists because, apart from the humanitarian arguments long used to provide school meals for children, there was also a practical political issue at stake contained within the phrase 'abnormal periods' which had been used by the Board of Education, for two out of the three periods so described related to industrial disputes. Back in 1906, when arguing for school meals provision, Will Thorne had told the Gasworkers' Conference:

> If the organized workers who were out on strike were perfectly sure that their children are getting plenty of food, it would give them more energy and encouragement to fight on until they got what they were fighting for.[63]

Board of Education circulars had hinted that children whose parents were involved in industrial disputes should not receive free meals; in July 1922 the Scottish Education Department issued Circular 51 which was more explicit. It sought to '... free Education Authorities from many of the anxieties which they have had to face in times of general distress due to the existence of industrial disputes'. 'There will be universal agreement' the Circular went on to explain, 'that a parent cannot be, within the meaning of the first proviso of Section 6, 'unable by reason of poverty' to supply sufficient and proper food or clothing for his child if he voluntarily abstains from work.... It thus appears that the responsibility which remains with Education Authorities is virtually that of dealing with cases where the question of neglect arises.'[64]

At the Southport TUC in September delegates were quick to respond to a move which might have been inspired by a desire to balance the books of the Board of Education but which clearly had fundamental political overtones. J. Campbell of the NUR warned delegates of an 'important feature which the Labour movement should particularly note in relation to the children of men on strike'. He saw it as 'an indication that the Government, at the instigation of the Federation of British Industries, are exploring every avenue with a view to bludgeoning the workers back below the 1914 standard'.[65] Neil Maclean of the Workers Union and C.J. Ammon of the Post Office Workers were quick to support Campbell and warn delegates of the consequences for Labour of the Geddes cutbacks.

By setting cash limits the Government were able to dictate terms to local authorities, especially as the provision of meals was permissive. At the same time such measures would not affect the more prosperous parts of the country which had, in general, never provided meals. As Campbell commented bitterly upon the legislation:

> ... the feeding and clothing by the education authorities is to be remedial and not preventive. That is to say a child must be in actual ill-health before it can be fed. That is an instruction coming from people who have not known what it was to be hungry in their lives.[66]

The campaign to feed hungry children which had gained limited official blessing in 1906 was prevented from becoming a national system. Like many of the TUC's hopes this was still a generation away from fruition.

Just as the labour movement insisted on providing food for many poor children so they stressed the need to detect ill health as early as possible by medical inspection. Pioneering work in this field was carried out by Margaret MacMillan as an ILP member of the Bradford School Board and Dr. James Kerr appointed as school medical officer for London in 1902. Medical inspection was needed to show the authorities the extent of the problem. The lack of physical fitness in army recruits had become well known but many failed to realize that unfit recruits usually had a history of poor health going back to their childhood. At the same time it was necessary to detect carriers of infectious diseases, such as impetigo, in order to inform both parents and teachers so that treatment might be sought. The necessity for elementary hygiene to be understood by those often living in squalid housing was also seen as vital if ill health was to be prevented. There was a limit to the influence which might be brought to bear on parents, some of whom were ignorant or indifferent in such matters. Hence the attempts by the Labour movement to get the community to provide the necessary help through the school which the children attended.

The evidence of the Departmental Committee on Physical Deterioration provided the Labour movement with the necessary information to support their claims for welfare programmes in schools.[67] The Gasworkers Union put forward a detailed resolution at the 1905 TUC aimed at 'checking the evils revealed in the Committee's Report' and demanding that 'free medical advice and inspection be placed within the reach of all children', and that '... the Board of Education provide a statistical department charged with the collation and periodic publication of statistics relating to the health and mortality of school children'.[68] Speaking for the resolution Will Thorne claimed that 'a great number of convicts were better fed and housed than numbers of the working classes'.[69] The main points of the TUC resolution were incorporated into the TUC Education Bill of 1906, the last two clauses reading:

> Each education authority shall take steps to record the height, weight, and chest measurement of children attending elementary schools;
> Each education authority shall appoint a medical officer, or officers, whose duty it shall be to medically examine, and to treat such children as the teachers may consider in need of medical advice.[70]

The suggestion that the teacher should have the power of deciding which children should be medically examined made it clear that active trade unionists were well aware of the manner in which some working class children were at times neglected by their own parents. In such circumstances it was believed that the State had to take over the responsibility; as Benn Tillett suggested in the same year '... it is the duty of the State to look after the children's bodies, so that the healthy body shall contain a healthy mind'.[71]

The Government did take action in 1907 when the Education (Miscellaneous Provisions) Act was put before the House of Commons conceding the principle of the need to medically examine school children yet withholding the next obvious step, namely to treat them. This situation arose partly from the declared belief that it was up to the parents to see that their children received treatment once a medical officer had pointed out a defect in the child's health and also because it was felt that some private doctors might object to a possible loss of potential fees.[72] It was also believed that treatment would seriously increase the costs of any school medical service.[73] It was accepted that children of negligent parents who needed treatment would not get it. 'The children of such must generally continue to suffer.... Negligent parents are unfortunately common in many places but there is reason to hope that they will diminish as time goes on.'[74]

Active trade unionists could not accept such views partly because they were closer to the problem. As the 1907 Education Act was being debated the TUC was developing its education and welfare programme further. The core of demands from 1905 remained but growing emphasis was placed upon the eradication of poor living conditions. Realizing that rehousing in many areas would be a slow process, even if a Government was devoted to such a programme, the TUC once more focused attention on the school as an agent for reform. A new clause in the TUC Education Resolution now called for '... the establishment under every education authority of scientifically organized open-air recovery schools, the cost to be borne by the community as a whole and not in any part by charitable contributions'.[75] It was agreed that the only hope for many sick children, especially those suffering from 'consumption', was to avoid the polluted air of the town. This might be achieved at least during the day-time by bussing sick children to purpose built open-air schools on the outskirts of towns.[76]

In the 1911 PCTUC Deputation to the Board of Education, Will Thorne called for school clinics to be established to deal with sick children instead of sending them to hospitals; he pointed out that the only two school clinics in London relied upon charity. Ironically, in replying, W. Runciman, the President at the Board, quoted Bradford as an example of an authority which was providing a well organized medical service for school children; yet much of the Bradford programme was due to the work of ILP councillors who had often found their efforts to establish a comprehensive welfare programme opposed by councillors from the other political parties. The TUC were well aware of the virtues of the Bradford programme and wished to see them extended to other authorities because, as Thorne pointed out, inspections had shown 'an appalling amount of disease among school children'.[77] It was frustrating for trade unionists to know that insufficient funds were made available for child welfare when they learned from the International Congress on Consumption held at London in August 1911 that, with modern science, consumption could be eradicated in twenty years if the necessary facilities were provided.

The Board of Education also felt frustrated. Attacked by the TUC for their rate of progress in this field, the President of the Board believed that insufficient consideration was given to their achievements which had been accomplished at a time when public opinion seemed to be more in favour of spending on rearmament than on child welfare. By 1914, when the increasingly ambitious education programme of the TUC was put before the Board of Education. J.A. Pease as President expressed some annoyance with the PCTUC Deputation. He complained that Congress was passing resolutions which no longer applied.

> In the last two years the Government have given fifty per cent grants for medical inspection and treatment ... [he thought] ... it right that local people should also make contributions. If the TUC will not give the President credit for progress they could at least give themselves credit for the influence they have brought on the Government.[78]

Thorne interrupted the President to point out that they wanted 'adequate funds' from Central Government; fifty per cent was an improvement on the past but the ability of local authorities to raise the balance varied widely. Moreover, those which needed medical facilities the most were the very areas which were poorest in terms of income from local rates or even donations to private charities working in this field; a form of welfare always disliked by the Labour movement.

It has been shown that trade unionists wanted compulsory legislation to cope with neglectful parents yet unfortunately some of the systems established to help working class parents in general often worked to undermine their self-respect at the same time. The form filling 'abilities' required by the bureaucrats, the manner in which parents were sometimes kept waiting for hours for a five minute inspection of their child, the bus fares involved for a visit to the hospital and the subsequent loss of pay did not seem to be appreciated by many of those offering medical treatment. The attitude of some doctors and nurses ranging from impatience to rudeness towards poorly dressed parents, easily embarrassed in an unfamiliar environment, made some feel at times that the service was being offered as a duty rather than in a genuine desire to help them with their problems.[79]

By 1918 a call for dental treatment and the construction of school baths had become part of TUC Education Policy but the welfare programme in general had been reduced to take account of the provisions now made in terms of school meals, physical education and medical inspection. Grants for medical treatment had been made available in 1912 and with H.A.L. Fisher at the Board of Education it was felt that progress would continue. Indeed, medical treatment was to be offered in the secondary continuation schools proposed in Fisher's Education Bill. This feeling of progress is reflected by the fact that little discussion concerning child welfare arose at Congress and the matter was not raised in the PCTUC Deputation to the Board of Education in 1919, 1920 and 1921.

There was a passing reference to a call for hygiene to be included in the school curriculum at the 1922 Congress[80] but it was not until 1924 that TUC demands in school welfare began to expand once more with not only a repeat of calls for open-air schools but also for improved facilities in the form of playing fields, gymnasiums and purpose built dining halls. M.F. Titterington (Stuff and Woollen Warehousemen) took the initiative in putting forward the Education resolution at Congress and in talking on the health aspects of the policy to Eustace Percy at the Board of Education. To Congress delegates he explained that the old unsatisfactory buildings helped to spread contagious diseases:

> There were thousands of old and decrepit school buildings that ought to be destroyed. There were thousands overcrowded. There were thousands built on the barracks plan. There were thousands in the inner ring of towns and cities, out-of-date, in noisy and squalid surroundings with contaminated air and that did not compare with gaols, workhouses, industrial schools or reformatories in the matter of being healthy.[81]

Titterington argued that open air schools would be cheaper to build because land on the outskirts was not so expensive as the more central areas of the town. Such pleas might convince fellow trade unionists but they made little impression upon Eustace Percy who considered TUC demands as impractical:

> At the present time they were dealing with an appalling accumulation of thoroughly insanitary schools, always in the centre of the great

towns ... it was suggested that they should never approve of new schools unless they were built on the outskirts of towns ... in Birmingham and Liverpool it was totally impossible ... to approve no future school in these great towns which did not meet this test they would be holding up the improvement of the very bad present schools for years.[82]

It is true that the cutbacks in social services in 1925 were bound to thwart the implementation of the kind of comprehensive welfare programme proposed by the TUC. However, even if such 'economies' had not been adopted by the Government the TUC welfare programme would probably have remained as an ideal rather than a practical reality for several reasons. There was the scope of the problem outlined by Eustace Percy in which he was quick to admit that 'the members of the deputation knew better than he did what the problems were in the towns'.[83] Even for a Government committed to the TUC Education programme, at least a decade of intensive urban renewal would have been necessary before the proposals could have been carried out satisfactorily throughout the country.

At it was, there was still a belief that the Government should not provide on the scale demanded by the TUC. Voluntary help was still considered a good thing both in terms of economics and morality, as Percy was keen to point out to the GCTUC.[84] It is also possible to suggest, without implying any lack of sincerity, that many in Government looked back at the real improvements which had been made in the first quarter of the century and believed that the pattern and direction of such had been the best that could be achieved. Some felt that the State already did too much and that there was a danger of taking away the responsibility and initiative of parents. If the TUC was out of step with such thinking, impatient, even impractical as far as Eustace Percy was concerned, it was because as the latter had admitted, they were closer to the problems of poor living conditions in their everyday lives. For them, the argument that the country could only gradually tackle urban deprivation was largely academic. For the children involved, a delay of just a few years would be sufficient to affect adversely their opportunities for a better education and future.

Notes

1 'Report of the British Association to make a systematic examination of the Height, Weight and other Physical Characteristics of the Inhabitants of the British Isles 1878–83' quoted in the *Report of the Interdepartmental Committee on Physical Deterioration 1904*, p. 3, para. 14.
2 Dr. Francis Warner's studies were published as 'The Report on the Scientific Study of the Mental and Physical Conditions of Childhood with particular reference to Children of Defective Constitution: and with recommendations as to education and training' 1895. In the first study 50,027 children from 106 schools were examined.
3 *Ibid.*, p. 62.

4 *Ibid.*, p. 52.
5 *Report of the Interdepartmental Committee on Physical Deterioration 1904*, p. 15, para. 76.
6 *Ibid.*, p. 44, para. 239.
7 *Ibid.*, p. 56, para. 57.
8 *Ibid.*
9 *Ibid.*, p. 7, para. 38.
10 *Report of the Interdepartmental Committee on Medical Inspection and Feeding of Children attending Public Elementary Schools 1905.*
11 For descriptions of the catchment areas of the six elementary schools studied and for comparisons of the average height and weight of different ages of children, see Vol. II, Appendix V, Pt. 3, p. 2, Table 1.
12 See BARNARD, H.C. *A History of English Education from 1760*, p. 224 and LOWNDES, G.A.N. *The Silent Social Revolution*, p. 174 2nd Edit. 1969.
13 HOBSBAWM, E.J. *Industry and Empire*, p. 137.
14 MCINTOSH, P.C. *Physical Education in England since 1800*, pp. 107–108.
15 For a detailed discussion on the origins and development of drill in English schools, see HURT, J.S. 'Drill, discipline and the elementary school ethos' in MCCANN, P. *Popular Education and Socialization in the Nineteenth Century.*
16 *Ibid.*, pp. 181–182.
17 MCINTOSH, P.C. *op. cit.*, p. 110.
18 LOWNDES, G.A.N. *op. cit.*, p. 27.
19 SPENCER, F.H. *An Inspector's Testament*, pp. 64–65.
20 LOWNDES, G.A.N. *op. cit.*, p. 27 and SMITH, W.D. *Stretching their Bodies: The History of Physical Education*, p. 92.
21 The Lads Drill Association was specifically founded in 1899 by Lord Meath to advocate compulsory military and patriotic training by a programme of 'the systematic physical and military training of all British lads, and their instruction in the use of the rifle'. See SPRINGHALL, J.Q. 'Lord Meath, youth and culture'. *Journal of Contemporary History*, 5(4) 1970, pp. 97–111.
22 *Report of the Interdepartmental Committee on Physical Deterioration 1904*, p. 91.
23 *Report of the Consultative Committee upon Questions Affecting Higher Elementary Schools 1906*, p. 11.
24 SMITH, W.D. *op. cit.*
25 Benjamin Lucraft protested within the LSB and W.Cremer to the LSB in 1875 about the practice of drill. See HURT, J.S. *op. cit.*, pp. 184–185.
26 *Manchester Guardian*, 19.9.1879.
27 TUC Report 1885, p. 44.
28 KENT, W. *Labour's Lost Leader*, p. 100.
29 MCINTOSH, P.C. *op. cit.*, p. 141.
30 BARKER, R.S. Ph.D. Thesis (London) 1968 *op. cit.*, p. 444.
31 *Ibid.*, pp. 445–446.
32 NUR Annual Conference Report 1918, p. 26.
33 Labour Party Annual Conference Report 1918, p. 22.
34 TUC Report 1920, p. 372.
35 TUC Report 1905, p. 151.
36 TUC Reports 1906, p. 175; 1907, p. 186; 1909, p. 191; 1910, p. 173; 1912, p. 175; and 1915, p. 143.
37 TUC Report 1918, p. 391, Appendix 5.
38 KENT, W. *op. cit.*, p. 20.
39 MACLURE, S. *One Hundred Years of London Education 1870–1970*, p. 57.
40 *Justice*, 11.4.1896.
41 BROWN, R. M.Sc. (Econ.) Hull 1966 *op. cit.*, p. 366.
42 *Report of the Royal Commission on the Elementary Education Acts 1888*, Minority

Report, p. 352.
43 *Justice*, 17.1.1891.
44 TUC Report 1897, p. 50.
45 Mass meetings were still being organized concerning school meals as late as 1906. The Gasworkers and General Labourers Union organized such a meeting in Liverpool (2.9.1906) the day prior to the opening of the TUC in that city. General Sec.'s Report ending June 30, 1906, p. 6.
46 *Justice*, 7.3.1896.
47 *Justice*, 29.11.1902.
48 *Justice*, 1. 11. 1902.
49 TUC Report 1904, p. 50.
50 HANSARD 1905, Vol. 145, Col. 556.
51 HANSARD 1905, Vol. 145, Cols. 543–544.
52 PCTUC Deputation to Board of Education 15.2.1912. Pease did not respond then but he did two years later by telling Thorne that the Board was against compulsion 'but hope to persuade LEAs as to the wisdom of providing meals'. PCTUC Deputation to the Board of Education 12.2.1914.
53 MEACHAM, S. *A Life Apart*, p. 209.
54 BARKER, R. Ph.D. 1968 *op. cit.*, p. 236 and WARD, L.O. (Ph.D.) *op. cit.*, p. 306.
55 BARKER, R. *Ibid.*
56 PCTUC Deputation to Board of Education. Mins., 15.2.1912.
57 PCTUC Deputation to Board of Education. Mins., 12.2.1914.
58 SIMON, B. *The Politics of Educational Reform 1920–40*, p. 54.
59 Circular 1261 Board of Education, 17.5.1922.
60 *Ibid.*
61 This may partly explain the slogan painted on a banner of the National Union of General Workers between 1910–20 which declared, 'No starving children in the Board Schools'. The Board Schools had been abolished by the 1902 Education Act but obviously many hungry children still remained. See GORMAN, J. *Banner Bright*, p. 180.
62 Circular 1273 Board of Education, 22.7.1922.
63 Gasworkers Biennial Congress Report 1906, p. 44.
64 Circular 51 Scottish Education Department 28.7.1922, pp. 3–4.
65 TUC Report 1922, p. 415.
66 *Ibid.*
67 '... the Report of the Interdepartmental Committee on Physical Deterioration affords ample justification for our agitation for Free Maintenance for the children, and provides a complete armoury of facts and arguments for the Socialist propagandist and assailant of existing social conditions.' *The Social Democrat*, 8(8) 15.8.1904, p. 451.
68 TUC Report 1905, p. 151.
69 *Ibid.*
70 A Bill to promote the improvement of education and the physique of children attending Elementary Schools. Introduced by Will Thorne and read for the first time on March 2nd, 1906. Clauses 8 and 9.
71 TUC Report 1906, p. 175.
72 *Report of the Interdepartmental Committee on Medical Inspection and Feeding of Children attending Public Elementary Schools 1905*, Vol. I, Pt. 2, Section III, p. 10.
73 *Ibid.*
74 *Ibid.*
75 TUC Report 1907, p. 186.
76 Some open air schools were built between the two World Wars. They often allowed the side of the classroom facing into a quadrangle to slide back to admit fresh air and sunshine. For illustrations of such schools, see SEABORNE, M. *Education: Visual*

History in Modern Britain Fig. 199; BOURNE, R. and MacARTHUR, B. *The Struggle for Education 1870–1970*, p. 80. *The Struggle for Education* also explains how dozens of classes were held in London parks in the 1920s with children being supplied with clogs to keep their feet dry, rugs to keep them warm and in winter slow combustion foot warmers.

77 PCTUC Deputation to the Board of Education. Mins., 15.2.1912.
78 PCTUC Deputation to the Boarrd of Education. Mins., 12.2.1914.
79 MEACHAM, S. *op. cit.*, pp. 210–211.
80 A.G. Maker (Shop Assistans Union) TUC Report 1922, p. 415.
81 TUC Report 1924, p. 418.
82 GCTUC Deputation to the Board of Education. Mins., 25.5.1925.
83 *Ibid.*
84 *Ibid.*

Chapter 6

School Boards, Higher Grade Schools and the 1902 Education Act

School Boards, Local Control and Higher Grade Schools

The School Board System

The School Board System, which lasted from 1870 to 1902, has been the subject of much writing;[1] Eaglesham's detailed study[2] in particular has traced the administrative chaos which gradually arose in the decades following the 1870 Education Act and described how J. Gorst, Robert Morant, Sydney Webb and A.J. Balfour intervened decisively to the detriment of the school boards in the last years of the nineteenth century, ostensibly in the name of rationalization but with distinct political motives in mind. There is no need to repeat the well known story of the establishment and development of the school board system; rather we shall examine the reactions to and attempts at participation by the labour movement within this new educational system.

The major argument surrounding the 1870 Education Act was concerned with who was to control the education of working class children in elementary schools, a responsibility which had in the past been largely the preserve of religious societies, especially the Church of England. Disagreement between the Church of England and the Nonconformists, which had prevented earlier education bills in 1853 and 1855 from getting through Parliament, finally seemed to reach a compromise solution in 1870. Where there were insufficient religious schools a school board would be established to provide schools on a non-denominational basis but religious societies were to be given a six month period of grace to enable them to plan for schools wherever they could. The result was that the applications for school building licences by the Church Societies which had numbered 226 in 1869 suddenly rose to 3003 in the last five months of 1870.[3] This period of grace was seen by some as an indication of the privileged treatment provided for the churches in the Act and the support of numerous Conservative MPs might be said to provide at least circumstantial evidence that the Bill contained no major threat to the Church of England.[4]

It is possible to argue that in terms of political power no Education Bill would have been successful without the support of both the Church of England and large numbers of Conservatives. In a country where the franchise had only recently been extended to male artisans, public opinion, even if known, was of little importance in such matters. In the long run a combination of vested interests in the form of the Established Church, the Roman Catholic Church, the Conservative Party, numerous rate payers and old grammar schools were to combine against the board schools and bring about their downfall. In 1870 such forces were not sufficiently united to prevent the Education Act from being passed, especially as an increasing number of people believed that something needed to be done to provide education for numerous working class children at the time. Nevertheless, although the Act was considered as being initially advantageous to the Church of England, this body worked from the outset to undermine the board schools.[5]

The Trades Union Congress acted through affiliated trades councils and continued to do so even after the latter had been excluded from Congress in 1895.[6] Therefore they took little direct part in the working of school boards although TUC delegates stood as trades council or socialist party candidates in school board elections. The PCTUC did write on one occasion to A.H.D. Acland asking for an extension of polling hours in school board elections[7] but inevitably the trades councils were in a better position to deal with the local school boards than any national body. However, in the late 1890s, when it became apparent that the school board system was under threat, the TUC did enter the national argument to defend the boards.

Trade Union Participation in School Board Elections

The most significant factor about the Education Act as far as trade unionists were concerned, apart from the means of providing more and better schools, was the opportunity provided through the establishment of elected school boards for the working class to participate in the running of the schools designed for their own children.[8] The *ad hoc* boards, which varied from five to fifteen members according to the size of the population in the school board district, were to be elected triennially and voting was to be on a cumulative basis. Ratepayers were entitled to vote and stand for election so some women were also able to participate. The cumulative voting system meant that minority groups could gain a seat by concentrating their votes on one or two members.

The labour movement was slow to organize itself, as also were the Liberals who failed to grasp the situation in their own stronghold of Birmingham and by putting up fifteen candidates found that control of the School Board in 1870 went to the Church Party who only put up eight candidates but encouraged their supporters to 'plump' for this smaller number. At first trade unionists voted for unsectarian candidates who were likely to be Nonconformists or Liberals like themselves. In London, of thirteen working class candidates, only one was successful in the 1870 elections[9] and that was Benjamin Lucraft a cabinet maker who stood in Finsbury. He was supported by the Working Men's School Board Central Committee which had been set up by the Labour Representation League, itself under the control of the Liberal Party. From the start the Liberal Party reluctantly accepted working men as candidates for the school board with just a little more enthusiasm than in the case of a parliamentary election, but made it clear that they were to stand as Liberals and not as Labour candidates.

There can be little doubt that the Church Party, a combination of Anglicans and Tories, was the best organized, as has been demonstrated by the Birmingham School Board elections. A major strength of this party was their promise to keep down the expenditure of board schools, which unlike the church schools, were financed from the rates. The motivation for such proposals might well have been to restrict the development of the board schools[10] and thereby to reduce the challenge to their own schools but for many voters, any offer of a reduction in rates was likely to prove an attractive argument regardless of the educational issues involved.

The national opponents of the Church Party were the Nonconformists and Liberals, and trade union participation in the elections was often 'hidden' within this movement. For example, in Manchester, Henry Slatter, General Secretary of the Typographical Society and a member of the PCTUC (1877–79) was also on the General Council for Manchester Liberal Association; he was a successful candidate in the 1879 election.[11] Both the Church Party and the Nonsectarian groupings were willing to use working class candidates in districts where it was considered advantageous: '. . . in Middlesbro' first election, for example, both a Church candidate and a National League candidate stood jointly also as working class candidates'.[12] Both were elected but support for working men varied between districts and within them at different times.

Standing independently was a more precarious venture for working men. In Stockton's second election the only candidate not returned was sponsored jointly by the trades council and the unsectarian party, and John Kane, leader of the Iron and Steel Workers Union standing as an Independent Working Man in Darlington, was unsuccessful in 1870 but elected in 1873.[13] At Hull, '. . . when, in 1877, a working man named Christie stood for the School Board he finished bottom of the poll, and there is no indication of any support for him among working class circles'.[14] However, when the Trades Council put up a member of their own, C. Jenning, in 1883, they were able to gain enough support for his election. This success encouraged their efforts so that three years later he was joined on the Board by Elvidge, a member of the Typographical Society, and from then onwards, in spite of a disastrous defeat of all three trades council members in 1895, there were always working men on the Hull School Board.[15]

Where sections of the Labour movement failed to get together with other progressive forces they ran the risk of being swept aside by the well organized

Church Party, as for example in Blackburn in the 1890s.[16] The best hope for trade unionists in the 1870s was to co-operate with the Nonconformists, as for example '. . . in Leicester where the liberal Registration Society, the Nonconformists and the Council of Trade Unionists decided jointly on candidates for the school board' in 1873.[17] Even where trade unionists did get onto boards by concentrating votes, as the Roman Catholics had quickly learned to do,[18] they were usually heavily outnumbered. An example of this and a further instance of the discipline of the Church Party was provided in 1893 in Lancaster where the nine places on the Board were distributed as follows; Church Party – five, Official Progressives, Roman Catholics, Skerton District Representative and Trades Council Representative one seat each. Even without the support of the Roman Catholics[19] the Church Party still controlled the Board although an analysis of the votes showed that they had only polled 12,982 votes compared with the unsectarian groupings 15,599. However the votes for the latter had been spread too thinly because the Progressives had put up three candidates, another person had stood as an 'Unsectarian' and the major had put himself forward as an independent.[20] The lesson was finally learned by the unsectarian grouping who gained control by concentrating their votes on fewer candidates in 1896 and retained control in 1899.

Apart from those already mentioned, trades council representatives were successful in 1870 in Plymouth, Nottingham, Hanley, Liverpool,[21] Longton and Walsall[22] and at Leeds and Bristol in 1886[23] whilst in '1889 the gasworkers put up two candidates for the Barking School Board, supported by an election committee of 1600, and celebrated their victory by a torchlight procession of 10,000'.[24] TUC delegates who gained places on school boards supported by trades councils and sometimes socialist parties included W.J. Davis, who stood as a Labour candidate in Birmingham[25] opposed by both Tories and Liberals in 1875, when he lost after collecting 10,000 votes, but on the same platform was successful in 1876, 1879 and 1882. Ben Turner gained a seat on Batley School Board in 1892 and G.H. Roberts was successful at Norwich in 1899. In 1896 Henry Broadhurst was unopposed for the Cromer School Board; a different story to his earlier unsuccessful attempt at Greenwich in 1873 when he stood as Secretary of the Labour Representation League and polled 6,000 votes. He claimed that his defeat was just as well as he could never have given '. . . the necessary time to the educational requirements of so vast, and in some parts so densely populated a district as the metropolis'.[26]

Whilst one can list outstanding trade unionists elected onto school boards they were not particularly numerous in the 1870s and 1880s. There were certain factors working against representatives of the Labour movement apart from the excellent organization of the Church Party. Many of the elections were dominated by religious arguments[27] which seemed irrelevant to many working people but which seemed to be forever to the forefront of middle class minds.[28] In the early years, especially in the large towns, it took considerable courage publicly to oppose well known local dignatories who possessed the confidence that success usually brings. Trade unionists were in a small minority among working men; they were even a smaller proportion of the population at large but the PCTUC were certain that it was 'equally important for the wage earners to be represented on School Boards and Boards of Guardians'.[29] It was an opportunity for Labour representatives to gain the very experience of local office which they so frequently lacked.

Apart from the problem of finding the time and energy to campaign after long hours of manual labour, working class men were not only faced with unpaid work but, unlike many professional and business people, lost pay for attending the Board, a point made by Frederic Rogers writing of his experience in London:

> The work meant often much pecuniary sacrifice to me, which, however, I did not begrude. Days or half-days away from my work – albeit on public service – were stopped out of my wages, and sometimes perhaps my enthusiasm grew cold, but never for long.[30]

Throughout the period, in national terms, trade unionists and socialists did not become a major force on the school boards. The numbers of voters turning out for such elections declined gradually[31] although by contrast the better organization of the labour movement, especially in the 1890s, brought them greater electoral successes. It is possible to sepeculate that this limited success would have been much greater in the twentieth century if the school board system had endured; a suggestion based upon the success at both local and Parliamentary level of the labour movement in elections in the first quarter of the twentieth century. The possibility of Labour capturing many of the school boards and favouring a generous policy of education must have been at least one reason why the Church Party was anxious to replace a system of voting for school boards with one of appointing education committees.

Higher Grade Schools

When the Education Act of 1870 was passed it was undoubtedly aimed at providing elementary education for working class children. The curriculum was laid down precisely by the revised code and for some children from poor home circumstances who were infrequent attenders it was more than they could do to reach the basic standard necessary to qualify for grant payable to the school. There were, however, children, especially those from the homes of artisans, shopkeepers and clerks, who, with parental support, rapidly worked their way through the standards, even after an extra seventh standard had been added in 1882, and had completed them by the age of eleven or twelve. If they remained at school they could earn extra grant by taking 'specific subjects' or 'class subjects'.

By the 1880s provision was being made, especially in the northern and midland industrial towns, for classes above standard VII to be taught; in some cases in the same school, in others in schools specially built to bring such children from a town together to be taught in what came to be known as

Higher grade schools. Sheffield is credited with being the first to establish such a school in 1876 and, whilst there was considerable variation between schools which taught beyond the basic standards, schools similar at least in this purpose were built in many towns including Barrow, Bradford, Birmingham, Nottingham, Halifax, Leeds and Brighton. London was late in establishing such schools and did not begin to develop such institutions until the 1890s.

These schools were formed due to local demand from parents, teachers and industry with the support of the Board of Education.[32] In addition they had taken advantage of earning the higher grants available from the Science and Arts Department of South Kensington. In time they not only turned out pupils who were well grounded in basic subjects but also often had the necessary skills to enter local industry. This was a result of the bias in their curriculum towards the sciences. In some schools students were prepared for entrance to technical colleges and even university places were gained. In London the curriculum often emphasized commercial subjects. There can be little doubt that the education provided in these 'higher tops' of elementary schools or in the purpose built higher grade schools receiving pupils after standard VI or VII was secondary in all but name and that it met a real need. This was seen as a success story by the board schools and many of their Liberal supporters in industrial Britain; the labour movement also supported and encouraged what they saw as the provision of a form of secondary education which had been denied working class children in any reasonable proportion by the traditional fee paying grammar schools.

The success story of the school boards was not greeted enthusiastically by all. The Church Party protested about the provision of post-elementary education by board schools at an early date complaining alongside ratepayer pressure groups that it was an unnecessary extravagance.[33] It was feared that the continual development of board schools would inevitably force the religious schools out of existence. These traditional enemies of the board schools were joined by a third group: the headmasters of old endowed grammar schools[34] who were finding that the higher grade schools were attracting a considerable number of parents by their efficiency, low fees of up to ninepence per week and their curriculum which seemed more relevant to industrial Britain. By contrast the traditional classics curriculum offered by many grammar schools and the inclusion of some poor teaching among the weaker ones was leading to a decline in the numbers of pupils coming forward. These were the forces which began to line up against the higher grade schools.

As a result of the numerous and often conflicting forces involved in the provision of some form of secondary education the Bryce Commission was established in 1894 to consider '... the best methods of establishing a well-organized system of secondary education in England, taking into account existing differences...'. Among the seventeen members of the Commission chaired by James Bryce, Liberal MP, were two trade unionists; Charles Fenwick, Secretary of the PCTUC 1890–93 and Liberal MP, and James Yoxall, Secretary of the NUT and also a Liberal MP. A memorial signed by Henry

Broadhurst and George Howell and forty-eight others[35] from the Trades and Labour Council was submitted to the Commission. It was clear that the trade unionists favoured the kind of relationship established in board schools, already favoured in the minority report of the Cross Commission of 1888, in which secondary education was a natural step from the elementary education which had gone before:

> Secondary education, in our view, must be defined and therefore administered, as the education which follows and continues primary or elementary education.
>
> Secondary schools, which provide this Secondary Education, should accordingly be so related to primary or elementary schools that their curriculum will proceed upon the course of instruction given in the latter, and be a continuation and development of it.... The distinction of primary and secondary schools should be in our opinion, strictly and solely educational, marking the successive stages of an educational curriculum; and not social, marking merely different grades of social rank.
>
> We conceive that it would be highly beneficial to all classes of the community if their children were to attend a common school.[36]

The Bryce Commission, which reported in 1895, recommended that one authority should be established to supervise both elementary and secondary education for although it did not in fact support the suggestion that there was considerable overlapping between higher grade and grammar schools,[37] it did suggest that the system by which the Education Department, the Science and Art Department and the Charity Commissioners were all involved in secondary education was unhelpful. This view was responsible for the formation of the Board of Education in 1899.

In 1895 the Conservatives were returned to power. They wished to help their Anglican allies and in 1896, Sir John Gorst, vice president of the Committee of the Privy Council on Education, introduced an education bill into the House of Commons proposing to remove 'secondary' education from the School boards and provide greater financial assistance to religious schools. *Justice* was worried that progressive forces did not seem to perceive the dangers inherent in the Bill:

> Already it is quite plain that not only the adherents of the Church of England, but the Catholics, and not a few Nonconformists are in favour of the measure. The measure bristles with insidious bribery at the same time that here and there it does remedy serious injustice.... It is all very clever and politically smart. The religionists are gratified by subventions, while the ratepayers are promised direct control over the School Board rate. We are very much afraid that as matters stand, the party of theology and reaction will win all along the line.[38]

The Bill was withdrawn, partly because it attempted to introduce religious tests for teachers in board schools, thereby arousing the animosity of the NUT.

However, in 1897, an Education Act was passed providing further financial assistance to religious schools.

The Labour movement continued to give its support to the Higher Grade schools. At the Gasworkers Conference of 1896 a detailed resolution was submitted by the London branches concerning Higher Grade schools in the Metropolis. They wished to see a complete scheme introduced for London and for fees to be abolished in such schools.[39] It was suggested that financial support should not come by an increase in school board rates, a measure known to be unpopular, but by central government grants, grants from the City Guilds and Technical Education Board, and by taxation of ground values.[40]

Another attack on the school boards was launched in the form of the Cockerton Judgement in June 1899 which threw the whole future of the Higher Grade schools into the melting pot.

Cockerton, the auditor of the London School Board, was encouraged by Sir John Gorst[41] to challenge the legality of expenditure by the LSB on higher education financed from the rates. The LSB appealed to the high court but Cockerton's view was upheld. It was established that the LSB could only meet the cost of elementary education for children from the rates. This effectively prevented the Board from offering secondary education to children or adults in evening schools. However much Sir John Gorst and his private secretary Robert Morant may have pleaded that the education system needed rationalizing there is little doubt that both were hostile to the successful manner in which the board schools had developed. Although Sir John Gorst was the chief architect behind the challenge to the London School Board's expenditure on 'higher' education in 1899 he denied involvement to the House of Commons.[42] Morant's part in the event is less clear:

> At first ... Morant seems to have accepted the policy of limitations and subordination [of the school boards] and only later, when he was more sure of his powers, did he press for abolition.[43]

The destruction of the Higher Grade schools may not have been the intention of the Government at the time, but it can be shown that this was in fact one such result of the 1902 Education Act.

The Cockerton Judgement had spread alarm among the school boards and their supporters. A deputation supporting the Higher Grade Schools was received by the PCTUC in July 1900 and in the discussion which followed '... it was ultimately decided that the result of their deliberations should be formulated in circular form.[44] This circular published on behalf of the PCTUC ran to more than 1,000 words[45] and began with a warning: 'The time has come to draw your attention to the conspiracy against the education of your children which has been developing during the last five years'. This was not just a circular of conventional protest but a real cry of alarm at the realization that a complete change in education policy had taken place since the Tories were returned to power. Previously, all governments after 1870 had gradually introduced reforms in education which quickly gained approval from most sections of society; compulsory education in 1880, abolition of fees in most elementary schools in 1891, and the final abolition of the 'revised code', or at least its most depressing features, a short while later. 'But now', the circular claimed, 'the power of the Government is turned against the people'.

By the Cockerton Judgement the Government were able to direct grants originally provided by the Science and Arts Department for 'the industrial classes' away from Higher Grade schools to middle class grammar schools. This prompted the PCTUC to declare in their circular that,

> ... it is in regard to the higher education of children of humble birth that the greatest mischief is being accomplished. Six sevenths of the nation pass through the elementary schools: does anyone suppose that all the highest intelligence is confined to the other seventh? ... The present Government ... has withdrawn these grants from many of the scholars of 'the industrial classes', and has diverted them to middle class schools. The other grants given for advanced (specific) subjects have this year been withdrawn, although these grants provided last year higher instruction for nearly 350,000 scholars.

To soften the blow the Government had formulated a new category of school called a 'Higher Elementary School', but this was not just to be another name for the Higher Grade Schools but a way of ensuring that they did not continue with 'secondary education' as their fore-runners, the Higher Grade Schools had done. In London, of the seventy-nine Higher Grade Schools which might have assumed that they would at least be included now as Higher Elementary Schools, only four were recognized as such.

The 1900 Congress approved of the PCTUC circular and a lengthy resolution was passed unanimously asking the Government to restore the system of grants to children beyond fifteen years of age at board schools. Comparisons were made with the Scottish system which gave grants to pupils up to eighteen years of age and it was decided 'that a copy of these resolutions be forwarded to the Prime Minister, The First Lord of the Treasury, the President and Vice President of the Board of Education, and further, that the trades representatives in every district be requested forthwith to communicate these resolutions to their respective MPs and to take strenuous action there on'.[46]

Protest meetings were arranged throughout the country by various educational authorities and three members of the PCTUC, including Will Thorne, attended a Conference the following February at St. Martin's Town Hall to give the declared support of the TUC.[47] In May a similar group of members joined a School Board Association deputation to the Duke of Devonshire and Sir John Gorst,[48] and three representatives from the PCTUC attended a National Conference of Progressive Educationists held on the 6th June at the Holborn Restaurant which was attended by people of nearly every shade of political opinion.

Within the trade union movement hostility towards the Tories increased and there was growing disenchantment with the Liberals which culminated in the formation of the Labour Representation Committee in 1900 from a meeting of the TUC, SDF, ILP and Fabian Society. Most of the attention of the TUC was taken up by the Taff Vale case in 1901, which posed a threat to the right of trade unionists to strike, but the education problem was not forgotten. A Bill introduced by the Government had been withdrawn but it was obvious that another would soon be drafted. C.W. Bowerman in his Presidential address at the Swansea Congress in 1901 pointed out that the Boer War had enabled the Government conveniently to shelve internal questions such as Old Age Pensions, and Working Class Housing but in Education:

> ... legislation of the most retrograde character has been attempted, with the apparent object of depriving their children of some of the advantages which they have hitherto enjoyed under the Board School system ... no excuse can be given for indirectly attempting to filch from the children of the workers an essential part of the educational system which has grown up under the Education Act of 1870 ... it remains for the workers to exercise the power they are continually being reminded they possess, by demanding for their children similar educational facilities to those freely granted in Continental countries ...[49]

W. Harvey of the Derbyshire Miners in moving the thanks of the Congress to the President claimed, 'they were faced by the danger of having elementary education snatched away from the children of the workers at the order of Lord Salisbury',[50] a remark which shows how clearly was the division between elementary and secondary schools for in fact Harvey's protest was about the loss of higher grade 'secondary education'; ironically it was precisely elementary education which the Government was proposing to offer to the vast majority of working class children.

The Education Bill of 1902 and the TUC's concern over Democratic Local Control

The PCTUC, in spite of its radical circular of 1900, did not seem to be willing to involve all the forces available to the Labour movement in their campaign against Government Education Policy. They had agreed to send their chairman, W.J. Davis, as a representative to a Conference called by the newly formed National Labour Education League[51] but at a meeting of the PCTUC in the new year there was disagreement as to the part the TUC should play in the education protests that had been suggested. After some discussion it was agreed that the PCTUC should call a conference of trade unionists following the introduction of the Government's Education Bill but some arguments ensued over the composition of the Conference. Davis and Bowerman, the Secretary, did not wish the trades councils to be invited whilst Thorne and Hobson believed that they should be involved. The remainder of the Committee supported Davis and Bowerman, in spite of the fact that it was the trades councils which had been most involved in campaigning for Labour candidates to be elected to school boards, including TUC delegates. The decision also seemed strange when it is considered how frequently the TUC had appealed to trades councils to fight for Congress Policy in many matters, including education. The decision probably reflected the usual anxiety of the TUC leadership over the radical views expressed by rank and file trade unionists through many of the trades councils. Finally, it was agreed to set up a sub-committee including Davis, Bowerman and Thorne to organize the Conference.[52]

The Government Bill was introduced on 24th March 1902 by A.J. Balfour and immediately widespread opposition arose. Nonconformists were quick to challenge the contents of the Bill. The Labour movement, with the exception of the Fabians and the NUT, protested alongside the Nonconformists but concentrated on the two issues central to TUC Education Policy: democratic control of local education and access to secondary education for working class children. The issue of control was fundamental. The Bryce Commission had suggested that, '... it is well ... to recognize ... that political control goes necessarily with the bestowment of public money'.[53] The TUC wished to ensure that political control should take place at local level as the board schools had allowed. The Circular had made this clear concluding that 'the only safeguard of democratic interests is a democratic franchise and a free, direct, and efficient popular control'. This view was emphasized further in the resolution, introduced by Davis at a further meeting of the PCTUC, for discussion by the Conference they had arranged. It stated:

> That as the Government Bill will destroy popularly constituted bodies of education this Conference expresses its dissent to the Government's policy on Education and further it is of the opinion that the abolition of School Boards will be detrimental to the interests of the people and take away the advantages which the workers have in its direct representation in the management of Board Schools.[54]

The Conference, which was held on the 28th May, with W.C. Steadman in the Chair, and included delegates representing over one million workers, expressed their approval of the resolution.

Early in June the Government Bill went into the Committee Stage and by the '7th August, when the House was adjourned, twenty-two days had been spent on the first seven clauses'.[55] The Bill attracted widespread coverage in the newspapers. A series of articles, by Dr. J. Clifford of the National Reform Union, which appeared between 12th August and 10th September in the *Daily News* were collected together and sold in pamphlet form. Clifford claimed that although '... the Bill was called an Education Bill, and deals professedly with primary and secondary education by the State; ... the educational aspect of the Bill is completely eclipsed by the tremendous political and administrative issues raised'.[56] He also pointed out that the proposals would have a disastrous effect upon the representation of women in local education: 'Women are not eligible for election to the Council'.[57]

As expected, when the TUC met in London in the first week of September, they stressed the attack on local democracy in education now apparent in the Government Bill. In a lengthy resolution, W.A. Appleton stated 'that this Congress condemns the Government Education Bill now before the Country because it does away with the principle of direct representation'.[58] The resolution demanded that '... all grades of education, in districts of suitable size, be under one local authority, directly elected, and elected solely for educational purposes'.[59] To reinforce these proposals it was also claimed '... that the principle of taxation without representation might justifiably be met by the refusal to pay the taxes imposed'.[60] A call was also made for support to be withdrawn from any candidate at the next Parliamentary Election who refused to support TUC policy concerning democratically elected education bodies.

The Education Bill had also been the first subject to be mentioned by the President, W.C. Steadman, who had been fully involved in the TUC Education Lobby, when he addressed Congress:

> Not a single measure of benefit to the working classes was put upon the Statute Book during the past session; on the contrary, the Education Bill of the Government, is a decidedly reactionary measure; ... the Bill abolishes the School Boards ... this in itself being a blow to democratic representation.[61]

He argued that even an amendment which had been passed gave no solution to the question as to '... how secondary education was to be brought within the reach of the children of the industrial classes'.[62]

By now it must have been obvious that the Government intended to have their way in Parliament. There was plenty of protest in the country but although various factions supported joint meetings it was largely because they found themselves facing a common enemy; the Nonconformists were furious at the aid to be given to the Church of England whilst the labour movement was more concerned with the issue of local democratic control, although the two were really part of the same problem. *Justice* expressed annoyance at the religious arguments:

> Dr. Clifford, the stern unrelenting High Priest of dogmatic Non-Conformity, can disclaim for hours and hardly mention the children.... On the other hand Cardinal Vaughan rejoices and waxes exceedingly glad because the Bill enables him to teach 'dogmatic Christianity' ... the whole discussion of the educational problem is developing into a wrangle between church and chapel.[63]

This was certainly the issue that captured most attention in Parliament and the newspapers.

The two sections of the labour movement which had supported the Bill were the NUT and the Fabian Society. They were in effect on the margin of the Movement, for the NUT would not affiliate to the TUC and the Fabians had few working class members; W.C. Steadman and Will Crooks were probably the most well known trade unionists in the Society. The NUT supported the Bill because many of their own members were in the poorly equipped religious schools and they knew that they would only enjoy a higher salary if greater financial aid was given to the religious societies. Support by them for the Nonconformist cause would have encouraged a split in the union on religious grounds, something British trade unions have avoided, unlike their Continental brethren. There were also particular clauses in the Bill favourable to NUT wishes, such as the promise to consider the issue of extraneous duties, so that such concessions made it difficult for the leadership to refuse support, even if it was not the ideal Bill that the Union would have drawn up itself.[64]

The Fabian attitude had nothing to do with trade union principles and realities but was a matter of their 'behind the scenes' approach to political and social problems. 'Morant was on terms with the Webbs, and Balfour the Prime Minister an old friend of Beatrice – and it 'happened' that Sir John Gorst asked for sufficient copies of the proofs of Tract 106 before it was published to circulate among the officials of his department'.[65] There is little doubt as to the personal involvement of the Webbs in these machinations:

> . . . it is certain both that the Fabian tract CVI, 'The Education Muddle
> and the Way Out' (1901) was essentially the fruit of Sidney's thinking
> and that this tract and the lobbying pressures brought to bear by
> Sidney greatly influenced the drafting of the Education Bills.[66]

Indeed the Fabians were quite proud of their work and had stated earlier in the year:

> The Fabian Society made its education policy so prominent a feature of
> last year's work that the members will naturally desire to compare the
> newly introduced Government measure with Tract 106. It will be at
> once seen that there is a considerable amount of similarity between the
> two.[67]

A few months later they were pleased to print a summary of Fabian Resolutions issued in May and compare them favourably with the amendments made to the Education Bill.[68] Such achievements were precisely in accordance with Fabian philosophy:

> There is no doubt that the story of the Education Act is very nearly the
> dream of Fabian 'permeators' come to life – proposals drafted by
> intelligent hard-working Fabians, conveyed to puzzled or sympathetic
> administrators, and carried into effect by a Conservative
> Government.[69]

This was no surprise to those who believed that the Webbs were more devoted to 'efficiency' than socialist or trade union ideals. The leader in *Justice* declared 'The [Education] Bill is admittedly a bad one; it only needed the blessing of the Fabian Society to damn it entirely. Socialists must oppose it vigorously...'.[70] On the 20th November the Bill finally passed through the Committee Stage in Parliament. A few days later the ILP called a meeting at Essex Hall in the Strand at which a resolution was passed echoing the main points of TUC Education Policy, including the demand '... that schools and colleges, if maintained at public expense, should be the property of the community and under complete and direct popular control...'.[71]

The outcry by the Labour movement against the Bill continued with *Justice* frequently attempting to expose the nature of Fabianism to supporters of Labour:

> We have previously shown the Fabian influence in the anti-democratic Education Bill of the Government. Their ideal of an educational authority is the Technical Education Board of the LCC,[72] and this is completely removed from popular control as any such body could possibly be. The public does not know who composes the Board, and the LCC is too busy to exercise any supervision.[73]

All protest was now too late to stop the Bill and it finally received the Royal Assent on 18th November. *Justice* called the Bill a 'Clerical Triumph'.[74]

The Labour movement had regarded the 1870 Education Act as a platform upon which to build a national system of education but just when the major part of the construction was near completion the whole framework had been destroyed by the 1902 Education Act. A few years earlier *Justice* had looked back to 1870 as a golden opportunity which was lost: 'More than ever do we regret, however, the late Mr. Forster's treacherous compromise of 1870. The whole thing might have been settled once and for all'.[75] The 1900 TUC Circular had expressed a belief that the education problem could be solved if the board school system was completed nationally instead of being destroyed:

> The scheme of National Education foreshadowed by the Act of 1870 shall be completed and made secure by the appointment in every district of Education Authorities elected as freely and democratically as other municipal bodies.[76]

The PCTUC had already proposed that:

> Steps should be taken at the next Parliamentary elections to secure the defeat of every Member of the present House of Commons and all Parliamentary candidates who may not promise to vote for a solution of the education problem in accordance with the declared policy of the Parliamentary Committee's Report.[77]

For the next three years TUC Education Resolutions were prefixed with the sentence '... this Congress condemns the educational policy of the Government, as laid down in the Act of 1902, and in the subsequently issued Minutes and Regulations...'.[78] Yet, when the sweeping Liberal victory at the polls came in 1906, fundamental changes to the 1902 Education Act did not follow.

The size of the Liberal Parliamentary majority even without the support of the newly elected Labour MPs was sufficient for them to be able to disregard protests from the Church of England, Roman Catholic Church and the Grammar School lobby. Given the strength of feeling among Nonconformists with regard to the 1902 Education Act it is surprising that the new Government did not take measures to curtail State expenditure on religious schools or at least demand greater control at national or local level. In fact the power of religious schools continued to increase throughout the years to come.[9] The failure of the Liberals to restore democratic control in education at the local level might be explained by their observation of the growing strength of the Labour movement, especially through the trade union movement's new political infant – the Labour Representation Committee – which had just returned twenty-nine MPs in the 1906 Election. This success had been achieved against a background of victories in local elections also. It could therefore be argued that the Liberals calculated that a return to a locally elected board school system would in the long run benefit the Labour movement more than themselves.

Notes

1 Some of the most interesting and controversial writings concerning the development and demise of the school boards include: BANKS, O. *Parity and Prestige in English Secondary Education*, Ch. 1–4; EAGLESHAM, E.J.R. *The Foundations of 20th Century Education in England*; SIMON, B. *Education and the Labour Movement 1870–1920*, Ch. 4, 6 & 7; STURT, M. *The Education of the People*, Ch. 14–19; WEST, E.G. *Education and the State*.

2 EAGLESHAM, E.J.R. *From School Board to Local Authority*.

3 STURT, M. *op. cit.*, p. 304.

4 Some thought the Bill gave preferential treatment to the Established Church but there is little doubt that Gladstone as Prime Minister and a pillar of the Church would not have agreed to any Bill which seemed to undermine the Church of England. John Stuart Mill at a meeting in St. James' Hall, London, commented upon the Education Act, '. . . a more effectual plan could scarcely have been devised by the strongest champion of ecclesiastical ascendancy for enabling the clergy of the Church of England to educate the children of the greater part of England and Wales in their own religion at the expense of the public'. (25.3.1870)

5 'The hostility of the "Church Party" to Board Schools never ceased, one clerically minded member of the [London] Board saying in 1893 that the School Board system "as it exists" was "the great enemy of the Christian religion in the land".' RUBINSTEIN, D. *School Attendance in London 1870–1904*, pp. 29–30.

6 See note 65.

7 PCTUC Mins., 11.10.1894.

8 The questioning of Mr. Powell, the school board visitor and trade unionist, by the Cross Commissioners revealed the attitude that trade unionists would support the extension of board schools because they had some say in the control of such schools, whereas they resented the development of voluntary schools because they were excluded from the management in terms of democratic representation. *Report of the*

Royal Commission on the Elementary Education Acts 1888, Vol. 17, p. 404.

9 George Potter standing for Westminster claimed that wilful delay at polling booths had prevented many of his supporters recording their votes. A protest meeting was held in Pimlico, but to no avail. Mr. E. Jenkins, a barrister who chaired this meeting gave evidence of 'very loose arrangements' at Eburybridge polling-place and Potter complained of the procedures at Horseferry Road polling-place. See *Beehive*, 3.12.1870. Potter was successful at the 1873 School Board Election.

10 'The Bishops reflected the attitude of the Established Church against the need for board schools. The Bishop of Salisbury publicly gave thanks that there was only one board school in a section of his diocese, and the Bishop of Chester led an effort to thwart the creation of a school board in his cathedral town.' RICHARDS, N.J. 'Religious controversy and the school boards 1870–1902'. *British Journal of Educational Studies*, 18 (2) June 1970, p. 186.

11 BATHER, L. *A History of Manchester and Salford Trades Council*, Ph.D. 1956, p. 70.

12 RATCLIFFE, K.G.M. 'Elections and the school boards: Tees-side 1870–1902' *Journal of Educational Administration and History*, 2 (2) June 1970, pp. 34–35.

13 *Ibid.*

14 BROWN, R., *The Labour Movement in Hull 1870–1900 with special reference to New Unionism*, M.Sc. (Econ.) 1966, p. 33.

15 *Ibid.*, p. 34. Even in 1895 George Belt was elected to the Board on an ILP ticket.

16 PUGH, D.R. 'A Note on school board elections: Some North-Western contests in the nineties'. *History of Education*, 6 (2) June 1977, p. 117.

17 RICHARDS, N.J. *op. cit.*, p. 182.

18 'In the School Board election of 1870 the Catholics achieved considerable success. Catholic candidates headed the poll in Birmingham, Manchester (1st and 2nd places) and Sheffield. Four Catholics obtained seats in Liverpool, three were elected on to the London Board, and two in Salford, Bootle and Leeds.' SELBY, D.E. 'Manning, Ullathorne and the school board question 1870–76' *Journal of Educational Administration and History*, 5 (1) Jan. 1973, pp. 22–23.

19 The Catholics could be considered politically progressive in that they often supported working men (see Chapter 3.) but educationally Conservative. In the 1885 General Election Cardinal Manning and several bishops urged Catholics to vote for a Conservative Government. See PLATTEN, S.G. 'The conflict over the control of elementary education 1870–1902 and its effect upon the life and influence of the church'. *British Journal of Educational Studies*, 23 (3) Sept. 1975. SIMON, A. 'Joseph Chamberlain and free education in the election of 1885' *History of Education*, 2 (1) Jan. 1973.

20 PUGH, D.R. *op. cit.*

21 Liverpool's first School Board in December 1870 was not based upon a competitive election but a compromise agreement; two artisans were selected alongside five merchants, three gentlemen, three professional men and two manufacturers. In denominational terms there were seven Anglicans, four Catholics and four Nonconformists. See PRITCHARD, P.B. 'After sixty weeks: The significance of the Liverpool school board by-election of January 1872'. *History of Education Society Bulletin*, No. 23, Spring 1979.

22 McCANN, W.P. Ph.D. 1960, *op. cit.*, pp. 71–72.

23 CLINTON, A. Ph. D. 1973, *op. cit.*, p. 83.

24 From *Justice*, 19.10.1889 quoted in THOMPSON, P. *Past and Present*, 1964, *op. cit.*

25 For a fighting speech by W.J. Davis in favour of independent Labour representation see DALLEY, W.A. *op. cit.*, p. 48.

26 BROADHURST, H. *op. cit.*, p. 64.

27 Leeds, Liverpool and Manchester were all dominated by religious conflicts in 1870. See RICHARDS, N.J. *op. cit.*, *British Journal of Educational Studies*, 1970.

28 MUNSON, J.E.B. 'The London school board election of 1894' *British Journal of*

Educational Studies, 23 (1) Feb. 1975, p. 17

29 Parliamentary Committee Address to the Officers of Trade Societies and Trades Councils. TUC Report 1885, p. 7.

30 ROGERS, F. *op. cit.*, p. 58.

31 RATCLIFFE, K.G.M. *op. cit.*, p. 30.

32 Whilst support was given for many years there was surprise expressed later as to the manner in which the system had been allowed to develop. See First Morant Memorandum which gives clear account of the development of Higher Grade Schools – even if it was written in order to argue against their continuation. EAGLESHAM, E.J.R. *From School Board to Local Authority*, Appendix A.

33 RUBINSTEIN, D. *op. cit.*, p. 33. Among other examples an interesting one from the *School Guardian*, 21.9.1878 is quoted: 'In September 1878 it pointed out portentously that Germany, whose educational system was so often held up as an example, had the fastest growing socialist vote in the world.' A warning to Church Party leaders that greater knowledge encouraged socialism; was the opposite view also held, that ignorance encouraged Conservatism? See SUTHERLAND, G. *op. cit.*, p. 31. Expenditure on education for working class children was often seen as an extravagance. An ironic example is provided in Hull where the school board voted in 1887 by a majority of one to build a higher grade school. It was opposed by the Roman Catholics, the Church Party led by the Rev Malet Lambert, Tory vicar of Newland and the local newspaper which referred to 'that extravagant School Board of ours'; in fact Hull spent less on education per pupil than any town in England, the figures being 3/8½d in Hull compared with an average for England and Wales of 16/3d, whilst London spent nearly 30/-. The result of this 'extravagance' was seen several years later when an HMI reported in 1898 that the Hull School Board had done 'what is absolutely necessary, but nothing more'. BROWN, R. M.Sc. (Econ.) 1966, *op. cit.*, pp. 92–93 & p. 414.

34 The Headmasters Association was formed in 1890 to campaign against higher grade schools and sent a memorial to this effect to the Duke of Devonshire in 1896. Their political lobbying was helped by the numerous connections made possible by many of their 'old boys' who were sympathetic to their cause.

35 The other signatures of the Memorial included representatives of trades councils in Nottingham, Manchester and Salford, Preston, Halifax, Dundee, Long Eaton and from Co-operative Unions including Lincoln, Doncaster and Nottingham. A complete list is given in the *Report of the Royal Commission on Secondary Education 1895* (The Bryce Report), Vol. V, pp. 494–497.

36 Memorial to Bryce Commission from Trades and Labour Councils. *The Bryce Report*, 1895, Vol. I, p. 495.

37 SIMON, B. *Education and the Labour Movement 1870–1920*, p. 185.

38 *Justice*, 11.4.1896.

39 Other sections of the labour movement wished to see the Higher grade school fees abolished for they averaged 9d per week and in some schools this figure was arrived at by charging less for the first year or more of attendance but above that figure for the higher classes. In Hull, Richard Hoyle Brown, an Independent Working Man Candidate on the School Board, opposed a higher grade school in 1886 because he claimed it would only benefit the middle class. There was evidence to show that few children from very poor families attended such schools and that the children of unskilled workers were not found in proportion to their numbers in the schools.

40 Gasworkers Conference Report 1896, p. 56.

41 '[Gorst] . . . had served as an organizer for the Conservative Party. He had a genuine interest in education but while he was Vice President this did not always show itself to the best advantage since he was liable to let his political opinion cloud his vision.' GOSDEN, P.H.J.H. 'The Board of Education Act 1899' *British Journal of Educational Studies*, 11 (1) Nov. 1962, pp. 46–47.

42 EAGLESHAM, E.J.R. *Foundations of Twentieth Century Education in England*, p. 34.
43 BANKS, O. *Parity and Prestige in English Secondary Education*, p. 22.
44 PCTUC Mins., 11.7.1900.
45 See Appendix IV.
46 TUC Report 1900, p. 90.
47 PCTUC Mins., 12.2.1901.
48 PCTUC Mins., 13.5.1901.
49 TUC Report 1901, p. 30.
50 *Ibid.*, p. 37.
51 PCTUC Mins., 4.12.1901.
52 PCTUC Mins., 5.2.1902.
53 *The Bryce Report*, 1895, *op. cit.*, Vol. I, p. 87 and Vol. III, p. 467.
54 PCTUC Mins., 26.5.1902 and 27.5.1902.
55 SIMON, B. VOL. 2, *op. cit.*, p. 220.
56 CLIFFORD, J. *The First Against the Education Bill: What is at Stake*, p. 7.
57 *Ibid.*, p. 44.
58 TUC Report 1902, p. 70 see Appendix IIIb.
59 *Ibid.*, p. 71.
60 This suggestion received little support. TUC Report 1902, pp. 70–72.
61 TUC Report 1902, p. 32.
62 *Ibid.*
63 *Justice*, 1.11.1902.
64 For the NUT attitude and approach to the 1902 Education Bill see TROPP, A. *The School Teachers*, Chapter 10.
65 COLE, M. *The Story of Fabian Socialism*, p. 105.
66 JUDGES, A.V. 'The educational influence of the Webbs' *British Journal of Educational Studies*, 10 (1) Nov. 1961, p. 44; also MACKENZIE, N. *Socialism and Society: A new view of the Webb Partnership.* Apparently, at an earlier date when 'Fabian Essays in Socialism' was published (i.e. 1889) Sidney Webb favoured the school boards 'as the instruments in whose hands educational advance could continue to be trusted'. BRENNAN, F.T. 'Educational engineering with the Webbs' *History of Education*, 1 (2) June 1972, p. 177.
67 *Fabian News*, 12 (4) 1902.
68 *Fabian News*, 12 (8) 1902.
69 COLE, M. *op. cit.*, p. 107.
70 *Justice*, 1.11.1902.
71 *Justice*, 29.11.1902.
72 Sidney Webb was Chairman of the Technical Education Board 1892–8, 1901–2, and Vice Chairman 1899–1901.
73 *Justice*, 13.12.1902.
74 *Justice*, 27.12.1902.
75 *Justice*, 11.4.1896.
76 See Appendix IV.
77 TUC Report 1902, p. 42.
78 TUC Report 1903, p. 86; 1904, p. 119; 1905, p. 142.
79 See CANNON, C. 'The Influence of religion on educational policy 1902–44' in MUSGRAVE, P.W. (Ed) *Sociology, History and Education*.

Chapter 7

Education for Trade Unionists

The Labour movement was involved in the provision of education in its widest sense, for working class adults during the 19th century.[1] For example, in the early years, the Co-operative Movement provided classes in basic literacy[2] whilst in 1868 the Amalgamated Society of Carpenters and Joiners ran courses for technical drawing and building. The earliest contribution of the TUC came when the PCTUC in its 1879 Annual Report, included a short list of books which it recommended to trade societies, trades councils and workmen's clubs in the expressed belief that their 'perusal will repay the labour and expense incurred and enable our friends to more fully understand and appreciate the work in which we are engaged'.[3]

In the twentieth century the TUC showed considerable interest in adult education. It began by becoming involved with Ruskin College and several other educational bodies concerned with trade union education in the Edwardian era, went on to try and bring these organizations together in order to establish a TUC College in the 1920s and came near to setting up such a college at Easton Lodge in Essex in this decade. For a variety of reasons attempts to establish a TUC College failed. One major factor was the lack of financial support which some trade unions were willing or able to give. However, even if that problem had been overcome, there was still the central issue concerning the aims and curriculum to be adopted by a TUC College. This issue understandably was a matter of heated debate among education organizations, trade union students and TUC delegates. In some ways the conflicting views were simply incompatible although genuine attempts towards a compromise solution were sought in the negotiations which took place between the TUC and various educational organizations in the 1920s.

To understand the major areas of disagreement it is necessary first to consider Ruskin College. The full story of this College and the 1909 dispute which led to the establishment of the Central Labour College has been told elsewhere in detail[4] but certain facts need to be related here for two reasons. Firstly, the PCTUC was represented on Ruskin College Council from its foundation and therefore received what might be considered as the official view of developments at this College, including the Strike of 1909. Secondly, many of the issues which arose at Ruskin College were at the core of discussions concerning education for trade unionists both at the time and again in the 1920s when the TUC was seeking to develop a College of its own. Trade unionists took sides and brought influence to bear both upon their individual unions and as delegates at the TUC as to which view of education would best serve the interests of the Labour movement. Certain aspects of this dispute even affected the negotiations later over Easton Lodge, especially the question of whether a stately home in a remote rural area was really the ideal site to provide trade union education.

Ruskin College and Some Problems of Education for Trade Unionists

Charles Beard, one of the three American founders[5] of Ruskin Hall as it was first known, had made contacts with people in the Labour movement while he was studying at Oxford University. One of the first with whom he became acquainted was C.W. Bowerman, a member of the PCTUC and, at the well attended inaugural meeting of Ruskin Hall in Oxford Town Hall, representatives from trades councils, trade unions and co-operative societies made up the majority of the audience, which included Ben Tillett and James Sexton. The founders envisaged trade unionists as forming the bulk of the student population and, although this did not happen in the early years,[6] the desire for trade union participation was reflected in the appointments made in February 1899 of seven trustees of whom C.W. Bowerman, Ben Tillett and A. Sellicks (Chairman of the ASE) were from the trade union world and W. Millerchip represented the co-operative societies.

There was however considerable ambiguity both in the TUC relationship with Ruskin College and the way in which the aims of the College could best be realized as far as the teaching staff were concerned. When the Warden wrote to the PCTUC eight months after the College had been established asking them to appoint three trustees, Will Thorne, alone, questioned the *bona fides* of the founders[7] but, on the understanding that there would be no monetary responsibility, C.W. Bowerman, F. Chandler and A. Wilkie were elected. They were, however, prepared to call upon affiliated unions to provide support for the College. For the best of motives, namely the belief that a College had been established specifically to help working class adults, especially those from organized Labour, the PCTUC became involved with the College although at no time did they seek a mandate from Congress to gain approval for their actions. This was to be questioned by delegates in later years.

The problems at Ruskin College arose from several sources. There were conflicts between the staff both in terms of wide differences of opinion and in clashes of personality. Once the founders had returned to their homeland the College experienced financial insecurity and several of the staff were concerned to gain the academic approval of Oxford University for the work of the students. After the first few years students tended, increasingly, to come from trade unions and to be active members well versed in the practical experiences of industrial disputes. They expected to find tutors in sympathy with the aspirations of the Labour movement. This was often not the case; hence another source of friction became apparent.

The appointment of Denis Hird as Principal by the founders was based upon his principled stand against the Established Church rather than his membership of the SDF.[8] Together with Alfred Hacking, a fellow lecturer and Oxford graduate, he believed the College should provide education from a socialist point of view to help future leaders of the labour movement in their struggles within a capitalist society. There were, however, far more influences at work opposing such a philosophy. The majority of the staff were not in sympathy with Hird's views. For example, H.B. Lees-Smith, born in India the son of a British major, was a product himself of the Royal Military Academy at Woolwich and a graduate of Queen's College, Oxford. When he became vice-principal he expressed some sympathy for socialist ideas but gradually moved politically to the right before joining the Liberal Party. He was at pains to point out to members of the public that whilst Ruskin was a Labour College this did not imply that it was socialist: 'All the teaching is carefully impartial, and all its tutors are not socialists'.[9] The College Constitution from the beginning had stated that there should be no teaching of 'party politics'.

Charles Buxton and H.S. Furniss, were also Oxford graduates, and appointed to the staff by H.B. Lees-Smith. Neither had any experience of working class life nor any knowledge of the Labour movement. Furniss, a leading member of the Gladstonian Liberal League, admitted he encountered difficulty in dealing with working class students, especially socialists.[10] He complained about students singing the 'Red Flag', whilst Bertram Wilson, another Oxford graduate on the staff, criticized Hacking for drinking with the students. Both Furniss and Wilson objected to students expressing their political views in public, especially at the Martyrs' Memorial in Oxford, which became the scene of heated meetings and some physical violence when more prosperous younger Oxford undergraduates clashed with older Ruskin trade union students advocating socialist ideas. One major problem for the College, therefore, was that those formally qualified to gain teaching posts at the College rarely had much experience of working class life or much understanding of the political and social aspirations of many active trade unionists. Wilson, Buxton and Furniss might view the socialist philosophy of Denis Hird and some of the students as partisan; what they failed to appreciate was that their own anti-socialist and anti-Marxist views were considered equally partisan by the Principal and socialist students. Therefore relationships both between staff, staff and students, and among some of the students themselves often suffered due to differences of ideology.

A further problem was the question of finance. Many trade unions would not or could not offer sufficient financial aid to the College. This was one reason why Wilson turned for assistance to those outside the Labour movement, among whom were the 'Dukes of Fife and Norfolk, Lords Avebury, Crewe, Monkswell, Ripon, Rothschild, Tweedsmouth, Northcliffe and Roseberry, the Rt. Hon. Sidney Buxton (father of the vice principal), C.B. Harmsworth, A.J. Balfour and Rupert Guinness...'.[11] These private donors had little sympathy for the Labour movement and inevitably conditions were sometimes attached to donations; Lord Roseberry refused to help a student when he found out he was a socialist,[12] the Rev. A. Baillie of Rugby expressed difficulty in supporting an institution in which 'the whole spirit of the education is agnostic',[13] and F.W. Gilbertson, a colliery owner refused to renew his subscription.[14] Such pressure from those 'paying the piper' was a further factor influencing the curriculum.

Finally there was the problem of gaining academic respectability. This was necessary if appeals for financial aid were to be made outside the Labour movement, especially when one considers the titled and influential people from whom Wilson sought help. They were more likely to give such help to a college which followed an orthodox academic path. Several of the teaching staff were also keen to strengthen ties with the academic world with which they were more familiar. Wilson was keen on establishing links with Oxford University and visits to Ruskin College were made by A.L. Smith, fellow and tutor of Balliol, and Lord Curzon, Chancellor of the University and past Viceroy of India. Some students believed that Labour's new show of strength in the 1906 General Election was partly responsible for the greater interest being taken in the College by Oxford University. Formal links were, however, initially a result of a joint meeting of the WEA, Ruskin College and University representatives, entitled 'Oxford and Working Class Education'.[15] One result of this meeting was to allow some Ruskin students to study for the University's Diploma in Economics or Political Science. This move was seen as a means of increasing the prestige of Ruskin College; inevitably at the same time it increased the influence of academic orthodoxy in the teaching.

All these moves were seen by H.B. Lees-Smith and his supporters as merely sound moves in strengthening the College academically and financially. They were not viewed in this manner by Denis Hird and many of the students. Increasingly after 1902–03 the student intake included trade unionists who had first participated successfully in a correspondence course and been sent by their trade union because of their active membership. In addition, such students were more likely now to be socialists of some kind, well versed in the ways of industrial disputes, with quite a few ideas of their own about the economic and political structure of the country. Fired by the pioneering work of the ILP, Clarion and the hopes of the new Labour Party, such students were seeking more than a description of contemporary society; they were searching for a prescription for radical changes. Yet they found a College which seemed to be moving away from any attempt to provide an alternative critical working class view of society towards an embrace with academic orthodoxy which came down usually on the side of the *status quo*. Hence some strong disagreements within the College seemed inevitable: the result was the Strike of 1909 and the establishment of an alternative Labour College committed to socialist teaching under the Principalship of Denis Hird.

During this first decade of the twentieth century some financial support from affiliated unions had been provided for Ruskin College from the ASE, London Society of Compositors and the British Steel Smelters, Mill and Tin Plate Workers' Association. The PCTUC continued to call for delegates to support the College which had 'done a vast amount of good educational work, especially in the Labour and Co-operative section of the movement',[16] whilst at the same time letting the College know that it had 'no power to grant any money for such an object'.[17] The relationship between the College and the PCTUC in these early years, therefore, was one in which the latter gave open approval of the aims of the College. At this time Ruskin College might be described as a college *for* trade unionists but not one *of* trade unionists. Hence although certain members of the PCTUC were involved with the College there is no evidence to suggest that it was seen by most of the Labour movement as its own College.

It is not known for certain how far events leading up to the Ruskin College Strike were familiar to all members of the PCTUC, for no mention of the matter appears in this Committee's Minutes. However, with C.W. Bowerman and D. Shackleton as members of the College Council it can be assumed that the version given of events was favourable to Wilson and his supporters. The PCTUC representatives had also attended a meeting in October of that year presided over by H.B. Lees-Smith, now a Professor at Bristol University, to consider 'The Democratic Control of Ruskin College'. It was at this meeting that a new Constitution was agreed upon to strengthen the position of working class representation on the College Council; there were now to be two members each from the PCTUC, Co-operative Union and GFTU plus one from the Working Mens' Club and Institute Union. At least one more sign of the official political attitude of the College was the inclusion of the Club and Institute Union which was not a part of the Labour movement although it had a considerable working class membership; at the same time a motion to include representatives of the Labour Party was defeated by twenty-seven votes to four.

The PCTUC were now a little more hesitant to recommend financial support for the College to Congress. In 1908, in reply to an appeal fund for £20,000 from the College, the PCTUC Secretary was instructed to reply that 'no statement can be permitted to Congress, but any literature sent would be distributed and a list of delegates sent if required',[18] but in 1911 the PCTUC agreed to endorse, through their two representatives on the College Council, an appeal for trade unions to subscribe to the founding of Trade Union Scholarships.[19] A request from the College 'to allow their representatives to interview the Executive Committee of Trade Unions for financial help'[20] was rejected by the PCTUC in 1912 on the grounds that if it were granted other movements would seek similar treatment. This cautious approach was probably adopted in the light of disputes between trade union supporters of Ruskin College and the Central Labour College, during which time the former continued to request official PCTUC backing for its financial appeals as well as involving them wherever possible in joint meetings, such as a Conference which took place in July 1913 bringing together representatives of the College, PCTUC and GFTU.[21] A few days later the new Principal called upon the PCTUC and arranged for a reference to this recent Conference to be included in the next PCTUC Report to Congress. It was clear that Ruskin College was going to be presented to delegates as the officially recognized TUC College.

Recent cautious replies from the PCTUC to Ruskin College were also related to their responses to the Central Labour College. This College, supported enthusiastically by the monthly magazine *Plebs* and financed jointly by the ASRS and SWMF (both of whom had transferred their grants from Ruskin College), had requested the PCTUC to include in its forthcoming programme a notice concerning a meeting to be held by the College. This was rejected by the PCTUC[22] who also refused to receive a deputation from the College two years later;[23] this probably explains why they felt obliged to reject a similar request from Ruskin College four months afterwards. In addition, for some reason, the Quarterly Report of the PCTUC in December 1912 included extracts from a critical report in the *Times* (18.11.1912) describing a disagreement which had arisen within the CLC.[24]

At the 1913 Congress Edward Gill and Frank Hodges, both of the Miners Federation and the latter a dissenting Ruskin College student of 1909, questioned C.W. Bowerman, Secretary of the PCTUC and Chairman of the Ruskin College Executive Council (joint offices which were bound to be a factor in his support for the latter), about statements concerning Ruskin College in the PCTUC Report. They were informed that there would be time to discuss this later and, finally, during the last fifteen minutes of Congress time on Friday, Bowerman asked Congress to endorse a resolution approving of statements made in the PCTUC Report concerning Ruskin College and expressing '. . . satisfaction that the government of the College is entirely in the hands of representatives of working-class organizations, such as the PCTUC, the GFTU, Co-operative Societies and the Trade Unions having students at the College. . .'.[25] The resolution included a request for Unions to sponsor students at the College.

Bowerman's supporting speech showed a clear awareness of both past and present criticisms of Ruskin College. The Labour pedigree of Dr. Slater, ex Mayor of Woolwich and now Principal of the College, was emphasized, reference made to the 'good financial support . . . being given to the College by the Cooperative movement, and also by the Club and Institute Union' and delegates informed that 'you yourselves, through your Committee, have two representatives upon the Board; and the General Federation has two representatives upon it also. That being so, I do not think that anybody can say that the College is not being controlled in a truly democratic manner'.[26] The new building programme was also enthusiastically described.

The picture of the democratic involvement of the Labour movement painted by Bowerman was not really accurate and he must have been aware of this fact. The Club and Institute Union's relationship to the Labour movement was ambiguous; it was not committed politically to Labour and in fact had Tory clubs affiliated to it.[27] Whilst financial support was afforded from sections of the Labour movement, as has already been shown, financial contributions were also received from anti-Labour movement sources. As for TUC representatives this was completely misleading. What had begun in 1899 as a well intentioned arrangement by the PCTUC to send members to Ruskin College had long since developed into what looked suspiciously like appointments arranged to avoid the scrutiny and approval of Congress delegates. Hodges questioned such placings by the PCTUC: 'We find no resolution has been carried here to give them that authority . . . if they do represent the Parliamentary Committee, they cannot in any sense represent us'.[28] Even Bowerman's statement that 'ever since the dispute, Ruskin College has been controlled in an absolutely democratic manner' also implied that this had not been the case before this event.

PCTUC support for Ruskin College can be explained for two reasons. There was the question of loyalty encouraged by the habit of long association, especially on the part of Bowerman, towards a College which had been among the first to show an interest in the education of working class adults. More important by 1913, however, was the fact that most of the PCTUC, and certainly their two representatives on the College Council, were far more in political sympathy with the views of this College preaching gradual social reform than they were with the ideas expressed by the Socialist and Marxist Central Labour College. Congress surprised the PCTUC by providing stronger opposition to Bowerman's resolution, which he had attempted to push through in the last moments of Congress, than they had foreseen. This opposition was voiced partly because, as Edward Gill pointed out, ' . . . there are delegates in this Congress representing unions affiliated with the Central Labour College that far outweigh the numbers of unions that support Ruskin College'.[29] The resolution was finally lost on a show of hands and attempts to call a card vote rendered impractical as delegates were on the move assuming that the debate was all over.

On the Saturday morning the President explained that a strong desire had been expressed for the PCTUC to undertake an enquiry into both Ruskin and Central Labour Colleges. He recognized the division within Congress over the matter and told delegates that ' . . . by dividing the support of Congress in this way no effective good would be done to either institution'.[30] At last the disagreements which had taken place in many sections of the Labour movement had received their first airing at Congress and the PCTUC's method of appointing members to Ruskin College Council challenged.[31] A promise had been given that the claims of the Central Labour College would now also be considered. The way was now clear for a fresh approach to both colleges; an approach which would be subject to the approval of Congress delegates.

Moves Towards a Unified TUC Education Scheme

The First World War had led to the temporary closure of both Ruskin and Central Labour Colleges. In 1915 the TUC promised equal treatment to both colleges after the President, in replying to James Winstone, confessed that, whilst a report on Ruskin College had been included, one by the CLC had been omitted 'in error and not by design'. From then onwards both colleges were afforded similar consideration by the TUC and, although rivalry continued to exist, much fiercer arguments were to develop between what were often considered equivalent organizations offering part-time education; the WEA/WETUC and the National Council of Labour Colleges.

From its inception in 1903[32] the Association to promote the Higher Education of Men, later to be known as the Workers' Educational Association, approached the PCTUC for co-operation. Its provisional meeting in July 1903 was initiated by Albert Mansbridge and inspired by his three articles which appeared in the *University Extension Journal*; these concerned the educational needs of working class adults and outlined his plans for a new organization. Two representatives from the PCTUC attended the Conference[33] which included members from the academic world, the Church, the Co-operative movement and trade unions. In January 1905 Mansbridge wrote to the PCTUC asking them to appoint a representative to the Committee of the Association, and Shackleton was elected, his expenses to be paid 'if necessary'.[34] Like early appointments to Ruskin College the Committee acted on their own initiative and for the same reason; well meaning people were asking them to co-operate in developing education for working class adults. In the Autumn the Committee reported their response to Congress:

> Your Committee elected Mr. Shackleton to attend provisionally. His report was submitted to a full meeting of your Committee, who decided to appoint two of their members, Messrs. Shackleton and Bell, to represent them upon the Advisory Committee of the Association.[35]

The PCTUC continued to keep Congress informed about their relationship with the WEA. For example, in 1909 Congress were told that the PCTUC had been invited to take part in a joint enquiry as to the means of bringing universities more within the reach of the workers of the country.[36] The WEA did most of the work, largely because of the connections they already had with the academic world and the resulting Memo drawn up by Mansbridge was circulated to every member of the PCTUC for consideration.[37] Eventually the PCTUC decided to associate themselves with the demand for an enquiry concerning this matter and 'take part in any deputation or work having that end in view'.[38] This much co-operation was forthcoming from the PCTUC yet in October when the WEA sent an invitation for the PCTUC to send a representative to its AGM at Reading the Committee 'decided not to be represented' although providing no explanation.[39] It is possible that the repercussions of the Ruskin dispute were beginning to be felt but this does not seem altogether a plausible explanation because a few years later and only months after the 1913 Congress had challenged the legality of PCTUC relationships with Ruskin College, an application for the PCTUC to receive a delegation from the WEA was acceded to[40] and the resulting request for financial aid[41] subsequently granted.[42] At this time the WEA was not associated with the Ruskin and CLC rivalry; the PCTUC granted them £50 in 1915[43] and a further five guineas the following year, although it was pointed out that this must be regarded as a grant and not an affiliation fee.[44]

In fact the WEA enjoyed a good relationship with many trade unions at the local level:[45]

> The Reading branch of the WEA . . . had a Trades Council representative on its board from the time of its foundation. The Belfast branch was set up when the Trades Council approached the University jointly with the Co-operative Society, and the trades councils at Leicester, Northampton, Derby and Blackpool convened the meetings that started local branches in those towns. The Glasgow Trades Council also began the WEA in Scotland.[46]

Inevitably exceptions to the good relationships established between the Labour movement and the WEA can be found, such as the time in Leeds when some of the University members of the WEA condoned blacklegging in the Municipal Strike of 1913, thereby earning themselves the wrath of many working people.[47] In general, however, the organization showed itself in full sympathy with the Labour movement and its pamphlet entitled 'What Labour Wants from Education', published in 1916, was fully endorsed by the PCTUC.[48] Similarly an invitation from the WEA to a Conference in 1917 on 'Post War Education Reconstruction' was accepted by the PCTUC; Bowerman and Gosling attended as representatives.[49]

In October 1919 the WEA formed an association with the Iron and Steel Trades Confederation entitled the Workers Education Trade Union Committee[50] in which the former were to administer and teach courses for members of the Confederation. The idea arose from discussions between Arthur Pugh, General Secretary of the Confederation who knew both MacTavish and G.D.H. Cole of the WEA well. The scheme initially amounted to the WEA providing education specifically for trade unionists as a group instead of just hoping that they would join in local classes. The WETUC included members from both the WEA and Trade Union world: A. Pugh (Chair), MacTavish (Sec), E.W. Wimble (Asst. Sec. WEA), Arthur Greenwood (V. Chair WEA), H.H. Elvin (Clerks Union) and G.D.H. Cole, then a tutor at the Extra-Mural Department of London University. Like the Council of Ruskin College, Pugh believed the WETUC should try to obtain government and local authority grants wherever possible, arguing that this was only fair as 'millions per year are granted from the Treasury to equip the experts who run capitalist industries'.[51]

The WETUC had been designed to enable other trade unions to join and within the next few years the Union of Post Office Workers,[52] Railway Clerks' Association (which had been involved with the WEA since 1913), Association of Engineering and Shipbuilding Draughtsmen and NATSOPA had joined the scheme. By 1921 a similar, and in many ways a rival, organization developed entitled the National Council of Labour Colleges,[53] usually staffed by ex-CLC students and supported by the Plebs League. It soon gained the affiliation of the Amalgamated Union of Building Trade Workers and the Amalgamated Engineering Union. Very soon a war of words sprang up between the NCLC and both the WEA and WETUC. The last two organizations, like Ruskin College, claimed to teach from an 'independent' and 'neutral' point of view whilst the NCLC, like the CLC, proudly proclaimed that they were committed to a socialist approach in their teaching. By 1925, the NCLC claimed to be the largest education body of its kind in the world; a claim admitted by the WETUC with reservation because the length of courses and type of work was not easily comparable between the NCLC and WETUC.[54] These two organizations often became associated in people's minds as non-resident equivalents of the CLC and Ruskin College respectively; this was not quite accurate for unlike Ruskin College the WETUC included G.D.H. Cole who was well known for his left wing views and there is no evidence to suggest that WETUC tutors saw the organization as a stepping stone to higher places in the academic world as had been implied about some earlier tutors at Ruskin College.

Hence, in the early 1920s, there were several organizations providing education for trade unionists: the two residential colleges of Ruskin and CLC; the WETUC which hired premises for part time classes and the NCLC which did the same but also possessed buildings in Glasgow. All invited trade unionists on to their governing bodies and all sought financial aid and affiliations from individual trade unions and the TUC. Each could claim the allegiance of certain trade unions and there were frequent arguments as to which education body a union should support. Each organization had its slogans and in support of their claim to neutrality both the WETUC and Ruskin College liked to say 'we teach you how to think not what to think'. The NCLC, admittedly partisan, asked 'what's the use of having a trade union ticket in your pocket if the boss has your head in his?'[55] (see also Figure 1). One saying that could have been used by any of the organizations was to be found inside the cover of a pamphlet by H.J. Laski entitled 'Democracy at the Crossroads'. It read: 'He will be a smart policeman who will arrest the spread of ideas, but apathetic members of the Working-Class Movement do it daily'.

The TUC became one of the forums where protagonists of each educational organization put forward their ideas hoping to convince fellow delegates. In order to avoid this constant friction the Trades Union Education Enquiry Committee was set up by the WETUC and produced a lengthy document[56] which was sent to the PCTUC and every individual trade union for consideration in March 1921. It provided a review of recent trade union history and the varied educational provisions for trade unionists by the different colleges and organizations which had developed during the first twenty years of the twentieth century, together with many of the problems which had beset them, such as finance, variations in subjects offered and attainments of students, the suitability of some tutors for the work and the need to qualify wherever possible for official grants. Special consideration was given to the nature of the education to be provided and the different needs of particular groups; seafarers, agricultural workers and women trade unionists. Detailed recommendations were made covering the co-ordination of the educational activities of trade unions, ensuring that control of the education provided remained with the working class and asking all trade unionists to contribute towards a Trade Union Education Scheme. The last point was of great importance because the financial burden of trade union education was unevenly spread; for instance the NUR and the SWMF between them provided the bulk of the finance for the CLC.

At the Autumn Congress a resolution was proposed by C.G. Ammond (UPW) which suggested that the Trade Union Education Enquiry Committee offered the basis for a scheme which would meet the varied educational needs of trade unionists. It instructed 'the General Council to co-operate with the Trade Union Education Inquiry Committee as to the best means of giving effect to the aims and objects of the inquiry, including the taking over and running of existing Trade Union Colleges, including the CLC and Ruskin Colleges'.[57] The resolution was seconded by Frank Hodges (Miners Federation), who asked with reference to continued friction between the organizations, 'Why should this internecine warfare go on?'.[58] He suggested that now the pioneer days of these organizations were over a new period of organization was needed, '... if the Labour movement as a whole does not now begin to attempt to co-ordinate educational activities for the benefit of its young men it is doing an injustice to the forthcoming generations'.[59] There were no disagreements expressed in the debate and the resolution was carried. It was now up to the General Council to develop a scheme acceptable to all the varying organizations. The most persuasive argument they possessed was their ability to provide the finance that was desperately needed by the education bodies; the CLC and NCLC especially relied solely upon trade union subscriptions.

In response to the 1921 Congress resolutions the General Council set up an Education Committee comprised of members from the General Council Sub-Committee (A. Pugh, G. Hicks, J.W. Bowen, A.H. Findlay, C.W. Bowerman, F. Bramley and W. Bolton – thereby ensuring all education bodies were represented) and the TU Enquiry Committee (J.W. MacTavish, T.W. Burden, G.D.H. Cole, A. Creech-Jones and Mrs. Calthrop). The first meeting took place on 23rd February 1922 with Pugh as chairman. It was decided to interview representatives from Ruskin and the CLC and seek the opinions of the Co-operative Education Committee, WEA and NCLC as to whether they wished to be included in a joint Trade Union Education Scheme. MacTavish was asked to produce a memo as to how support from public funds might best be obtained.[60] He readily provided this and also suggested 'that the General Council of Congress be empowered to instruct its Sub Education

A FOOL'S PARADISE!

Oxford University (to Ruskin College) — "Come and dwell
with me, my boy — and forget all about nasty things like
wages and class struggles. They are *so* sordid!"

Committee to enter into negotiations with all bodies concerned in the wider scheme with a view to taking over: (a) Ruskin College (b) CLC (c) WETUC'.[61] A whole series of related suggestions followed concerning necessary organizational considerations for such a scheme.

During 1922 the General Council Education Committee contacted all the organizations suggested but, whilst general approval and a desire to co-operate was forthcoming, reservations were also voiced. In March a CLC deputation including W.W. Craik, Ablett, Lowth plus Millar (Scottish Labour College) and Hamilton (NCLC) – the last two had not been invited but asked if they might attend – called upon the GCEC. Mr. Ablett stressed the importance they attached to independent working class education:

> The Labour College was not prepared to modify any of its principles with regard to independent education… Their greater concern was that the workers should have the control of their teaching and should not be interfered with … they taught on a clear Marxian basis and must preserve the independence of their view in teaching in that way.[62]

Craik said they wanted a united educational front 'but a unified front depended upon unity of principle'.[63] In 1922, therefore, the CLC were willing to consider the TUC Education Scheme but only if they did not have to surrender any of their independence in teaching and propaganda.

Three months later it was the turn of the Ruskin College deputation of H. Sanderson-Furniss, F. Smith and W. Temple (Working Mens' Club and Institute Union) to put their views to the GCEC. Furniss expressed their reservations:

> They had never been an exclusively Trade Union College. They also received a good deal of support from bodies such as the Club and Institute Union and the Co-operative Movement and would not like to come into any scheme which would cut them off from those bodies. The College was non-party in politics … if such a body as the Labour Party, for instance were included in the Scheme, it would have to be considered, whether they could change the constitution of the College, and whether it would be wise to do so.[64]

The Club and Institute Union representative stressed that they existed for social purposes and made it clear that they would not send members 'to certain colleges', obviously referring to the CLC.

Such remarks from the CLC and Ruskin College meetings with the GCEC give an indication of the problem confronting the TUC. One college clearly represented a left wing socialist approach to the education they provided and the other was at least reluctant openly to support the political views of the Labour movement. Critics of Ruskin pointed to a contradiction because, whilst Furniss proclaimed that Ruskin College should be of service to the Labour movement, the College would have nothing to do with the political party of the Labour movement; it would not even allow a representative from the Labour

Party on to the Governing Council of the College. It would not be unfair either to say that the College was hostile to Marxism, if only because Marxists were constantly critical of the College, and the day before the Ruskin College deputation called upon the GCEC the Principal had proposed 'the reduction of the time spent on Marxian Economics'; a proposal which was readily accepted.[65] Deputations from the Co-operative Union and the WEA calling upon the GCEC expressed an interest in the Trade Union Education Scheme and the latter wished to be involved through the WETUC.[66]

Following the interviews and discussions, the GCEC produced a report on Trade Union Education which it presented to Congress in 1922:[67] it included a brief description of German Trade Union Education which was considered to be better organized than the various British schemes. The Report outlined the purpose and character of working class education:

> The workers want knowledge, both for the immediate and practical purposes of the labour movement, and also as a means to the enlargement of their mental and social outlook. They seek a knowledge, not only of economics and industrial history, but also of the general and social history of their own and other people, of literature, and the arts and sciences.[68]

However, it was also recognized that specialist education was necessary for their class because of the industrial and political changes which had taken place in the UK that now meant 'the administration of branch business is a training for wider responsibilities and provides opportunities of graduating for positions on the District and National Committees of Trade Unions, local Authorities, and the House of Commons'.[69] Two important things were being recognized here: one was that active participation in a trade union was an education in itself; another was the need for working class representatives fully to understand wage agreements, insurance legislation, industrial hygiene, banking and finance so that they would possess the 'technical knowledge' necessary to represent their members well at the place of work. This was obviously an aspect of education vital to trade unionists but the Report believed that the efficiency of trade unionists also had political implications:

> The extent to which Labour will win control over local and national affairs will for some time to come be determined by the extent to which the average wage-earner thinks it is more capable of managing every-day affairs than those who oppose it.[70]

A constant source of argument in working class education had been the provision of teachers. At its crudest the alternatives suggested were well qualified academics indifferent to or ignorant of the working class or working class tutors committed to the Labour movement but lacking the necessary academic background. The Report pointed out that 'it is essential to the success of working-class education that a large number of teachers should be men and women who have had personal experience of wage-earning conditions. Universities do not always provide the best atmosphere for the training of such teachers'.[71] This view, reflecting more the CLC approach, was qualified by some acknowledgement of the opposing Ruskin College view:

> Advanced students . . . prefer the qualified teacher, if he is a master of his subject and can 'deliver the goods' (even if he is anti-Labour) to the sympathetic teacher whose mastery of the subject is not so complete.

It was institutionally recognized and approved knowledge that was being assumed by the word 'qualified'; a distinction with which all would not have agreed. Moreover whilst a working class pedigree had a certain emotional appeal and might well provide the best experience of what it was like to be 'an appendage of machinery' there was plenty of evidence both then and in later years to show that working class careerists could act against their own class when in office. There were also examples of middle class people who gave much of their energy and time to improve conditions for lower income groups; especially was this true of certain educationists, for example, H.J. Laski, G.D.H. Cole and R.H. Tawney.

The importance of winning women to the views of the Labour movement was stressed, a factor which had become increasingly important since women over thirty years of age had been enfranchised in 1918. 'No increase of male members will ever overcome the influence of women hostile or indifferent to Labour principles, more especially those who are wives or mothers, whether engaged in industry or not.'[72] It was essential when men were engaged in industrial disputes to feel that they could rely upon support from home and there can be little doubt that the failure, for a variety of reasons, to bring large numbers of women into the labour movement, especially the trade union world, was to cost the Labour Party dearly in many General Elections in the future.

Provision of the comprehensive education scheme outlined in the Report would ultimately depend upon the financial resources of the trade union movement and any other sources which could be tapped. This had been a critical area of disagreement between education bodies in the past. Those who took the Marxist view of the State as the apparatus by which the Ruling Class rules inevitably argued that such a State would hardly contribute funds to teaching designed to undermine it. Indeed, provision of such funds was, they believed, a guarantee that the education being offered by an organization was 'acceptable' to the Ruling Class. The way out of such a dilemma suggested by the Report was to obtain public money to finance some classes, perhaps those of a technical nature or in the natural sciences where the facts were less likely to be in dispute, whilst classes which had a strong political element critical of the *status quo* could be financed entirely by trade union funds.[73]

It was also hoped that even classes critical of the capitalist system might receive public finance:

> . . .the Trade Union movement has won for itself a recognized status

within the capitalist State. Its functions have become essential to both social and industrial well being. It does not, however, regard the present industrial system as permanent. It is of the opinion that the social relations denoted by the terms wage earner and capitalists must be fundamentally changed, and that to effect these changes in a constitutional way is a legitimate function of Trade Unionism... We submit that just as public funds are used to educate men and women to serve capitalist industries without any inquiry as to the social values of these industries, so public funds ought also to be available for the education of Trade Unionists as such, without any interference with the opinions or social theories of students or tutors.[74]

If this view appeared naîve to some it is partly explained by the outlook of individuals such as Pugh, who believed that trade union education could safely be left to 'the professionals'[75] and partly by the realization that trade unions were less likely to have the scale of funds necessary for such a programme of education in the future; the end of the post war boom meant that more workers were taking industrial action to defend their standard of living, a factor recognized by the Report, which referred to the depletion of trade union funds due to unemployment and attacks on wages.[76] A final reason for seeking public finance was the recognition that 'at present many teachers give their services free or accept low fees to assist voluntary education movements. But immediately the Trade Union movement accepts responsibility, it will be expected to apply Trade Union principles, and offer reasonable conditions of service'.[77]

The cautious recommendations of the GCEC Report, especially in terms of finance, reflected the sudden change in the post war industrial and political situation. The take over of the two residential colleges by the GC was given no time limit but agreed to in principle 'as soon as satisfactory financial and other conditions can be agreed upon' and the GC were prohibited from increasing any affiliation fees 'without authorization of the Congress itself'. An annual report to Congress on future progress to be made towards the setting up of the Trade Union Education Scheme together with a special study of the educational needs of young workers was also promised by the TUCEC. One can trace through the next two years a strong desire upon the part of the GCEC to negotiate an agreement between the education bodies as fast as possible before the deteriorating industrial situation overtook them. It is clear that the CLC and the WETUC were also aware of the necessity for a quick agreement to be reached. Ruskin hesitated because of its constitution; it wanted TUC approval and financial aid without losing its other supporters. Apart from political consideration, it believed that a variety of sources[78] provided a sounder financial base than one exclusive supporter, and the apparent unwillingness of some trade unions to subscribe to any education body must have helped to make them apprehensive. It might also be argued that their link with Oxford University by which certain students studied for a Diploma meant that they were not so independent academically as the CLC. The NCLC stood unyielding. It might be that their view of independent socialist education for trade unionists was correct but it was abundantly clear that many TUC delegates were not in favour of this approach if only because some already felt loyalty to other institutions with which they had become involved. The TUC was trying to bring together bodies with different and sometimes conflicting views but the NCLC seemed determined to stress the conditional terms they considered necessary for any agreement.

In terms of collecting factual information, such as college expenditure, some progress was being made, but the NCLC representatives did not make matters easy. Typical of the arguments heard was that which took place in May 1923. Mark Starr of the NCLC pointed out the special nature of his organization and could not resist a jibe at both Ruskin College and the WEA, both of whom had representatives present:

> ... the work of the NCLC entitles it to extra special consideration when it comes to making financial provision... The NCLC will never be able to issue an appeal such as Ruskin College issued, signed by such good friends of labour as A.J. Balfour, Robert S. Horne and Lloyd George. We have no Cassel grant to draw upon such as the WEA... We shall have to depend on Trade Union support. We are prepared to allow the TUC a share in the control of our work ... but if you say to us that ... we are not to go about and say of the WEA – we think it is in that stage of working class education, which, in the political sphere, is known as the Lib Lab, ... [and] ... we must not denounce this Mr. Facing Both Ways, we should consider such financial support as being too dearly bought.[79]

There can be little doubt that such remarks made negotiations difficult and G.D.H. Cole pointed out the dilemma caused: 'We do not want to rule out the Labour Colleges; but they want to rule us out'. He felt that the NCLC view was based upon some misunderstandings and speaking on behalf of the WETUC argued that there was place for both approaches to education:

> We differ neither in aim, nor in the main in teaching method, but in attitude ... I am a Socialist and a Marxian, and I want my students to believe what I hold to be true; but I try to keep my own bias under, and to draw them to make their own decisions; even against my view of the truth. The Labour Colleges have a different method. I do not say it is less legitimate ... but I do not see why we should fight.[80]

W.W. Craik also believed there was room for both approaches and pointed out that 'the TUC must be Catholic'. It was this factor which the NCLC seemed to ignore in the negotiations.

The Report made to the 1923 Congress reflected some of the uncertainties expressed in past discussions between the various bodies involved. A general desire for a TUC Education Scheme was confirmed by Congress and it was agreed to set up an educational fund of £1000; this represented approximately one per cent of TUC Annual Income. A full debate took place concerning the type of education needed by trade unionists; this was partly sparked off by a discussion the previous day on the need to support the *Daily Herald*, a matter which some delegates believed was related, for it was argued that just as the Labour movement needed to control a newspaper of its own so it needed to control its own educational institutions.[81]

Those supporting what might be termed as committed education were most vociferous: W.J. Nichol (ASW) and M.F. Titterington (Stuff/Woollen Ware-housemen) were both wary of simply more education being offered because the latter believed 'education to-day is merely making for efficiency under the present system of production: our education makes us efficient wage slaves'. Hence the former's open support for class conscious education:

> I am absolutely sick and tired of listening to people on 'Labour' problems talking about 'broadness'. The spirit of the movement is based upon the narrowest of conceptions, and that is that the working classes produced the wealth and ought to be entitled to it. I believe that the movement as a whole is based upon that. Certainly if education within our own ranks is not directed to that end then it misses its point altogether. Instead of working-class education being broad in concep-tion, it ought to be working class education, education in two or three specific subjects such as will fit the rank and file to take their part in the class struggle [82]

The call for what was in fact a socialist approach to education made sense to some trade unionists who believed that capitalism was the cause of the industrial and political problems confronting them. There were however numerous trade unionists, especially those in leading positions on the General Council, who saw themselves as merely in a position of bargaining with employers. They approved of solidarity when wage negotiations were under way but dis-approved of talk which included references to class struggle or worker control. J.H. Thomas for example showed no dislike for those described by some of his colleagues as the ruling class; he dined with them frequently and made it clear to Congress that he would be glad for the NUR to be free of the CLC; this was ostensibly for financial reasons[83] but their teaching can hardly have been to his liking either. Even the once radical Ben Tillett now seemed confused and anxious to avoid militant action of any kind; he offered his services to the Conservative Premier Stanley Baldwin in 1923[84]

It would seem that most members of the General Council would have been happier linked to Ruskin College and the WETUC. Apart from their tradition-al association with the former and Pugh's involvement with the latter, few favoured the teachings of the CLC and even less the NCLC. If it were not for the fact that the NUR and SWMF were involved with the CLC and the AUBTW with the NCLC it is quite possible that the GC would have ignored them both. However, the railwaymen and miners were too powerful to be ignored. It must be admitted that the TUCEC itself did its best to be impartial and the presence of G.D.H. Cole was a major factor in smoothing negotiations for, whilst he was with the WETUC, both in his views and discussions he showed considerable sympathy for the CLC and NCLC. He had in fact written an article in *Plebs* in 1916 pointing out that he was quite willing for the WEA to sever its links with bodies outside the Labour movement:

> The sooner Labour can stand on its own educational legs, the better for itself and the worse for the capitalist system. I do not believe that Oxford and Cambridge or the new Universities are going intentionally to help Labour to secure emancipation. I am only waiting until Labour is prepared to take over the WEA and to run it as a definitely Labour concern – and to pay for it.[85]

What seemed unrealistic about the NCLC in negotiations is that they must have known that their views did not accord with those of many trade union leaders but instead of quickly getting under the umbrella of the TUC they continued to argue their points and criticize those who were expected to work alongside them.[86]

Negotiations concerning the TUC Education Scheme continued slowly; a meeting of all unions which had educational schemes (but not those involved with full time colleges) was held in March 1924 and in the same month[87] it was recommended that the Joint Educational Committee should give way to an Educational Advisory Committee which would broaden the membership to include appointees of the GC; one representative from each affiliated union which had a definite scheme of educational work in operation, two representatives each from the Co-operative Union, WEA and NCLC, and one each from Ruskin and the CLC. The new committee faced precisely the same problems as the old: to produce a TUC Education Scheme acceptable to all the educational organizations involved with trade unionists. The discussions took the same form. The same arguments were repeated.[88] Similarly, the 1924 Congress heard familiar pleas, including a forceful speech by George Hicks on an amendment to make all trade union education follow the principles of the CLC and NCLC;[89] he withdrew the amendment the next day after a request from A.J. Cook in the interest of trade union unity.[90]

The Education Advisory Committee were able to get the various organizations to agree, sometimes only after considerable compromise by representatives, to a series of suggestions concerning residential colleges, tutors, organizers and the rights of criticism and propaganda; the latter was later interpreted differently by the WEA and NCLC. When it came to objectives however, there was an *impasse*. Ruskin College and the WEA made a brief statement which included the view that the education offered should be designed '. . . to assist the working class in its efforts for social and industrial emancipation'. The NCLC responded with the aim '. . . to educate them for the purpose of bringing to an end the system of Capitalism, thus enabling the working class to achieve its social and industrial emancipation'. Finally a compromise was accepted omitting any reference to capitalism, to allow for the constitution of the WEA.[91] This outcome displays once more a predicament among educational organizations which genuinely wished to help in the education of members of the Labour movement yet could not bring themselves to take their side. In the class divided Britain of the 1920s many of the problems facing the working class were seen by many workers as products of capitalism. The CLC and NCLC were outspoken in their desire to see an end to such an economic system. By continuing to give it tacit support, both Ruskin and the WEA's genuine support for the working class interests were open to question.

1925 was a significant year for the TUC Education Scheme. It really began to look as if past difficulties between the educational institutions might be overcome. Within individual bodies views had not basically changed; Fred Bramley of Ruskin College, who had considerable doubts as to whether the TUC could or should finance its own college[92] complained bitterly about the way the NUR and SWMF provided the CLC with £8,000 annually whilst his College 'was starved of funds', overlooking the fact that these two unions actually owned the CLC.[93] In spite of such remarks, within a month both colleges had stepped closer than ever to the plan for the TUC to take them over. Preliminary discussions first took place between the TUCEAC and the joint owners of the CLC[94] and a few weeks later a second meeting resulted in the handing over of a document from the latter stating the terms on which they were prepared to surrender the CLC to the TUC.[95] The theoretical basis of the teaching was to be safeguarded, the two unions agreed to send their usual complement of students for the next two years, they would donate £1,000 and they requested that their newly acquired site at Kew should be considered for development.[96] It was agreed that the site might be sold if new premises for a TUC College were found elsewhere and that after two years the NUR and SWMF would subscribe to a TUC Education Fund in the same manner as other unions. Such an offer was considered to be constructive by the TUCEAC and at the same time would remove the disproportionate financial burden the two unions had been carrying in providing working class education.

Discussions with Ruskin College also proceeded smoothly. In May the College wrote to the TUCEAC offering to co-operate 'wholeheartedly', whilst at the same time asking for a donation,[97] and in June the College repeated the conditions considered necessary by the Governing Council for control to be handed over to the TUC.[98] These conditions were put in the form of a resolution unanimously carried at a meeting of the Ruskin College Governing Council and forwarded to the GCTUC. Like the CLC, they wished to safeguard their teaching aims. They also wished for non trade union bodies such as the Co-operative Union and the WMCIU to have representation in any new scheme in which they were involved.[99] In fact the Co-operative Union had by now established its own College at Holybrooke, near Manchester, so that this section of the Labour movement was not likely to play a major part in any future TUC College.[100] Ruskin College was worried about the future site of a new College, being content with Oxford but prepared to accept London as an alternative.

By the late Summer of 1925 the take-over of Ruskin College and the CLC by the TUC seemed inevitable. By coincidence both colleges were without a Principal[101] and it was agreed to hold back from any appointments in the belief that soon only one would be needed. Further evidence that all was going well can be deduced from the fact that the TUCEAC deferred a proposal to pay fifty per cent (that is £100) of the cost of each trade union student accepted by any one of eighteen Cambridge colleges participating in a scheme organized by the Extra Mural Studies Department of Cambridge University.[102] They clearly believed that such a scheme would not be necessary now that their own trade union education plans were nearing fruition.

Following the approval of the 1925 Congress to the proposed development of the TUC Education Scheme, the TUCEAC prepared a circular to be sent to all the affiliated societies. It pointed out that the GC could only carry out Congress instructions provided that financial support was forthcoming '. . . and in this connection the Education Committee feels that one of the best methods of assistance will be adopted if the vacancies for students at the residential colleges . . . can be speedily filled'.[103] Smaller unions wishing to send students were offered some financial help from the TUC.[104] The worry for the TUCEAC was that Congress approved easily enough the proposed new education scheme but response from some trade unions to provide the necessary financial aid was less than enthusiastic. The growing anxiety of the Committee could be understood from the proposals they were expected to act upon:

(a) A grant of now £2,000 *per annum* from Congress to an Educational Fund.
(b) The taking over the maintenance of Ruskin College and the CLC.
(c) Raising levies from affiliated unions in addition to (a) to finance the working of the proposed scheme.

The TUC and the Easton Lodge Scheme

Towards the end of 1925 a new factor entered into the situation which seemed at first glance to some trade unionists to provide a solution to the problem of setting up a TUC College. A letter was received by the TUCEAC from Lady Warwick stating 'that she was desirous of handing over the whole of the estate of Easton Lodge, with the exception of two rooms which she would wish to retain for her own use, to the Trade Union movement as a Central Labour College'.[105] It was agreed to follow up this 'extremely generous offer' and arrangements were made for the Committee to visit Easton Lodge,[106] much to the delight of Lady Warwick who enthusiastically replied 'I am so glad that there is a chance of our Central Labour College becoming a fact!'.[107]

Pugh, though very pleased with the offer, was a little more cautious and suggested that it might be premature for her land agent to attend at their meeting 'to go into figures and ask *Technical* questions about the property'.[108] The TUCEAC knew that they had to consider not only the situation of Easton Lodge but the continuing financial problem of Ruskin and CLC which were in effect experiencing a 'hand to mouth' existence hoping that help would soon be on its way from the TUC. The former College now became disturbed at information which had somehow been 'leaked' to the *Morning Post* which ran an article stating that '. . . if the gift is ratified, . . . the Labour College, London and Ruskin College will be sold and merged into a Socialist University . . .'.[109] Ruskin College had agreed that London would be an acceptable site but Essex was less attractive and so was reading about private negotiations in a daily newspaper,[110] especially one constantly hostile to the Labour movement. Once the news was out the TUC received numerous tenders for necessary alterations at Easton Lodge from builders and plumbers, including an application from a Birmingham firm to supply badges for future students. A letter was even received from Fenner Brockway, Secretary of the ILP, asking if there might be a vacancy for his cousin, 'a socialist gardener', when the College was established.[111]

Rather inevitably suspicion for the leak fell upon Lady Warwick who was rarely averse to publicity and whose son, Maynard, worked for the *Morning Post*. She wrote to Walter Citrine protesting her innocence in the matter:

> Will you please tell your TUC Education Committee that the newspaper announcements had nothing to do with *me*! Since your visit I have maintained absolute silence. . . . My younger son rang me up on Friday saying the Press Association had the news and asking me to explain. I said it was perfectly true – but negotiations were in their infancy, and I could say nothing definite without *your* consent – I referred him to *you*. As I hear there is a full account in the *Morning Post* (I never see the Rag) I supposed you satisfied him and yesterday every newspaper in the country rang me up. . . .[112]

Compared to Oxford and London, Easton Lodge in rural Essex was a remote spot. Doubts were expressed by the TUCEAC '. . . as to whether the teaching staff would be sufficiently in touch with educational developments if residing in such a place, and, further, the isolation of students at Easton would be a subject for consideration'.[113] A meeting at Ruskin College discussed this issue[114] although, to Bowen, the danger was of 'students running wild in London' if a Trade Union College was established there. Creech-Jones doubted the wisdom of 'working class students being taken out of their environment into an atmosphere of the kind which prevailed at Easton Lodge', an accusation also made about Ruskin College being in Oxford, by TUC delegates! To the question of schooling for tutors' children, H.H. Elvin (Clerks Association) believed that this problem 'was not insurmountable, because there were boarding schools and the usual preparatory schools'. Such familiarity with the private fee paying school system and seeming approval of it, at least for the children of tutors if not trade unionists, seemed incongruous for a trade unionist discussing working class education. It was this kind of statement which provided circumstantial evidence about the commitment of some elements at Ruskin College to independent trade union education.

In the same month the approximate costs necessary to convert parts of Easton Lodge were listed and found to total nearly £40,000.[115] Two days later Walter Citrine informed Lady Warwick that the GC had accepted her offer and were going to appeal to the Unions to raise £50,000;[116] Lady Warwick then invited them to spend a couple of days as her guests 'perhaps for the last time on your own premises'.[117] In fact there was less reason for continued optimism than the correspondence warranted, for appeals to the trade unions for funds were not proving very successful: the London Society of Compositors wrote to tell Citrine that they 'are unable to give any guarantee or grant at present';[118] the Amalgamated Society of Woodworkers told him that 'financial assistance to educational schemes was submitted to the membership of this Society on two occasions, but the proposition did not carry'[119] whilst the Operative House, Ship Painters and Decorators replied, 'In view of the fact that our members have definitely turned down the proposals for the provision of a Working-Class Education Scheme, the question will not arise'.[120] The one letter of support came from the Tailor and Garment Workers Union who sent £50 in March.[121]

Little enthusiasm seemed to be aroused at Ruskin College either. The students passed a resolution 'deprecating the removal of the College from Oxford' whilst the acting Principal, A. Barratt Brown expressed considerable reservations in a report he made following upon his visit to Easton Lodge.[122] This in turn brought a critical response from Citrine who wrote to the College explaining that 'the GC were extremely disappointed that the representatives of the two Colleges (that is, Ruskin and CLC) had made the most of the objections and too little of the possibilities'. Citrine's frustrations concerning past quarrels between the different education bodies was also apparent. He said that the GC 'had made up its mind to go on with Easton Lodge and to develop an educational institution in the form of a Trade Union College rather than a Labour College'.[123]

Lady Warwick was also now conscious of the doubts being raised. She wrote to Citrine:

> Things are difficult all round – Aren't they? Press is untruthful, Friends and Comrades are antagonistic. *My* 'relations' are furious and jealous, and now I believe Mr. Henderson has discovered obstacles.[124]

The 'obstacles', in fact, were the new conditions she was now demanding which meant, as Henderson had pointed out, that the TUC 'in effect of the proposals now made would be deprived of all the usual rights of ownership. There would be no power either to sell or mortgage the whole or any part of the property'.[125] It seemed that Lady Warwick wanted the TUC to finance her stately home whilst she still retained control over it for she wrote 'in my life time I have promised to keep intact the legacy of my ancestors.... Of course I have no shadow of right to impose conditions *after my death*'.[126]

Perhaps trying to force the pace, she offered October 1st for the TUC take over of Easton Lodge.[127] She realized that the miners lock out was dragging on and that the whole trade union movement was being bled white in the struggle. A Trade Union College hardly seemed a top priority now: '... the psychological moment passed long ago' she wrote to Citrine, 'and I imagine that a levy *now* would produce consternation'.[128] The following month a lengthy debate ensued at the 1926 Congress over the TUC Education Scheme for Easton Lodge. The sum of £50,000 for capital costs alone staggered many delegates in a year when they were in dire financial straits following the General Strike in May and it was the scale of this commitment which doubtless frightened many away from a decision to act upon the report placed before them. Mrs. Anne Laughlin (NUTGW) felt that such expenditure would leave little money in the hands of unions to provide 'educational facilities for the rank and file in regard to evening classes ...'.[129] Unions would still be required to finance scholarships for residential students and when this sum was added to the capital costs Arthur Henderson believed that over the next two years the TUC would have to raise £60,000 to £70,000 to finance the scheme adequately. He told delegates that for many unions

> any question of a levy on their funds at the present moment, in view of the financial experience we have just had in relation to the national strike, must, of necessity, be very carefully reviewed ... it is in no cheeseparing frame of mind that we, the Transport Workers, have some hesitation ... until we have some assurance from the GC, some greater detail of the proposal, and know how money is to be spent....[130]

Bowen asked the unions to pay for the scheme and Pugh, in a long speech explaining the history of the negotiations finally put it to Congress that 'either we must go forward or we must stop.... We must have from you ... definite instructions on this matter; and we can only construe, I regret to say, a reference back to this report as a recommendation that we are not to proceed'.[131] On a card vote Congress decided for the reference back by 2,441,000:1,481,000.

The financial burden was the major cause of worry among delegates; this mood of apprehension was capitalized upon by J. Jones who gave a speech which brought laughter from delegates and, whilst it made little mention of money, appealed to the emotions of rank and file delegates, helping to sway opinion away from support for the TUC Education Scheme. That many delegates probably wanted to be persuaded is possible; that Jones had the talent to do it seems fairly certain. In many ways he was only repeating some of the views expressed by committed socialists in the past, partly caricatured for this occasion. The audience responded to the pictures he painted of 'workmen who have gone up to Ruskin College dressed as workmen, who have come back with halos, dressed in plus fours, and immediately wanting to be general secretary of their union [laughter]'. He continued, '. . . if we are going to subsidize education, let us subsidize it in industrial centres, where the workers will go to evening schools. I know nothing about Easton Lodge except that I have been to see it . . . the Labour Movement is not going to be saved by the kind of people produced at such places'.[132]

Jones thought that location and roots were vital; Ruskin at Oxford was no more suitable as a place of study for trade unionists than Easton Lodge in Essex. He favoured West Ham, a working class constituency in which he enjoyed a majority of 10,000 as a much better place for working people to study in. He had no wish to '. . . drive our people down to where they have to associate with the class against whom we are fighting. . . . We want education from our own class standpoint . . .'.[133] Jones' speech helped to decide the issue. The Easton Lodge scheme was dead. Only the formalities of burial remained. Lady Warwick wrote to Citrine describing the TUC decision as 'a devastating blow' and declared that now 'the incident is closed'.[134] A letter from her solicitors quickly followed confirming that 'the matter is at an end'.[135]

It was, however, more than the Easton Lodge scheme that had expired at the 1926 Congress. Within two years the CLC had closed[136] and Ruskin College was to know only lean times for years to come. Following the Congress decision, Citrine wrote to Ruskin College informing them that '. . . it was necessary to face the fact that little financial support could be expected from the General Council, apart from their present commitment *in view of the present industrial situation* . . . the College should not look too optimistically to assistance from Trade Unions for at least another twelve months'.[137] This gloomy picture from Citrine was reinforced by news that the Durham Miners' Scholarship would not be taken up now and a scheme for an exchange between Ruskin College and Belgian students had to be cancelled.[138]

The General Strike had not only crippled the Labour movement financially; it had dealt a shattering blow to morale. Membership of unions affiliated to the TUC shrank by half a million between 1926–28. The argument about trade union education, however, remained and attempts to summarize the arguments, based upon the experiences related, inevitably lead to conjecture.

It is difficult to avoid the view that Ruskin College was governed and staffed for much of the period considered by those who largely wished for little more than the *status quo* in society. In seeking to attain academic respectability, and the approval of student work by Oxford University they inevitably embraced a conservative force which may have had some sympathy for working class students as scholars but showed little interest in ideas aimed at emancipating Labour. To have done so would have been considered 'taking sides' and therefore against Liberal academic traditions. By the same token there were those who believed that to hold to the *status quo* or even adopt a neutral pose also meant taking sides, whilst in the sciences, whatever claims for impartiality natural scientists might be able justifiably to make, such a claim could not be maintained in the social sciences, nor in some of the arts.

It is not difficult to find examples of life experiences amongst those connected with Ruskin College which showed little concern for Socialism. The question that needs to be put here, though, is whether many of the leading trade unionists equated trade union education with some form of Socialist ideology anyway; the answer for a considerable number of the prominent members connected with trade union education would have to be that they did not. Arthur Pugh, C.W. Bowerman, J. Sexton and J.W. Bowen, for example, were not enamoured with Socialism and were positively hostile to Marxism.

Ben Tillett made an interesting speech at the laying of a foundation stone at Ruskin College in 1912 in which he stated:

> We talk so much about what the working class is, what it ought to be, and what should be done to it, but up to now we have been rather patronized, and the workers of the country love a Lord – they love the sight of opulence and the sight of office and distinction, but I am hoping that this College is going to kill that form of flunkeyism, at least in everyone who comes to it...

Such sentiments gained approval on such an occasion but they were never fulfilled. Many associated with the College embraced that very flunkeyism that Tillett claimed to despise: Sanderson-Furniss became Lord Sanderson, William Bowen accepted a knighthood,[139] whilst Lees-Smith, the vice principal who had clashed so fiercely with Denis Hird and exchanged political parties made a doubtful contribution to the education of new Labour MPs in 1924:

> 'They had to be taught how and when to bow when leaving and entering the Chamber of the House of Commons. They had to know how to address other MPs correctly.... So a class in deportment was started. The instructor was Professor Lees-Smith'.[140]

To socialist trade unionists such activities were anathema. They did not believe it served any useful purpose for trade union leaders to ape the mannerisms and habits of the higher income groups they were supposed to be opposing.[141] More than one trade union leader used his own trade union organization, not necessarily in his earlier years of commitment, but later, as a means of obtaining social mobility. If Ruskin College did little to refute such actions it may well have been because many of those involved with the College believed that such activities were quite legitimate. It is also obvious that some academics had no conception of a 'class war' and could not readily understand why some trade unionists might adhere to such a doctrine; or at least believed that once they had received the benefit of higher education such ideas would evaporate in the light of new knowledge.

Socialists and Marxist trade unionists at CLC and NCLC did gain the support of many rank and file members. The question that needs to be posed is whether they could have gained the support of many more workers, enough at least to save the CLC. When industrial disputes pressed hard upon the financial resources of a worker and his family, many saw full-time education at least as an expensive luxury. The struggle to persuade the organized working class to support their own political party, their own Co-operative Movement, their own newspaper and their own education movement was to be a never ending struggle. These institutions could only expect to raise money from among their own ranks. What ruling class would provide money to support an institution which might in some way undermine it, the Marxists frequently asked. Hence when Ruskin College received financial aid from the Board of Education in 1920 that was evidence enough for some that the education provided could not be unduly critical of the existing social order.

Moreover there is evidence to show that there were elements within the higher echelon of the State who were apprehensive about working class education, whether provided by Ruskin College, the CLC, the TUC or even school teachers supportive of trade unionists. In 1920 George V expressed his concern to H.A.L. Fisher who wrote in his diary, 'The King most disturbed about Labour colleges, Socialist Sunday Schools'.[142] Representations made by the NUR concerning the reinstatement of railway workers who wished to study at a Labour College were all rejected by the employers;[143] this was a way of both intimidating workers from pursuing further education and safeguarding against the re-employment of active trade unionists who might otherwise return to their jobs even better informed. Even the TUC Education Scheme of 1925 brought forth hostile remarks from Lord Percy at the Board of Education who singled out for comment, in particular, the NCLC who were included in the Scheme. He believed them to be the real enemies of education: 'In opposing the NCLC we are fighting no political battle ... but in very truth a battle against spiritual wickedness'.[144] Others arousing suspicion were the Teachers Labour League, which supported the strikers in 1926. They were duly placed under police surveillance.[145]

It might seem that the General Strike and its aftermath led to a great reduction in trade union education and certainly prevented planned expansion from taking place. In a formal sense it did but it must be remembered that the experience obtained by living through the industrial and political struggles of the time was an education in itself, especially for the activists within the Labour movement. Some might see it as a more important and appropriate education for trade unionists than any College could ever provide, no matter what the calibre of the staff or the place in which it was situated. To that extent trade union education was not reduced. It took a practical turn and may for that reason have been of greater significance in the long run.

Notes

1 See, for example, the detailed study of adult classes in nineteenth century Yorkshire in HARRISON, J.F.C. *Learning and Living 1790–1960* or Workers' Movements and Education between 1832–1850 in SIMON, B. *Studies in the History of Education*

1780–1870. Chapter V.

2 COLE, G.D.H. *A Century of Co-operation*, pp. 227–228.

3 The seven books and pamphlets recommended ranged in price from 3d to 13/6d and were largely confined to legal matters concerning trade unions. For example, George Howell's *Handy Book to the Labour Laws* and Henry Compton's *Industrial Conciliation*, TUC Report 1879, p. 15.

4 See HUGHES H.D. *The Story of Ruskin College*, (rev'd 3rd ed); CRAIK, W.W. *Central Labour College*; YORKE, P. *Ruskin College 1899–1909*; SIMON, B. *Education and the Labour Movement 1870–1920*, pp. 318–342.

5 The founders were Walter and Anne Vrooman, and Charles Beard. In the early years it was largely financed by Anne Vrooman whose family were wealthy newspaper proprietors.

6 In the first few years many foreign students came for a few weeks because at 12/6d per week full board it was such a cheap place to stay and learn English. Students from Church societies were also numerous. See. YORKE, P. *op. cit.*, pp. 7–9.

7 There was some disagreement over the PCTUC's support for Ruskin Hall in 1899. For one thing C.W. Bowerman and James Sexton had gone to North America lecturing as PCTUC delegates on the need for such a college to be established there. Some TUC delegates objected to this activity on the grounds that it had not been authorised by Congress. TUC Report 1900, p. 55.
It was also suggested that the motive for some of this criticism was because the LTC believed any Labour College should be in London.

8 Denis Hird had been a clergyman in Battersea until forced to resign by Dr. Frederick Temple, the Bishop of London, because he would not give up his membership of the SDF. His outspoken support for socialist ideas was also considered to be an embarrassment to the Church.

9 YORKE, P. *op. cit.*, p. 3.

10 *Ibid.*, p. 33.

11 *Ibid.*, p. 30.

12 *Ibid.*, p. 31.

13 *Ibid.*, p. 30.

14 *Ibid.*, p. 31.

15 The PCTUC were invited and sent C.W. Bowerman and D.J. Shackleton. PCTUC Mins., 16.10.1907. They reported in some detail to the PCTUC and some details of the Oxford meeting were published in the Annual Congress Report. See PCTUC Mins., 19.11.1908 and TUC Report 1909, pp. 11–12.

16 TUC Report 1903, pp. 49–50.

17 PCTUC to Ruskin College, 23.7.1903.

18 PCTUC Mins., 17.6.1908.

19 PCTUC Mins., 25.5.1911.

20 PCTUC Mins., 14.2.1912.

21 PCTUC Mins., 21.5.1913.

22 PCTUC Mins., 30.8.1909.

23 PCTUC Mins., 5.9.1911 & 18.10.1911.

24 PCTUC Quarterly Report 1912, p. 85.

25 TUC Report 1913, p. 332.

26 *Ibid.*, p. 333.

27 CRAIK, W.W. *op. cit.*, p. 85.

28 TUC Report 1913, p. 334.

29 *Ibid.*, p. 333.

30 *Ibid.*, p. 337.

31 Small wonder that the PCTUC decided 'to take no action' when approached a few months later by the London Working Men's College for a representative to serve on the Governing Body. PCTUC Mins., (7.1.1914) and (11.3.1914).

32 For a short history of the WEA see STOCK, M. *The Workers' Educational Association.*

33 See SIMON, B. *Education and the Labour Movement 1870–1920*, p. 306. The PCTUC Mins. mention a letter being received from the Association but no record was made of response in terms of sending representatives. PCTUC Mins. 2.9.1903.

34 PCTUC Mins., 19.1.1905.

35 TUC Report 1905, p. 91.

36 TUC Report 1909, pp. 10–12.

37 PCTUC Mins., 28.2.1910.

38 PCTUC Mins., 19.5.1910.

39 PCTUC Mins., 12.10.1910.

40 PCTUC Mins., 24.2.1914.

41 PCTUC Mins., 12.3.1914.

42 PCTUC Mins., 8.4.1914.

43 PCTUC Mins., 15.12.1915.

44 PCTUC Mins., 1.9.1916.

45 There were early opponents, especially Mrs. Bridges Adams and at first George Lansbury. STOCKS, M. *op. cit.*, pp. 48–49.

46 CLINTON, A. Ph.D. (London), p. 86.

47 *Ibid.*

48 PCTUC Mins., 25.5.1916.

49 PCTUC Mins., 21.3.1917.

50 For a history of the WETUC see CORFIELD, A.J. *Epoch in Workers' Education.*

51 *Ibid.*, p. 15.

52 In 1919 the Union of Post Office Workers applied to the NUR to see if they could become part owners and controllers of the CLC to enable them to establish scholarships and send members to the College. A decision was deferred because at the time the College was full and it was suggested that information should first be sought as to how many other unions might be interested in such an idea. This delay was probably regretted later when the UPOW joined the WETUC. Gen. Sec.'s Report NUR Conference Report 1919, p. 90.

53 A detailed account of the NCLC has been written by J.P.M. Millar entitled 'The Labour College Movement' but the book printed in 1977 has not been put on sale. The writer has seen a copy and some references will be made to the edition listed in the bibliography. (Since published 1979, see bibliography).

54 There was some move towards the NCLC and away from the WEA in the 1920s. CLINTON, A. Ph.D. 1973, *op. cit.*, p. 300.

55 Cover page of AUBTW pamphlet c. 1922 (Marx Memorial Library).

56 Reprinted in full in Appendix 2. CORFIELD, A.J. *op. cit.*

57 TUC Report 1921, p. 362.

58 *Ibid.*, p. 364.

59 *Ibid.*, p. 363.

60 TUC Education Committee Mins., 23.2.1922. (TUCEC Mins.)

61 TUCEC Mins., 27.4.1922.

62 TUCEC Mins., 30.3.1922.

63 *Ibid.*

64 TUCEC Mins., (22.6.1922) & (8.2.1923). See also Ruskin College Mins., (20.2.1923).

65 Ruskin College Mins., (21.6.1922). A request by Mr. Temple for more time to be spent on the study of trade unionism, the Co-operative movement and the labour movement was objected to by the Principal and rejected by the Executive Committee Ruskin College Mins., (10.1.1923) & (23.3.1923). The Principal suggested the ending 'of Marxism lectures' and that 'it might be left to the College's own Economics lecturer to give what he considered Marx's place in the general scheme'.

Ruskin College Mins., (24.6.1927).

66 TUCEC Mins., 1.6.1922.
67 TUC Report 1922, pp. 187–197.
68 *Ibid.*, p. 188.
69 *Ibid.*
70 *Ibid.*, pp. 189–190.
71 *Ibid.*, p. 191.
72 *Ibid.*, p. 192. See also TUCEC Mins., (5.3.1923) for discussion on education between TUCEC and deputation from Women Workers' Group represented by Miss J. Varley and Miss I. Cowell.
73 TUC Report 1922, p. 193.
74 *Ibid.*
75 CORFIELD, A.J. *op. cit.*, p. 14.
76 A Report from Ruskin College 1922 also drew attention to 'the smaller number of students ... partly to be accounted for by the non-renewal of certain Trade Union scholarships owing to the effect of industrial conditions on Trade Union funds....' The 1923 Report of the Scottish Labour College told a similar story. TUC Report 1923, p. 146.
77 TUC Report 1922, pp. 192–193.
78 Ruskin College sources of income in 1925 included:
    (a) Cassell Grant since 1920 (£1000, 1921: £500, 1922)
    (b) Sara Hall Trust £250 p.a. to be used as salary for Robert Owen Lecturer
    (c) Board of Education Grant: £20 p.a. per student
    (d) Some renewable subscriptions
    (e) Scholarships from trade unions and other societies £1250 p.a. approx.
    (f) Rowntrees: occasional grants to individual students
    TUCEC Mins., 8.7.1925.
79 TUCEC Mins., 5.5.1925.
80 *Ibid.*
81 See E. Williams (Miners Federation) speech: TUC Report 1923, pp. 257–258.
82 *Ibid.*, p. 256.
83 *Ibid.*, p. 257.
84 For evidence of this allegation and hypocrisy of J.H. Thomas regarding comments made about J. Bromley (ASLEF) see FARMAN, C. *The General Strike*, p. 65.
85 MILLAR, J.P.M., p. 79.
86 See GCTUC Mins., 9.4.1924 for letter from WEA alleging misrepresentation by the NCLC of financial aid received from the Carnegie Trustees. No action was taken.
87 TUCEC Mins., 4.3.1924.
88 TUCEC Mins., 26.6.1924 & 18.7.1924.
89 TUC Report 1924, pp. 421–426.
90 *Ibid.*, p. 427.
91 TUCEC Mins., (16.1.1925), (24.1.1925), (26.2.1925) (7, 28.2.1925).
92 TUCEC Mins., 12.3.1925.
93 Ruskin College Mins., 16.4.1925.
94 TUCEC Mins., 24.4.1925.
95 TUCEC Mins., 12.6.1925.
96 An artist's impression of proposed new buildings for a Labour College on the Kew site is contained in CRAIK, W.W. *op. cit.*, between pp. 96–97.
97 TUCEC Mins., 13.5.1925. £150 grant was recommended.
98 TUCEC Mins., 10.6.1925.
99 Ruskin College Mins., 26.6.1925. At this meeting the Principal did express the belief that there would be less chance of friction if Ruskin and the CLC were not in the same building.

100 TUCEC Mins., 20.7.1925. The Co-op Union pledged support for the TUC Education Scheme but informed the Committee that they had now established their own College.

101 By the end of Nov. 1925 it was agreed that Ruskin College could appoint their Vice Principal, Mr. Barratt Brown to the Principalship on the understanding that new arrangements might be necessary when the TUC Education Scheme came into operation. TUCEC Mins., 30.11.1925. This temporary appointment was made permanent in 1926.

102 TUC Report 1925, p. 252.

103 A report had revealed that there were few students in residence at Ruskin and the position at the CLC unknown. TUCEC Mins., 6.11.1925.

104 Originally suggested as fifty per cent of scholarship to either college; later reduced to unspecified offer of help. TUCEC Mins., 30.11.1925.

105 TUCEC Mins., 6.11.1925.

106 TUCEC Mins., 9.11.1925. Party of Pugh, Bowen, Hicks, Citrine and Firth visited Easton Lodge, 28.11.1925.

107 Lady Warwick to A. Pugh, 11.11.1925.

108 Lady Warwick to Mr. Firth (Acting Asst. Sec.) 20.11.1925 and reply 23.11.1925.

109 That is Easton Lodge. *Morning Post*, 5.12.1925.

110 J. Smith (Sec. Ruskin College) to A. Pugh, 5.12.1925.

111 Fenner Brockway to TUC 1.2.1926.

112 Lady Warwick to W. Citrine 6.12.1925. See also Lady Warwick to Mr. Firth, 8.12.1925.

113 TUCEC Mins., 18.1.1926.

114 Ruskin College Mins., 19.1.1926.

115 Approximate costs of proposed scheme:

East Wing 60 students: 30 each sex, two storeys	£11,500
Entrance, Billiards Room, Common Room	£3,500
North Wing	£6,000
West Wing	£11,000
Colonnade, lay-out of quadrangle	£3,000
Dining Hall, Kitchen alterations	£3,750
Interior alterations	£500

TUCEC Mins., 25.1.1926.

116 TUCEC Mins., 27.1.1926.

117 Lady Warwick to W. Citrine, 29.1.1926.

118 Naylor to W. Citrine, 17.2.1926.

119 Wolstencroft (Gen. Sec.) to Citrine, 17.2.1926.

120 J.A. Gibson (Gen. Sec.) to A.S. Frith, 23.2.1926.

121 £25 on 3.3.1926 and a further £25 the next day.

122 Ruskin College Mins., 18.2.1926.

123 *Ibid*. A Trade Union College was defined by Citrine as 'A Centre in which the curriculum was such as to enable people to be turned out who would be useful to the Trade Union Movement'.

124 Lady Warwick to W. Citrine, 19.3.1926.

125 Shaen, Roscoe, Massey and Co. (TUC Solicitors) to Godfrey Payton Land Agent for Lady Warwick. March 1926.

126 Lady Warwick to TUCEAC, 22.3.1926.

127 Lady Warwick to W. Citrine, 29.7.1926.

128 Lady Warwick to W. Citrine, 29.8.1926.

129 TUC Report 1926, p. 350. W.W. Craik claimed that the NCLC had pushed this argument hard for several weeks before in *Plebs*. CRAIK, W.W. *op. cit.*, p. 142.

130 *Ibid*.

131 *Ibid*., p. 358.

132 TUC Report 1926, p. 353.
133 *Ibid.*
134 Lady Warwick to W. Citrine, 12.9.1926.
135 Frene Chomeley and Co. (Solicitors to Lady Warwick) to Shaen, Roscoe and Massey (Solicitors to TUC), 15.9.1926.
136 See CRAIK, W.W. *op. cit.*, Chapter 12.
137 Ruskin College Mins., 14.10.1926.
138 *Ibid.*
139 There is considerable evidence to suggest that a number of trade unionists easily embraced titles. The five volumes of Bellamy and Saville's *Dictionary of Labour Biography*, show nearly thirty with titles.
140 HAMILTON, W. *My Queen and I*, p. 104.
141 J.R. Clynes' *Memoirs*, illustrate the attitude of some trade union leaders who were overwhelmed by a comment from the Monarch (see Vol. II, p. 22) and rationalized their ready adoption of court dress by suggesting that such actions proved they were as good as the Tories who had previously worn such costumes (*op. cit.*, p. 25). Although Ramsay MacDonald was primarily responsible for Labour Ministers continuing the tradition of ceremonial dress there is little evidence to suggest that he faced much serious opposition in the Cabinet to this practice. An interesting illustration of R. MacDonald, D. Kirkwood, A. Greenwood and J.R. Clynes in court dress, including ceremonial swords, is provided in SHINWELL, E. *The Labour Story*, facing p. 145.
142 DEAN, D.W. 'Conservatism and the national education system 1922–40' *The Journal of Contemporary History*, 6 (2) 1971.
143 NUR Conference Report 1923, p. 100.
144 MILLAR, J.P.M. *op. cit.*, p. 70.
145 DEAN, D.W. *op. cit.*

Chapter 8

Education, Trade Unions
and Trade Unionists at the TUC

One union concerned directly with education could have played a major role at the TUC. However the NUT refused to affiliate and this prevented it from having as much influence as it might have done. A few NUT branches had joined trades councils[1] but affiliation to the TUC was rejected at the NUT Conference of 1895 and although negotiations were instigated again between the NUT and TUC in 1917[2] at the request of F. Goldstone, an executive member of the NUT, insufficient support among the teachers prevented them from linking up officially with Congress. A few years later a resolution calling for an alliance with the Labour Party was also rejected at the NUT Conference by 29,743 to 15,434 votes. The fact is that the majority of teachers were Conservative at the time[3] although this allegiance was to undergo considerable change in the 1920s.[4] Notwithstanding the rather aloof position the NUT seemed to take with regard to the Labour Movement they did hold meetings with the TUC to discuss matters of mutual interest, such as the matter of vocational education in primary schools which both rejected in the belief that the first priority for all children was a general education.[5]

There was a minority group of teachers who did affiliate to the TUC. They were members of the National Union of School Teachers, largely composed of uncertificated and supplementary teachers who were excluded from the NUT and made up about one third of the teaching force. They have not previously attracted much attention in the Labour movement but this is not surprising as comparatively little has been written about various groups of teachers in the past, in spite of a long history of organization among teachers. The leader of the NUST was Miss Walsh who encouraged branches to join trades councils and told an audience in Wolverhampton that 'the uncertificated teachers were mainly interested in the education of working class children, she had found from experience that the assistance they required for gaining of their rights was more likely to be secured through the assistance of the Trades and Labour Councils than from either Tories or Liberals'.[6] Less obvious was the reciprocal assistance the NUST would be willing and able to provide to the TUC.

There was a paradoxical situation for Congress: sympathy for a group of teachers willing to join with other working people at trades councils and the TUC yet, among the craft unions at least, a reluctance to support claims that 'unqualified' teachers should receive the same salary as those qualified by certificate. Miss Walsh exploited her position at Congress by using every opportunity to state the claims of her members. She made major speeches at Congress in 1919, 1920 and 1921, and was included in PCTUC Deputations to the Board of Education in 1920 and 1921, when on both occasions she put forward her complaints to H.A.L. Fisher. In general the claim of the NUST was that uncertificated teachers were treated unfairly. The major demands were made at the 1919 TUC in which Miss Walsh called for equal pay for all teachers whether certificated or not, the same examination for teachers whether they attended college or not, equal representation with the NUT on all local and national education committees and a public inquiry into the situation of uncertificated and supplementary teachers. The resolution and others similarly worded were passed at the three Congresses she addressed although not without expressed opposition from some delegates. She received little sympathy from H.A.L. Fisher.

Two of the claims seemed to be justified. One was that in negotiations over pay uncertificated teachers were excluded from the talks and therefore their certificated colleagues set the rates. The second was that in theory an official ratio of staff to pupils was laid down emphasizing the differences in teacher status; one certificated teacher to sixty pupils, one uncertificated teacher to thirty-five pupils and one supplementary teacher to twenty pupils. Miss Walsh claimed however that 'it is common knowledge that this rule is entirely ignored in practice, and the numbers of children in classes in no way depend upon the description – or so-called grade – of the teacher'.[7] Moreover it would seem that 'economy minded' local authorities sometimes favoured the engagement of uncertificated teachers because they were less expensive to employ. This accusation was made by G. Titt (Workers' Union) who told delegates that '. . . the average Education Committee has utilized the position of the uncertificated teacher merely as a means of sweating a very important sector of the working class community'.[8] Church schools in particular were blamed for this situation because it was claimed they 'preferred to employ young girls and women who were not entirely dependent upon their own financial resources. . .'.[9]

Congress expressed sympathy for the lack of representation by the NUST in pay negotiations and agreed that if uncertificated teachers did the same work as certificated colleagues it was not fair that they should only receive a half to two thirds of the latter's pay. Both J. Battle of the Operative Cotton Spinners in 1919 and George Hall at the 1921 Congress underlined the manner in which the NUST had related itself to the Labour movement whilst the NUT had stayed outside. There were, however, objections to some of the claims of Miss Walsh and, whilst E.L. Poulton as Chairman in 1920 called for a vote, thereby preventing these from being raised, what might be seen as the craft point of view was expressed at the Glasgow and Cardiff Congresses. Both T.W. Church (London Compositors) and A.W. Tapp (Ship Constructors and Shipwrights

Association) argued in 1919 and 1921 respectively that uncertificated teachers had every opportunity to gain a certificate. Church told delegates, 'if these women want certificates they can get them without going to a training college; and if they cannot, or will not, make themselves efficient, they should not be in the teaching profession at all'[10] whilst Tapp explained that:

> If the uncertificated teacher has passed the preliminary certificate, that is a part-qualification. After two year's experience, if they have failed in the interval, they can take their certificate at the examination set by the Board of Education. Some education authorities ... have given special expenses or special grants to teachers as late as ten years after they have passed the preliminary certificate, in order that they might go to college and get their certificates ... if the uncertificated teacher is going to be years and years teaching and not get up to the educational standard, in the interests of education itself it is better that he is removed from the sphere of teaching...'[11]

H.A.L. Fisher rejected all of the arguments Miss Walsh presented as a member of the PCTUC Deputations. In the matter of representation he pointed out that the Board of Education had no say in the appointment of representatives to the Burnham Committee whilst such bodies as the Consultative Committee were made up of eminent individuals, not representatives, because technical matters were discussed, such as psychological tests. As for equal pay Fisher's views provided no encouragement for Miss Walsh:

> ... generally speaking the difference between the Certificated and Uncertificated teacher corresponds to the difference of qualification and capacity.... Certificated teachers, taking them as a class, having regard to the collegiate training they have, are undoubtedly better teachers than Uncertificated teachers.... The Acting Teachers Examination ... is open to all Uncertificated teachers, and if they pass it they get certificates. Many of them have tried to pass it and have failed. Is it seriously suggested that it would be in the interests of the children to lower the standard I have mentioned.[12]

The following year Fisher was just as firm. Indeed after several interruptions from Miss Walsh he turned on her and said 'I have listened to you; I am afraid I must ask you to listen to me', going on to point out that 'the supplementary teacher, being an unqualified teacher, ought either to make up her mind to obtain qualification, or ought to take up some other occupation...'.[13] As Fisher was doing his utmost at the time to build up the quality of teaching in schools, claims on behalf of uncertificated and supplementary teachers were not likely to be received sympathetically as they ran counter to his designs.

There was just no way in which a minority of teachers, generally in the lowest positions, were going to be given equal pay with teachers enjoying higher status at the time. There were signs of injustice which seemed to ring true, such as the claim by Miss Walsh that a sick uncertificated teacher paid

£4.10s was temporarily replaced by a certificated teacher who was paid £9 per week.[14] The pattern of work allocated to different grades of teacher did not always seem to follow that laid down by the Board of Education. It was also claimed by A.A. Purcell (Furnishing Trades), as a member of the 1921 PCTUC Deputation to Sir E. Phipps, Principal Assistant Secretary at the Board, that the better qualified teachers were allocated to schools in the more affluent areas of the town in which he lived:

> *Mr. Purcell*: ... when they opened a new school in a better class district ... they ran all certificated teachers in there; all of them.
>
> *Sir E. Phipps*: This is a new point. Certificated teachers in better class districts.
>
> *Mr. Purcell*: There is no question about it. Most working class children could not get up there. [that is to the schools in prosperous areas] ... they have a larger number probably almost entirely certificated teachers there, and in other districts they are mixed, and sometimes there is a majority of uncertificated teachers...[15]

Sir E. Phipps claimed no knowledge of 'certificated teachers in better class districts' but Purcell was able to support his claim from a good knowledge of the various districts in Manchester and Salford. In many areas the best schools were to be found in the more prosperous and pleasant neighbourhoods and inevitably attracted the best qualified teachers. This was also a distinction to be found between small towns and rural areas, the latter having poorer school facilities, poorer qualified teachers and a higher turnover of staff.[16] Both the uncertificated teachers and poorer children were victims of a system in which teachers were graded and so were schools by the district in which they were situated.

Uncertificated teachers had been forced to organize themselves because NUT membership was not open to them. In 1919 the NUT Conference narrowly agreed to remove the barrier and approximately 10,000 uncertificated teachers joined. The NUST remained in being partly perhaps in the thought that their minority views would be lost in the NUT but also due to the strong personality of the Secretary, Miss Walsh, who continued to run a union of steadily dwindling numbers until her death in 1945. It is probable that the members of the NUST were closest to working class children and the poorest districts but their membership of the TUC seemed to be used solely to complain about their own particular grievances; only occasionally did a wider educational issue arise indirectly out of their campaign. They must have embarrassed the NUT with the way they were able to use the TUC platform but there is no evidence to show that they made any real contribution to TUC Education Policy.

The contribution of various other trade unions to the development of TUC

Education Policy, other than that associated with trade union education, is rarely reflected in the histories of individual unions.[17] This is partly because dramatic industrial conflicts make better reading but also because such events did stand out more vividly in the minds of members or receive greater publicity at the time than debates arising from resolutions on education at the TUC. An examination of such resolutions submitted to Congress and listed in Appendix II does provide some evidence of the trade unions[18] who were to the forefront in pressing for changes in education.

Prior to 1895, the geographical area of speakers to resolutions and not their trade union, was usually recorded in Congress Reports. After this date it became customary for the union represented by any speaker in the debate to be stated. By examining these details it is easy to see that the Gasworkers dominated educational proposals during 1895–1905 and played a prominent part also between 1908–16 in education debates.[19] Will Thorne and Pete Curran were responsible for most resolutions between 1895 and 1911; the former proposing seven and seconding two whilst the latter proposed three. No other union took such an active part although various individual textile unions when placed under a common umbrella can be seen to have also played a substantial role, especially the lacemakers, whose Secretary, W.A. Appleton proposed six resolutions and seconded one on education between 1901 and 1907.

There is no easy explanation in terms of skilled or unskilled workers' unions pushing for educational reform: the Gasworkers were the proto-type of what is often referred to as the New Unionism whilst unions such as the Amalgamated Lacemakers and the Typographical Association, who also played a leading role in moving resolutions on education, had long histories of craft unionism behind them. It seems more likely that prior to 1914 it was easier for leading personalities to put forward resolutions on education acceptable to both their own union conferences and the TUC. Some explanation for the Gasworkers dominance in this matter is to be found in the political affiliation of its two leading members; Thorne was a member of the SDF and Curran owed allegiance to the ILP. A 'common core' of educational proposals can be traced through these two socialist parties *via* the Gasworkers Conference to the TUC. That there was common support for them from delegates has been shown, as also has the minority opposition to such aspects as secular education and the raising of the school leaving age. It is difficult, however, to think of a time when a call for improvement of educational facilities was not fully endorsed by all unions. One might expect the proposals of Appleton to be more cautious than Thorne's but, in fact, no major distinction can be seen between the two.

Schooling of Individual Trade Unionists

The way in which individual trade unionists, such as Thorne, Curran and Appleton were able to submit radical proposals on education from their trade unions has been mentioned on several occasions. The source of these radical proposals has been sought in the joint membership of trade unionists with such pressure groups as the NEL in the late 1860s, the SDF and ILP in the 1890s. However this only explains the presentation of a resolution, it does not explain widespread Congress support for radical ideas in education when, in general, the TUC has been shown to be dominated by cautious Liberals for most of the nineteenth century, and given the weakness of socialists both on the PCTUC and as delegates throughout the period under consideration. The answer seems to be in the personal experiences of so many delegates when they were of school age. It is for this reason that an attempt has been made to trace the schooling received by as many trade unionists as possible.

With a few exceptions, such as Applegarth and Cremer, most trade unionists in the nineteenth century looked upon education in a fairly restricted manner. Skilled workmen sometimes saw it in close relation to learning a trade, hence their demands for an expansion of technical education or apprenticeship schemes. Nearly all equated education with formal schooling and it seems that their attitude towards the many TUC resolutions tabled on education from 1885 were determined by the experience of their own childhood and school days.

Such is the sparcity of biographical information relating to the education of many trade unionists that it has only been possible to gather some details of sixty-nine TUC delegates of whom fifty-one served on the PCTUC. Whilst it is not claimed that they form a perfect cross section of nineteenth century trade unionists there are factors which suggest that their backgrounds were typical of large numbers of working class children of that century. A map plotting their place of birth or early childhood illustrates a reasonable regional spread (see Figure 2), admittedly with London somewhat under-represented, whilst a glance at the father's occupation provided for many in Appendix I gives a wide range from cotton mill manager to numerous labouring jobs. Miners and those involved with the mine as a place of work are most numerous but a breadth of skilled trades is also to be found; stonemason, shoemaker, cooper, journeyman machine maker and weaver as well as such livelihoods as hawker, poacher, soldier and sailor.

The general lack of information available about trade unionists until recent years[20] is largely a matter of the sociology of knowledge in that attitudes to the question of who should be considered worthy of biographical attention have changed over the years. Prominent men such as Joseph Arch, George Potter and Alexander MacDonald were not included in major encyclopaedias although about half the list in Appendix I are included in the *Dictionary of National Biography*.[21] By contrast numerous titled people whose careers were rarely more influential have automatically been accorded a place in the past. It seems that only when a trade unionist became an MP was he considered of sufficient eminence to be included among the famous in the nineteenth century. It is for this reason that a fuller detailed list could not be compiled.

Of the sixty-nine trade unionists listed, at least twelve wrote autobiographies and an additional nine were the subject of biographies.[22] Yet when the majority of these books are considered one searches in vain for any substantial writing about their schooldays. One or two, such as Arch and Rogers, contain up to a paragraph or a few phrases more but many hardly mention their school experiences. Sexton for example only tells how he attended Low House School for three pence per week plus six pence per month for heating (coke) until he left at eight years of age. Tillett's biography mentions only that he left school at a similar age whilst Thorne, who was the staunchest advocate of education at the TUC, never mentions a school, merely suggesting that he never attended one. This could hardly have been an exaggeration as he was working full-time at six years of age. This general lack of schoolboy memories suggests that for most working class men such time as they did spend at school was too brief and infrequent for it to have been of major consequence. For those who therefore recorded their lives later the sentence or two afforded to their time spent at school was in proportion to its significance in their lives.

Approximately sixty-five per cent of the trade unionists studied left school before the 1870 Education Act came into force and an examination of their leaving ages and scanty descriptions of school reinforces the view that circumstances prevented many working class children from regularly attending the elementary schools which were provided. They do nothing either to suggest that the education given was anything but meagre and rudimentary, providing little or no opportunity for social mobility.

An examination of the school leaving ages (see Figure 3 p. 234) does not provide an absolute rule that they rose as the century progressed although a general pattern in that direction is indicated. Allan and Guile, born within a year of each other, 1813 and 1814 respectively, stayed at school until twelve years of age, whilst Thorne, born a generation later in 1857 left school at six years and Hardie born just a year before Thorne left at seven years of age. As in the case of Thorne, death of one or both parents was often a factor forcing children prematurely on to the labour market and, of the fifteen trade unionists listed who had left school by eight years of age, five had suffered such a loss. In general the school leaving age did rise steadily. For those who left school before 1870 more than half were nine years of age or less: for those leaving school after 1881 the only example of a child under twelve was a half-timer. Even between 1870 and 1880, of the four children leaving at nine years of age, three were half-timers. Geography provides no pattern of school leaving age; the higher leaving age in Wales is largely explained by the later dates and the comparatively lower leaving ages in textile areas, a product of the half-time system. (See Figure 2)

From the information obtainable it is quite clear that prior to 1870 most children had left school by their tenth year. Some of the exceptions can be explained. Broadhurst was one of two trade unionists listed who attended a private school, for six pence per week, as compared to the penny or two pence charged by most elementary schools. One can only assume that his father experienced some prosperous years as a stonemason. Cremer's mother ran a dame school so may well have emphasized education and been able to maintain

Figure 2

Major area of schooling and school leaving age of leading trade unionists.

+ Continued as half-timer.

Those who left school after 1870 in italics.

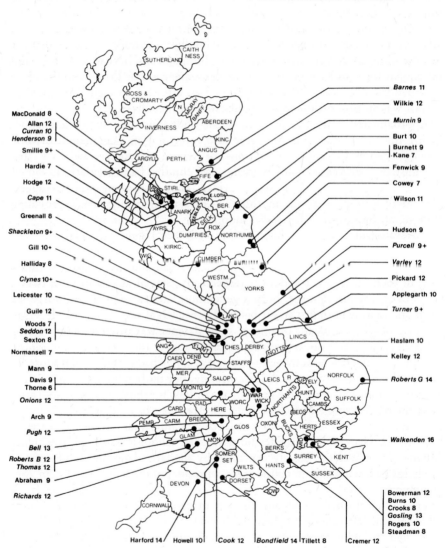

Barnes 11
Wilkie 12
Murnin 9
Burt 10
Burnett 9
Kane 7
Fenwick 9
Cowey 7
Wilson 11
Hudson 9
Purcell 9+
Varley 12
Pickard 12
Applegarth 10
Turner 9+
Haslam 10
Kelley 12
Roberts G 14
Walkenden 16

MacDonald 8
Allan 12
Curran 10
Henderson 9
Smillie 9+
Hardie 7
Hodge 12
Cape 11
Greenall 8
Shackleton 9+
Gill 10+
Halliday 8
Clynes 10+
Leicester 10
Guile 12
Woods 7
Seddon 12
Sexton 8
Normansell 7
Mann 9
Davis 9
Thorne 6
Onions 12
Arch 9
Pugh 12
Bell 13
Roberts B 12
Thomas 12
Abraham 9
Richards 12

Bowerman 12
Burns 10
Crooks 8
Gosling 13
Rogers 10
Steadman 8

Harford 14 Howell 10 Cook 12 Bondfield 14 Tillett 8 Cremer 12 him at school a few years longer whilst Pickard was the only one mentioned who attended a grammar school.[23] As his father was a miner it is assumed that Pickard won a scholarship; nevertheless when he left at twelve years of age he still went down the pit like other local boys. Kelley also stayed on until twelve years of age as a pupil teacher in his village school before taking up an apprenticeship as a lithographic printer in York. Even allowing for these exceptions early school leaving seemed to be a common experience for most working class boys.

School leaving age was an unreliable guide to education, at least until the 1890s, for, unless attendance was regular, little progress could be made at school. Thus, although Appleton is credited with a leaving age of ten years three months, he recalled in later years that 'I don't think I ever went to school for more than a few days'.[24]

Many working class children only attended school when they were not required to work. This was true for Henderson whose 'schooling was brief and often broken into by obligation to help – by work for a few pence'[25] and even Broadhurst's attendance at a private school did not exclude him from this common experience: 'Happily, my services were frequently needed at home'; he was thus able to 'escape the taskmaster' who provided 'plenty of teaching combined with plenty of stick'.[26] Even where attendance could be kept up, long and regular hours of part-time work prevented many children from giving proper attention to school work. J.H. Thomas for example, worked two hours before school and a further two hours after school plus all day Saturday from nine years of age until he left school at twelve.[27] Wilson's leaving age is probably the most misleading for whilst he did not leave school until eleven years of age he never stayed in any one district for more than six months because his father was a poacher and had to keep moving. He therefore experienced plenty of schools but it is doubtful whether he was able to make much progress.

Thomas Burt attempted to put his total schooling into perspective. A few months before his sixth birthday he went to school.

> Now began my brief and rather fitful schooling. The whole period, when the many interruptions are deducted, could not have extended over two years. The first interruption was due to the outbreak of the miners' strike of 1844.[28] I was then a little over 6 years and had been at school only a few months.[29]

Tom Mann also later related a story of broken attendance when young:

> I must explain that I only had a very short time at school as a boy, less than three years all told; about a year and a half at Foleshill Old Church Day School and about a year at Little Heath School, Foleshill. As by this time I was nine years of age [and] considered old enough to start work.[30]

The major reason for non-attendance in rural areas was inclement weather for where children only possessed one pair of shoes and possibly an ill-fitting threadbare top coat, they were unlikely to venture miles along unmade roads through rain or snow. The practical problem of drying clothes in time for school the next day was often beyond families lacking adequate heating; at the other end of the journey wet clothing draped around a single school stove provided both a familiar sight and smell in classrooms during winter months. Burt's journey to school was six miles and for a six year old such a journey from pit village to school in a Northumbrian Winter was out of the question with obvious consequences: '. . . severity of the winter had greatly interrupted my attendance'.[31] Like Broadhurst, he was not further encouraged to attend a school where a master gave him 'frequent beatings'.

It might be suggested that in later life some trade unionists had exaggerated the brevity of their schooling to emphasize the obstacles they had overcome in earlier years but whilst this is obviously possible the general picture of nineteenth century education obtainable by working class children suggests that the cases that have been cited are in no way extraordinary. Raymond Williams has suggested 'an average duration of school attendance, in 1835, of one year . . . [which had been raised]. . . . By 1851 . . . to two years'.[32] That poor attendance was a major problem is confirmed by Robert Lowe's Revised Code of 1862 which stressed attendance as a vital prerequisite for earning grant: 'For every scholar who has attended more than 200 morning and afternoon meetings of their school. . .'[33] the school was to receive four shillings, which was nearly two thirds of the grant available to a child under six years of age and one half of the grant available to a child over six years of age, subject to a successful examination.

This emphasis on attendance in the Code suggests that the earlier optimistic picture presented by the Newcastle Commission the previous year was not considered to be entirely convincing; an opinion verified by HMI Reports following the introduction of the Code in the 1860s in which 'a canvas in Birmingham showed: 8044 children age 3–12: 887 at work; 3972 at school; 3185 neither at school nor at work . . . [whilst]. . . . In Liverpool a survey taken in certain sample streets showed that 5890 children attended school and 4761 did not . . .'.[34] Any doubts concerning the true picture of attendance were dispelled by the reports of experienced HMIs specifically sent by W.E. Forster to Birmingham, Leeds, Liverpool and Manchester where '. . . the great towns showed that in every case, less than a tenth of the population was in school . . . while the schools provided reasonably well for one district, they left another almost destitute'.[35] W.E. Forster spelt out the full picture to the House of Commons in his speech introducing the 1870 Education Act:

> . . . only two.fifths of the children of the working classes between the ages of six and ten years are on the registers of the Government schools, and only one-third of those between the ages of ten and twelve. Consequently, of those between six and ten, we have helped about 700,000 more or less, but we have left unhelped 1,000,000; while

of those between ten and twelve, we have helped 250,000, and left unhelped at least 500,000.[36]

One of the poorest types of schooling prior to 1870 was that provided in Dame Schools; which varied from a low standard of child minding to some teaching of the basic three Rs.[37] At least ten of the trade unionists listed attended such schools. Apart from Cremer, who naturally went to that run by his mother, Applegarth, Davis, Guile, Potter, Rogers, Shackleton, Turner and Wilson all spent their earliest school years in dame schools. Applegarth is believed to have gained a 'little education' from his brief stay in one[38] whilst Potter attended such a school before going on to 'Arlidge's Charity and endowed school on Abbey Hill.... There he learned to read and write'.[39] This seems to imply that he had not learned such skills at the dame school. Guile is credited with having learned his ABC at a dame school.[40]

The fullest description of a dame school is provided by Turner who also reinforces the general view that little of substance was really learned in them:

> The first school I attended was known as a 'Dame School'. It was a one-roomed barnlike place, with an iron stove in the middle and hard forms without backs for us youngsters to sit on. The little children were at one end of the room and the older ones at the other. We paid school pence for our training, and the old lady taught us the ABC but not much more.[41]

In searching out the sparse comments about schooling made by trade unionists themselves or their biographers it becomes obvious that in most cases only the rudiments of elementary education were obtainable by most working class children before the passing of the 1870 Education Act. Some did a little better than their peers. Guile, the son of a skilled worker, moved to a Wesleyan Free School at seven years of age, 'where one penny was paid ... for learning to read and spell, and when promoted to writing in a copybook a half penny per week extra was paid towards the cost of pens, ink and paper'.[42] Burt 'made fair progress in reading and writing'[43] at a boys' school before he was seven but like so many others did not progress much further because he did not attend regularly.

Arch was conscious of the brevity of school life available to rural children: 'a village boy was given the bare chance of picking up a few scraps of rudimentary knowledge – the three Rs as we used to say – or of going without'.[44] Normansell's schooling was less than that experienced by Arch, and later described as 'what his Aunt caused him to receive at a Wesleyan Methodist Sunday School, where he got through the alphabet and where a little reading of rather a difficult and puzzling kind was the highest scholastic accomplishment he managed to acquire'.[45] Odger's education, undergone a decade earlier, '... was limited to the rustic school of his native place, and consisted of its simplest materials',[46] probably a euphemistic description of a poorly equipped village school. In any case Odger left 'at an early age' to help with the family budget.

Howell attended the local village school 'where the rudiments of reading were taught by a local school mistress, the primer being the New Testament'.[47] To use the authorized version of the Bible as a standard reading book for children of primary school age suggests that much of the learning must have been done by rote, an impression confirmed by Rogers, one of the few trade unionists to describe the teaching methods he experienced in the mid nineteenth century:

> In my brief school days the method of teaching was simply to memorize passages from the grammar or geography, and repeat them at the proper time. If the monitor could explain anything he did. It was a crude method enough....[48]

As for achievement it is difficult to know. Burn's biographer tried to assess the extent of his education:

> The receipt of a volume of physiology[49] as a prize does not denote that the subject was on the school curriculum. It is most unlikely that he was taught this or any other science ... the sum of his acquirements was the three Rs and perhaps a small knowledge of the geography of England.[50]

Turner's experience in the 1870s suggests a similar picture. Leaving school at nine years of age to become a half-timer in the woollen industry, he later wrote that at his 'fully equipped' National School he '... learnt to do sums there and to know a bit about geography'. The vicar arrived each day to give Bible readings and Turner claimed that he '... read the Bible through twice in [his] school days, right from Genesis to Revelations'.[51] Pugh, who attended school in the 1880s believed he was more fortunate than many of his colleagues: 'I did go to school up to the fourth standard, and learnt to read, write and do easy sums'.[52] In fact this was no great achievement as there were six standards until the year Pugh left school when a seventh was added. It may be, however, that in the rural area of Ross-on-Wye where he grew up to reach the fourth standard was an above average achievement.

Some of the trade unionists when young were able to acquire hardly any knowledge at school. Hardie was illiterate at seventeen years of age, being unable to sign his name when joining the Templars.[53] Normansell and Thorne both signed the marriage register with a cross, as did Thorne's wife.[54] Some who attained basic literacy were able to supplement their education by attending evening classes. This was true of Burns who 'was assiduous in attending "night" school',[55] and developed a passion for books which led him to amass a large private library formidable by any standards.[56] Woods, who owed his reading ability to attendance at Sunday School left school at seven years of age to work for the next twenty years in the pits. He managed to attend Owen's College, Manchester, part-time, where he gained a First Class Certificate in mining management. W.J. Davis obtained a Queen's Prize of South Kensington Art and Science Department by attending Barr Street Improvement Society. J.H. Thomas went to Mrs. Smart's Bible Classes each Tuesday as a young man.

Thorne was helped to improve his reading and writing principally by Eleanor Marx; these were skills he desperately needed as secretary of the newly formed Gasworkers Union.

Perhaps the most remarkable stories of self-discipline in education are those of the two Scottish miners; Alexander MacDonald and Keir Hardie who left school at eight and seven years of age, although separated by a generation in time. Hardie joined the Templars as a young man where he was taught to read and write. Whilst still in the pits he taught himself shorthand, practising with a piece of chalk by using the coal face as a 'black board'. MacDonald, whilst working in the pits in the 1830s prepared himself for university entrance and in 1846 entered Glasgow University. He supported himself financially by returning to the mines during vacations and, upon obtaining his degree, became a schoolmaster in 1850. After seven years he turned his attention to the miner's cause, organizing the Scottish Miners and becoming President of the Union in 1863, a post he held until his death in 1881.

There were trade unionists who used their literacy to educate themselves solely by reading without any help from outside organizations. Hence Arch explains how upon leaving school at nine years of age with

> barely three years of regular schooling to start me on my way in life
> ... I bought books, and studied hard, and educated myself when I
> came home of an evening from the fields ... so that with the help of
> my mother and my books – books purchased out of my scanty wage –
> I managed to pick up piecemeal what was then considered a fair
> education.[57]

Rogers, in a completely different environment, went through the same process explaining how 'it was not easy for a London errand boy to get reading then [1856] ... but I got a good deal'.[58] Will Crooks was also faced with formidable personal problems in trying to get an education. His father had been a ship's stoker but lost an arm in an industrial accident and had to take a poorly paid job as a night watchman. Will was one of seven children and the poverty of the home was such that they were all put into the Poor House;[59] during this time he attended Sutton Poor Law School. His illiterate mother took in sewing and saved enough money to retrieve the children and then he attended George Green School. Once he could read '... he read and read. He read the Bible and Pilgrim's Progress. . . .'.[60] Later in life as a well known trade unionist he spoke at meetings held regularly by East India Dock Gates; meetings which became known by the dockers as 'Crook's College'. His reputation attracted crowds of working men who were able to obtain knowledge at this 'College' that was rarely available at more orthodox learning establishments.

There is also some evidence from a handful of trade unionists who entered Parliament, some of whom later achieved positions in Government, to suggest that their own lack of the kind of formal education their new-found colleagues and political rivals had received, caused them apprehension at times. George Howell wrote, in a draft of his unpublished autobiography:

> Let those educated at Rugby or Eton, preliminary to Oxford or
> Cambridge, sneer. They are put through courses of study early; I had
> to begin where they left off. I had to feel my way, in spare hours, with
> spare means, and no real guide to help me or point the way – Books,
> only books were my masters, teachers, counsellors and friends at that
> early date.[61]

Broadhurst, in describing his feelings upon his appointment as Under Secretary
to the Home Office in February 1886, wrote later:

> I realized as I had never done before the irretrievable loss which the
> lack of education in my early days involved. Visions of humiliation
> arising from the duties of my new office and my meagre capacity and
> endowments rose before me with startling vividness.[62]

At times, leading trade unionists were cruelly reminded of their lack of
schooling and rough accents. Thus the Birmingham *Daily Gazette* reporting
the Parliamentary election at Boardesley in 1892 wrote of W.J. Davis, the
independent 'Labour' candidate: 'He aims at an accent of culture, [but] he is
not yet sufficiently advanced to tackle the aspirates' and the writer of 'Current
Topics' in the same paper, in May 1891, writing of Mr. Davis, said: 'He was
very anxious to impress his hearers with the fact that, if they sent him to the
'ouse of Commons, he dare not do as he liked.'[63] What effect such remarks had
upon W.J. Davis is not known but Will Thorne was '. . . particularly stung in
1916 when Snowden wrote of his unlettered ignorance and unfitness for
Parliament'.[64]

Leading trade unionists had no illusions about their own lack of formal
education. J.H. Thomas as a member of the PCTUC Deputation to H.A.L.
Fisher at the Board of Education said, with respect to his fellow trade
unionists: 'We, everyone of us round here, have had no education . . . I was at
work at nine. . .'.[65] Whether this implied that they had still made progress is
doubtful when the personality of Thomas is taken into consideration but
Crooks made it quite clear on another occasion that he did not think that
formal education was the only measure of a person's ability to take on
responsible work:

> I am the last to despise education. I have felt the need of more
> education all my life. But I do protest against the idea that only those
> who have been through the Universities or public schools are fit to be
> the nation's rulers and servants. Legislation by the intellectuals is the
> last thing we want.[66]

Burns, too, was unlikely to have been over-impressed with formally educated
colleagues. Humbleness was never one of his characteristics and in any event
both his considerably successful political life and his prolific reading meant
that he had little cause to defer to those of wealthier or more powerful family
origins.

The examination of the schooling and later education of numerous trade unionists suggests two major factors. The first is that, due to a variety of social circumstances well down until the 1890s, regular schooling was impossible for many working class children. Hence they were rarely able to obtain anything more than the basic rudiments of literacy. This is clear from the experiences related and it needs to be remembered that trade unionists such as Arch, Burns, W.J. Davis, Hardie and MacDonald had tremendous powers of self-discipline and determination. To varying extents they were able to overcome the paucity of educational provision in their youth. Most working people were not and it seems quite obvious from the information considered that, allowing for some exceptions, the opportunities for acquiring a good elementary education in England and Wales prior to 1870 were slender for working class children.[67]

The second and most crucial factor in terms of understanding TUC Education Policy is that most delegates had experienced similar kinds of educational deprivation when young. They therefore knew the circumstances which prevented many working class children from receiving a sound education. It was because they were able to identify so readily with these problems that the TUC not only welcomed the 1870 Education Act as a first important remedial step but also explains how a cautious Congress, dominated by Liberals virtually until the turn of the century, was willing to support both educational and welfare proposals at the TUC as radical as any of the smaller socialist parties, such as the SDF and ILP. Moreover, if most of those attending Congress could be considered 'successful', at least within the Labour movement, they were likely to be the very members of the working class who realized the scale of educational provision necessary if their children and grandchildren were to receive a better start in life than they had themselves.[68] This explains the deep feelings and passion aroused by some speakers in TUC Education debates. By the same token, it could be suggested that the greater caution and appeal for gradualism in national educational provision by those confronting TUC Delegations at the Board of Education was partly due to the fact that most of the Government Ministers and Civil Servants had no personal knowledge of public elementary education, nor was there much likelihood that their offspring were destined for such schools. 'People think differently who live differently'[69] and to that extent the kind of schooling trade unionists experienced when young was the major factor in determining the way they thought about educational provision as adults.

Notes

1 CLINTON, A. Ph.D. 1973, *op. cit.*, p. 55.
2 PCTUC Mins., 21.3.1917.
3 DEAN, D.W. M.Phil. 1968, *op. cit.*, p. 164.
4 The 1924 Conservative Party Conference expressed concern at the number of teachers who had left the Conservative Party to join the Labour Party. DEAN, D.W. 'Conservatism and the National Education System 1922–40' *The Journal of*

Contemporary History, 6 (2) 1971, p. 152.

5 PCTUC Mins., (8.4.1914), (7.1.1915) and (16.12.1915).
6 *The Schoolmaster*, 27.10.1917.
7 TUC Report 1921, p. 366.
8 TUC Report 1920, p. 370.
9 A claim made by T.W. Church (London Compositors) TUC Report 1919, p. 348.
10 TUC Report 1919, p. 348.
11 TUC Report 1921, p. 369.
12 PCTUC Deputation to the Board of Education. Mins., 5.2.1920.
13 PCTUC Deputation to the Board of Education. Mins., 10.2.1921.
14 PCTUC Deputation to the Board of Education. Mins., 5.2.1920.
15 PCTUC Deputation to the Board of Education. Mins., 10.2.1921.
16 For example, in a study of selected West Sussex schools across the Weald between 1810–1914 the most urbanized, Bognor Regis had three head teachers between 1872 and 1914 whilst East Dean near the scarp face of the South Downs had fifteen, Eastergate had seven and Lodsworth had eighteen. A similar picture is reflected in the number of assistant teachers. GRIGGS, C. M.A. (Educ.) 1969, *op. cit.*, see Appendix 6, Teaching Staff.
17 e.g. HILTON's *History of the Building Trade Workers*, HYMAN's *Story of the Workers Union*, and MUSSON's account of *The Typographical Association*, have nothing to say about trade union attitudes to schools. Bagwell's history of the NUR and Page Arnot's work on the SWMF deal with trade union education but make little reference to trade union attitudes to schooling.
18 The minutes of the Gasworkers Union and National Union of Railwaymen have been examined as examples of two unions which expressed a concern for education but the bare outlines of Conference decisions do not provide further details as to how resolutions arose or the nature of any discussion which might have followed. To pursue numerous other individual trade union minutes and conference reports would have been impractical due to the scale of the task involved. Note, The Gasworkers Union was officially known as the General Workers Union by the 1920s and joined with the National Amalgamated Union of Labour and the Municipal Employees Association to form the General and Municipal Workers' Union in 1924.
19 In its foundation year the Gasworkers Union put up two candidates for the Barking School Board; both were elected.
20 The compilation of the *Dictionary of Labour Biography*, under the editorship of Joyce Bellamy and John Saville at Hull University is helping to provide information about many members of the Labour movement who have been neglected in the past. Volume I was published in 1972 and since that date five more volumes have appeared.
21 Encyclopaedia Brittanica 1974 (ed) lists only nine of those included in Appendix I, Barnes, Burns, Clynes, Cook, Cremer, Hardie, Henderson, Mann and Tillett. Neither Chambers (1950) nor Everyman (1968) Encyclopaedia mention Joseph Arch for example. In Encyclopaedia Britannica William Crawford, the miners' leader, is not included but Joan Crawford the film star is. There is no need to labour the point for the *Dictionary of Labour Biography*, would not have been necessary if traditional reference sources had provided relevant information on leading members of the labour movement in the past.
22 This would be increased to eleven if the biographies of Will Thorne and J.H. Thomas who wrote autobiographies were included. See Bibliography.
23 The *Dictionary of Labour Biography*, gives Kippax Grammar School; the *Dictionary of National Biography*, mentions only a 'colliery school'.
24 *Seventy Years of Trade Unionism*, p. 43.
25 HAMILTON, M.A. *op. cit.*, p. 2.

26 BROADHURST, H. *op. cit.*, p. 4.
27 BLAXLAND, G. *op. cit.*, p. 17.
28 The strike lasted seventeen weeks involving 22,000 men and boys in Northumberland and Durham.
29 BURT, T. *op. cit.*, p. 31.
30 MANN, T. *op. cit.*, p. 3.
31 BURT, T. *op. cit.*, p. 32.
32 WILLIAMS, R. *The Long Revolution*, p. 157.
33 MACLURE, S. *Educational Documents: England and Wales 1816–1967*, p. 79.
34 STURT, M. *The Education of the People*, p. 296.
35 STURT, M. *op. cit.*, p. 301.
36 Hansard 3rd Series CXCIX Col. 441. (17.2.1870)
37 It is possible to suggest that for working class children in rural areas in the nineteenth century to obtain a good grounding in the three Rs was a considerable achievement on the part of a dame school – and the most that would be expected of any school at the time. Some individuals later indicated that they were encouraged to read a number of standard classics at such schools. Even allowing for the possibility that many working people readily identified with these 'domestic extensions of the home' it must also be remembered that numerous villages possessed no school at all and that such schools were just as readily plagued by the problems of attendance as much as other schools in rural areas. Dame schools were usually a local response to schooling and not by any means a rural system of schooling. See HIGGINSON, J.H., 'Dame Schools' *British Journal of Educational Studies*, 22 (2) June 1974.
38 COLE, M. *Makers of the Labour Movement*, p. 145.
39 BELLAMY, J.M. and SAVILLE, J. (Eds) *Dictionary of Labour Biography*, Vol. I.
40 FYRTH, H.J. and COLLINS, H. *The Foundry Workers: A Trade Union History*, p. 49.
41 TURNER, B. *About Myself*, pp. 22–23.
42 FYRTH, H.J. and COLLINS, H. *op. cit.*
43 BURT, T. *op. cit.*
44 ARCH, J. *op. cit.*, p. 28.
45 *Various Labour Biographies*, p. 134.
46 *Ibid.*, p. 122.
47 LEVENTHAL, F.M. *op. cit.*, p. 2.
48 ROGERS, F. *op. cit.*, p. 50.
49 Huxley's *Instructions in Physiology*.
50 KENT, W. *op. cit.*, p. 6.
51 TURNER, B. *op. cit.*, p. 23.
52 *Seventy Years of Trade Unionism*, p. 59.
53 COLE, M. *op. cit.*, p. 206.
54 BELLAMY, J.M. and SAVILLE, J. *Dictionary of Labour Biography*, Vol. I, p. 315.
55 COLE, G.D.H. *John Burns: Biographical Series No. 14*, p. 6.
56 The remains of this library are at present held by the TUC.
57 ARCH, J. *op. cit.*, p. 29.
58 ROGERS, F. *op. cit.*, p. 6.
59 Ironically, in later life, Crooks became Chairman of the Poor Law Guardians of Poplar (1878–1906) and must have been one of the few to hold such a position with personal experience of Poor House life.
60 STAFFORD, A. *A Match to Fire the Thames*, p. 46.
61 LEVENTHAL, F.M. *op. cit.*, p. xv.
62 BROADHURST, H. *op. cit.*, p. 189.
63 DALLEY, W.A. *op. cit.*, p. 11.
64 BELLAMY, J.M. and SAVILLE, J. *op. cit.*, Vol. I.
65 PCTUC Deputation to the Board of Education, Mins., 12.3.1919
66 HAW, G. *From Workhouse to Westminster: The Life Story of Will Crooks MP*, pp.

16–17.

67 E.G. West for example has argued in *Education and the State*, Institute of Economic Affairs 1965, that the 1870 Education Act was not necessary because school provision was already adequate. To a large extent the massive school building programme undertaken after 1870 by both religious bodies and the school boards would seem readily to refute his thesis but above all it is the numerous stories of working class children whose attendance at school was brief and irregular that make it clear that in England and Wales legislation and intervention by the State were imperative to provide at least elementary education on a scale the Churches had not been able to meet. Even then it took a generation to tackle the distractions of child labour and the threat of a World War to provide the kind of social services which would enable all children to benefit from the schooling offered.

68 Referring to the hard manual work he experienced, especially in the munitions factory where his hands were burnt by acid, Thorne later recorded that '. . . at the age of fifteen he swore to do all he could to help and prevent other children from going through the same hardships'. BELLAMY, J. and SAVILLE, J. *Dictionary of Labour Biography*, Vol. I., p. 315.

69 . . . no one who studies the legislation of a state can doubt its relativity to the demands of the class which acts in its name. The history of trade union law in England, of freedom of contract in America, of agrarian legislation in Russia, are all instances of the way in which a dominant economic class uses the state to make ultimate those legal imperatives which best protect its interests. This is not to deny for one moment a desire in the governing class to act reasonably or justly. But men think differently who live differently; and in the approach to the problem of what legal imperatives are ultimately desirable in the interests of the community as a whole, each class approaches the question with an unstated and half-conscious major premise at the back of its mind which is of fundamental importance to its view of reason or justice . . . and since the main item in our experience is gained in the effort to make our living, the way in which that living is earned is that which most profoundly shapes our notions of what is desirable. LASKI, H. *An Introduction to Politics*, p. 18.

Chapter 9

Conclusion

Trade union leaders were extraordinary people. Their distinction however was not in their experiences which were common to many of their fellow workers: little formal schooling, long hours of work at an early age, seeking work by tramping as in the case of Broadhurst or walking from Birmingham to London, like Thorne, to seek employment at the Old Kent Road Gasworks. What marks out many of the leading trade unionists is that they still made time to read,[1] organize other workers and regularly attend meetings. However they led their unions or branches, this ability to overcome harsh conditions has to be admired.

Many leading trade unionists started out as radicals critical of early injustices which they had witnessed. Some lost their radical attitudes later in life either because they believed a less strident approach in particular circumstances might be better tactically for the union to adopt or because later respectability, comfort and higher income insulated them from the conditions experienced by their members. The election to high office in the union or to Parliament was a considerable achievement when one considers the disadvantaged early years which many underwent, there is some evidence that they viewed their careers in this manner. One has only to consider the titles or subtitles given to the autobiographies of such men to see that this was so: George Barnes' *From Workshop to War Cabinet* or Henry Broadhurst's *From Stonemason's Bench to Treasury Bench*. Such writings showed pride in the struggle faced by the author and often implied that success in society was possible for those able or willing to display similar qualities. Their very success suggested there was less need now for radical change than there had been in their youth. To the extent that working conditions were better in the second half of the nineteenth century than the first half, this was true. It might be argued that high office in the Labour movement blunted the cutting edge to the socialist views of men like Ben Tillett[2] and Will Thorne; the latter, for example, retained his membership of the Marxist SDF for most of its existence yet in the 1920s went along with the Executive of his Union in refusing to associate with trades councils affiliated to the National Minority Movement because it contained Marxists.[3]

Frequently TUC members have been blamed for not holding socialist views later which they never aspired to in the first place. The PCTUC was dominated by Liberals throughout the nineteenth century; only Sexton and Thorne saw themselves as socialists and they seemed rarely able to come to any agreement between themselves. Howell, Broadhurst and Fenwick all carried out actions precisely in accordance with Liberal Party principles. To argue that the TUC might have made more progress if it had adopted socialist ideas is another issue altogether and one that provides little help in understanding the situation as it was. It could be argued that much of the history of the twentieth century Labour movement has been characterized by the struggle of a minority of socialists to convert the Movement to such a philosophy but for the period under consideration little success in this direction was achieved in the Co-operative Movement, the TUC, many trade unions and the Labour Party itself, although socialists did achieve considerable influence on some trades councils and in some trade unions.

Pragmatism seemed to be the major influence at work in the PCTUC. To some extent external events forced such an outlook upon them. It also allowed them to work with organizations on specific issues which those with firm ideological commitments might have found impossible to do. Hence, having expelled the trades councils in 1895, the PCTUC still continued to work with them and seek their help when the occasion demanded. Also, the refusal of the NUT to affiliate to the TUC did not prevent negotiations taking place between the two bodies on areas of mutual interest whilst a PCTUC Deputation was quite willing to support higher wages for teachers at the Board of Education.[4] It was the broad federal structure of the TUC that enabled it to survive and grow whilst smaller sectarian groups within the Labour movement declined. This broadness of the TUC also needs to be borne in mind when one writes about TUC declared views for they were often founded upon policies finding general agreement rather than strict and narrow programmes to which only a minority of working people could agree.

Whatever their religious or political ideologies trade unionists demonstrated a concern for the provision of educational and associated welfare programmes. Principally it would seem that this arose from their own early experiences of school and work. They really knew what it was like to go early to the pits, the mill or the field. This was why they were able to unite on a progressive programme for education even though it had been initiated outside the TUC in organizations such as the NEL, SDF or ILP. This did not bother delegates who readily accepted the adopted and adapted TUC Education Programme as the kind of system necessary for working class children at the time. By the 1890s the programme was distinctly socialist and was to remain so in terms of the British Labour movement throughout the period studied. One might suggest that secondary education for all would have been a true test of socialist purity but, in a movement which readily accepted different grades at work and corresponding pay differentials, to ask for equality of opportunity was as much as any section of the Labour movement was promoting in the 1890s. They were trying to sketch out a fairer system of education against a model which was almost solely divided in terms of social class. In this context equality of opportunity was a revolutionary idea.

One can find, readily enough, examples of TUC influence on the thinking and action of political parties and governments, especially the legislation cited by George Howell[5] and examples such as the Trade Disputes Act of 1906. Does this also apply to education? This is less easy to demonstrate because whereas the Liberal Government knew in 1906 that failure to amend the legislation which had led to Taff Vale would mean organized hostility from the TUC which would invite defeat at the next General Election, they might well surmise that failure to reverse the 1902 Education Act would evoke less response because it did not threaten the essence of trade unionism.

Yet there is evidence of educational legislation being influenced by the TUC. If Congress was too small to influence the 1870 Education Act it was certainly a factor in Conservative proposals to abolish fees in most elementary schools in 1891. This might seem a marginal matter but it did show how the Government was responding to the newly enfranchised rural voters and TUC lobbying for free education. 1902 was a real test of strength but on this occasion the Conservative Government were not willing to concede at all because their allies wanted the board schools abolished, the religious schools given more finance and the secondary schools strengthened. There was no room for negotiation with the TUC on this occasion, for what was at stake was the way in which all state schooling would develop in the twentieth century. Any continuation of an elected school board system held too many dangers for the Conservatives. They were opposed to the widespread development of secondary schools and this might easily have taken place in school board areas if the Labour movement had captured them at election time; this was increasingly possible if local and national election successes of the Labour movement in the early years of the twentieth century are considered. The failure of the Liberals to overturn the 1902 Education Act which they had argued so strongly against was also due in some measure to the realization that the Labour movement was beginning to show its potential strength electorally.

When the Conservatives believed that only cut backs in public expenditure, including education, could aid the economy in the 1920s, they were again willing to confront the TUC and ignore their views. Indeed confrontation eventually led to the industrial disputes which became known as the General Strike which lies outside the area of this study. Suffice to say that when the occasion arose the GCTUC showed little liking for the conflict and some reluctance to establish the kind of organization necessary to make its actions most effective.[6] This provides at least circumstantial evidence that whilst the TUC did possess power its leaders were never willing or confident enough to use it.

It is in the field of gradual reform that the PCTUC felt most at ease and were most successful. Once permissive legislation was passed, such as that concerning school meals and medical inspection, they beavered away to get it expanded. The same occurred with the free place system in secondary schools. Evidence of their success came from remarks made by J.A. Pease, who felt that the PCTUC Deputation was too critical of Government measures: 'If the TUC will not give the President credit for progress they could at least give themselves credit for the influence they have brought on the Government'.[7]

It was always known that whilst the PCTUC could legitimately claim to speak for millions of workers it did not follow that all the membership of affiliated unions agreed with their views; still less the larger number of workers outside the TUC, whether unionized or not. The views of the PCTUC were seen as those of the most respected and well organized of the working classes; at least this was true of Committees or Government Ministers who made contact with them. The Cross Commission of 1888 accepted that trade unions reached '... the more prosperous class of working people'[8] and showed no inclination to disagree with the views of Mr. Powell, a first class visitor of the LSB for Southwark, that 'they are better disciplined, more self respectful'.[9] However the Consultative Committee on Attendance at Continuation Schools thirty years later suggested that 'a distinction must be made ... between resolutions passed at such meetings as those of the TUC and the real attitude of the average Labour mind', although it was accepted that they had 'distinct effect on public opinion among the workers...'.[10]

It was this power to influence other workers which H.A.L. Fisher valued so much in his early years at the Board of Education.

> We here at the Board who are anxious to promote educational reform
> are conscious that in the last resort we cannot outstep public opinion;
> and it is upon the trade unionists of the country in a very large measure
> that the direction of public opinion into useful channels will depend.[11]

This optimistic view of TUC influence did not seem to take into account other sources of influence, such as the FBI or the newspapers, although John Mill, a PCTUC representative on the Deputation did ask the President whether 'we should get Lord Northcliffe on our side to create some public opinion'.[12] The remark brought laughter but by the 1920s the popular press showed their power to influence by helping to create an atmosphere that made the recommendations of the Geddes Commission more readily acceptable[13] and many of the aims of the 1918 Education Act unobtainable.

Whilst the TUC continued to press for changes in schooling and welfare for children, the abolition of the school boards denied an outlet for many trade unionists to express their ideas on education or influence schooling at the local level. Whether this was a factor in diverting some attention to adult education is not certain, for, although the PCTUC was involved with Ruskin College from 1899 onwards, it was only in the Edwardian era that trade union education began to attract wider interest among Congress delegates. Here the TUC was finally forced to come to terms with the curriculum in a way they had never done with regard to schools.

It does seem as if the General Council of the TUC believed that a college of their own would be a practical proposition and a worthwhile acquisition. Considerable progress can be traced in negotiations between the various bodies already involved in providing education for trade unionists; Ruskin College, the Central Labour College, the WETUC and the NCLC. Yet in the long run, even if the necessary finances had been forthcoming and no industrial dispute on the horizon, future success of such a venture seemed doubtful. Problems of accommodation and suitable teaching premises could probably have been agreed upon but it is not easy to contemplate two colleges such as Ruskin and the CLC existing smoothly side by side in the same building. Their approaches to the curriculum were diametrically opposed. Ruskin College and the WEA might well suggest that all was not well with capitalism but there was little suggestion as to how socialism might be introduced or urgency expressed about its necessity. After all, the TUC had constantly campaigned for the Government to come to their aid with legislation for both trade union activity and many aspects of schooling and child welfare. They sought the protection of Government against what they believed had been forces sometimes opposed to working class interests; the Church, private schools and industry.

At times Government did provide legislation in accordance with TUC wishes but governments were also capable of introducing legislation which seemed to be against the interests of the working class; the 1902 Education Act and the Geddes cut back were seen in this light by Congress. There was enough dissatisfaction with governments for the TUC to help in establishing an independent political party for organized Labour in the hope that this would eventually capture power and rule in the interests of working people. Compare this with the Socialist and Marxist outlook of the CLC which saw different governments as part of the same State apparatus by which the ruling class ruled and believed that the actions of some leading members of the GCTUC were more inclined to support the *status quo* than bring about necessary radical changes in society. Such views were to be expressed within the Labour movement, especially in the newly formed Communist Party, but there was little hope that leading members of the General Council would encourage such ideas in any college over which they had some say. Still less was there likely to be any chance of State or local authority support for any part of a college designed to expose and undermine that State.

Ruskin College and the WEA did receive State aid. For those, such as A. Pugh, who believed that technical knowledge to argue the workers' case was the most practical type of education for trade unionists, Government aid was openly courted. This financial support together with a greater acceptance of the *status quo* and a less critical outlook of Labour leadership made such a college a far greater attraction to the General Council than the CLC who would have to rely solely on trade union funds and therefore prove a greater financial burden. All of these difficult questions, at least difficult at a Congress attended by supporters of both colleges, were not quite put to the test for external events provided some kind of solution; namely the continuation of Ruskin and the demise of the CLC.

The TUC believed the country could and should provide a better educational service, hence their programme to expand facilities and opportunities for school children. They must have been pleasantly surprised in 1917 when H.A.L. Fisher told representatives of the PCTUC 'that if the nation really wants a good system of education, this country, war or no war, is perfectly rich enough to pay for it'.[14] It was not the TUC who needed persuading as to the validity of such a view but the FBI and successive governments, all of whom were willing to concede by the 1920s that elementary education should be available for all children. Apart from that, with the exception of a few very intelligent working class children, anything beyond basic education should only be available on the same principle as other goods or services, strictly related to ability to pay the relevant fees.

It can be accepted that the TUC failed to solve the problem of providing an agreed syllabus for trade union education. At the same time disagreements concerning the curriculum in any rapidly changing society are the norm rather than the exception. By bringing education for children before Congress delegates had to consider a fundamental issue outside their daily world of industrial struggles. It is true that education was never a priority at Congress but it did receive a considerable amount of debating time over the years and the PCTUC and GCTUC did do their best to press Congress Education Policy before Ministers at the Board of Education. Delegates showed, by their very knowledge of education for working class children both in terms of personal experience and their present relationships with the living and working environment in which many schools were located, an awareness of the problems facing most children; these were problems sometimes known to those at the Board of Education and in Parliament only through official surveys and reports. The picture given of problems facing young children at school by Congress delegates were frequently substantiated by such surveys and reports.

TUC resolutions on education were idealistic yet proven by later events to be practical, as might be expected from working people whose lives were dominated by practicalities. Free education from infant school to secondary school (later extended in 1906 to include universities), physical education divorced from military influences, raising of the school leaving age to fifteen years without exemptions, introduction of the metric system, free school meals, medical inspection and treatment were all part of TUC Education Policy at times and all were achieved, at least partially,[15] even if many of these reforms were not achieved until years after 1925. Other parts of TUC Education Policy were not successful, such as secular education, reduction of class sizes to a maximum of forty pupils, national control of educational endowments or democratically elected *ad hoc* committees to organize education locally.

Whatever criticisms might be made of the TUC – and clearly a large federal body which has lasted for so many years had problems, made mistakes and experienced leadership under trade unionists motivated by various ideas – it would be difficult to deny that their steady and persistent demands for reform in the education and welfare of children brought positive benefit to thousands.

Those seeking greater achievements may be disappointed but one good meal at lunch time for a hungry child, some physical ailment cured by early medical inspection and treatment, the opportunity for just a minority of working class children to gain more than a basic elementary education can all be rated as positive achievements because they affected the lives of individual children in poor circumstances for the good. That conditions for children both at school and work were better in 1925 than in 1868 was due in no small measure to the willingness of Congress delegates to give time and involve themselves in efforts to improve the lives of the ordinary children of Britain.

Notes

1 For a vivid description, born of experience, of the problems facing manual workers trying to pursue any serious reading in their spare time during the nineteenth century see Jack London's *Martin Eden*.

2 In a debate following a resolution introduced by Ben Tillett on Compulsory Arbitration, the Dockers' leader remarked: 'Some people would remark that it was very peculiar for an extremist to believe in constitutional government, [laughter]' and later in the debate, Mr. Ward, a delegate from Manchester, replied: '... speaking as a strong arbitrationist, [he] was pleased to see that Mr. Tillett of today was not the Mr. Tillett of ten years ago'. [Laughter]. TUC Report 1899, p. 73. Yet later when addressing Transport Workers in the 1912 Transport Strike Tillett declared: 'Capitalism is capitalism as a tiger is a tiger; and both are savage and pitiless towards the weak'. MEACHAM, S. *A Life Apart: The English Working Class 1890–1914*, p. 145.

3 RADICE, E.A. and RADICE, G.H. *Will Thorne: Constructive Militant*, p. 105.

4 PCTUC Deputation to Board of Education Mins., 15.2.1917.

5 Howell listed 123 enactments between 1868–1901 favourable to working people and wrote: 'In the series of Congresses – 1868–1901 inclusive – every measure of importance affecting workmen has been considered, and the Parliamentary Committee initiated, promoted, advocated and supported Bills introduced'. HOWELL, G., *Labour Legislation, Labour Movements and Labour Leaders*, Vol. II, pp. 469–472.

6 See FARMAN, C. *The General Strike*, Chapter 10.

7 PCTUC Deputation to the Board of Education, Mins., 12.2.1914.

8 Report of the Royal Commission on the Elementary Education Acts (The Cross Report), Vol. 17, p. 404.

9 *Ibid.*

10 *Report of the Consultative Committee on Attendance at Continuation Schools 1909*, p. 142.

11 PCTUC Deputation to the Board of Education, Mins., 15.2.1917.

12 *Ibid.*

13 See SIMON, B. *The Politics of Educational Reform 1920–40*, Ch. 1. Pt. 2.

14 PCTUC Deputation to the Board of Education, Mins., 15.2.1917.

15 School meals were only made free for children whose parents received below average incomes.

Figure 3 School Leaving Age of Sixty-seven Trade Unionists Listed in Appendix I

School Leaving Age	6	7	8	9	10	11	12	13	14	14+
Left School Before 1870	x	xxxx x	x*x*xx xxxxx	x†xxx xx-x	x†xxx xxxxxx	x	xxxx xxxxx		x	
Left School 1870–1880				x†x†x	x†xx	xx	xxx	xx		
Left School 1881+				x†			xxxxx		xx	x

x* 'early age'
x† half-time – for 2/3 yrs.

At least ten attended dame schools for some time.

65.2% left school before 1870
21.2% left school between 1870–1880
13.6% left school 1881 onwards

Appendix I Schooling of Prominent TUC Delegates

*Column 4 M = Death of Mother, F = death of Father, O = Orphan b~ 10 years of age.

Dates	Name	Father's occupation	*M, F or O	School Leaving Age	School Attended	First Work/ Apprenticeship	Trade Union	Other Details
1842– 1922	Abraham W.	Miner		9	Received 'scanty' education	9 yrs in Colliery until 29 yrs	Miners	First Welsh Miners' M.P. Rhondda (1885–1920)
1813–74	Allan W.	Manager, Cotton Mill		12		Piecer in Cotton Factory, 15 yrs App. Engineer	Engineers	
1834– 1924	Applegarth R.	Quartermaster R.N.		10	Dame School	Bookmakers errand, odd jobs then Carpenter	Carpenters	1870 Lambeth School Board election – unsuccessful. Exec. Committee of N.E.L.
1859– 1940	Appleton W.A.	Farmworker?		10	'Few days of attendance'	Evening Classes as youth	Lacemakers	
1826– 1919	Arch J.	Farmworker		9	Local National School	Scaring crows at 9 yrs, ploughboy then hedger.	Agricultural Labourers	Taught mainly by mother
1859– 1940	Barnes G.	Journeyman, Machine Maker		11	Church School, Enfield Highway, Mdx.	Clerk in Jute Mill & 11 yrs, Apprentice Eng. @ 13 yrs.	Engineers	Attended evening classes for Technical Drawing/ Machine Construction
1859– 1930	Bell R.	Quarryman		13	Church School. & Board School	Clerk, Shunter @ 16 yrs, Porter @ 17 yrs., Guard.	Railwaymen	
1873– 1953	Bondfield M.	Foreman Lacemaker		14	Chard Elem. School	Pupil Teacher @ 13 yrs., Apprentice Shop Asst.	Shop Assts. N.U.G.M.W.	
1851– 1947	Bowerman C.W.	Tinplate Worker		12	Five Years at Barnsbury National School.	Worked for watchmaker @ 12 yrs, Apprent. Printer at 14 yrs.	Compositors	Keen supporter of education – opposed 1902 Education Act. Assoc. with Ruskin College from its foundation until his death. Opposed CLC.

Dates	Name	Father	Code	Age	School	Work	Union	Notes
1840–1911	Broadhurst H.	Stonemason		12	'Private school at 6d. per week'	Blacksmith's Forge @ 12 yrs., Apprent. Stonemason to father 13 yrs.	Stonemasons	Candidate Greenwich Sch. Ed. 1873 unsuccessful Elected Cromer Sch. Bd. 1896.
1842–1914	Burnett J.	Engineer	O	9?	Duke of Northumberland's Charity School	Errand boy, Apprent. Engineer	Engineers	Member Newcastle Mechanics' Institute
1858–1943	Burns J.	Engineer	F	10		Candle Factory, Buttons, Apprent. Engineer	Engineers	Amassed very large private library
1837–1922	Burt T.	Miner	F	10	Dame School., Elem. School in Durham, Attended 2 out of 4 years	Began as Trapper Boy, Putter then Heaver	Miners	No more than two years schooling
1868–1947	Cape T.			11?	Great Broughton Endowed School.	Scaring crows @ 11 yrs., Colliery Boy at 12 yrs.	Miners	'The school years for Thomas Cape were very brief'
1859–1949	Clynes J.R.	Farmworker		10+		10–12 yrs. Half-Time in Textile Mill	Gasworkers	'Detested' Elem. Sch. 12–14 yrs. paid 8d. for 2 nights tuition from ex-schoolmaster.
1884–1931	Cook A.J.	Soldier		12	Elem. School	Colliery South Wales	Miners	Attended C.L.C. 1911, Financial difficulties prevented him completing a second year
1839–1903	Cowey E.			7		Trapper Boy, Royal Navy then Colliery again	Miners	
1833–90	Crawford W.			10		Joined Colliery @ 10 yrs.	Miners	

Dates	Name	Father's Occupation	M F or O	School Leaving Age	School Attended	First Work/ Apprenticeship	Trade Union	Other Details
1828–1908	Cremer W.R.		F	12	Dame School, then Church School, Farnham, Hants.	Pitch boy in shipyard, apprent. Carpenter	Carpenters	Attended Dame School kept by his mother.
1851–1921	Crooks W.	Ship's Stoker		8	George Green School E. India Dock R.C. & Poor Law School Sutton	Milk round, errand boy @ 8 yrs, Apprent. Cooper at 14 yrs.	Dockers	Famous for Sunday morning meetings at E. India Docks known as 'Crooks' College'
1860–1910	Curran P.			10		Junior Hammer Driver, became Blacksmith's Striker	Gasworkers	
1848–1923	Davis W.J.	Publican		9	Dame School, for 2½ years	Entered Brass Trade at 13 yrs.	Brassworkers	Gained Queen's Prize S. Kensington Art & Science When teenager. Candidate B'ham Sch. Bd.: 1875 Unsuccessful; Elected 1876, 1879, & 1882.
1850–1918	Fenwick C.			9	Village School, Cramlington, Northumberland	Worked on surface at Colliery @ 9 yrs., underground at 10 yrs.	Miners	Received little formal education.
1861–1930	Gosling H.	Lighterman	M	13	8 yrs. of schooling, B. & F. School, Marlborough St. Blackfriar.	Apprent. to father @ 14 years	Lightermen	Mother schoolteacher but died when he was seven years old. In his school one master often taught 250 boys.
1856–1914	Gill A.	Cotton Spinner		10+	St. Mary's School Balderstone	10–13 yrs. Half-Timer, then full-time.	Textile Workers	Represented Trades Council on Bolton Tech. Education Board.

Dates	Name	Occupation		Age	School		Trade Union	Notes
1814–83	Guile D.	Shoemaker		12	Dame School until 7 yrs., then Weslyan Free School	Apprent. Ironfounder at 13 yrs.	Ironfounders	
1857–1937	Greenall T.	Miner		8		Bottle Factory at 8 yrs., Hauling Tubs under harness in pit @ 12 yrs.	Miners	Few years of schooling but learned to read and write.
1835–1919	Halliday T.	Miner	F	8		Worked at Pit @ 8 yrs., then Half-Timer in Textile Mill, returned to Pits	Miners	
1837–98	Harford E.	Policeman		14	Tiverton Factory School	Apprent. Confectionery Trade, Policeman, Railwayman	Railwaymen	
1856–1915	Hardie K.	Carpenter		7		Errand boy, Trapper boy @ 10 yrs.	Miners	Real father miner, Hardie educated himself down Pit, taught himself shorthand.
1842–1913	Haslam J.	Shoemaker		10	Stable School, Clay Cross	Worked on Pit Brow @ 10 yrs., underground at 16 yrs.	Miners	Meagre education.
1855–1937	Hodge J.	Puddler, Ironworks		12	Hutcheson Boys' Grammar School, Glasgow	Many jobs including Solicitor's Clerk, then Ironworks	Ironfounders	
1863–1935	Henderson A.	Cotton Spinner		9/12	Returned to school when moved from Scotland to Newcastle	Apprent. Foundryman	Ironfounders	'Schooling brief and often broken into by the obligation to work'.
1853–1910	Howell G.	Stonemason		10	National Elm. School, Bristol	Ploughboy, helped Father, Apprent. Shoemaker at 14 yrs.	Builders	Attended Evening Classes in London – 1850s.
1852–1935	Hudson W.	Gas Stoker	O	9	Workhouse School then Richmond National School	Worked on farm until 20 yrs. then Railway	Railwaymen	Attended Sunday/Evening Classes as youth

Dates	Name	Father's Occupation	M. F or O	School Leaving Age	School Attended	First Work/ Apprenticeship	Trade Union	Other Details
1852– 1936	Jenkins J.H.	Shipwright			Elementary School	Apprentice shipwright	Shipwrights	Taught in Cardiff Ragged Schools, Superintendent for 15 years.
1819–76	Kane J.	Attorney	O	7	Mr. Tait's School, Alnick	Tobacco Factory @ 7 yrs, Apprent. Gardener at 12 yrs. Ironworker at 17 yrs.	Ironfounders	Returned to school from 9–12 years of age. Candidate for Darlington Sch. Board; 1870 unsuccessful; 1873 elected.
1848– 1911	Kelley G.D.	Cooper		12	Village School Rushinton, Lincs.	Pupil teacher then apprentice Lithographic Printer	Printers	Pupil teacher for 2½ years, unsuccessful candidate for Manchester School Board 1891.
1825– 1903	Leicester J.	Glassblower		10	National School, Warrington	Apprent. to father @ 10 yrs.	Glassmakers	Outstanding craftsman; three prizes from Society of Arts for Artistic work in Glass.
1821–81	MacDonald A.	Sailor		8		Into pits @ 8 yrs., worked in mines for 16 yrs. and studied.	Miners	Whilst a miner successfully studied for university entrance. Attended Glasgow University and became a school teacher then worked for miners.
1856– 1941	Mann T.	Colliery Clerk	M	9	Foleshill Old Church Day School; Little Heath School.	In pits @ 9 yrs., then apprentice Engineer.	Engineers	
1865– 1932	Murnin H.	Miner		9	Elementary School	Entered pits @ 9 yrs., worked underground for 21 years.	Miners	

Dates	Name	Occupation	Age started	School	Work history	Trade	Notes
1830–75	Normansell J.	Miner	O	Wesleyan Methodist Sunday School	At 7 yrs. pushing tubs underground, then worked regularly in pits.	Miners	Illiterate; could not sign name on marriage register.
1820–77	Odger G.	Cornish Miner	O	Roubro' Elem. School, Devon	Apprentice Shoemaker	Shoemakers	
1854–1934	O'Grady J.		'early age' 10	St. Mary's R.C. School – few years	Mineral Water Factory, Apprentice Cabinet Maker @ 15 years.	Furnishing Trades	
1858–1921	Onions A.	Miner	12	St. George's Church School	In pits at 12 yrs., N. Staffs.	Miners	Member Myhyddyslwyn Sc. Board 1888, Bedwellty Sch. Board 1899.
1847–96	Patterson W.	Quarryman			Worked in pits	Miners	Methodist local preacher when teenager; elected Durham Sch. Board 1884, took active interest in Durham Mechanics Institute.
1842–1904	Pickard B.	Miner	12	Kippax Grammar School	Hurrier in pits when 12 yrs.	Miners	
1832–93	Potter G.	Carpenter	'early'	Dame School, then Aldridge's Charity School	Ploughboy, errand boy, apprent. carpenter @ 16 yrs.	Builders	Candidate L.S.B.: Unsuccessful 1870; successful 1873–82, Fought for free education, founded The Beehive when 29 years of age.
1870–1955	Pugh A.	Engineer	O	Elem. Educ. up to Standard IV	Apprent. to farmer, then butcher. Entered Steel Trade @ 24 yrs.	Ironfounders	Chairman W.E.T.U.C.: Took great interest in Trade Union Education.
1872–1935	Purcell A.	French Polisher	9+	Keighley Elem. School, Yorks.	Half-timer at Woollen Mill from 9 yrs., apprent. Fr. Polisher @ 18 yrs.	French Polishers	
1853–1931	Richards T.	Miner	12	Beaufort British School Ebbw Vale	In pits from 12 years	Miners	

Dates	Name	Father's Occupation	M. For O	School Leaving Age	School Attended	First Work/Apprenticeship	Trade Union	Other Details
1897–1964	Roberts B.	Mining Engineer		12		Delivery boy, then in pits for 13 years.	Miners/N.U.P.E.	Evening classes, CLC in 1920. Moved from Wales to become General Secretary N.U.P.E.
1869–1928	Roberts G.H.	Shoemaker		14	St. Stephen's National Elem. School	Apprentice Printer	Printers	Evening classes at Higher Grade & Tech. Schools in Norwich. Elected Norwich Sch. Board 1899.
1846–1915	Rogers F.	Shop Assistant		10	Dame School	Errand boy, then apprentice bookbinder at 15 years.	Bookbinders	Worked for L.S.B. but does not give details; assume elected as trade union candidate?
1868–1939	Seddon J.	Nail Maker		12	Huyton & Prescot National & Board Schools	Grocer's Assistant, Commercial Traveller, Shop Assistant.	Shop Assistants	
1856–1938	Sexton J.	Hawker		8	Low House School	Worked first in Market then in Gas Works at 9 yrs., then docks.	Dockers	Stowed away to San Francisco when 12 yrs. of age. Organised R.C. opposition to secular educ. @TUC.
1863–1938	Shackleton D.J.	Power Loom Weaver		9+	Attended Dame School at 5 yrs., Longholme Wesleyan Day School at 6 yrs.	Half-timer Hull Carr Cotton Mill, Full-time at 13 yrs.	Textile Workers	
1857–1940	Smillie R.		O	9+	Infrequent Attendance	Errand boy, Half-timer Spinning Mill, Miner at 17 yrs.	Miners	Evening classes as youth, elected Larkhill Sch. Board 1888–1900, member Plebs League, supported C.L.C.
1851–1911	Steadman W.C.	Shipwright		8	Local National School	Various jobs including Errand boy, Apprentice Shipwright @ 15 yrs.	Barge Builders	

Thomas J.H.	1874–1949	Seaman	O	12	St. Paul's National Elem. School Newport.	Part-time Shop Assistant, Engine Cleaner @ 15 yrs.	Railwaymen	Chairman A.S.R.S. Branch at 23 yrs. & President Newport Trades Council.
Thorne W.	1857–1946	Brickmaker	F	6	No formal education	Hard manual work; brick yards, munitions factory, gas works.	Gasworkers	Illiterate – signed marriage register with X. Leading advocate of education in own union and behind formation of TUC Education. Programme.
Tillett B.	1860–1943	Labourer	M	8	Only a few days at National School in Stafford, Dismissed.	Worked in brickyard @ 6 yrs., joined Circus at 8 yrs., R.N. at 13 yrs.	Dockers	Could hardly read until 17 yrs. of age. Attended Bow and Bromley Institute Evening Classes.
Turner B.	1863–1942	Hand Loom Weaver		9+	Dame School, Liphill Bank Elem. School	Half-timer 10–13 yrs.	Textile Workers	Attended Mechanics Institute; supported Secular Sunday Schools.
Varley J.	1871–1952	Mill Worker		12	St. Andrew's School Bradford & Quaker Sunday School.	Part-time Mill Worker then Weaver	Textile Workers	Helped in organisation of school meal system, Bradford. Active in Nat. Fed. Women Workers.
Walkden A.	1873–1951	Railway Clerk		16	Merchant Taylor's School, Ashwell.	Railway Clerk, gained rapid promotion.	Railway Clerks	Member of Newcastle School Board for several years.
Wilkie A.	1850–1928		O	12	Sound Elem. Education – won prizes.	At 13 yrs. apprent. ship building yards.	Shipwrights	
Wilson J.	1837–1915	Labourer/ Poacher	O	11	Dame School at 6 yrs., Variety of schools due to travelling.	Quarry, errand boy then pit at 13 years.	Miners	
Woods S.	1846–1915	Miner		7	Education supplemented by attending Evening Classes.	Into pits @ 7 yrs. looked after pit ponies at 13 yrs.	Miners	Some further education 9–13 yrs., learned to read at Sunday School. Obtained 1st Class Cert. Mining Management @ Owen's College, M'ster.

Appendix II   TUC Resolutions on Education 1868–1925

Year	Major subject matter of Resolution	Proposer/ Seconder	Other Details
1868	Technical Education		
1869	1. National, unsectarian, compulsory system of education	W.R. Cremer	Carried unanimously
	2. Limitation of Apprentices (Indirect)	G. Potter (LMWA)	Carried
1870	No Congress		
1871	Primary education for all children, Technical education for all engaged in industry.	G. Potter (LMWA)	Unanimous
1872	No time for paper on Forster's Education Bill to be read. Resolution allowed to be proposed/seconded only.	A.W. Bailey?	Assume resolution passed?
1873	Reduction in working hours of women/young children to 54, Half-timers to commence at 10 instead of 8. (Indirect)	A.W. Bailey C. Williams	Unanimous
1874	1. Limitation of Apprentices (Indirect)	M. Donell (Manchester) Hodges (Birmingham)	Carried
	2. Establishment of Technical schools in all industrial centres	W. Owen (N. Staffs.) Lester (Sheffield)	Unanimous
1875 1876 1877 1878	(Jan. & Oct. Congresses)		
1879	Objections to National Society Reading Book	A. Simmons (Kent Agric. Labourers)	Deputation to Archbishop of Canterbury and (?) President, Board of Education.
1880	1. ditto	A. Simmons (Kent Agric. Labourers)	Letter to National Society from PCTUC.
	2. Limitation of Apprentices (Indirect)	Nannetti, Owens	

Year	Major subject matter of Resolution	Proposer/ Seconder	Other Details
1881	1. Amendements to Educational Endowments Bill (Scotland) to allow for direct/complete control in election of governors.	Thom Inglis (Glasgow)	Unanimous
	2. Objections to National Society Reading Book	A. Simmons (Kent Agric. Labourers), Jack (Glasgow)	Unanimous
1882	Creches for married mothers working	T.R. Threlfall (Typo. Assoc.), Holmes (Burnley)	Withdrawn Too controversial at time!
1883	Support for discretionary powers to fine parents for non-attendance of their children	Powell (London) Merrick	Carried
1884	In favour of Sunday Opening for Museums, Art Galleries, etc. (Indirect)	Inskip (Leicester)	passed 40:21
1885	1. Sunday Opening of Museums, etc.	Inskip?	Amendment to extend hours in week to 10 p.m. passed, 78:21
	2. Free Education for all children attending Elementary Schools	Bisset. G. (Aberdeen) Richards (Southport)	Unanimous
	3. Objections to Military Drill in schools	Morrison (London) Howarth S. (Bolton)	Carried by large majority
1886	1 Free Elementary Education	Knight R. (Newcastle) Miller (Blyth)	Carried 'with few dissentions'
	2. Establishment of Evening/ Recreative/Instructive Classes for young persons who have left school	Davidson R. (Liverpool) Spencer W. (London)	Carried Unanimously
1887	1. Demand for National System of Free Education	Myers J. (Barrow in Furness) Holmes (Leicester)	Unanimously agreed
	2. Establishment of Evening Recreative Classes (vid. 1886)	Horobin (Leicester) Holmes (Leicester)	Adopted
	3. Sunday Opening of Museums, etc.	Freak (London) Cameron (London)	Motion carried 45:24

Year	Major subject matter of Resolution	Proposer/ Seconder	Other Details
1888			
1889	1. Government Grants to Elementary Schools to give intellectual youths chance of college/university education so that future Labour Representatives in Parliament would be well educated.	Callow J.	Resolution lost by large majority
	2. Demand for Evening Continuation Schools for children of working classes	Keywood J. (Notts.) Another Notts delegate	Unanimously passed
	3. Education of Blind . . . 'to obtain for that class such assistance as shall tend to the amelioration of their condition'	Keir J. (Aberdeen – blind himself) Livingston (Aberdeen)	Unanimous
1890			
1891	Amendment to delete demand for ROSLA to 12 in debate on Factory Inspectors	Holmes (Lancs.)	Against Amendment 79:301
1892	Objections to National Society Reading Book (vid. 1879 & 1880)	Drummond (Glasgow) Leitch (Glasgow)	Resolution adopted
1893			
1894			
1895	1. Demand for democratic control of education to secure principle of equality of opportunity	Thorne W. (Gasworkers)	Agreed to
	2. Abolition of child labour to 15 (Amendment to 14 yrs by Glover T. Lancs.) Abolition of Night Work up to 18 years	Clynes J.R. (Gasworkers) Bland (Bradford)	Resolution adopted
1896	Same Resolution as Thorne W. 1895 plus secular education (Implied in 1895 but not named – now spelt out clearly) Amendment similar to Resolution	Curran P. (Gasworkers) Turner (Batley) Rogers Owen (Burslem)	Amendment carried unanimously
1897	1. Abolition of Child Labour under 15, Night-work under 18. (vid. 1895)	Curran P. Gasworkers Johnson H. (London)	595,000 For 274,000 Against (Mainly Lancs opposed to ROSLA)
	2. Condemnation of Government Education Policy-Demands: a) Equality of Opportunity	Brabham, Proctor	Carried by large majority – textile workers opposed.

Year	Major subject matter of Resolution	Proposer/ Seconder	Other Details
1897 Cont'd	b) School Meals c) Abolition of half Time & ROSLA to 16 with maintenance grants d) Secular Education etc.		
1898	Ditto	Woods W. (Leeds.) Templeton (Glasgow)	Unanimously adopted
1899	1. Ditto	Picard H. (Gasworkers) Davis R. (Leicester) (Navvies)	Proposition carried
	2. Child Labour in Factories – Abolition up to 14 years	Curran P. (Gasworkers) Bell R. (Railwaymen, ARS)	Carried:- 587,000 For 171,000 Against
1900	1. ROSLA 15 years	Hurley T. (Oldham) Gasworkers Bowman A. (Belfast) (Гlaиdroooore)	Motion carried 'a number of hands ... held up against' (Lancs. Textile Workers)
	2. Opposition to recent Government proposals – support for Higher Grade Schools, Representatives of Labour to Board of Education Put pressure on MPs	Jenkins J. (Cardiff) (Assoc. Shipwrights) Sherwood W. (Sunderland) (Gasworkers)	Carried unanimously
1901	1. Prohibition of children under 15 in employment	Sherwood W. O'Grady J. (London)	Carried 171:71 (Textile workers opposed)
	2. National System of Education ROSLA 15 yrs. etc.	Appleton W.A. (Amal. Lace Makers) Wignal J. (Swansea)	
1902	1. Composite Resolution: a. Demands to oppose Government Education Bill b. Education, through democratically elected authorities c. No fees in Elementary, Higher Education Continuation & Technical Schools	Appleton W.A. (Amal. Lace Mkrs.) Bowerman C.W. (London) (Compositors)	Carried by large majority after amendment for reference back rejected 64:185

Year	Major subject matter of Resolution	Proposer/ Seconder	Other Details
1902 Cont'd	d. No Maximum leaving age to be fixed e. Free scholarships for children upon principle of intelligence & attainment f. Adequate provision for teacher training free from sectarian bias or control etc. 2. Prevention of children under 15 working in textile or non-textile factories	(Gasworkers)	Passed
1903	Composite Resolution: a. Full popular control over all state aided schools & abolition of all school fees b. Secular education in all state aided schools c. Primary, Secondary & Technical Education to be free d. Free maintenance scholarships for all attending Secondary Schools e. Adequate provision for all children to continue at school until 15 yrs. f. Establishment of Technical Schools for industrial training of capable blind g. Proper management of educational endowments	Appleton W.A. (Amal. Lace Makers) Thorne W. (Gasworkers)	Opposition to Secular clause by some but amend defeated 567,000 to 327,000 Congress adjourned
1904	1. Condemnation of Government Educational Policy: All schools to be under popular control Primary, Secondary & Technical education to be free All state aided education to be secular Proper management of educational edowments	Appleton W.A. (Amal. Lace Mkrs.) Michaels S. (London) (Cabdrivers)	Carried unanimously
	2. Provision of one school meal per day for children in state supported schools Children under 14 not to be	Thorne W. (Gasworkers) Keens A.W. (Cab. Makers)	Carried Unanimously

Year	Major subject matter of Resolution	Proposer/ Seconder	Other Details
1904 Cont'd	employed before/after school TUC Educ Policy to all MPs to ascertain their support or otherwise		
1905	1. Condemnation of Government Education Policy: All grades of education to be free & state maintained Attendance in primary & secondary schools to be compulsory All children to stay at school until 15 Provision to continue education of able students through university courses School performance to be judged by continuous performance and not competitive exams Only candidates supporting TUC Education policy to be supported for Parliament, etc.	Appleton W.A. (Amal. Lace Mkers.) Gordon J.C. (Tinplate Workers)	Resolution with slight amendment agreed to
	2. Due to findings of Interdepartmental Committee on Physical Deterioration-Demands: a. One free school meal per day b. Free medical inspection/ advice for all children c. Efficient P.T. for all children d. Regular information of health of school children etc.	Thorne W. (Gasworkers) O'Grady J. (Furnishing Trades)	Motion adopted
1906	1. State maintenance of school children Physical Education with Medical inspection National system of education under full popular control, free & secular from primary school to university Secondary & Technical education for *all* children up to 16 years. Restoration of	Appleton W.A. (Lace Makers) Tillett B. (Dockers)	Resolution carried almost unanimously

Year	Major subject matter of Resolution	Proposer/ Seconder	Other Details
1906 Cont'd	misappropriated education endowments. etc. 2. Repeat of Thorne's Resolution passed in 1904 & 1905.		
1907	Repeat of Appleton's Resolution of 1906, etc.	Appleton W.A. (Lace Makers) Roberts J.H. (Typo. Assoc.)	Card Vote:- For: 1,239,000 Against: 126,000
1908	Demands Parliamentary & Municipal Recognition of TUC Education Policy (Appleton's 1906 Resolution)	Roberts G.H. (MP) (Typo. Assoc.) Thorne W. (MP) (Gasworkers)	Carried
1909	1. Abolition of Half-Time System	Dawtry F. (Steam Engine Mkrs.) Gordon J.C. (Sheet Metal Wkrs.)	
	2. Establishment of Technical schools for apprentices to attend on some days during week	Barnes R. (Litho. Artists) Richards TF (Boot & Shoe Operatives)	Resolution agreed to
	3. Demands for Parliamentary & Municipal Recognition of TUC Education Policy (As proposed by Appleton in previous years)	Gwynne I.H. (Tin & Sheet Millmen) Gee A (Tex. Workers)	Carried by large majority (Sexton led opposition to secular educ.)
	4. Abolition of fees in Secondary schools & Technical Colleges	Walls P. (Blast-furnacemen) Turner B. (Weavers)	Carried?
	5. TUC Educ Policy similar to 1905, 1906 etc.	Thorne W. (Gasworkers) Cuthbertson J. (Metal, Wire & Tube Workers)	Carried unanimously
	6. Day time classes to be available for young people 16–18 years to learn theoretical/ practical side of their work	Elvin H.H. (National Clerks) Chandler A.E. (Railway Clerks)	Resolution agreed to
	7. End to imprisonment for non-payment of industrial school fees	Sexton J. (Liverpool) (Dockers) Hutchcroft T. (Liverpool) (Dockers)	Unanimously agreed to
1910	1. Abolition of Half-Time System	Dawtry W.F. (Steam Eng. Mkrs.) Booth	For: 1,259,000 Against 153,000 (Opposition from Lancs Textile

Year	Major subject matter of Resolution	Proposer/ Seconder	Other Details
1910 Cont'd		F.W. (Typo. Assoc.)	Workers.)
	2. Demands for Parliamentary & Municipal Recognition of TUC Education Policy	Cuthbertson J. (Metal Workers) Walls P. (Blast-furnacemen)	Resolution agreed to
	3. Abolition of fees in Secondary schools	Hall J. (Blast-furnacemen) O'Grady J. (Furnishing Trades)	
	4. Ballot of TUC Members as to the wish to retain secular education in TUC Educ Policy	Sexton J. (Dockers)	Resolution defeated For: 666,000 Against: 725,000
	5. End of imprisonment of parents for non-payment of industrial school fees	Sexton J. (Dockers) Kilkelly F. (Dockers)	Resolution agreed to
	6. TUC Education Policy: a. State maintenance of school child. b. Scientific P.E. & Medical Inspection c. Secondary & Technical Education for all children d. ROSLA to 16 years e. Establishment of teachers training colleges in connection with universities f. Education costs to be met by Exchequer & restoration of education endowments etc	Thorne W. (Gasworkers) Cross J. (Northern Weavers)	Resolution agreed to
	7. Free & Secular Education	Cuthbertson J. (Metal Workers) Gwynne I.H. (Tin & Sheet Millmen)	For: 827,000 Against 81,000
1911	1. TUC Education Policy (As above)	Thorne W. (Gasworkers) Cooper B. (Cigar Makers)	For 717,000 Against: 120,000 (Bitter scenes with Sexton on Religion)
	2. Abolition of fees in Secondary schools	Gwynne I.H. (Tin & Sheet Millmen) Cuthbertson J. (Metal Workers)	Resolution Carried For: 397,000 Against: 180,000
	3. Compulsory Day	Elvin H.H.	

Year	Major subject matter of Resolution	Proposer/ Seconder	Other Details
1911 Cont'd	Continuation Classes plus ROSLA to 16 yrs.	(National Clerks) Chandler A.E. (Railway Clerks)	
1912	1. Abolition of Half-Time System	Dawtry W.F. (Steam Engine Mkrs.) Turner B. (Weavers)	Resolution Carried
	2. TUC Education Policy: a. National system of education under full public control from primary school to university b. Adequate maintenance of school children c. Scientific P.E. & annual medical inspection d. Establishment of teachers training colleges in connection with universities e. Education to be paid for by Exchequer & restoration of education endowments f. Public Commission to examine endowments Nb. Secular education excluded to prevent dissent	Wright S.J. (Gas workers) Barker G. (Miners' Fed.)	Resolution Carried
	3. Secular Education no longer to be discussed	Butler J. (Miners' Fed.) Doonan J. (Miners' Fed.)	For: 952,000 Against: 909,000
	4. Abolition of fees in Secondary Schools	Walls P. (Blast-furnacemen) Gwynne J.H. (Tin & Sheet Millmen)	Resolution Carried
	5. Compulsory Day time classes for children	Elvin H.H. (N.U. Clerks) Gates E.C. (Postal Tel. Clerks)	For: 397,000 Against: 180,000
1913	1. TUC Education Policy: (Same as 1912)	Glyde C.A. (Gasworkers) Battle J. (Spinners)	Resolution Carried
	2. Compulsory Day time Classes	Elvin H.H. (N.U. Clerks) Grundy A. (Carters & Motormen)	Resolution Carried
	3. Maintenance Grants for	Gwynne J.H.	Resolution Carried

Year	Major subject matter of Resolution	Proposer/ Seconder	Other Details
1913 Cont'd	Children attending Secondary Schools	(Tin & Sheet Millmen) Walls P. (Blastfurnace-men)	
	4. Abolition of Half-Time System	Dawtry W.F. (Steam Eng. Makers) Cuthbertson J. (Metal Workers)	Resolution Carried
1914	No Congress		
1915	TUC Education Policy: a. 3 meals per day including holidays, for necessitous children b. Specialist P.E. teacher for all schools c. Provision of bathing facilities in schools & public places d. ROSLA to 16 yrs e. Finances of endowed institutions to be examined f. Treasury grants increased rather than decreased g. Maximum of 40 children in any one class h. Compulsory day time continuation classes	Jones J. (Gasworkers) Elvin H.H. (National Clerks)	Carried Unanimously
1916	1. TUC Education Policy: (As 1915)	Clynes J.R. (Nat. Gen. Workers) Winstone J. (Miners' Fed.)	Unanimous
	2. ROSLA 14 yrs with local authority bye-laws for 16 yrs. Wage earning work prohibited under 16 Compulsory day time classes (Continuation) for 16–18 yr olds	Hoffman P.C. (Shop Assts.) Carmichael D. (Shop Assts.)	Resolution Carried
	3. Depriving children of educational facilities due to local authority 'economies'	Elvin H.H. (Nat. Clerks) Hall A.B. (Nat. Clerks)	Resolution Carried
	4. Industry & Technical Education	Hodge J. (Brit. Steel Sm'ters.) Farrah R.H. (Nat. Gen. Workers)	Carried
1917	Demand for complete reorganization of education	Beadle G. (Iron & Steel Trades)	Resolution Carried by general assent

Year	Major subject matter of Resolution	Proposer/ Seconder	Other Details
1917 Cont'd	system from primary school to university, with special attention to health, school meals, medical facilities etc.	Thompson F. (Dock & Riverside)	
1918	TUC Education Policy: Nursery Schools ROSLA to 16 yrs Maximum class size 40, in 5 yrs 30 Employment of children out of school prohibited Secondary school fees abolished Continuation Classes for under 16 yr olds 18 yr olds limited to 25 hrs work per week P.E. & Medical facilities in all schools Universities – generous maintenance grants for students & public enquiry into endowments of Oxbridge	Cramp C.T. (NUR) Pearson, Mrs. (Women Workers)	Carried Unanimously
1919	1. Introduction of metric system into schools	Gwynne J.H. (Tin & Sheet Millmen) Handley G. (Textile Wkrs.)	Resolution Carried
	2. Equal representation of Uncertificated teachers with Certificated teachers on all local/ national bodies plus same salaries & conditions	Walsh E. (Miss) (N.U. School Teachers)* Battle J. (Operative Cotton Spinners)	Resolution Carried
1920	1. Position of Uncertificated teachers (As 1919)	Walsh E. (Miss) (N.U. School Teachers)* Titt G. (Workers' Union)	Resolution Carried
	2. Maintenance Grants for all children who qualify for secondary schooling.	Tapp A.W. (Ship Constructors & Shipwrights Assoc.) Mather D. (U. Patternmakers)	Carried Unanimously
	3. Continuation Classes but not run by employers	Lappin R.J. (Eng/ Shipbuilding Draughtmens' Ass.) Houghton	Carried Unanimously

*Not the National Union of Teachers

Year	Major subject matter of Resolution	Proposer/ Seconder	Other Details
1921	1. Free access to secondary schools for all children who pass qualifying exams	J. (Scottish U. of Dock Labourers) Tapp A.W. (Ship Con. & Ship Wrights' Assoc.)	Resolution Carried
	2. Education for trade unionists	Mather D. (U. Patternmakers) Ammond C.G. (P.O. Workers)	Resolution Carried
	3. Position of Uncertificated teachers (As 1919)	Hodges F. (Miners' Fed.) Walsh E.E. (N.U. Sch. Teachers)*	Resolution Carried
	4. Facilities to enter	Hall G. (Workers' Union Gwynne J.H. (Iron & Steel Trades Fed.) Coyle O. (Iron & Steel Tr. Fed.)	Carried?
1922	1. Demand for implementation of 1918 Education Act & opening of all educational facilities to those capable of taking advantage of them.	Bowen J.W. (U. of P.O. Workers) Hill J. (Boilermakers)	Carried Unanimously
	2. Grant of £250 to each of: Ruskin College Central Labour College W.E.A.	Mason C.E. (Lond. Compositors) Cook C. (Lond. Compositors)	Carried
1923	Reports of Joint Education Committee concerning: a. Labour Colleges b. Proposals for education of Trade Unionists c. Education for young workers		Reports endorsed: Detailed Reports carried by Joint Educ. Comm. concerning Adult Education (pp. 136–146)
1924	1. Welcomes new spirit of Labour Government but also recommends: a. All future elementary schools to be open air planned with playing fields, dining rooms b. ROSLA to 15 yrs with maintenance allowance where necessary c. Fees to Secondary Schools	Titterington M.F. (Stuff & Woollen Warehousemen) Hoffman P.C. (MP) (Shop Assts. U.)	Resolution Carried

*Not the National Union of Teachers

Year	Major subject matter of Resolution	Proposer/ Seconder	Other Details
1924 Cont'd	to be abolished within 5 years		
	d. Extension of scholarship system to provide complete free system of Secondary Technical & University Education		
	e. Continuation Schools to be obligatory for all up to 18 yrs, in employers' time.		
	2. TUC to take more active part in furtherance of working class education in conjunction with Ruskin, CLC, NCLC, WEA & WEATU Committee	Creech-Jones A. (T & G.W.) Walker J. (Iron & Steel Trades Fed.)	Resolution Adopted
	3. Industrial Workers Charter: Detailed resolution dealing with Nationalization, Wages & Hours of Labour, Unemployement, Housing, Industrial Accidents, diseases, Pensions & Education	Turner B. (Weavers Bately) Bowen J.W. (UPW)	Carried Unanimously
1925	Composite Resolution No. 13 dealing with working class education withdrawn. Education policy of TUC outlined in Report of Deputation to the Pres of the Board of Education (25.5.1925)		
	a. Future elementary schools to be open air		
	b. ROSLA 15 yrs Plus maintenance Grants		
	c. Secondary School fees to be removed within 5 yrs		
	d. Extension of scholarship system with eventual aim of free elementary, secondary, technical and university education		
	e. Education in continuation schools up to 18 yrs. to be obligatory upon employers.		

Appendix III   (a)   1897 TUC Education Resolution

48. This Congress emphatically condemns the education policy of the present Government, and declares –

1. That in this question of the education of the nation's children the workers should ever keep in view as their ideal the democratic principle of 'Equality of Opportunity,' and should not be satisfied until the highest educational advantages which the country affords are within the reach of all.

2. That as it is a duty which the community owes to posterity to see that no future citizen lacks the requisites to a healthy development of body and mind, a measure should be brought before Parliament which shall empower school boards to provide food for the many thousands of starving and underfed children who are to be found in the people's schools throughout the country.

3. That the half-time system be abolished; that the school age be raised to sixteen years, and such maintenance provided by the State as shall place secondary education within the reach of every worker's child; that the system of providing secondary education only for the very small proportion of the workers' children who can come to the top, after severe competition with their school fellows, is to be strongly condemned
    (a) on educational grounds, and
    (b) in that it tends to foster feelings of antagonism and jealousy, which are such a serious obstacle in the way of that union among the workers which their highest welfare demands, and which it is the object of trade unionism to promote.

4. That such reforms be at once made in the method of training the teachers of the nation's children as shall ensure that in no case shall the difficult task of training the minds of young children be entrusted to those whose minds are undeveloped.

5. The cost of educating the nation's children should be defrayed out of the National Exchequer, and should be met by the democratic administration of educational grants and endowments and graduated income tax on all incomes over £300, and graduated death duties.

6. That sectarian strife should be dissociated from the question of education, and this can only be done by debarring theologians from raising sectarian strife and by the State providing for the teaching of secular subjects and social duties, leaving the teaching of creeds and dogmas to the religious denominations.

7. That the Parliamentary Committee be instructed to form a deputation, which shall wait upon the Education Minister, and urge the pressing necessity for the reforms here indicated.

(Resolution moved by Mr. Brabham; seconded by Mr. Proctor.)

Appendix III   (b)   1902 TUC Education Resolution

Mr. W.A. Appleton (Amalgamated Lace Makers) moved:

That this Congress condemns the Government Education Bill now before the country, because it does away with the principle of direct representation; will increase sectarian jealousy; repeals the Acts which stand alone in giving statutory recognition to the need for manual instruction in the application of special branches of science and art to specific industries and employment; and will prevent women educationists from being elected upon the Education Committee.

Therefore, this Congress calls upon the organized workers to use every effort to secure the rejection of the Bill, and the inauguration of such a system of national education as will afford the children of British parents opportunities at least equal to those enjoyed by the children of other nations, the cost of such system to be a charge upon the National Exchequer.

This Congress, therefore, recommends:

(a)   That in order to secure the 'effective' improvement and full extension of education in England and Wales, and especially with the view of securing economical administration and the provision of the various types of schools required by the special circumstances of different localities, as well as the prevention of unnecessary overlapping, it is essential that all grades of education should, in districts of suitable size, be under one local authority, directly elected, and elected solely for educational purposes, and that the Parliamentary Committee be instructed to oppose any Bill which does not provide for the election of such an authority.

(b)   That adequate provision be made for the efficient education of all children under the age of fifteen years, and that no maximum age limit be fixed; and, further, that no fees be charged in any of the elementary, evening continuation, higher grade or technical schools, and that all grants to any of these schools recently withdrawn or reduced be re-established.

(c)   That, in order to provide opportunities for the children of the working classes, free scholarships shall be available to those parents who are anxious to continue the education of their children, the governing principle of these scholarships being that of intelligence and attainments of the child.

(d)   That the obstacles to the continuance of free and properly-equipped evening schools be abolished.

(e)   That there be adequate provision of training colleges for teachers, such colleges to be free from sectarian bias or control.

(f)   That the Parliamentary Committee be instructed to prepare and, in conjunction with co-operative societies and other friends of a democratic system of education, introduce at the earliest opportunity a Bill embodying these recommendations.

The Congress expresses the opinion that the principle of taxation without representation might justifiably be met by the refusal to pay the taxes imposed, and it declares its conviction that steps should be taken at the next Parliamentary election to secure the defeat of every member of the present House of Commons and all Parliamentary candidates who may not promise to vote for such a solution of the educational problem as is indicated by the foregoing resolution.

Appendix IV   TUC Circular 1900: Higher Grade Schools

THE TRADES UNION CONGRESS PARLIAMENTARY COMMITTEE
19 Buckingham Street, Strand, London W.C. August, 1900

IMPORTANT CIRCULAR. As an outcome of the representative deputation which waited on the Parliamentary Committee in July on the subject of High Grade Education, and referred to in the Parliamentary Committee's Report, the following circular has been drawn up by a sub-committee of the Parliamentary Committee for the careful consideration of delegates.

To the Officers of Trade Societies.

GENTLEMEN, – The time has come to draw your attention to the conspiracy against the education of your children which has been developing during the last five years.

Every child in Scotland has the chance of efficient and suitable education up to eighteen years of age, free of charge and under proper control, while in England and Wales such privilege is only enjoyed up to fifteen years of age. Similar advantages have for generations been enjoyed by the working classes of Germany and America, and much of the success and prosperity of these nations comes from the provision made by the State for the efficient education of the workers. The wealth of a nation is not in money bags, but in the power of labour and the cultivated intelligence of the workers.

In England and Wales the elementary education of the people has many enemies. Some of the 'upper classes' and some of the churches have always been a drag on the wheels of progress. But in the course of years their oppositions has been overcome. Until the present Government took office, whatever political party has been in power, progress was made. But now the power of the Government is turned against the education of the people.

In 1870 local authorities elected on a democratic franchise were empowered to provide and maintain schools for the people, but the establishment of such authorities was optional, and their creation has been for thirty years successfully resisted in many places. Since 1870 universal local self-government has been created in every parish for such matters as drains, water supply, gas, police, and every other local matter affecting the welfare of the people, and we claim that the time has come to complete the work of 1870 by giving in every district the same democratic control over education.

The present Government instead of helping this reform has thwarted it on every possible occasion. By the settlement of 1870 the schools established by the clergy for sectarian purposes were secured from competition so long as they were efficient and so long as the proprietors provided half the cost of maintenance. The present Government has destroyed this settlement. It has given huge doles to the clerical schools until they are now almost entirely supported by public money, and it has removed nearly all the safeguards for efficiency. We do not object to clergy and capitalists managing the schools of the people if they are responsible to the people and are elected from time to time by a popular vote, but we object to the education of the people being controlled by irresponsible persons who have other interests to serve and who are known to be antagonistic to popular aspirations. The present Government, while resisting to the utmost the creation of any democratic body, has covered the country with clerical organizations, has given them power to make the schools more sectarian, and has endowed them for this purpose with a grant of nearly £800,000 per annum.

But it is in regard to the higher education of children of humble birth that the greatest mischief is being accomplished. Six-sevenths of the nation pass through the elementary schools: does any one suppose that all the highest intelligence is confined to the other seventh? Even 'hewers of wood and drawers of water' need foremen and managers better equipped than themselves, and all history shows that not only foremen and managers, but some of the greatest masters in trade and manufacture, and even in the professions and in art and science, have struggled painfully upwards from the humblest ranks of society. Who can estimate the value to the nation of those who rose through ignorance and poverty and years of manual toil to their proper work? And, still more, who can estimate the national loss in the crushed intellects of those gifted sons who never surmounted the initial difficulties of life? This is above all others the greatest problem of National Education. This is the problem which the democratic School Boards in the great towns have, during the last thirty years, attempted to solve by creating 'Higher Grade' Schools and classes in which those scholars who remained at school could acquire more advanced knowledge. These schools have been mainly supported by grants for specific subjects and by the grants of the Science and Art Department, which was established many years ago to promote instruction in Science and Art 'especially among the industrial classes'. The present Government have struck these words out of the Directory. It has withdrawn these grants from many of the scholars of 'the industrial classes,' and has diverted them to middle-class schools. The other grants given for advanced ('specific') subjects have this year been withdrawn, although these grants provided last year higher instruction for nearly 350,000 scholars.

The Government has attempted to declare the expenditure from rates on Science and Art illegal. It has moved Parliament to give it power to withdraw all or part of the Government subsidy secured by the Free Education Act of 1891 for the free education of every child up to fifteen years of age. These changes apparently involved (as they were designed to do) the destruction of the Higher Grade Schools, and aroused such opposition that the Government pretended to retrace their steps and proposed to recognize and give a new grant to a new kind of 'Higher Elementary School' which would take their place. The public agitation was thus outflanked, but the insincerity of the concession is being rapidly proved. The new scheme is surrounded by so many restrictions and regulations that it is useless. The London School Board asks for its seventy nine Higher Grade Schools to be continued under the new rule, and the Government offered to recognize four only. Other Boards are being treated similarly, and the pretended concession is now proved to be nothing put an instrument of destruction. A Bill has also been introduced which would divert most of the money available for the technical education of the working classes, under the County and Urban Councils, to middle-class schools and universities. Much has been done and much more is threatened.

The retrograde steps of the last five years has revealed the weakness of our position, and before the ruin of all the slowly-built edifice of popular education is accomplished we appeal to the workers of England and Wales to speak out.

The education of the nation is a national interest. Equality of opportunity free and ungrudgingly given to every child is of vital concern. The rights of those of humble birth are too precious to be left at the mercy of warring sects or social prejudices. The only safeguard of democratic interests is a democratic franchise and a free, direct, and efficient popular control.

We, therefore, demand that –

1. The scheme of National Education foreshadowed by the Act of 1870 shall be completed and made secure by the appointment in every district of Education Authorities elected as freely and democratically as other municipal bodies.

2. That they shall be empowered to provide efficient and suitable education for all who require it.
3. That clerical managers and clerical organizations shall not be allowed to control the education of the people to serve sectarian purposes.
4. That the elementary and higher education of the people shall be at the public expense, free, unsectarian, and under the management of the elected representatives of the people.

I am, yours faithfully,
On behalf of the Parliamentary Committee,
S. WOODS,
Secretary.

Appendix V   TUC Education Bill 1906

(Introduced by Will Thorne, and read for the first time on March 2nd, 1906)

A BILL

TO PROMOTE THE IMPROVEMENT OF EDUCATION AND THE PHYSIQUE OF CHILDREN ATTENDING ELEMENTARY SCHOOLS.

Be it enacted by the King's most excellent Majesty, by and with the advice and consent of the Lords Spiritual and Temporal, and Commons, in this present Parliament assembled, and by the authority of the same, as follows:

1. On and after the 1st of January, 1907, all (Elementary) schools receiving Government grants shall be placed under the local education authority of their respective districts and boroughs.

2. The education authority shall be empowered to make such arrangements for the purchase or hiring of any denominational or privately owned school as may be mutually agreed upon, subject to the approval of the Education Department. Failing the making of such arrangement, the local authority shall provide a new school, and within one month of the opening of the same grants to the denominational schools shall cease.

3. The instruction in all State-aided schools shall be in secular subjects only, and no theological or denominational tests shall be applied to any of the staff of officers of the school or of the educational authority.

4. Provision shall be made by the local authorities for secondary and technical instruction for all who desire to avail themselves of it; and a sufficient number of free maintenance scholarships shall be provided by grants from the Board of Education to enable all who have fitted themselves, by their previous work, to continue their studies at technical institutes or universities until they attain adult years.

5. Each education authority shall make suitable provision for the technical training necessary to complete the equipment of the teachers in State schools.

6. The cost of carrying out the provisions of this Bill shall be met by grants from the Imperial Exchequer, and by the restoration of educational endowments.

7. Each education authority shall provide at least one free meal a day for children attending the schools in their respective areas.

8. Each education authority shall take steps to record the height, weight, and chest-measurement of children attending elementary schools; and shall furnish the first returns thereon to the Board of Education not later than December 30th, 1906.

9. Each education authority shall appoint a medical officer, or officers, whose duty it shall be to medically examine, and to treat such children as the teachers may consider in need of medical advice.

This Bill shall be cited as the 'State Education Act, 1906'.

Drafted by Parliamentary Committee, Trades Union Congress, in accordance with the instructions from Trades Union Congress, Hanley, September, 1905, and backed by Messrs. Barnes, Roberts, Parker, Hudson, Henderson, Wilson, Walsh, and Richards.

Bibliography

Correspondence, Minutes and Diaries

The Broadhurst Papers: London School of Economics & Political Science S.R. 151.
The Howell Collection: Bishopsgate Institute, London.
Correspondence between the National Society and the Trades Union Congress 1879:
National Society Archives.
Correspondence between Lady Warwick and the GCTUC: Congress House, 813–3.
Minutes of PCTUC Deputation to the Board of Education: 16.3.1911 Ed. 24/289.
25.2.1912, 12.2.1914, 17.2.1916, 15.2.1917, 12.3.1919, 5.2.1920, 10.2.1921, Ed. 24/
1384.
Minutes of the GCTUC Deputation to the Board of Education: 25.5.1925 Ed. 24/1384
Minutes of the FBI Deputation to the Board of Education 6.2.1918 and resulting
correspondence, including internal correspondence within the Board of Education:
Ed. 24/657 and Ed. 24/1187.
Minutes of the PCTUC 1888–1921.
Minutes of the GCTUC 1921–1925.
Minutes of the Education Committee of the TUC 1922–25.
Minutes of the PCTUC Deputation to the Board of Education 2.3.1909 (TUC Report
1909, pp. 55–59).
Minutes of Ruskin College Vol. IV December 1921 – June 1925.
Minutes of Ruskin College Vol. V. July 1925 – January 1928.
Minutes of the FBI Education Committee 21.11.1917 & 28.11.1917. FBI/C/81 Vol. 173.
Tait Diaries 1879: Lambeth Palace.

Theses

BARKER, R.S. (1968) *The Educational Policies of the Labour Party 1900–61* Ph.D.
(London)
BATHER, L. (1956) *A History of Manchester and Salford Trades Council* Ph.D.
(Manchester)
BROWN, R. (1966) *The Labour Movement in Hull 1870–1900 with special reference to
New Unionism* M.Sc. (Econ) (Hull)
CLINTON, A. (1973) *Trade Councils from the Beginning of the Twentieth·Century to the
Second World War* Ph.D. (London).
DEAN, D.W. (1968) *The Political Parties and Development of their Attitude to
Educational Problems 1918–42* M.Phil. (London).

Articles/Papers

BALL, N. (1973) 'Elementary School Attendance and Voluntary Effort Before 1870'. *History of Education*, 2(1) Jan.

BRENNAN, F.T. (1972) 'Educational Engineering with the Webbs' *History of Education* 1(2) June.

CANNON, C. (1970) 'The Influence of Religion on Educational Policies 1902–1944' in MUSGRAVE, P.W. (Ed) *Sociology, History and Education.*

CLINTON, A. (1974) 'The History of Trades Councils' *Society for the Study of Labour History Bulletin* No. 29 Autumn.

DEAN, D.W. (1970) 'H.A.L. Fisher, Reconstruction and the Development of the 1918 Act'. *British Journal of Educational Studies* 18(3) Oct.

DEAN, D.W. (1971) 'Conservatism and the National Education System 1922–40'. *Journal of Contemporary History* 6(2).

DENT, H.C. (1971) 'To Cover the Country with Good Schools: A Century's Effort'. *British Journal of Educational Studies* 19(2) June.

EAGLESHAM, E.J.R. (1962) 'Implementing the Education Act of 1902' *British Journal of Educational Studies* 10(2) May.

EAGLESHAM, E.J.R. (1963) 'The Centenary of Sir Robert Morant' *British Journal of Educational Studies* 12(1) Nov.

ELLIOT, B. (1978) 'School Boards and Industrial Schools: a neglected aspect of the 1870 Education Act' *History of Education Society Bulletin* No. 22 Autumn.

ELLIS, A.C.O. (1973) 'Influences on School Attendance in Victorian England' *British Journal of Educational Studies* 21(3) Oct.

FIDLER, G.C. (1977) 'The Liverpool Trades Council and Technical Education in the era of the Technical Instruction Committee' *History of Education* 6(3) Oct.

GOLDSTROM, J.M. (1966–7) 'Richard Whately and Political Economy in School Books, 1833–80' *Irish Historical Studies* 15.

GOMEZ, G. (1974) 'The Endowed Schools Act, 1869 – A Middle Class Conspiracy? The South West Lancashire Evidence' *Journal of Educational Administration and History* 6(1) Jan.

GOSDEN, P.H.J.H. (1962) 'The Board of Education Act 1899' *British Journal of Educational Studies* 11(1) Nov.

GOSDEN, P.H.J.H. (1977) 'The Origins of Co-optation to Membership of Local Education Committee' *British Journal of Educational Studies* 25(3) Oct.

GRANT, A C. (1968) 'A Note on Secular Education in the Nineteenth Century' *British Journal of Educational Studies* 16(3) Oct.

GREEN, H. (1974) 'A Howkie Gans to Parliament' *Marxism Today* 18(3) March.

GRIGGS, G. (1981) 'The Attitude of the Labour Movement towards Drill in Elementary Schools, 1870–1925 *Bulletin of Physical Education* 17(2) Summer.

GRIGGS, C. (1981) 'H.A.L. FISHER, the 1918 Education Act and the Trades Union Congress' *History of Education Society Occasional Publication* No. 6, 1981.

GRIGGS, C. (1981) 'The Trades Union Congress and the Controversy over the National Society's Standard V Reading Book in 1879' *British Journal of Educational Studies* 29(3) Oct.

GRIGGS, C. (1981) 'The Trades Union Congress and the Question of Educational Endowments 1868–1925' *History of Education Society Bulletin* No. 28, Autumn.

HARRISON, B. (1967) 'Religion and Recreation' *Past and Present* No. 38 1967.

HAYWOOD, W.A. (1971) 'MPs and the 1870 Education Act: A Study in Human Motivation' *Journal of Educational Administration and History* 4(1) Dec.

HIGGINSON, J.H. (1974) 'Dame Schools' *British Journal of Educational Studies* 22(2) June.

HORN, P.L.R. (1974) 'The Agricultural Children Act of 1873' *History of Education* 3(2) Summer.

HURT, J.S. (1977) 'Drill, Discipline and the Elementary School Ethos in McCANN P. (Ed) *Popular Education and Socialization in the Nineteenth Century*

JUDGES, A.V. (1961) 'The Educational Influence of the Webbs' *British Journal of Educational Studies* 10(1) Nov.

LEE, A.J. (1979) 'Conservatism, Traditionalism and the British Working Class 1880–1918' in MARTIN, D. and RUBINSTEIN D. (Eds) *Ideology and the Labour Movement.*

McCANN, W.P. (1969) 'Elementary Education in England and Wales on the Eve of the 1870 Education Act' *Journal of Educational Administration and History* 2(1) Dec.

McCANN, W.P. (1970) 'Trade Unionists, Artisans and the 1870 Education Act' *British Journal of Educational Studies* 18(2) June.

MACKENZIE, N. (1978) 'Socialism and Society: a new view of the Webb Partnership'. Lecture given at LSE 15.5.1978: printed by LSE 1978.

MacLEOD, R.M. (1966) 'Social Policy and the Floating Population 1877–99' *Past and Present* No. 35 Dec. 1966.

MARCHAM, A.J. (1976) 'The Birmingham Education Society and the 1870 Education Act' *Journal of Educational Administration and History* 8(1) Jan.

MARSDEN, W.E. (1977) 'Education and the Social Geography of Nineteenth Century Towns and Cities' in REEDER, D.A. (Ed) *Urban Education in the Nineteenth Century.*

MORTON, A.L. (1973) 'A French View of William Morris' *Marxism Today* 17(5) May.

MOXLEY, F. (1963) 'Railwaymen and Working Class Education', Appendix A, in BAGWELL, P.S. *The Railwaymen.*

MUNSON, J.E.B. (1975) 'The London School Board Election of 1894' *British Journal of Educational Studies* 23(1) Feb.

MUSGRAVE, P.W. (1970) 'The Definition of Technical Education 1860–1910' in MUSGRAVE, P.W. (Ed) *Sociology, History and Education.*

NEVILLE, R.G. (1976) 'The Yorkshire Miners and Education 1881–1930' *Journal of Educational Admin. & History* 8(2) July.

PATTISON, R. (1973) 'The Birrell Education Act of 1906' *Journal of Educational Administration and History* 5(1) Jan.

PELLING, H. (1964) 'Religion and the Nineteenth Century British Working Class' *Past and Present* No. 27 1964.

PICKERING W.S.F. (1967) 'The 1851 Religious Census – A Useless Experiment?' *British Journal of Sociology* 18(4) Dec.

PLATTEN, S.G. (1975) 'The Conflict over the Control of Elementary Education 1870–1902 and its effect upon the Life and Influence of the Church' *British Journal of Educational Studies* 23(3) Sept.

PRITCHARD, P.B. (1979) 'After Sixty Weeks: the significance of the Liverpool School Board By-Election of January 1872' *History of Education Society Bulletin* No. 23 Spring 1979.

PUGH, D.R. (1968) 'The 1902 Education Act: The Search for a Compromise' *British Journal of Educational Studies* 16(2) June.

PUGH, D.R. (1977) 'A Note on School Board Elections: Some North-Western Contests in the Nineties' *History of Education* 6(2) June.

RATCLIFFE, K.G.M. (1970) 'Elections and the School Boards: Tees-side 1870–1902' *Journal of Educational Administration and History* 2(2) June.

RICHARDS, N.J. (1970) 'Religious Controversy and the School Boards 1870–1902' *British Journal of Educational Studies* 18(2) June.

ROBERTSON, A.B. (1972) 'Children, Teachers and Society; The Over-Pressure Controversy 1880–86' *British Journal of Educational Studies* 20(3) Oct. 1972.

ROPER, H. (1975) 'Towards an Elementary Education Act for England and Wales 1865–68' *British Journal of Educational Studies* 23(2) June.

SCOTLAND, N. (1977) 'Methodism and the "Revolt of the Field" in East Anglia 1872–96 *Wesley Historical Society Proceedings* Vol XLI Feb. and June.

SELBY D. (1973) 'Manning, Ullathorne and the School Board Question 1870–76' *Journal of Educational Administration and History* 5(1) Jan.

SELBY, D. (1976) 'Cardinal Manning and Free Education 1885–91' *History of Education Society Occasional Publications* No. 2 Summer.

SHARP, R.P. (1974) 'The Origins and Early Development of Local Education Authority Scholarships' *History of Education* 3(1) Jan.

SHERINGTON, G.E. (1974) 'R.B. Haldane: The Reconstruction Committee and the Board of Education 1916–1918' *Journal of Educational Administration and History* 6(2) July.

SHERINGTON, G.E. (1976) 'The 1918 Education Act: Origins, Aims and Development' *British Journal of Educational Studies* 24(1) Feb.

SILVER, H. (1973) 'Education and the Labour Movement: A Critical Review of the Literature' *History of Education* 2(2) June.

SILVER, H. (1977) 'Aspects of Neglect: The Strange Case of Victorian Popular Education' *Oxford Review of Education* 3(1).

SILVER, H. (1977) 'Ideology and the Factory Child: Attitudes to Half-time Education in McCANN P. (Ed) *Popular Education and Socialization in the Nineteenth Century*.

SIMON, A. (1973) 'Joseph Chamberlain and Free Education in the Election of 1885' *History of Education* 2(1) Jan.

SIMON, B. (1977) 'Education and Social Change: A Marxist Perspective *Marxism Today* 21(2) Feb.

SMITH, A.W. (1968) 'Popular Religion' *Past and Present* No. 40.

SPRINGHALL, J.O. (1970) 'Lord Meath, Youth and Culture' *Journal of Contemporary History* 5(4).

THOMPSON, P. (1964) 'Liberals, Radicals and Labour in London 1880–1906' *Past and Present* No. 27.

THOMS, D.W. (1975) 'The Emergence and Failure of the Day Continuation School Experiment' *History of Education* 4(1) Spring.

WARD, L.O. (1973) 'Joseph Chamberlain and the Denominational Schools Question' *Journal of Educational Administration and History* 5(2) July.

WARD, L.O. (1973) 'Technical Education and the Politicians 1870–1918' *British Journal of Educational Studies* 21(1) Feb.

WARD, L.O. (1974) 'H.A.L. Fisher and the Teachers' *British Journal of Educational Studies* 22(2).

WILLIAMS, A.R. (1973) 'A Deputation of the National Education League 1870' *History of Education Society Bulletin* No. 12 Autumn.

Books and Pamphlets

ANDREWS, L. (1976) *The Education Act, 1918* Routledge and Kegan Paul.

APPLETON, W.A. (1925) *Trade Unions: Their Past, Present and Future* Allan and Co. Ltd.

APPLETON, W.A. (n.d.) *What We Want and Where We Are: Facts not Phrases* Hodder and Stoughton.

ARCH, J. (1966) *The Autobiography of Joseph Arch* MacGibbon and Kee.

ARNOT, R.P. (1967 & 1975) *South Wales Miners: A History of the South Wales Miners Federation*: Vol. I 1898–1914 (pub. 1967) Vol. II 1914–1926 (pub. 1975) Allen and Unwin.

ATKINS, J. (1981) *Neither Crumbs Nor Condescension* Workers Educational Association.

BAGWELL, P.S. (1963) *The Railwaymen: A History of the National Union of Railwaymen* Allen and Unwin.

BAMFORD, T.W. (1967) *The Rise of the Public Schools* Nelson.
BANKS, O. (1955) *Parity and Prestige in English Secondary Education* Routledge and Kegan Paul.
BARKER, R. (1972) *Education and Politics 1900–1951* Oxford, Clarendon.
BARNARD, H.C. (1961) *A History of English Education from 1760* University of London Press 2nd Ed.
BARNES, G. (1924) *From Workshop to War Cabinet* London, Jenkins.
BELLAMY, J. and SAVILLE, J. (1972–1979) *Dictionary of Labour Biography* Vol.1 (1972); Vol. 2 (1974); Vol. 3 (1976); Vol. 4 (1977); Vol. 5 (1979); Vol. 6 (1982) MacMillan.
BERNBAUM, G. (1967) *Social Change and the Schools 1918–44* Routledge and Kegan Paul.
BEST, G. (1971) *Mid-Victorian Britain 1851–75* Weidenfeld and Nicolson.
BIRCH, L. (Ed) (1968) *The History of the TUC 1868–1968. A Pictorial History of a Social Revolution* General Council TUC.
BLAXLAND, G. (1964) *J.H. Thomas: A Life for Unity* Frederick Muller Ltd.
BOOTH, C. (Ed) (1892) *Life and Labour of the People in London* MacMillan.
BOURNE, R. and MACARTHUR, B. (1970) *The Struggle for Education 1870–1970* Schoolmaster Publishing Co.
BRIGGS, A. (1965) *Victorian People* Penguin.
BROADHURST, H. (1901) *Henry Broadhurst MP: The Story of his life from a Stonemason's Bench to the Treasury Bench* Hutchinson.
BURT, T. (1924) *Thomas Burt: An Autobiography* Fisher Unwin Ltd.
CASEY, (C. 1912) *The Burston School Strike* Labour Leader Pamphlet.
CHALLINOR, R. and RIPLEY, B. (1968) *The Miners' Association – A Trade Union in the Age of the Chartists* Lawrence and Wishart.
CHANCELLOR, V.E. (1970) *History for their Masters* Adams and Dart.
CLARK, G.K. (1973) *Churchmen and the Condition of England 1832–1885* Methuen and Co. Ltd.
CLEGG, H.A., FOX, A. and THOMPSON, A.F. (1964) *A History of British Trade Unions since 1889 Vol. I 1889–1910* Clarendon, Oxford.
CLIFFORD, J. (1902) *The Fight against the Education Bill: What is at Stake* National Union Reform Pamphlets 13.9.1902.
CLYNES, J.R. (1937) *Memoirs* Vol. 1 1869–1924; Vol. 2 1924–1937; Hutchinson and Co.
COLE, G.D.H. (1943) *John Burns* Biographical Series No. 14; Gollancz and Fabian Society.
COLE, G.D.H. (1944) *A Century of Co-operation* Allen and Unwin.
COLE, G.D.H. (1948) *A Short History of the British Working Class Movement 1789–1947* Allen and Unwin (Revised Edition).
COLE, G.D.H. (1965) *British Working Class Politics 1832–1914* Routledge and Kegan Paul 4th Impress.
COLE, M. (1948) *Makers of the Labour Movement* Longmans, Green and Co.
COLE, M. (1963) *The Story of Fabian Socialism* Mercury Books.
COLLINS, H. and ABRAMSKY, C. (1965) *Karl Marx and the British Labour Movement* MacMillan and Co.
COOMBES, B.L. (1939) *These Poor Hands* The Autobiography of a Miner Working in South Wales, Victor Gollancz.
CORFIELD, A.J. (1969) *Epoch in Workers' Education* Workers Educational Association.
CRAIK, W.W. (1919) *A Short History of the Modern British Working Class Movement* Plebs League.
CRAIK, W.W. (1955) *Bryn Roberts and the National Union of Public Employees* Allen and Unwin.
CRAIK, W.W. (1964) *The Central Labour College 1909–1929* Lawrence and Wishart 1964.

CROSS, C. (1966) *Philip Snowden* Barrie and Rockliff.

CRUICKSHANK, M. (1963) *Church and State in English Education* 1870 to the present day, Macmillan.

DALLEY, W.A. (1914) *The Life Story of W.J. Davis J.P.* Birmingham Printers Ltd., Birmingham.

DAVIS, W.J. (1910) *The British Trades Union Congress: History and Reflections* Co-operative Printing Society Ltd.

DAVIS, W.J. (1916) *The British Trades Union Congress: History and Recollections* Volume II Co-operative Printing Society Ltd.

DUNLOP, J. and DENMAN, R.D. (1912) *English Apprenticeship and Child Labour* T. Fisher Unwin.

EAGLESHAM, E.J.R. (1956) *From School Board to Local Authority* Routledge and Kegan Paul.

EAGLESHAM, E.J.R. (1967) *The Foundations of Twentieth Century Education in England* Routledge and Kegan Paul.

EDWARDS, B. (1974) *The Burston School Strike* Lawrence and Wishart.

FARMAN, C. (1974) *The General Strike: May 1926* Panther.

FAY, C.R. (1945) *Life and Labour in the Nineteenth Century* Cambridge University Press.

FISHER, H.A.L. (1940) *An Unfinished Autobiography* Oxford University Press.

FLINN, M.W. (1965) *Readings in Economic and Social History* MacMillan.

FRASER, W.H. (1974) *Trade Unions and Society: The Struggle for Acceptance 1850–1880* Allen and Unwin.

FROW E. and KATANKA, M. (Eds) (1968) *1868 Year of the Unions.* A Documentary Survey Michael Katanka (Books) Ltd.

FROW, E. and FROW, R. (1970) *A Survey of the Half-Time System in Education* Morten, Manchester.

FYRTH, H.J. and COLLINS, H. (1959) *The Foundry Workers.* A Trade Union History, Amalgamated Union of Foundry Workers. Manchester.

GILBERT, B.B. (1970) *British Social Policy 1914–39* B.T. Batsford Ltd.

GOLDSTROM, J.M. (1972) *The Social Content of Education 1808–1870* Irish University Press.

GORMAN, J. (1976) *Banner Bright* Penguin.

GROVES, R. (1949) *Sharpen the Sickle! A History of the Farm Workers' Union* Porcupine Press.

HALL, P. (1971) *Social Services of England and Wales* Routledge and Kegan Paul Ltd. (8th Ed.).

HAMILTON, M.A. (1938) *Arthur Henderson: A Biography* William Heinemann Ltd.

HAMILTON, W. (1975) *My Queen and I* Quartet Books

HANNINGTON, W. (1937) *The Problem of the Depressed Areas* Victor Gollancz.

HARRISON, J.F.C. (1954) *A History of the Working Men's College 1854–1954* Routledge and Kegan Paul.

HARRISON, J.F.C. (1961) *Learning and Living 1790–1960.* A Study in the History of the English Adult Education Movement, Routledge and Kegan Paul.

HAW. G. (1907) *From Workhouse to Westminster: The Life Story of Will Crooks M.P.* Cassell and Co.

HILTON, W.S. (1963) *Foes to Tyranny.* A History of the Amalgamated Union of Building Trade Workers, A.U.B.T.W.

HIRD, F. (1898) *The Cry of the Children* James Bowden.

HOBSBAWM, E.J. (Ed) (1948) *History in the Making.* Vol. 3 Labour's Turning Point, Lawrence and Wishart.

HOBSBAWM, E.J. (1968) *Industry and Empire: An Economic History of Britain since 1750.* Weidenfeld and Nicolson.

HOBSBAWM, E.J. (1968) *Labouring Men: Studies in the History of Labour* Weidenfeld and Nicolson.

HOFFMAN, P.C. (1949) *They Also Serve: The Story of the Shop Worker* Porcupine Press.

HOLYOAKE, G.J. (1906) *Sixty Years of an Agitators Life* T. Fisher Unwin.

HORN, P. (1971) *Joseph Arch: The Farm Workers' Leader* Kineton: The Roundwood Press.

HORRABIN, J.F. and HORRABIN, W. (1924) *Working Class Education* Labour Publishing Co. Ltd.

HOWELL, G. (1876) *The Policy of the School Board for London and its Opponents* Handbill, November.

HOWELL, G. (1900) *Trade Unionism: New and Old* Methuen.

HOWELL, G. (1905) *Labour Legislation, Labour Movements and Labour Leaders* 2 Vols. Fisher Unwin (2nd Ed.).

HUGHES, F. (1953) *By Hand and Brain.*A Story of the Clerical and Administrative Workers' Union, Lawrence and Wishart.

HUGHES, H.D. (1968) *The Story of Ruskin College* University Press, Oxford (3rd Revised Edition).

HUMPHREY, A.W. (1913) *Robert Applegarth: Trade Unionist, Educationist, Reformer* National Labour Press. Manchester and London.

HUTT, A. (1937) *The Post-War History of the British Working Class* Victor Gollancz Ltd.

HUTT, A. (1962) *British Trade Unionism 1800–1961* Lawrence and Wishart (5th Edition).

HYMAN, R. (1971) *The Workers' Union* Clarendon Press, Oxford.

INGLIS, K.S. (1964) *Churches and the Working Classes in Victorian England* Routledge and Kegan Paul (2nd Imp.).

JEFFERYS, J. (Ed) (1948) *Labour's Formative Years* History in the Making Vol. 2. 1849–1879, Lawrence and Wishart.

JONES, G.P. and POOL, A.G. (1959) *A Hundred Years of Economic Development in Great Britain (1840–1940)* Gerald Duckworth and Co. Ltd.

KELLY, T. (1970) *A History of Adult Education in Great Britain* Liverpool University Press (2nd Ed.)

KENT, W. (1950) *John Burns: Labour's Lost Leader* Williams and Norgate.

KUCZYNSKI, J. (1972) *A Short History of Labour Conditions Under Industrial Capitalism in Great Britain and the Empire 1750–1944* Frederick Muller.

LANE, T. (1974) *The Union Makes Us Strong* Arrow Books.

LASKI, H. (1951) *An Introduction to Politics* Allen and Unwin (Revised Edition).

LAWSON, J. and SILVER, H. (1973) *A Social History of Education in England* Methuen.

LEESON, R.A. (1971) *United We Stand.* An illustrated account of Trade Union Emblems, Adams and Dart, Bath.

LEVENTHAL, F.M. (1971) *Respectable Radical: George Howell and Victorian Working Class Politics* Weidenfeld and Nicolson.

LINDSAY, K. (1926) *Social Progress and Educational Waste: Being a Study of the 'Free Place' and Scholarship System* Routledge.

LOVETT, W. and COLLINS, J. (1969) *Chartism.* A New Organization of the People embracing a Plan for the Education and Improvement of the People Politically and Socially, Leicester University Press.

LOWNDES, G.A.N. (1969) *The Silent Social Revolution* Oxford University Press (2nd Ed.).

McCANN, P. (Ed) (1977) *Popular Education and Socialization in the Nineteenth Century* Methuen.

McINTOSH, P.C. (1952) *Physical Education in England since 1800* G. Bell and Sons Ltd.

MacKENZIE, N. and MACKENZIE J. (1977) *The First Fabians* Weidenfeld and Nicolson.

MACLURE, S. (1970) *One Hundred Years of London Education 1870–1970* Allen Lane.

MACTAVISH, J.M. (1916) *What Labour Wants from Education* Workers Educational Association.

MANN, T. (1923) *Memoirs* MacGibbon and Kee.

MARTIN, D. and RUBINSTEIN, D. (Eds) (1979) *Ideology and the Labour Movement* Croom Helm.

MARWICK, A. (1967) *The Deluge: British Society and the First World War* Penguin.

MARX, K. (1954) *A Critical Analysis of Capitalist Production* Vol. 1, Foreign Languages Publishing House Moscow.

MARX, K. and ENGELS, F. (1955) *On Britain* Foreign Languages Publishing House Moscow.

MEACHAM, S. (1977) *A Life Apart: The English Working Class 1890–1914* Thames and Hudson.

MILLAR, J.P.M. (1979) *The Labour College Movement* NCLC Pub. Society Ltd.

MILNE-BAILEY, W. (1929) *Trade Union Documents* G. Bell and Sons Ltd.

MITCHELL, B.R. and DEANE, P. (1962) *Abstract of British Historical Statistics* Cambridge University Press.

MORRIS, M. (Ed) (1948) *History in the Making Vol. 1 1815–48* Lawrence and Wishart.

MORTON, A.L. and TATE, G. (1956) *The British Labour Movement* Lawrence and Wishart.

MURPHY, J. (1971) *Church, State and Schools in Britain 1800–1970* Routledge and Kegan Paul.

MUSGRAVE, P.W. (1968) *Society and Education in England since 1800* Methuen and Co. Ltd.

MUSGRAVE, P.W. (Ed) (1970) *Sociology, History and Education* Methuen.

MUSSON, A.E. (1954) *The Typographical Association: Origins and History up to 1949* Oxford University Press.

MUSSON, A.E. (1968) *The Congress of 1868: The Origin and Establishment of the Trades Union Congress* Centenary Edition TUC.

NISBET, R.A. (1970) *The Sociological Tradition* Heinemann.

PALGRAVE, R.H.I. (c. 1880) *Political Economy Reading Book – Adapted to the Requirements of the New Code* National Society.

PARKINSON, M. (1970) *The Labour Party and the Organization of Secondary Education 1918–65* Routledge and Kegan Paul.

PELLING, H. (1963) *A History of British Trade Unionism* Pelican.

PELLING, H. (1968) *Popular Politics and Society in Late Victorian Britain* MacMillan.

PERCY, E. (1958) *Some Memories* Eyre and Spottiswoode.

PINCHBECK, I. and HEWITT, M. (1973) *Children in English Society Vols. I & II* Routledge and Kegan Paul.

POSTGATE, R.W. (n.d.) *The Builders' History* Labour Publishing C.

RADICE, G. and RADICE, L. (1974) *Will Thorne, Constructive Militant* Allen and Unwin.

REEDER, D. (Ed) (1977) *Urban Education in the Nineteenth Century* Taylor and Francis Ltd.

REID, T.W. (1970) *Life of the Rt. Hon. W.E. Forster* 2 Volumes, Adams and Dart.

REYNOLDS, G.W. and JUDGE, A. (1968) *The Night the Police Went on Strike* Weidenfeld and Nicolson.

RICH, E.E. (1970) *The Education Act 1870: A Study of Public Opinion* Longmans.

ROBERTS, B.C. (1958) *The Trades Union Congress 1868–1921* Allen and Unwin.

ROGERS, F. (1913) *Labour, Life and Literature* Smith, Elder and Co.

ROWNTREE, B.S. (1901) *Poverty – A Study of Town Life* MacMillan.

RUBINSTEIN, D. (1969) *School Attendance in London 1870–1904: A Social History* University of Hull.

RUBINSTEIN, D. and SIMON, B. (1969) *The Evolution of the Comprehensive School 1926–66* Routledge and Kegan Paul.

SCHULLER, T. (Ed) (1981) *Is Knowledge Power? Problems and Practice in Trade Union Education* Aberdeen People's Press.

SEABORNE, M. (1966) *Education* Studio Vista.

SEXTON, J. (1936) *Sir James Sexton – Agitator* Faber and Faber Ltd.

SHINWELL, E. (1963) *The Labour Story* MacDonald.

SILVER, H. (1975) *English Education and the Radicals 1780–1850* Routledge and Kegan Paul.

SIMON, B. (1965) *Education and the Labour Movement 1870–1920* Lawrence and Wishart.

SIMON, B. (1966) *Studies in the History of Education 1780–1870* Lawrence and Wishart.

SIMON, B. (Ed) (1972) *The Radical Tradition in Education in Britain* Lawrence and Wishart.

SIMON, B. (1974) *The Politics of Educational Reform 1920–40* Lawrence and Wishart.

SMITH, H.L. and NASH, V. (1889) *The Story of the Dockers' Strike* T. Fisher Unwin.

SMITH, W.D. (1974) *Stretching Their Bodies: The History of Physical Education* David and Charles.

SPENCER, F.H. (1938) *An Inspector's Testament* English Universities Press Ltd.

STAFFORD, A. (1961) *A Match to Fire the Thames* Hodder and Stoughton.

STEWART, W. (1921) *J. Keir Hardie: A Biography* Cassell and Co.

STOCKS, M. (1968) *The Workers' Educational Association* Allen and Unwin.

STURT, M. (1967) *The Education of the People: A History of Primary Education in England and Wales in the Nineteenth Century* Routledge and Kegan Paul.

SUTHERLAND, G. (1973) *Policy-Making in Elementary Education 1870–1895* Oxford University Press.

TAWNEY, R.H. (1922) *Secondary Education for All: A Policy for Labour* Allen and Unwin & The Labour Party.

TAYLOR, A.J.P. (1966) *English History 1914–1945* Oxford University Press.

THOMPSON, P. (1967) *Socialists, Liberals and Labour: The Struggle for London 1885–1914* Routledge and Kegan Paul.

THOMSON, D. (1950) *England in the Nineteenth Century* Penguin.

THOMSON, D. (1965) *England in the Twentieth Century* Penguin.

THORNE, W. (1926) *My Life's Battles* George Newnes Ltd.

TILLETT, B. (1931) *Memories and Reflections* John Long.

TOBIAS, J.J. (1972) *Crime and Industrial Society in the Nineteenth Century* Penguin.

TORR, D. (1956) *Tom Mann and His Times*. Vol. I (1856–1890), Lawrence and Wishart.

TRESSELL R. (Noonan R.) (1955) *The Ragged Trousered Philanthropists* Lawrence and Wishart.

TROPP, A. (1957) *The School Teachers* William Heinemann.

TSUZUKI, C. (1961) *H.M. Hyndman and British Socialism* Oxford University Press.

TURNER, B. (1920) *Short History of the General Union of Textile Workers* Labour Pioneer and Factory Times.

TURNER, B. (1930) *About Myself* Humphrey Toulmin.

WEARMOUTH, R.F. (1959) *Methodism and the Trade Unions* The Epworth Press.

WEBB, S. (1901) *The Education Muddle and the Way Out* Fabian Tract No. 106.

WEBB, S. and WEBB B. (1902) *The History of Trade Unionism* Chiswick Press also 1919 Edition.

WEBB, B. (1948) *Our Partnership* Longmans, Green and Co.

WEST, E.G. (1965) *Education and the State* Institute of Economic Affairs.

WIGHAM, E.L. (1963) *Trade Unions* Oxford University Press.

WILSON, J. (1910) *Memories of a Labour Leader* T. Fisher Unwin.

YORKE, P. (1977) *Education and the Working Class. Ruskin College 1899–1909* Ruskin Student's Labour History Pamphlets No. 1.

YOXALL, J.H. (1901) *The Coming Education Bill; The Need For It. The Best Lines For It* National Union of Teachers.

Fifty Years of the National Union of General and Municipal Workers NUGMW 1939.
Sixty Years of Trade Unionism 1868–1928. Souvenir of the 60th TUC, TUC General Council.
Seventy Years of Trade Unionism 1868–1938 TUC 1938.
Various Labour Biographies TUC Publications (n.d.)

Name Index

Ablett, N. 189
Abraham, W. 236
Acland, A.H.D. 160
Adams, B. Mrs. 205
Adamson, W. 37, 65
Addison, C. Dr. 149
Allan, W. 6, 215, 236
Ammon, C.J. 64, 151
Ammond, C.G. 187, 256
Applegarth, R. 6, 8, 23, 25, 27, 84, 105, 110, 114, 119, 135, 214, 219, 236
Appleton, W.A. 26, 34, 45, 63, 88, 106, 128, 170, 213, 217, 236, 248, 251, 262
Arch, J. 11, 25, 35, 78, 80, 83, 85, 86, 88, 94, 214, 215, 219, 221, 223, 224, 236
Asquith, H.H. 50, 72
Ayre, J.W. 99
Avebury, Lord 180

Bailey, A.W. 10, 245
Baillie, A. Rev. 180
Baker, H.R. Rev. 99
Baldwin, S. 66, 194
Balfour, A.J. 24, 117, 159, 169, 171, 180, 193
Barker, G. 253
Barnes, G. 26, 145, 224, 227, 236, 268
Bartley, G. Sir. 148
Battle, J. 210, 253, 255
Beadle, G. 254
Beard, C. 178, 204
Bedford, W.W. Bishop, 107
Bell, R. 18, 37, 39, 184, 236
Bellhouse, G. 71
Belt, G. 174
Bevin, E. 26
Birrell, A. 29
Birtwhistle, T. 26
Bisset, G. 113, 246
Block, M. 100
Bolton, W. 187
Bonaparte, N. 144

Bondfield, M. Miss. 236
Booth, C. 2, 34, 70, 114, 141, 148
Booth, F.W. 116, 251
Bowen, J.W. 131, 187, 198, 200, 202, 207, 256, 257
Bowerman, C.W. 49, 71, 88, 168, 169, 178, 181, 183, 185, 187, 202, 204, 236, 248
Bowman, A. 42, 48, 248
Bradlaugh, C. 85, 86
Bramley, F. 187, 196
Broadhurst, H. 4, 11, 14, 15, 26, 28, 33, 72, 86, 97, 99, 105, 113, 119, 120, 122, 162, 165, 215, 217, 218, 222, 227, 228, 237
Brockway, F. 198
Bromley, J. 206
Brougham, H. 118
Brown, A. Barrett 199, 207
Brown, R.H. 175
Bruce, W. 61, 145
Bryce, J. 164
Burden, T.W. 187
Burgwin, E.M. 146
Burnett, J. 26, 237
Burns, J. 14, 16, 26, 28, 85, 112, 145, 146, 220, 222–224, 237
Burt, T. 7, 35, 217, 218, 237
Butler, J. 253
Buxton, C. 179
Buxton, S. 180

Callow, J. 247
Calthrop, E. Mrs. 187
Campbell, J. 151
Cape, T. 34, 237
Carlile, E.H. 43
Carmichael, D. 254
Cecil, E. 115
Chamberlain, A. 62
Chamberlain, J. 109, 112
Chamberlain, N. 67, 76
Chandler, A.E. 73, 252, 253

Subject Index

Agnosticism: 4, 103, 180
Agricultural Children's Act: 1873, 32
Amalgamated Lacemakers: 213
Amalgamated Society of Carpenters & Joiners: 177 v. also Amalgamated Society of Woodworkers
Amalgamated Society of Engineers : 115, 147, 181, 186
Amalgamated Society of Railway Servants: 17, 182 v. also N.U.R.
Amalgamated Society of Woodworkers: 80, 199 v. also Amalgamated Society of Carpenters & Joiners
Amalgamated Union of Building Trade Workers: 186, 194
Apprentices/Apprenticeships: 23, 36, 37, 214, 217
Assessment, Continuous (Overall): 126, 127
Associated Society of Locomotive Engineers & Firemen: 136
Association of Engineering & Shipbuilding Draughtsmen: 186

Beehive: 6, 9, 84, 85, 119, 135
Birmingham Daily Gazette: 222
Blackleg Labour:
    Ascot Village, 1873: 78
    Leeds Municipal Strike, 1913: 185
    Sheffiield Outrages, 1866: 98
Boer War: 168
Bradford Charter: 65, 139
Brassworkers Union: 81
British & Foreign School Scoeity: 102
British Socialist Party Conference 1918: 74
British Steel Smelters, Mill & Tin Plate Workers Association: 181
Bryce Commission 1894: 122, 164, 165, 169
    and Trades & Labour Councils & Coop Societies Memorial to: 19, 122, 164

Burston Strike School, 80, 104 v also Strikes:
Building Industries Federation: 115

Canal Boat Children: 33
Capitalism: 192, 196, 231
    and criticism of: 23, 179, 191, 194, 195, 233
    support for: 78
Central Labour College: 23, 177, 181–183, 189, 192, 194–196, 202, 203, 231
    and TUC: 22
    Trade Union support: 187
    Proposed takeover of: 23, 187
    Closure: 201
Charity Commissioners: 124
Chartist Convention, 1851: 110
Child/Juvenile Labour: 21, 31–43, 48–50, 52, 68, 70, 71, 79
Christian Socialists: 79
Church of England: 17, 77, 78, 80, 81, 83–85, 88–90, 92, 94, 101–105, 109, 111, 114, 159, 160, 165, 170, 173, 179, 184, 231
    and Disestablishment: 84
    and School Boards: 160, 173, 174
    Alliance with Conservative Party: 77, 114
Church Schools: v Schools, Religious
Church Times: 78, 82
Circulars:
    Board of Education: 1190; 66
                          1228; 62
                          1238; 133
                          1261; 149, 150
                          1273; 150
    Scottish Education Department: 51; 150 v. also PCTUC Important Circular, 1900
Clarendon Commission, 1864: 118, 119
Clarion: 180
Clerical Committee, 1879: 94, 95, 97, 99, 100
Cockerton Judgement: 166, 167
Communist Party: 231